*TRABELIN' ON*_____

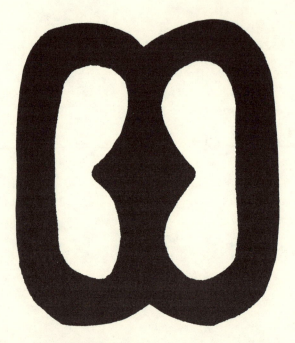

NYAME, BIRIBI WO SORO, MA NO MEKA ME NSA
O God, there is something above, let it reach me

A pattern hung above the lintel of the King of Ashanti. The king would touch the lintel, his forehead, and his breast, repeating the words three times.

Source: J. B. Danquah, *The Akan Doctrine of God* (London: Frank Cass & Co., 1968), p. 187.

TRABELIN' ON
THE SLAVE JOURNEY TO AN AFRO-BAPTIST FAITH

Mechal Sobel

Princeton University Press
Princeton, New Jersey

Published by Princeton University Press, 41 William Street,
Princeton, New Jersey 08540
In the United Kingdom: Princeton University Press, Chichester, West Sussex

TRABELIN' ON The Slave Journey to an Afro-Baptist Faith, by Mechal Sobel. Originally
published, with appendix, in the Greenwood Press series, Contributions in Afro-American
and African Studies, No. 36, Westport, CT, 1979. Copyright © 1979 by Mechal Sobel. All
rights reserved.

This abridged edition omits Appendixes I–III of the original edition. Reprinted by
arrangement with Greenwood Press.

First Princeton Paperback printing, 1988

LCC 87-32808
ISBN 0-691-00603-2

Printed in the United States of America

10 9 8 7 6 5 4 3 2

COPYRIGHT ACKNOWLEDGMENTS

Grateful acknowledgment is made to the following for permission to reprint previously published and facsimile material:

Alan Lomax: For an excerpt from *The Folk Songs of North America*, published by Doubleday & Co. (Copyright 1960 by Alan Lomax.)

American Folklore Society: For excerpts from "Hoodoo in America" by Zora Hursten, reproduced by permission of the American Folklore Society from *The Journal of American Folklore,* vol. 44, 1931.

The First Baptist Church of the City of Washington, D.C.: For excerpts and photocopies of the manuscript minutes of the church.

International African Institute: For excerpts from *Conversations with Ogotemmêli* by Marcel Griaule. (Copyright 1965 by International African Institute.)

Jonathan David Publishers, Inc.: For an excerpt from *The Encyclopedia of Black Folklore and Humor*, edited by Henry D. Spalding. (Copyright 1972 by Jonathan David Publishers, Inc.)

Macmillan Publishing Co., Inc.: For an excerpt from *Army Life in a Black Regiment* by Thomas Wentworth Higginson. Introduction by Howard N. Meyer. (Introduction: © Macmillan Publishing Co., Inc., 1962.)

United Church Press: For excerpts reprinted by permission of the publisher from *God Struck Me Dead: Religious Conversion Experiences and Autobiographies of Ex-slaves,* ed. Clifton H. Johnson. Copyright © 1969 United Church Press.

University of Wisconsin Press: For an excerpt from *The Atlantic Slave Trade: A Census* by Philip D. Curtin. (Copyright 1969 by the University of Wisconsin Press.)

For Mindy, Daniel, Noam and Zvi who have crossed over the *grandywater*; and for Minn

CONTENTS

ILLUSTRATIONS_____

TABLES

*ACKNOWLEDGMENTS*_____

I would like to thank many individuals and institutions for their help over the years in which I worked on this book. Haifa University provided a sabbatical year and funds that supported my research. The Historical Commission of the Southern Baptist Convention in Nashville, Tennessee, was extremely helpful, providing services and materials both in Nashville and via the mails. In particular, I wish to express thanks to Marian Keegan, archivist, as well as to Reba McMahon, Lynn E. May, Jr., and Ronald Tonks.

I owe a very special debt to Eugene Genovese, who read an early version of the manuscript. His questions, comments, and encouragement were crucial. The exchange of ideas with my friend and colleague Noam Flinker was indispensable, as was the yeoman service of Brian Stonehill.

C. Eric Lincoln, John H. Ness, Jr., Mary Overby, Lawrence Jones, Harrison Daniel, S. E. Grimstead, Miles Kinghorn, Edward C. Starr, Norman Maring, Rivka Kluger, Labelle Prussin, John R. Woodard, E. Earl Joiner, Earnest C. Bolt, Jr., Reverend Charles O. Walker, Reverend Charles S. Lee, Reverend Dale Dicks, Vardit Salinger, Helen Conger, Mrs. Ashley Graves, Ilana Flinker, and Eve Shoresh all provided advice and aid that was much appreciated. The library of the Eastern Baptist Theological Seminary, Philadelphia, Pennsylvania, which served as a base for a year's research, was extremely helpful, as were the staffs of the Dargan-Carver Library, Nashville, Tennessee; the American Baptist Historical Society, Rochester, New York; the Library Company of Philadelphia and the Historical Society of Pennsylvania, Philadelphia; the Library of the University of Pennsylvania, Philadelphia; Haverford College Library, Haverford, Pennsylvania; the Library of Congress, Washington, D.C.; the Virginia Baptist Historical Society, Richmond, Virginia; the Southern Historical Collection at the University of North Carolina at Chapel Hill; Perkins Library, Duke University, Durham, North Carolina; the Presbyterian Historical Society, Philadelphia; the Georgia Baptist Historical Society, Macon, Georgia; the Alderman Library, University of Virginia, Charlottesville; the North Carolina Baptist Historical Collection, Winston-Salem, North Carolina; the Schomburg branch and the main branch of the New York City Library; and the Haifa University Library, Haifa, Israel.

Genoveva Breitstein typed an early version of this manuscript. The final version was done by Beverly Lapkin who, under the pressure of time, edited the appendix with great precision and concern for accuracy. I am much indebted to both of these women.

I want to thank my older children, Mindy and Daniel, for their patience and to give special thanks to my youngest child, Noam, who, as he says, "suffered" (which is a play on the meaning of our name) so that I might do this research. And I thank my husband, Zvi Sobel, who washed the windows, bought the groceries, ate cold cake, and "listened" critically as this book was written.

I want to thank the writers cited in the notes as well as the people remembered in this book; I am deeply indebted to them. Ralph Ellison has noted that

> each of us has no special grasp upon reality, but that each of us lives a special part of it. It is owed to the rest. We must all learn from it. We must be able to partake of it if we would . . . . I learned to walk in a certain way because I admired Milton Lewinson, who ran a clothing store in Oklahoma City. It was not just that I liked this walk. I liked his principles. He happened to be a Jew. But I know that much of Milton Lewinson is Ralph Ellison.[1]

I would like to think that as a result of my contact with the lives of the people remembered in this book, I walk a little bit differently, too.

Mechal Sobel
Haifa, Israel
February 1977

INTRODUCTION_____

This volume is a study of value adaptations, cultural growth, and institutional development as reflected in the religious history of slaves and free blacks in antebellum America. The central thesis of this book is that Africans brought their world views into North America where, in an early phase of slavery, the core understandings, or Sacred Cosmos, at the heart of these world views coalesced into one neo-African consciousness—basically similar yet already significantly different from West African understandings. Over time, white cultural elements, some of which were Christian and many of which were based on conflicting values, were syncretically blended into this world view, creating a dichotomy that was often overtly reflected in black behavior. Nevertheless, blacks in America, under the enormous pressures and hardships of chattel slavery, came to achieve a new coherence which preserved and revitalized crucial African understandings and usages regarding spirit and soul-travels, while melding them with Christian understandings of Jesus and individual salvation. A coherent Afro-Christian faith was created, and its reality was reflected in a vibrant and known institution, a black Baptist church, the history of which goes back to the 1750s.

This book is divided into two sections, each of which is very different in method and materials. The first, dealing with African values and ideas and their transmission and early development in America, is an interpretive essay on the structure of early Afro-American history, utilizing published sources. The second, dealing with black Christian consciousness and black Baptist churches (to 1864), is based on much new evidence taken largely from black narratives and white church records. This section presents a new analysis of black Christian belief and black churches, contradicting much of what has been widely accepted as black church history to this point. These data substantiate the thesis that the so-called hidden institution, the black church of the slave period, was not hidden at all; that the black church was a known and well-established institution; and that it can be seen again after a long period of obfuscation. Extensive minutes from white churches, as the few minutes extant from black churches, reveal broad aspects of the lives of the members of these churches and their patterns of social organization:[1]

1. Blacks established independent churches beginning in the middle of the eighteenth century. They were often formally organized, with written covenants, written membership rolls, and written minutes.
2. The formally organized black churches, some numbering thousands of parishioners, existed in both the upper and lower

South, and in both urban and rural areas. Smaller, often weaker, churches were organized in the North and later in the Midwest.

3. Both slaves and free blacks organized, joined, and led these churches; whites recognized both the churches and their leadership.

4. A large leadership group of formally recognized black preachers, deacons, and deaconesses emerged at an early date. By 1800, black preachers, both lay and ordained, served black, mixed, and occasionally even white churches. Hundreds of these men are known by name, and many of their biographies can be written in detail.

5. Black churches grew both as institutions that were totally independent from the outset and as subchurches under the roof of white churches.

6. Independent black churches were recognized as having "freedom in Christ." Their covenants were between themselves and God and did not involve white intermediaries.

7. Black churches, both early and late, joined mixed church associations (generally known as "white" associations) in both the South and the North. Beginning in the mid-1830s, the Midwestern churches of newly freed blacks began to organize separate black church associations.

It is ironic that white records provide the key evidence for the above conclusions, in that whites did not see the black church as an institution. Generally, the whites overlooked black values and black churches, making these "invisible" in their eyes at the very same time as they were recording their vital statistics and preserving their records. These statistics and records have been collected here into an index of all the known black Baptist churches. While presented as an appendix to the book, it is actually a key section in the volume. It documents the reality of the churches and of the black leadership that emerged as both father figures and role models for the community.

Clearly, blacks in America had found spiritual space and time to forge a black institution: an Afro-Baptist denomination. Statistics, however, reveal only the institutional reality; they cannot answer questions about the nature of the black religious experience. To suggest that it was Christian is correct but insufficient. What was the nature of black Christianity in the slave period?

Most studies of slave culture that have attempted to answer this question have not considered developments over the more than 200 years of American slavery and have essentially lacked a time orientation. The current reevaluation of the changing nature of black American culture in the seventeenth and eighteenth centuries brings into question the broadly accepted view that the American context is sufficient to explain the content of black Christianity. The African component of the earliest slave cultures was so overwhelming that, with growing awareness of it, it has become impossible to explain black religion in America without exploring continuities with African understandings.[2]

In *Roots*, Alex Haley recounts his extraordinary visit to his forefathers' Gambian village where the local oral historian, the groit, told him of the last time his great-great-great-great grandfather, Kunta Kinte, had been seen there. Haley went on a unique journey where time past was revealed to him in very real terms; yet, strangely, I feel that while doing research for this book I experienced a significant part of what Haley felt. With the help of Geoffrey Parrinder, serving as a near-groit for an outsider coming to African culture, I took a spiritual journey, leading to an overwhelming shock of recognition and surety about the African soul in Afro-American Christianity.[3]

American blacks, in talking and writing of their experiences in converting to Christianity, have handed down a tradition that, on first appraisal, appears highly parallel to the white conversion experience. However, there is one jarringly different element, found only in the black recitals and found there with great consistency. It is the reference to "the man in the man," "the little me in the big me," "the little Mary in the big Mary," "the little John in the big John." For blacks, there was a twofold spiritual participation in the actual conversion experience that was not known to whites and, in each case, it was the "little me" inside the "big me" who traveled to visit God in Heaven during the ecstatic vision experience.

The key to the significance of this most important concept, and a basic proof of the continuity of the West African and black American ethos, can be found in Geoffrey Parrinder's work. Parrinder suggests that the West African separates form and content; that in each object or thing or person is the "thing in itself," the "essential being," its soul. Man in himself, man's essential being, is spiritual, and the spirit's "real life is spent in touch with the supreme Spirit." Parrinder, apparently unaware of the Afro-American use of these terms, suggests the way in which an African might verbalize this complex concept: "The African might say that *'in each thing is another thing,'* and *'in every man there is a little man.'*" He explains that the African accepts that this little man, the "thing in itself," existed before birth and continues to exist after death: "Africans would not say that what subsists after death is a part of man; it is rather himself, 'the man himself,' and this is 'the little man' who was hidden behind the outward appearance, the man himself whose existence continues in one way or another into the afterworld.''[4]

This idea, perhaps the most important concept in the West African world view, clearly retained its central importance for Africans in America. Not only did this man himself continue to exist in the African afterworld, but he also lived in Georgia, Virginia, and, in fact, wherever blacks lived. The "little man," the "thing," hidden behind the outward appearance remained the touchstone and the key to the African soul. He did not die with the trans-Atlantic passage but was harbored in the adversity of enslavement and refreshed in contact with Christian faith. It is this "little man" who is the touchstone of the thesis that to an important extent the African Sacred Cosmos was preserved, altered, and perhaps revitalized in a new integrity in an Afro-Christian Sacred Cosmos. It was then the "thing" in itself, hidden and yet very real, that was in fact *the* reality.

This book begins with a survey of the basic elements common to West African world views. In this assay at establishing universals, at combining ideas which were not exactly the same, it is suggested that they were similar enough to have become one under the impact of slavery. This is, in a sense, weighting the issue in the direction it is seen as having gone later. It is posited that the various West African world views can be understood as variants of one "ideal-type" West African world view, a construct that did not exist in West Africa but that does seem to have heuristic value for understanding the similarities (and differences) of various West African views.

In doing this, the stage is being set for what apparently happened in the early phases of black adjustment in America: (1) The many West African world views had the potential to coalesce and can be understood as one whole; and (2) a process of unification (and change) apparently occurred in America.

The book moves in time to the first stages of slave adjustment. Here the suggestion is made that African languages and African world views were clearly brought into America and that there was adequate time and spiritual space for one African world view to be compressed from the many different, but similar, world views brought to the New World. Perhaps as early as 1750, first-generation Afro-Americans had created a new quasi-African world view—although this clearly is a metaphor. Its reality must be looked for in language, symbols, and action.[5]

The evidence of the survival of an African or quasi-African world view in an obviously African form is limited and explains why E. Franklin Frazier, Timothy Smith, and many other scholars could, with impunity, maintain that black Christians had no African values and that black

Christianity was the result of white missionary work.[6] The one obviously neo-African faith is Voudou, which shared African and Afro-Haitian understandings of God, the divinities, souls, and the use of spirit-workers. However, its proven extent was limited, and its formative stages occurred outside North America.

While the retention of obvious African forms was very restricted, it is suggested that *a quasi-African body of values functioned in almost every African household in America.* There is an increasing body of evidence that slaveowners interfered as little as possible in the nonwork lives of their labor force. Clearly, the radically new situation from the first moment of enslavement began to alter the world views of Africans, but, just as clearly, the value system of African-born parents, speaking African tongues and perhaps Pidgin English, had to, willy-nilly, be the value system with which they socialized their slave-born children. It would appear that eighteenth-century slaves retained contacts with blacks from their own peoples and that their languages and values continued to find expression. The original mixing of slaves, which probably occurred less than was once assumed, hastened the destruction of separate black world views but abetted the creation of a single quasi-African slave world view. It did not lead to the destruction of all earlier values, as has been assumed.

The succeding chapters of this book follow the hypothetical development of the black world view as it came in contact with the white Anglican and then the white Baptist world views, each of which is considered both separately and in its relationship to the black Sacred Cosmos. Afro-American slaves, at the same time as they were forming a singular quasi-African world view, were gradually internalizing some contradictory white values and priorities, making for a significant dichotomy. As a result, the Sacred Cosmos itself was subject to an unconscious attack, with the key understandings of the nature of spirit, or Nyama, and of man as he is dependent on Nyama, as the chief victims. For many blacks, it became unclear where power was in the world, who could control it, and for what ends. The increasing influence of "white values" was not the result of a purposive attempt to civilize slaves. By and large, the white slaveowner remained primarily concerned with the black as laborer, and his patterns of behavior outside of working time continued to be, within certain very significant limits, his own affair. Thus, a neo-African value system could continue to function within this severely limited and altered time and space, but its content had to undergo change. Under these circumstances, while many folkways were maintained, much of what had been done as purposive action in Africa, action which maintained the social system (such as honor to spirits and forefathers in pre-paration for one's own entry into these ranks) became relatively routinized and had a significantly less organic connection to the new social system.

In this process, the new neo-African Sacred Cosmos began to lose its coherence. It increasingly incorporated contradictory demands and essential confusions, although a large body of the rules of behavior it had engendered remained operative. What remains open to question is to what extent the quasi-African world view was sustained into the nineteenth century. By that period did the slaves still know the spirits, or did they carry out proscriptions and taboos without that knowledge? People who knew the spirits received a gift of power in dealing with them; one who compulsively repeated a set formula when he performed a particular act could not have had the same reward.

The first slaves to come into meaningful contact with Christianity were probably socialized with a neo-African world view that had already absorbed many contradictory values. In their confrontation with Christianity, they developed an African/Christian faith structure that was not yet a coherent whole. The nature of the Sea Islander's Christianity, which has been studied, suggests that comparable to the creole speech pattern they preserved, which had earlier been a general black speech pattern, they also preserved an African/Christian religious development that had once been the more common black one. In this neo-African plantation-Christianity, many separate Christian elements existed along with purely African ones, but hierarchical values were confused or contradictory.

In-depth reintegration of the black soul took place in the creation of the black or Afro-Baptist faith, which began as early as the 1750s but which was at different stages of development in different black communities. This is the concern in the second half of this book. It is suggested that this process involved the creation of a new Sacred Cosmos, one which integrated African and Baptist elements into a unified whole, so that the black was at one and the same time at home again and whole with himself in America. "Free at last"—his soul free to know God in the Pauline sense, and yet free to achieve its own fulfillment in the African sense. The "little man" could go home to Jesus and find him sitting in a green field surrounded by lambs "mourning" a neo-African dirge and shouting and dancing in a neo-African religious drama.

The new character of black Baptist possesion rituals exemplifies this new entity, as much as does the content of the visions alluded to above. In Christian individualistic terms, wherein every soul must come to Christ, every black looked forward to experiencing "that thing." The trance became a far more private affair than it had been in Africa, notwithstanding its American revival function, and individual blacks heard their own drummers and shouts, often alone in the woods or in their cabins. More importantly, they were not taken over or "mounted" by God, as an African is mounted or used as a mouthpiece by a divinity, but they met and talked with God who then came to be and remained in their hearts. They had gotten "that thing." They had come in contact with POWER and they had become what they should have become, fulfilling the African goal. The spirit's real life was being spent in touch with the Supreme Spirit who was now known as Jesus.

In traveling to a Christian Heaven, while yet alive, Afro-Americans made the future into time past, into an event that had already occurred. Thus, they used the African time sense (of present and past) to encompass the Christian's messianic sense of time future and to make it real.

Language was an integral part of this developmental process. Dillard has suggested that black language developed in three phases; this structure can be seen as comparable and related to the development of black religion. After enslavement, blacks continued to speak African languages, but while their new societies did afford some opportunities to talk in their native tongues, it was necessary to develop a *lingua franca* to use with whites as well as with blacks speaking unfamiliar languages. Dillard has shown that (1) the Afro-Americans' Pidgin English and (2) their children's language, creole, which later developed into (3) black English, all retained basic elements of taxonomy and time sense native to West African languages and culture. It can be posited that the first phase of religious development, (1) the quasi-African, was experienced during the period of the development of Pidgin English. This English was a second (or third) language for the blacks; it was the means of exchange at work and in "surface" matters. Spiritual life and the mind continued to function in the African mother tongues.

As the number and percentage of American-born blacks rapidly grew, English became a creole tongue—the first language spoken by children for whose parents English was a second language. Creole was a language that developed out of Pidgin English; it was not a corruption of standard English. Again, the taxonomy and time sense prove the significance of these statements. The period of creolization corresponds with the period of (2) African/Christianity, a period when values from both cultures coexisted but did not coalesce. Serious contradictions were readily apparent. (The misunderstanding of this language and religion helped to sustain the white image of the slave as ignorant, stupid, and primitive. The blacks were seen as speaking a strange and poor standard English, while their Christianity was judged to be primitive.)

The creation of (3) a black Baptist Sacred Cosmos corresponds with the development of black English. Both are integrative wholes. One is a full language and the other the heart of a coherent world view, and they dialectically support each other. Both express a hierarchy of values and a taxonomy, and both provide their full "participants" with the possibility of making sense out of their world and themselves. Using this English, many

Afro-Americans lost touch with the source of their images and their understanding. But lack of consciousness does not alter the black Christians' ties to the African Sacred Cosmos. Down through slavery and into the emancipation period, blacks apparently thought of the "little me inside me" and of going home to spirit, much as an African would. Divinities guided them to the beautiful pasture that was home, and Christ in his "breastplate, buckler, and shield" promised them glory.

Born again, the black Baptist knew he was a Christian, and yet he knew that he had a special ability to contact God. Neither blacks nor whites really appreciated the African aspects in this tradition, in part because of the extraordinary nature of their melding into a new Sacred Cosmos, a new whole.

The new Sacred Cosmos was expressed in a new and viable institutional structure and in new Christian biographies. Both individuals and institutions interacted with the Sacred Cosmos, altering it and strengthening it; it continued to grow and change, supporting both the individuals and the institutions. The first Baptist church community was formally organized in 1758, and by 1865 over 205 formal black Baptist churches and myriad less formal plantation congregations had been organized. Hundreds of black preachers (lay or floor preachers, licensed preachers, and ordained preachers) led the new people, now a black Christian people. Emerging as the new elders, the Baptist preachers provided the leadership and life-style examples for a constantly growing community. The black Baptist faith gave coherence to prewar slave society. It provided the possibility for meaningful lives with meaningful goals. It was a black creation, made in contact with the white Baptist faith and affecting that faith, but it remained the very special Sacred Cosmos of blacks, filled with spirit and joy and mourning and time past, all used to understand time present. Seeing themselves as the New Israel, waiting for God's redemption, black Baptists *knew* they would "emerge the conquerer."

I am a poor wayfarin' stranger
A trabelin' thru this world a woe
An there's no sickness toil or danger
In that fair land to which I go

I'm just a trabelin' over
    Jordan
I'm just a goin' over home

I'm goin' there to see my
    mother
I'm goin' there no more
    to roam
I'm just a goin' over
    Jordan
I'm just a goin' over
    home

part I | *The African world view and its enslavement*

1

THE WEST AFRICAN SACRED COSMOS

I

Every culture can be said to have a world view, by means of which the potential chaos of the social world is ordered and evaluated. This construct can be used in the study of American slaves through analysis of the developing world views of black Africans as they came into contact and interacted with the changing world views of white Euro-Americans.

In Thomas Luckman's fine analysis of the concept of world views, he maintains that all the myriad specific evaluations made in each culture are actually part of "an encompassing system of meaning" and can be subsumed under the categories of time, space, causality, and purpose. Luckman's four categories are a valuable analytic tool, but African world views seem to call for an additional category—concepts of being. Luckman further suggests that socialization can be viewed as the unconscious internalization of this system of meaning, accomplished by means of an integrally related style of thinking as objectified in symbols, movement, and, most crucially, language. Every language is seen as having an inner form which "may be said to represent a comprehensive model of the universe." This emphasis on the nominizing function of language is a seminal idea and has proven very important in relation to the study of blacks in America.

Luckman suggests that there is an inner core to every world view, a Sacred Cosmos, which is an evaluation of and a response to the mysterious or inexplicable. The "symbols which represent the reality of the sacred cosmos . . . perform, in a specific and concentrated way, the broad religious function of the world view as a whole." The internalization of this Sacred Cosmos is the crucial aspect of an individual's socialization and of his life. Through the internalization of a coherent Sacred Cosmos, the potentially chaotic and frightening infinity of events "falls in place," and the life of the individual assumes purpose and direction. The individual is given categories of meaning, ways of looking at and evaluating reality, an "inner hierarchy of significance." The world view is the "historical" and necessary "context within which human organisms form identities."[1]

The relationships between the world view, individuals, and social structure in a given culture are dialectical. In part, the world view "routinizes and stabilizes the individual's memory, thinking, conduct and perception." But it not only provides this "unthinking routine"; its structuring of significance provides taxonomy, models, and goals in relation to which the individual must evaluate reality and choose action. The individual's pattern of priorities is, in part, given to him by the world view, but the individual is, at one and the same time, a participant, a coproducer, and a dialectical taker and giver. He finds a system. In his taking it, however, he changes it, making it both his own and something different. The world view that emerges is changed by each and every individual. Similarly, social institutions are both dependent upon the world view and products of it; yet, they, too, transform and then transmit further a somewhat changed world view. By stabilizing or institutionalizing cultural elements, institutions change the relative importance of these very elements and create the need for new responses or new understandings. Thus, the world view of any culture holds within itself dynamic elements. Its transmission by individuals and institutions must lead to its change, although clearly different world views regularly generate change at different rates.[2]

In times of social trauma, the normative processes are altered and the individual, institutions, and interrelated world view all undergo development unusual for the particular culture, although dependent upon the nature of that culture prior to the trauma. The transporting of millions of Africans to the Americas and their enslavement in the new environment constituted social trauma and led to changes in the world views of both the black and white participants in this social reality. As a result, their world views, which were undergoing change prior to these historical events but to which the events are related, underwent unusual change and interaction.[3]

What were the world views of the participants in these events, and why and how did they change during and as a result of this history? An assessment of the function of the world view in the life of blacks in America must involve a tentative assessment of the African and white world views prior to racial interrelatedness, as well as the emerging world views of blacks and whites in North America. What follows is a preliminary analysis of the changing Sacred Cosmos of Afro-Americans, utilizing the categories of time, space, causality, and purpose, as well as the particularly African category of being. This analysis recognizes ritual, myth, movement, and, above all, language as the significant symbolic forms of transmission and content.

II

There was no one West African Sacred Cosmos. Each people had a separate world view, and sometimes the world views of subgroups incorporated significant differences paralleled by dialect differences in their languages. Nevertheless, it can be maintained that there was a shared basic outlook, either through common origin or because of cross influence or assimilation. This basic similarity allowed for the possibility of a melding into one single world view, and this is exactly what seems to have occurred under the conditions of slavery in North America. As suggested above, the positing of a single ideal-type West African Sacred Cosmos already weights the argument in favor of this conclusion, but the two theses are part of one whole: (1) It is possible to suggest a basic similarity between the different West African world views and to posit an ideal-type West African Sacred Cosmos, and (2) it is highly likely that West African slaves in America early melded their various Cosmos into a single one, a process that was possible because of the similar West African backgrounds but that was significantly shaped by the common slave experience.

The shared aspects of the West African world view are paralleled by the shared aspects of language in West Africa. In a comprehensive analysis of African tongues, Greenberg has found at least 800 separate languages. He nevertheless believes that African tongues comprise a single "linguistic area" united by similar use of "tone, the existence of nominal classification, and [shared] verbal derivations." Moreover, and more directly important for this analysis, Greenberg convincingly argues that these 800 languages fall into no more than four stocks "of apparently distinct origin." The vast majority of the slaves brought to North America came from one of these four language stocks. They spoke languages that had originally come from one source, the "Niger-Congo and Kurdofanian" language group, spoken in almost all of the slaving area from Gambia to Angola. While Greenberg divides this stock into eight substocks, each of which in turn is comprised of many languages, these all shared an inner logic and an inner structure. The Niger-Congo languages are all "conspicuously" characterized by their classification of nouns. This classification is not the familiar sex classification of masculine, feminine, and neuter; rather, it rests on a large number of complex taxonomic distinctions, "human beings in one class, animals in another, trees (along with other items not easily classifiable) in another," followed by other classes for which Greenberg was unable to discern the basis of meaning. The nature of being clearly made for the distinctions in the language and in the thinking, and it is this taxonomy of being that was apparently carried into the Americas.[4]

This shared reservoir of language structure and interrelated beliefs was to prove very important after the slaves were transported to the Americas. It is therefore crucial that the attempt be made to conceptualize the major shared viewpoints and differences. While the African languages were not generally spoken by second-generation Afro-Americans, it would appear that aspects of the inner logic were brought into the new tongue. Nor did a molding into one world view occur in Africa, although some peoples, such as the Dahomeans, had already integrated many ethnic patterns while in Africa. But the finding of the crucial common "denominator," the concern with being, and the perception of its inner nature as spirit or power running as a "stream" of water or fluid fills all of the varied West African Sacred Cosmos and is not simply a postfacto assertion.

III

A charming and yet disturbing anecdote told by Marcel Griaule about his extraordinary work with the Dogon, a West African people living in the bend of the Niger south of Timbuktu, epitomizes the problems involved in analyzing African world views. For some fifteen years, Griaule had been studying the Dogon, and in all that time they had provided simple and seemingly complete answers. Suddenly, at an indefinable juncture— apparently after Griaule had passed some test of honesty, presence, or concern—the elders formally "met together and decided that the more esoteric aspects of their religion should be fully revealed." Griaule had not even known the right questions to ask. He was not at all prepared for the complexity and depth of the philosophy revealed to him, and this after fifteen years of contact.[5]

Probably all who have done field work have had some sense of layers of reality and are prepared to appreciate another level of meaning than the one perceived at the moment. The informants' willingness to reveal themselves is only one factor in the complex process of doing history, sociology, or anthropology, and the researcher's original perception is another. The interaction of these two world views changes both the viewer's perception and the history itself, so that we "do" history, while it "does" something to us as well.[6]

The Dogon elder, Ogotemmêli, sat with Griaule for thirty-three days revealing a highly complex cosmogony symbolically reflected in decorations, structures, forms, and village layouts. These symbols had surrounded Griaule all the days he had been with the Dogon, and yet he had been unaware of their significance. Ogotemmêli revealed a system of astronomy, calendrical measurements, a formal pharmacopoeia, as well as extensive anatomical and physiological knowledge. Above all, he revealed the sacred heart of the Dogon world view, a Sacred Cosmos.

The Dogon Sacred Cosmos is filled with a life force, or "being," expressed in the idea of the high god Amma but conceived symbolically as water or *"the word."* "Being" is the origin of all things and persons. It

House in Djeneé, Mali. Motifs symbolically present complex male and female elements.
Source: Marli Shamir

penetrates both material and immaterial objects, and it accounts for the "tension of opposites" that are like a force-field that the Dogon finds within himself and in his spiritual world.

As Ogotemmêli very cautiously and carefully explained, God, or Amma, sought to approach his creation earth sexually but found that he had to excise the male element in the earth before they could cohabit. As a result, the issue was not dual, as had been planned. The progeny, a single jackal, introduced an improper, unpaired element into creation. The second issue, however, was properly dual: word or spirit as twin *Nummo.* The improper jackal then had incestuous relations with mother earth, thus beginning the history of evil, while the Nummo, "in Amma's place," made the first eight ancestors, four male and four female, but each bisexual. God symbolically gave man three "words" or dimensions of spirit, represented by natural strands of fiber for clothing (literally one-dimensional); weaving of warp and woof (two-dimensional); and drumming on a pot with a transmitting internal coil (three-dimensional). The seventh ancestor, master of speech, brought evil into the world of men by violating his own promise not to eat of a given fruit. It was then that God brought death into the world. The earliest ancestor, and then the oldest man alive after him, " 'had to die in order to pass into the same world . . . and so enable the purposes of God to be fulfilled. So he died.' " " 'But not really,' " as Ogotemmêli explained, " 'only in appearance. The common people were told that he was dead . . . to make them understand things better.' " This act symbolized the fact that earth, man, and God are unified.

For the Dogon, this unity of the world is symbolically viewed as a granary, a feature of every Dogon household. It is " 'the granary of the Master of Pure Earth.' " Everything in the world has its symbolic place in this symbolic granary, just as every real granary is a symbol of the world and has its structure and use is rigidly governed by ritual prescriptions. Spirit is the ultimate reality, and man shares in God's spirit as is symbolized and made "understandable" through the "eating" of the first ancestor by spirit. Ogotemmêli clearly conceptualized this symbolism:

> The seventh Nummo sacrificed himself. He alone could do it, he the master of Speech, which is to say the master of the world. Without him no reorganization was possible. He might say—he did not say it, but he might have said—"What I did, the work that I accomplished and the word that I spoke, is: . . . My head has fallen for man's salvation."

The seventh ancestor ate the man-like descendant of his eighth brother, mingling their life forces. " 'Their souls were joined together and, though they remain distinct, they are never parted.' "

Ogotemmêli had a vast oral tradition to transmit, although he was occasionally unclear about some facet of the ancient myths and consulted other elders; this was a shared Sacred Cosmos. Ogotemmêli recognized these ideas as symbolic and certainly did not view all the myths as literally true, although he respected their symbolic power. When Griaule naïvely asked how all the created animals could fit on the steps of the finite granary, as Ogotemmêli had described it, Ogotemmêli patiently explained: " 'All this had to be said in words, but everything on the steps is a symbol, symbolic antelopes, symbolic vultures, symbolic hyenas. Any number of symbols could find room on a one-cubit step.' "[7]

The Sacred Cosmos of many West African peoples is parallel to that of the Dogon. As with Griaule, most outsiders, even those who had been in long contact with West Africans, had been unaware of its nature, in part because West Africans preferred to hide their wisdom and in part because Western viewers, even those supposedly trained and scientific, could not think and evaluate in the language and meanings of another world view. All this was complicated, of course, by the underlying negative evaluation of blacks in the Western ex-slaveowning world. The contemporary situation is somewhat changed in that some elders are now willing to sit with us, both West Africans and people who have spent much of their lives in contact with the West African world view and who, as a result, have also passed the magical dividing line and have become aware of some of the complexities and realities.[8]

Mbiti (a Christian-African) defines the heart of the African world view and socialization much as Luckman does: "To live is to be caught up in a religious drama." For Mbiti the Sacred Cosmos of the African is man-centered but spirit-filled:

> God is the Originator and Sustainer of *man*; the Spirits explain the destiny of *man*; *Man* is the centre of this ontology; the Animals and Plants and natural phenomena and objects constitute the environment in which *man* lives, provide a means of existence, and, if need be, *man* establishes a mystical relationship with them.

There are five basic categories of being in this analysis of the Sacred Cosmos: (1) God, who is the first creator; (2) spirits, of the recent dead and of great predecessors; (3) man, who as we will see, has more than one spirit, or several aspects to his spirit; (4) animals and plants, which can also have spirits, but which, as well as man, can be inhabited by alien spirits, as can (5) phenomena and objects. This classification seems clear enough. However, Mbiti quickly complicates this taxonomy:

In addition to the five categories, there seems to be a force, power or energy permeating the whole universe. God is the Source and ultimate controller of this force; but the spirits have access to some of it. A few human beings have the knowledge and ability to tap it, manipulate it and use it.

This sixth element, this force, power, or energy, is not a category but pervades all the categories. It is, as we shall see, a crucial element of the West African Sacred Cosmos.[9]

What is the hierarchy of significance in this Sacred Cosmos? Man seems to be most important: every spirit and thing exists in its relationship to him and is actually defined as it relates to man. But force or spirit is the key to all control, to all power, and man is neither creator nor ultimate controller of force or spirit. The primary goal in this Sacred Cosmos is to get in touch with this force or spirit: *to be*, properly, so that one is spirit or actualized; to act properly, so that spirit is for you and not against you; to placate or invite spirit to be with you.

In the African Sacred Cosmos, time past and time present are *the* modes of concern; time future hardly exists. Space is connected to time and to its use. It is not an unrelated material object that can be simply abandoned. It participates in spiritual life and spirits are located in it—in earth, rock, and water.[10]

The basic spring of action, the nature of causality, seems to be found in a dialectic of creation: opposites are created within each whole, and the activity generated by the working out of these given contradictions leads to development. Purpose is tied directly to causality: man's spirit must develop and fulfill itself in order to live with the Supreme Spirit.

IV

In order to suggest an ideal-type West African Sacred Cosmos, it is necessary to present a very brief overview of the central beliefs of West African peoples. What follows is a reduction of a highly complex, infinitely rich, and multifarious tradition based upon what is, by now, an extensive library of works by anthropologists and Africanists concerned with these issues. It should be noted that this analysis is, in some respects, ahistorical in the sense that what is dynamic and ever-changing is presented uni-dimensionally. Changes certainly did occur in West African societies. However, I am assuming that the shared core of the West African world views remained relatively stable over a long period of time and that evidence from the slave period, as well as congruent evidence from later anthropological sources, can be validly used to analyze the traditional West African Sacred Cosmos. This analysis follows the African categories of being—God, divinities, man, and the pervasive element, spirit, or power—as well as Luckman's categories of time, space, causality, and purpose.[11]

GOD: "Let the Souls of thy People be Cool."

Prayers to the "High God" are common among all West African peoples. Some pray daily upon rising or retiring; some at ritual occasions as at planting, hunting, or before battle and others on private occasions only.

Our Father, it is Thy universe;
It is Thy will;
Let us be at peace;
Let the souls of Thy people be cool;
Thou art our Father;
Remove all evil from our path.

This is an extemporaneous Nuer prayer. The Nuer pray to God at most any time, although they suggest that they usually pray when happy. Mbiti, in his analysis of over 300 African peoples, found that all "have a notion of God as the Supreme being"; in-depth studies of many separate African faiths confirm this view. However, of all the West African peoples, apparently only the Ashanti practice a ritual worship of the High God. Ratray's study of the Ashanti found that they had professional priests dedicated to His service for life and many formal temples to the Supreme God, while fork-branched altars for this worship were traditionally found in every family compound. God's Ashanti name, Nyame, indicates His integral connection with Nyama—spirit, force, or power—and perhaps His creation of spirit. The symbolic representations of Nyame, using the sun, moon, and stars, associated Him with the sky, but He is not viewed simply as the strongest among spirits whose areas of power involve aspects of the universe. It is He "who made death eat poison"; who gave sickness and medicine; and who determines each man's destiny. Like the sky, He is omnipresent and as the Ashanti proverb tells us, "God needs no pointing out to a child."

The Ashanti are the only West Africans who had temples and priests to the Supreme Being, although there was a limited but formal Ewe High God cult at Abomey. Nevertheless, God's reality is affirmed in prayers, proverbs, folktales, and myths found among every African people.[12] For the Akan of the Gold Coast, who also had altars to God, Onyame (the root of whose name in their language means glory, dignity, majesty, and grace) is part of a trinitarian High God. Together, Onyame, Onyankopon, and Odoman Koma are Infinite Being, creator of light, sun, rain, goodness, and all other beings. Danquah suggests that a sophisticated Akan ontology and a questioning philosophy lay behind what have often been regarded as simplistic or "totemistic" references. In an Akan folksong, it is asked:

> Who gave word?
> Who gave word to Hearing,
> For Hearing to have told Ananse,
> For Ananse to have told Odomankoma,
> For Odomankoma
> To have made the Thing?

When "hearing" or ote is rendered as Logos or spirit, Ananse (the spider) as the Onyankopon element in the God-head (as the spider is often the creator of the world in Akan myths) and Odoman Koma as God in His Infinite Being, then Danquah's commentary becomes tenable. For him, this poem says

> how did the idea occur to God to create the Universe, the Thing? The process must have involved first a "hearing" or taking of notice, i.e., understanding; then a knowledge or cognition involving experience; and then an insight or apprehension of the entire idea or concept. . . . Of the three persons in the Trinity of Godhead, who first thought of creation?[13]

Most West African peoples view God as having removed Himself from intimate daily contact with men. There are many African myths about the golden age of creation, an Edenic time when God was closer or more intimate with man. The mythic explanations of His decision to separate Himself or move further away do not involve any sin on man's part but do involve man's bothering God, annoying Him as it were. One myth tells of how men were accidentally but constantly hitting into Him; another tells of His being "pestered" by man's constant requests. Many myths tell of a particular rule broken by men. Much as a father, with too many unruly children, God decides to retreat, but He does not abandon His children. He creates deities who are His subalterns and with whom the troublesome people must deal.

The Yoruba and the Mawu maintain an expectation of personal contact with God, but only after death. The Yoruba believe that "when we die we shall have to state our case in the hall of heaven." The good will be sent to the "good heaven," and the wicked to the "heaven of pot sherds." Most other African peoples, however, see the eventual contact with God in purely spiritual terms. The unique nature of God, his essential difference from all the divinities and spirits, is marked by man's different relationship to him. He does not enter into man's body and possess man as the divinities do. In fact, possession by the Supreme Being is "unthinkable." Nor is He to be persuaded or flattered; that is the intention of much of the ritual surrounding the lesser gods or spirits. While individuals pray to God daily, the important taboos and rituals related to marriage and death and the celebration of great festivals are not associated with God but belong to lesser divinities (God's creations) or the spirits of people who are dead. God is appealed to and people are aware of His presence, but He is not generally worshiped or given homage in this human way.[14]

God is seen as the creator and not as a king elevated to eternal life. He is spirit and essentially other. The general lack of God-oriented ritual is a sign of the acknowledgment of His power. He cannot be cajoled or controlled, but man's spiritual being, if properly realized, can participate in His spiritual being.

Spirit: Nyam or Da

As already suggested, the root Nyam is widely used in West Africa, both in conjunction with the Supreme God and in relation to spirit, force, or power. Father J. Henry, writing about the Bombara, characterized Nyama as

> a force, a power, . . . an energy . . . possessed by every man, every animal, every living being . . . which never disappears, for even after death it continues to exist. This energy, this fluid, is the envoy, the messenger of hatred, of vengeance, of justice, and it goes where a directing and ruling will send it, taking, rightly or wrongly, misfortune, poverty, sickness, death.

Among the Fon of Dahomey this power is called Da, "a force which manifests himself in the world in a number of ways": as the rainbow which creates all other Da, or as a serpent which "coiled himself round the inchoate earth [and] enabled it to be gathered together." Da is androgenous and the source of the gods that create men.

Every individual analyzing the various Sacred Cosmos of West Africans has recognized the reality of this force, but no one has yet adequately translated this concept into Western terms. It is the essence of being; it can be used for good or evil; it is the recognition of the presence of universal spirit; and it must always be taken into account. It can be in words (curses or blessings) and things, animals, people, spirits and divinities; it *is* God.

> "The sun's rays are fire and the Nummo's excrement. [Nummo is spirit, God's first creation.] It is the rays which give the sun its strength. It is the Nummo who gives life to the star, for the sun is in some sort a star.

"The rays drink up the little waters of the earth, the shallow pools, making them rise, and then descend again in rain.
To draw up and then return what one had drawn—that is the
life of the world!"[15]

Man: "The spirit of Man Is Without Boundaries."*

Becoming is a basic West African principle. Man's spirit both changes
and is irreducible. The "man in himself," the "little man" inside, the
essential being, always remains, but he can become more powerful
through the resolution of opposite tendencies, through realization that
involves dialectical growth.

The Dogon hold that both men and women have dual male-female souls
(the Kinndou-Kinndou) and that each individual must submerge one aspect
in order to emerge whole. The Fajulu see the dialectic in terms of the conflict
of an evil and a good soul; again resolution means growth in power. The
Ashanti, Fon, and Yoruba all see the soul as having several parts. Sometimes
the division is seen as between an outward-oriented personality soul, an
inward-oriented spirit soul, and a guardian oversoul; or between a personal
blood soul and a clan soul. Notwithstanding these differences, there is a
shared view that the soul is not unitary and that it is separate and
separable from the body. It is generally viewed as a gift to the body.
Among the Ibo, it is said that God entrusts each human being with a soul at
conception and that the soul's destiny is then in the human being's hands.
Loss of soul, which is seen as very possible, is always disastrous.

The Akan suggest that each individual is given a unique pure
"message" (nKrabea), or soul, ordained especially for him and with
unique potential. It is man's role to fulfill its possibilities for good. Should
he fail to fulfill his soul's good potential, he may have to be reincarnated in
order to continue development, but when fulfilled, death is a return to the
"source," and "it is a glad homegoing for the fully integrated soul."

Each person's uniqueness is symbolized by a name. Africans widely
accept that each and every individual has a particular, unchangeable name,
the word that is the key to his essence and that "shares in the spiritual
reality of a man's being." Among the Dogon, it is believed that simply "to
utter a name is to bring into existence a form and a habitation—the best
form and the most suitable habitation to receive the life-force of the being
invoked."[16]

---

* I have used the word *man* (meaning a person, male or female) and the personal pronoun
his throughout the book, as I find none of the genderless substitutes thus far suggested
appropriate.

This is a very widespread human understanding. The power of words and the uniqueness of identity have often been seen as coalescing in the individual's name. A biblical concern with this power, which would later be of relevance for the Afro-American, is found in God's first compact with Moses which involved God's knowing Moses by name and exchanging his secret name in return. With this knowledge Moses had a hold on God.[17]

For all Africans, naming a child is a very important act and is generally celebrated ritually. It identifies the individual at the same time as it establishes his or her clan relationship. In West Africa, a person is often regarded as twice born, the second birth bringing one into the adult communal group, a social birth as it were. An individual has blood links with clan and ancestors that firmly establish his place in the society, giving him both privileges and responsibilities. Humanity is seen as permanently divided "into clans founded by divine persons" who must be served by their descendants. "According to the myth, the basic structure of all social life is the clan, all the members of which share a common essence and practice the same cult—that of their founder." Most often the second birth into the clan life is enacted in public initiation rites. Ga boys are beaten and treated as corpses. Prepared for the grave, they are then reborn as new men who assume a place with the adults. Among the Yoruba, young men must submit to circumcision *as if they were dead*, while the Ibo reenact a formal dying of their old selves and a rebirth to a higher, better life. The Gikuya, an East African people, literally bind the initiate to his mother and then cut this symbolic umbilical cord while the reborn child (age six to ten) mimics birth cries.

As part of many different West African initiation rites, the initiates must leave the community to fast and suffer as a symbol of their deaths; later they return in joy, reborn. Girls are often secluded at puberty, to emerge fattened and as possessors of a new wisdom: new human beings.

Initiation into a West African priesthood often involves a formal celebration of a second birth. This practice is found among the Toge Ewe and the Dahomean Yoruba, with new names again symbolizing the initiate's new state. Among the Fon, the initiate is subjected to a lengthy convent training, the goal of which is "the complete change of personality of the neophyte."[18]

Thus, while each person has a unique essence, confirmed by his original name, he can and should change radically. Reborn, he is hastened on his proper course toward integration with spirit. While every person can make contact with God and spirit, it is accepted that people can be crucially helped and/or hindered. This potential for intervention is in the hands of the divinities and "living dead," whom men must learn to know and placate through the aid of experts and traditional wisdom.

The Living Dead and Divinities

Many different divinities inhabit each West African Sacred Cosmos. As suggested, they are viewed as God's creation, His intermediaries, whom in His withdrawal He has set to be the middlemen between Himself and human beings. Imasogie suggests the term *bureaucratic monotheism* as the best description for this Cosmos. This term is somewhat misleading, however, because it does not impart the significant difference between God and the divinities, a difference that affects every aspect of men's lives and influences the hierarchy of decisions men must make. God has appointed these divinities, but while they all participate in spirit and use force, they are not God-like. God is variously seen as either good or as partaking in the contest with evil forces, working towards good. In contrast, the divinities are by nature highly unreliable. They are most human in character, and they must be honored, placated, bribed, fed, married, and otherwise dealt with in order to avoid trouble.

Legba's character is well known, but his personality whims are not unique. Legba is an "arch individualist who loves mischief, knows no inhibitions, recognizes no taboos, dares to challenge injustices, even on the part of the creator, to expose them." The personalities adopted by possessed mediums in trances reflect the nature of the various divinities:

> *Ogun* (Yoruba) or *Gun* (Fon), god of blacksmiths, warriors, hunters, and all who use iron, is characterized by coarse and energetic manners; *Shango* (Yoruba) or *Hevioso* (Fon), god of thunder, by manly and jolly dances; *Orishala* (Yoruba), or *Lisa* (Fon), the creator God, by calm and serene behavior; *Shapana* (Yoruba) or *Sapata* (Fon), god of smallpox and the contagious diseases, by restless agitation; *Eshu Elegba* (Yoruba) or *Legba* (Fon), messengers of the other gods, by cynical and abusive attitudes.

Divinities may have been great men, mythic founders of clans and peoples, or the spirits of any of the dead. Mbiti makes an interesting and seemingly cogent discrimination. He suggests we abandon the term *ancestral spirits* and divide the worshiped spirits into (1) the divinities who are based on real or mythical personalities from the unknown distant past, and (2) the living dead, the spirits of those who have died relatively recently and who are still recalled by name and character. (When those who knew them in life are all dead, these spirits move into the general class of divinities, becoming more dangerous because of their lack of direct ties to the living.)

All of the spirits, but especially those of people recently alive, are regarded as personalities who function much as they did when alive. They have likes and hatreds, weaknesses and strengths, and must be dealt with as one deals with living persons, but they also have far greater power over spirit. They are, therefore, very dangerous, and it is wise, if possible, to find professional and experienced help in dealing with them. This is the role of what outsiders have called witchcraft, Juju, and Voudou. These are the techniques of trained professionals in handling divinities, the living dead, and Nyama. Thus, it is the role of ritual and, in particular, of ritual possession to find out the divinities' desires and to fulfill them.[19]

Time and Space

Running through the African Sacred Cosmos is the constant concern with the past, paralleled by a concern with the present—with the clan and with elders, who will soon be the living dead. But there is almost no concern with the future. Mbiti confirms that dimension of the Sacred Cosmos through reference to language, which, as Luckman has suggested, can be viewed as the symbolic re-creation of the cosmos. In the languages Mbiti studies, "there are no concrete words or expression to convey the idea of a distant future." Language can be at the most related to two years hence; later "events lie beyond the horizon of what constitutes actual time." It is a potential with which Africans are essentially unconcerned. It is the past that is of importance—the divinities and the dead who were once living, as well as the accumulated wisdom that teaches one the actual character of the spirits. One does not need to learn how things can work in principle. One needs to know the historical and unique character of particular spirits that lived in the past. No science can bring this knowledge because its character is not that of logical order. Each spirit is unique and has to be learned of through esoteric wisdom, handed down by those who have had experience of it. The distant past exists as a golden age, but there are virtually no myths about its reestablishment or the end of days.

Africans often use the same word when speaking of either time or space. In both cases, the language used is related to the use made of the time and space. The physical world is made meaningful through use, and its divisions are related to that content. Thus, even the world inhabited by spirits is envisioned as one of towns and villages, with each people having their rightful home. (John Atkins, on a slavetrading journey in Guinea in the 1720s, saw numerous slaves ready to die as "many of them think . . . that Death will send them into their own Country.")

Africans view spirits as having localized histories; the spirits inhabit fixed homes, rocks, rivers, and people. God is universal, but His emissaries come to a particular people in a particular place. This people is regarded as having a holy and communal relationship to their land and its spirits. Clearly, dislocation must cause basic trauma.[20]

Causality, Professional Assistance, and Possession

God is good, and there was once an ideal state. What then explains evil? By and large, West Africans seem to believe that evil is caused by some spirit or some person having violated the proper social order, either through forgetfulness or a deliberate act. In either case, the individual act has strong communal repercussions, as the individual exists only as a member of a large and intrinsically interrelated social group. "The principle of good is whatever makes for community welfare, while evil is the reverse."

In the Dogon cosmology, both the single jackal and the seventh Nummo violated order. The jackal committed incest, while the seventh Nummo, "the word," ate the self-forbidden fruit. This fruit or grain is still eaten by the Dogon, although it is planted and harvested under very singular circumstances. Its ritual cutting and its fixed storage place at the heart or womb of the granary is explained by its being an intrinsic part of God's creation. It is both good and evil, intertwined: " 'the seed also preserved its beneficent power, the good word God put into it when he created it.' "

Sexuality is the mode in which the nature of reality is worked out, and the creation of offspring is the continuation of God's word in the world. Family interrelationships are thus part of the sacred order, tied to the first ancestor and continuing through to the present. (The Dogon evil grain, Digitaria, is seen as symbolic of the menstrual blood flow, which is also a symbol of the primal evil.)

Morality is based on past and present kinship interrelations, and goodness on preserving the larger kinship structure. Thus, "wrongness" is opposition to the traditional, the communal, or the established order, and any individual opposition is a crime for which the community can suffer. The wrath of the spirits can affect everyone, and the offender is, therefore, called upon by the chiefs or elders to make amends. All antisocial action is responded to communally, although it affects the individual in a very personal way as well. Among the Mende, an antisocial "offender is believed to be as it were covered with rust, a condition which destroys his personality."

Since it is believed that nothing bad happens by chance, the evil cause or evil agent must be found. Misfortune is the sign that an evil act has been committed, and the cause must then be uncovered. The first suspect is the sufferer himself. Since there are elaborate systems of proper and improper behavior in each African society, there are endless possibilities for having violated the proper social order, offending either God, divinities, or men. But an outside agency may, of course, be at fault; or someone may be using sorcery to bring spiritual difficulty to an individual and his society. In all cases, the source of evil must be found, either through confession or counter-witchcraft, and it must be purged. This is, indeed, a dangerous business because it is the spirits who are the agents of evil, and if improperly treated they can bring further evil.[21]

West African life is permeated by ritual and by trained professionals who organize the rituals. Their roles are legitimated by their relationship with the divinities and the living dead, whose will they generally learn through messages these spirits send through mediums. Spirit possession is almost universally known to West African peoples, and it is ritually prepared for and ritually used to explain evil and legitimate change.

West African religious professionals are of many types and hold various status positions in their societies, ranging from priests and leaders of cults, through mediums, servants, and wives of gods, to witches, wizards, diviners, and herbalists. Their primary function is to get in contact with the divinities—to learn if the divinities are angered by the breaking of a taboo, or if they can be used to gain power or spirit. They are the chief means of communication with Nyama itself, with the divinities and with the living dead as well as with the spirits in animals, plants, rocks, water, soil, and objects. They provide access to the Sacred Cosmos. They learn to use spirit for good or for evil. They are, therefore, very powerful, and their honor is given a high priority in the West African hierarchy of values.

Parallel to the varied, yet similar, West African understandings of God, man, divinities, and spirits, possession is viewed somewhat differently in the various West African societies, but almost all are acquainted with it. In Ghana, the divinities, the living dead and spirits of rivers, wars, and things can possess a person. (It should again be emphasized that the High God does not possess men.) The spirits begin by calling the individual in an initial disassociational experience, and it is his or her task to discover who is calling. (Most West African mediums are women, and they begin their practice in the crucial identity-establishing period between the ages of seveteeen and twenty-eight.)

A Ghanean who felt called to serve a divinity would turn to a diviner for aid in establishing the source of the call and then train in the appropriate lore. Once initiated, trances take the medium out of himself, or as the Akamba initiates say, they have "lost themselves." Typically, the Ghanean medium does not consciously remember anything from the trance period. It is ostensibly the spirit that is acting in the medium's body. This trance is traditionally prepared for and carried out in a ritual fashion. It is preceded by a period of fasting, which is followed by a group experience involving drumming and rhythmic singing and clapping. The medium begins the possesion in a daze which is followed by hyperactive leaping, dancing, singing, and talking in tongues, although the particular character of the trance is related to the particular divinity involved.

In African cultures (as in the West Indies), the divinity or spirit is regarded as mounting or climbing on the medium, and the inhabited or possessed body adopts the behavior appropriate to the spirit that has come to subordinate her body. She is the "one climbed on" or the "horse" of the divinity. If possessed by Lisa, the medium always acts calmly and serenely, while if Legba is the mountee, the mounted person is cynical and abusive.

The various status groups among these professionals utilize ecstasy and possession in different forms and for different purposes. Among the Kalabari, "spirit dancing" is clearly the prerogative of highly trained priests, who express the divine power's concern for the whole community through public trances held at elaborate public festivals. In contrast, almost any member of the same society can express a call to "speak with the mouth of a Spirit," while individuals, usually women, can set themselves up as private professional mediums, offering their services, for a fee, to anyone who wants to contact "their" spirit. At will, they go into trance, calmly relaying the spirit's messages, although these may well be in tongues.

In all cases, the medium is but an agent, chosen by the gods, who returns to her old self after the possession ritual. She has power, but her own essential nature is not changed. She is the mounted steed, and the rider is the significant actor.[22]

Purpose

Notwithstanding all the dangers and dark possibilities, the purpose of life is to affirm joy. Man's task is to realize himself, to grow in power and possibility through intrinsic relations with all the physical and spiritual world around him. This is a difficult process, complicated by proscriptions, possible errors of commission and omission, spirit in the hands of enemies, and other forces powerful and dangerous. Life's goal is fulfillment. A sense of primal guilt is not an African complication, but this does not make the task easier.

The fulfillment that is sought as *the* goal in African life is individual, but it cannot be achieved outside of the communal structure. Both aspects should be emphasized. The African concern with the individual is often disregarded in the emphasis on clan or tribe. Each man is seen as part of a larger family, both alive and dead. This corporate group is crucial in every formal matrix of every individual's life, including birth, education, marriage, landholding, and death. "No one stands alone . . . as long as he has family and clan members," alive and dead, "at his side." But there is another, individualistic, aspect in the African world view, symbolized in the Dogon's use of private altars. In addition to all the public altars, each Dogon has two private altars: one for his head and one for his body. They mirror the duality running through the cosmology and the major symbols. They enable the individual to communicate with the first ancestor, who is seen as drinking at these private altars and who then returns to spiritual life. The individual can both influence and assimilate life force and thus can personally affect "the course of this world's destiny."[23]

Each man alone must be responsible for making himself and taking his proper place in the ongoing continuum. Every man is responsible for his own inner self, for the "little man" who existed before his body came into the world and who will continue to exist after his body dies.

West African peoples did not have one Sacred Cosmos. For the ethnographer concerned with Africa the differences between African views and their respective change over time are far more significant than an abstract of their similarities. However, for the study of American blacks, one of the significant questions is to what extent blacks shared values and understandings prior to their forced removal from Africa. This brief overview of African world views suggests that there was the potential for the creation of one quasi-African world view in America.

2

THE TRANSMISSION OF AFRICAN PEOPLES, LANGUAGES, AND WORLD VIEWS TO NORTH AMERICA

I

Having posited the thesis that West African world views could well be combined into one world view—that the basic understandings of god, spirit power, divinities, and man, as well as the senses of time, place, causality, and purpose were shared—can it be shown that these views survived the Middle Passage and the trauma of enslavement, and can their growth into one Sacred Cosmos be authoritatively established? In the South American and West Indian experience, it is easy to recognize that African faiths survived and assimilated neo-Catholic forms; but aside from Louisiana Voudou of the late eighteenth and early nineteenth centuries, the existence of other African faith systems in North America is not obvious. Can it be maintained that African beliefs were preserved while formal religious institutions were not? And what can account for this most basic difference between the various slave cultures?

The seminal study of the slave trade done by Philip Curtin and the recent revisions of his research provide clues and direct answers to some of these questions. Of the 8 to 11 million people transported from Africa in the 400 years from the midfifteenth to the midnineteenth centuries, only 596,000 were brought to North America. The great majority of these Africans were shipped directly from Africa to the Southern colonies, arriving in the period between 1700 and 1860, with the largest number purchased between 1740 and 1810. "This means that the African population in this country arrived, on the whole, much earlier than did the majority of settlers from Europe," and that the racial balance in the South altered radically in the middle decades of the eighteenth century.[1]

From an early period, the pattern of black population growth in North America was significantly different from that of South America and the West Indies. North American blacks began to reproduce themselves and early experienced a positive birth rate. In contrast, South American and West Indian slave populations did not have an adequate birth rate to maintain their numbers, and millions of Africans were transported there, in great part to maintain the slave population. In North America blacks rapidly became a community of second- and third-generation Americans, and the percentage born in Africa, while significant through the end of the eighteenth century, soon became a minor factor in the nineteenth. Fogel and Engerman maintain that from 1710 on the majority of slaves in America were born in America, notwithstanding a 1780-1810 peak in slave importation. At the end of the legal slave trade (1808) the black population already equaled a half million. By 1860 it had grown to 4.5 million although the total illegal importation (1808-1860) is estimated at only 54,000. These facts alone go a long way toward explaining the differences between North and South American slave cultures. In 1860 most North American slaves were second-, third-, and fourth-generation Americans, while South American slaves remained largely native Africans until near to the close of slavery.[2]

The changing market conditions in Africa, combined with planter prejudices in the New World, led to shifts in the ethnic origins of slaves imported into the Americas. South America, the West Indies, and North America were each populated by different combinations of African peoples, a difference Curtin suggests may also have been crucial for cultural development. Imports to any one area changed over time as well. Thus, the English slave trade of 1680 through 1688 was primarily with the Windward Coast; by 1713, the locus of trade had shifted to the Bight of Benin, by 1724, to the Gold Coast, and by 1752, to the Bight of Biafra, which, along with Central Africa (the Congo and Angola), remained particularly important through the end of the century.

The various colonial sections of North America were also populated by different combinations of peoples. Slaves coming to the Northern colonies were most often born in the West Indies. Of the 4,551 slaves imported into New York and New Jersey between 1715 and 1767, only 930 were born in Africa. In stark contrast, the South's slave population was primarily African-born and, as slavery grew, Africans were increasingly shipped directly to North America. Herbert Klein points out that between 1735 and 1769 86 percent of South Carolina slaves and 83 percent of Virginia slaves (the two largest slave populations) came directly from Africa.

Table 1
Slaves Imported into the North American
Mainland, by Origin

	Percent of slaves by identifiable origin imported by—			
Coastal region of origin	(1) Virginia 1710-69	(2) South Carolina 1733-1807	(3) British slave trade, 1690-1807	(4) Speculative estimate, all imported into North America (Pct.)
Senegambia	14.9	19.5	5.5	13.3
Sierra Leone	5.3	6.8	4.3	5.5
Windward Coast	6.3	16.3	11.6	11.4
Gold Coast	16.0	13.3	18.4	15.9
Bight of Benin	—	1.6	11.3	4.3
Bight of Biafra	37.7	2.1	30.1	23.3
Angola	15.7	39.6	18.2	24.5
Mozambique-Madagascar	4.1	0.7	*	1.6
Unknown	—	—	0.6	0.2
Total	100.0	100.0	100.0	100.0

*Included in Angola figure.

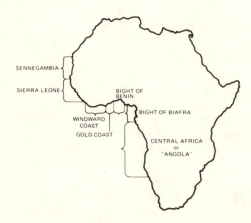

Slave-trading Areas in West Africa

SOURCE: Philip C. Curtin, *The Atlantic Slave Trade: A Census* (Madison: University of Wisconsin Press, 1969), 157.

Curtin's figures suggest that initially there may have been two relatively distinct Southern slave populations as well. The first came through South Carolina, reaching North Carolina and Georgia, and accounted for some 46 percent of the American slaves. South Carolinians preferred Senegambian and Gold Coast or Sierra Leone slaves; this preference distinguished them from the majority of English traders. The second slave population came into the country through the Chesapeake Bay and was sent to Virginia, Maryland, and the remaining slave areas. This second population was closer in origin to the average English trade distribution.[3]

Intercolonial and interstate slave sales later led to a general mixing of slaves, but most members of the black communities in the eighteenth century were apparently ethnically distinguishable, while many were ethnically localized.

Melville Herskovits, in his seminal study of Africanisms in American Negro life, maintains that import statistics, cultural "carryovers" in North America, and historical traditions in West Africa all support the thesis that the Akan and Ashanti of the Gold Coast, the Dahoman, the Yoruba of Western Nigeria, and the Bini of Eastern Nigeria were culturally the most important peoples for the North American black settlement. He holds that they came in the largest concentrated groups, established cultural hegemony over the Senegalese blacks earlier brought to America, and were able to preserve elements of their culture into the nineteenth century. There has been serious criticism of Herskovits' use of the construct of "cultural areas" in Africa, but Elizabeth Donnan's and Philip Curtin's figures substantiate the assessment that large groups of particular "peoples" or people exported from a particular port were imported in a given period. However, it has not yet been established exactly who was on any ship recorded as having come from a single port, and there is much conflicting evidence. We know that it was trader lore that slave populations should be mixed so that they might not have a *lingua franca* and would be forced to learn English more rapidly. But this supposed desideratum was not a direct concern of the African sources of supply. We have no records of traders turning down slaves on the basis of their sharing a common language, although Captain William Smith claimed that he followed the prudent pattern of trading "with the different nations, on either side of the [Gambia] River, and having some of every sort on board, [so that] there will be no more likelihood of their succeeding in a Plot, than of finishing the Tower of Babel."[4]

Yet, there was strong demand for slaves of a particular origin. There is evidence that it was actually easier in the short run to administer a plantation if a black overseer or driver, who could talk some English, was given a homogeneous group to control.

Certainly some shiploads brought polyglot groups. Alexander Falconbridge, a surgeon in the slave trade in 1758, testified before the Privy Council that on two occasions he had purchased slaves at Bonney (380 and 420) and that "these negroes, purchased from black traders who had brought them from the interior, were unable to understand each other." At least five different African peoples were aboard a single ship, the *Doris*, when it arrived in South Carolina, on January 30, 1806: "Mandingos, Soozees, Ballams, Bagos, [and] Naloofe Negroes," as they were then advertised. In 1835, Francis Moore reported that at James Fort, the English trading station on the Gambia River, black middlemen, Mandingo traders, regularly brought polyglot groups down river. "In some years Slaves to the Amount of 2000, most of which they say are Prisoners taken in War: They buy them from the different Princes who take them; many of them are Bumbrongs, and Petcharies, Nations who each of them have different languages, and are brought from a vast Way inland." A "vast way" is clearly a very imprecise term, and recent scholarship tends to suggest that an inland strip parallel to the coastal trading stations was the source of most slaves. However, some small numbers were indeed brought over vast distances, traded from people to people.[5]

Most of the slave shiploads brought to the Americas were advertised as if they were homogeneous groups, with the ethnic origins of the slaves generally a distinct item of concern in the lower South. In Georgia, slave origins were commonly advertised, as in the *Georgia Gazette* of August 2, 1764: "To be sold at publik vendue, for ready money, on Thursday the 9th inst. at the plantation late John Spencer's five miles from Savannah on the Augusta road, Nine New Negroe Men, as likely as any brought into this province, lately imported from the Gold Coast." Similarly, in the *Georgia Gazette* of January 14, 1767: "On Tuesday the 17th inst. will be sold at Savannah About 40 likely New Negroes, Consisting mostly of Men and Women, Lately from Gambia and Sierreleon."

Ethnic origins were a question of concern in South Carolina as well. The *South Carolina Gazette* of 1765 contained many such advertisements: "Now Selling, One Hundred and Fifty choice Gold-Coast Negroes. . . . Directly from the windward and Grain coast of Africa being such as are usually brought from Gambia."

In another South Carolina advertisement for a sale of the 280 slaves who arrived on the *Betsey*, coming from Angola on June 6, 1771, the peoples were described as: "mostly of the Masse-Congo country, and are esteemed equal to the Gold Coast and Gambia slaves."

When a shipment arrived on the *Unity*, the sale of August 5, 1772, was advertised, and "Whidah" was "talked up" as follows:

> Whidah is esteemed to be the finest Country in Africa and Slaves from thence, usually sell in all the West-India Islands for Five

Pounds Sterling per Head more than Negroes of any other country. Whidah, a Country greatly preferred to any other, thro'out the West Indies, and inferior to none on the coast of Africa.

We know that South Carolina and Georgia planters, as well as those on the Islands, were very conscious of the origins of their slaves and had strong opinions about tribal differences and the supposed relative value of the different groups. One can assume, therefore, that they attempted to buy those they "knew" to be best and that, as a result, plantation homogeneity was reinforced.

Henry Laurens has left us a detailed record of local prejudices in this regard. Ordering 100 slaves for resale in the fall of 1755, he put in a request for tall men eighteen to twenty-five and women fourteen to eighteen; but "There must not be a Callabar [Ibo] amongst them. Gold Coast or Gambia's are best, next to them the Windward Coast are preferred to Angola's."

Laurens claimed to have had direct experience with Callabars or Ibo, "which slaves are quite out of repute from numbers in every Cargo that have been sold with us destroying themselves." Laurens was willing to try to sell Callabars if no other cargo was on the market in competition, or if he could obtain a particularly young population as he did in May 1756: "it was a most butiful Cargo of the sort, chiefly young People from 15 to 20 which are not accustomed to destroy themselves like those who are Older."[6]

The Ibo slave Olaudah Equiano, better known by his slave name of Gustavus Vassa, confirms Laurens' judgment, at least in terms of his desire for death. The unpopularity of Ibo served to reinforce his isolation and depression, as he met with few who could speak his language. Of his arrival at a Southern plantation in 1756, Equiano later wrote:

I was now exceedingly miserable, and thought myself worse off than any of the rest of my companions, *for they could talk to each other*, but I had no person to speak to that I could understand. In this state I was constantly grieving and pining, and wishing for death rather than anything else.[7]

Both Georgia and South Carolina planters of the mideighteenth century had clear prejudices, and it would seem these overrode any lore about mixing slave groups. It was most important to get good workers, and if a particular people worked better and adjusted more easily, then they were purchased.

Donnan notes that in Virginia "les importance seems to have been attached to the section from which the Negroes came" than was the case in the lower South. Nevertheless, even in Virginia many advertisements did note slave origins: "Just arrived from Africa, the Snow *Nancy*, James E. Colly

Commander, with about two hundred and fifty five healthy Windward and
Gold Coast Slaves, the Sale of which will begin at Osborne's on James
River, on Wednesday the 29th Instant (July)" (*Virginia Gazette,* July 9,
1772).

In sharper contrast, Northern sales did not generally note tribal
origins but most often simply defined blacks as "likely Negros." This is as
would be expected inasmuch as small groups, born in or transhipped from
the Islands, were the basic source of supply in the North.

Once the slaves were purchased, however, owners in all states knew
their slaves' origins. Eighteenth-century advertisements for runaways list
this aspect as an important identifying feature:

> [H]e is a young Angola Negro; . . . a very Black Mundigo Negro
> Man; . . . a native of Madagascar; . . . a Congo Negro slave;
> . . . of the Suso country; . . . New Negro Fellow . . . calls him-
> self Bonna and says he came from a Place of that name in
> the Ibo country in Africa; . . . marked in the face as the Gold
> Coast slaves generally are.[8]

As early as 1625, the Reverend Jonas Michaelius, considering the New
Netherlands experience, singled out the Angolan slaves for particular
opprobrium, finding them "thievish, lazy and useless trash." This did not
mean Angolans could not be sold. By the 1730s, the Southern market was
readily absorbing Angolans, probably because of their cheaper price. They
were apparently rated as a good buy at the price, although certainly not
equal to the "first class" Whidah, or Gold Coast Ashanti (Coromantines),
who had the reputation of being brave and sturdy. Angolans were not seen
to be equal even to Gambians or to blacks from the Windward Coast. They
were approximately fifth in the ranking order, but far above Callabars
("bites" or Ibo) in the popular evaluation.

An anonymous pamphleteer of 1763, seeking to legitimate the slave
trade (and gain support for its extension) and to explain the relative
success of the French in their colonial ventures, credited the French
achievements to their superior slaves, who include "many Negroes from
the Gold Coast, Popo, and Whidah, which are the most valuable for the
laborious cultivation of the sugar-cane, and other plantation products."
His reasoning is sociological in nature:

> The Gold Coast, Popo and Whidah Negroes are born in a part of
> Africa which is very barren. . . . On that account, when able
> to take hoe in hand, they are obliged to go and cultivate the
> land for their subsistence. They also live hardily; so that
> when they are carried to our plantations (as they have been
> used to hard labour from their infance) they become a strong

robust people. . . . Indeed they live better in general in our plantations; and they are always ready, on arrival there, to go to the hard work necessary in planting and manufacturing the sugar cane.

On the other hand, the Gambia, Callabar, Boney and Angola Negroes are brought from those parts of Africa that are extremely fertile, where everything grows almost spontaneously. . . . They have every other necessary of life in great plenty. On that account, the men never work but lead an indolent life, and are in general of a lazy disposition and tender constitution; for the necessary work among them is done by the women.[9]

The Coromantines or Ashanti were highly regarded both in the West Indies and in the North American colonies. At the same time, they were feared as dangerous: as independent and potentially mutinous. By 1735, John Atkins had worked out a full-scale slave valuation:

Slaves differ in their goodness; those from the Gold Coast are accounted best, being cleanest limbed, and more docible by our Settlements than others; but then they are, for that very reason, more prompt to Revenge, and murder the instruments of their Slavery, and also apter in the means to compass it. . . .

To Windward [of the Gold Coast] they approach in Goodness as is the distance from the Gold Coast; so, as at Gambia, or Sieeraleon, to be much better, than at any of the interjacent places. . . .

To Leeward from thence, they alter gradually for the worse; an Angolan Negro is a Proverb for worthlessness; and they mend (if we may call it so) in that way, till you come to the Hottentots, that is to the Southernmost Extremity of Africa.

Different ethnic groups of slaveowners apparently had differing evaluations of slave populations, and slaves that would not sell well in one market were often found desirable or salable in others. For example, Angolans, low in demand in North America, sold well in St. Dominique and in other plantation areas. While market conditions were important, perhaps there were differing interactions between these particular African and slaveowner world views that affected sales.[10]

In what way does this evidence help us to evaluate the maintenance of tribal identity, language carryover, and, above all, the transmission of the Sacred Cosmos to America? It seems fairly clear that during the eighteenth century large enclaves of several tribal peoples existed from Maryland south, although among each group many languages were spoken. In 1708, Maryland Governor Seymour "reported that a considerable number of the 4,657 slaves in Maryland had come from 'Gambo and the Gold Coast.' "[11]

Gerald W. Mullin's fine study of slaves in eighteenth-century Virginia and Peter H. Wood's equally suggestive study of colonial South Carolina break new ground in regard to language and culture maintenance. A clearer picture is just beginning to emerge of the eighteenth-century African-ness of the American South. The New World population certainly looked different from any the blacks had known, while the blacks were, to all appearances, changing rapidly. Most blacks were given slave clothing and made unique adaptations at the outset, but occasionally an African still in traditional garb was recorded in America, some in long cloth gowns and others in "arse-cloths." Africans with facial and body scarification, teeth filed, and hair elaborately dressed were common sights. The mixture of African peoples was a new one, but the African would still find many familiar qualities in the strangely new surroundings.

In South Carolina, which, by the mideighteenth century had the highest density of blacks to whites in all of North America, it was not difficult for blacks to locate others who could speak their own language. Moreover, many blacks could often understand African tongues other than their own far better than their owners thought they could. Wood cites the rare interview material available from the *Amistad* mutiny which refers to a Bandi who could talk Mendii, a Mendii who could speak Vai, Kon-no, and Gissi, etc. We know that for trade purposes many West African blacks knew several languages. Hausa, Dyula, Woloff, and Arabic often served as trade languages before the European presence, with the addition of Pidgin Portuguese, Pidgin French, and Pidgin English afterwards. Curtin is certain that "multilingualism is widespread in Africa. Most Africans know at least two languages and some knew many more." Bilali, a slave on a plantation near Savannah, knew French, English, Fula, and Arabic and taught the first three languages to his children. Similar stories were repeated throughout the South. Black African "linguists" were for hire in the slave trade and served an important role as intermediaries between slavers and slaves.[12]

There is the fascinating story of Dick, a free black linguist, who served as the go-between on the slave ship *Rainbow* in 1758. He translated the white orders into an African tongue or tongues and reassured the slaves that they were being taken as laborers, and not as food or sacrifices. (Many slaves thought "themselves bought to eat.") Dick's contribution to order "was of great Consequence to the interest of the Voyage" until suddenly one of the crew, a man called Comer, apprised him that the captain intended to enslave him through sale in the West Indies. This allegation played on a conscious and real fear, as this was a fate that too often awaited "free" blacks involved in the slave trade. (Many upper-class Africans found themselves "illegally" enslaved as had Ayuba Suleiman Diallo or Job, a rare individual who succeeded in reestablishing his proper status and was returned from Maryland to Africa to continue as both an owner and trader of slaves.) When Dick heard of the cruel fate supposedly awaiting him, "Dick grew sulky and . . . the Slaves on Board refused their Victuals and would be under no Command as formerly." The captain inquired as to the cause of the major dislocation. When he learned of Comer's allegations, he informed Dick that they were groundless. According to the deposition of the white mate:

> Dick demanded satisfaction of the Said Comer, but the Captain told him he could give him no Satisfaction having no power to beat any White Person on board, but Dick being Disatisfied, and stormed and Raged upon Deck; and in the Deponents Opinion, the Captain apprehended danger from the Slaves, and therefore to prevent Insurrection Desir'd the said Dick to take Satisfaction of the said Comer.

After two whippings at the hands of the African linguist, the white seaman died.

It was quite unusual for whites to so openly acknowledge their dependence on the language skills of a black man. Generally whites were either unconscious of their dependence or unwilling to acknowledge it. We now know, however, that many Africans had extensive language skills and that whites were often dependent upon them in this regard.

Taking the fragmentary language evidence as a whole, it now seems possible to hypothesize, in a preliminary fashion and as a basis for further research, that as a result of transport and purchase policy, several African languages may well have survived the initial slave trade into the Americas. This language survival helped some Africans to maintain their separate Sacred Cosmos for a significant period of time after they were in America and provided a congenial milieu for the development of one black Sacred Cosmos.[13]

II

The suggestion that Africans may have maintained their African Sacred Cosmos for some time is not meant to imply that the move to America was not traumatic nor that it did not result in anomie and lasting disturbance. The sustaining conversation between an enslaved African and his society began to falter in Africa itself. Mungo Park reported the dejection of the blacks in the coffle he traveled with in 1799. Even in Africa the slaves were stimulated by black owners to engage in

> games of hazard, and sing diverting songs, to keep up their spirits; for though some of them sustained the hardships of their situation with amazing fortitude, the greater part were very much dejected, and would sit all day in a sort of sullen melancholy, with their eyes fixed upon the ground.

On the slave ships most Africans looked "dull and empty," "hopeless" or desperate, in the eyes of the whites. The often savage treatment in transit, and the process referred to as "seasoning" or "breaking in" on the Islands, whether intentional or not, began to alter the African world view.[14]

Africans were highly conscious of a breakdown in values. Abou Bekir Sadiki, "alias" Edward Doulan, a slave in Jamaica in 1834, painfully recognized his own marginality:

> My parents' religion is of the Mussulman, they are all circumcised and their devotions are five times a day, they fast in the month of Ranadan, [sic] they give tribute according to their laws, they are married to four wives but the fifth is an abomination to them, they fight for their religion, and they travel to Hedjaz (those that are capable). They don't eat any meat except what they themselves kill. They do not drink wine nor spirits as it is held an abomination so to do. They do not associate with any that worship idols, nor profane the Lord's name, nor do dishonour to their parents, or commit murder, or bear false witness, or who are covetous, proud or boastful for such faults are an abomination unto my religion. They are particularly careful in the education of their children and in their behaviour, but *I am lost* to all of these advantages since my bondage *I am corrupt* and I now conclude by begging the Almighty God to lead me into the faith that is proper for me for he alone knows the secrets of my heart and what I am in need of.[15]

While others may not have articulated their plight as well as Sadiki, many experienced his sense of loss and corruption.

The preceding evidence was presented to indicate that eighteenth-century slaves were likely to have been in the proximity of others with whom they could talk in African tongues and share world views. This evidence suggests that many of the slaves who arrived in North America in the mideighteenth century may have been able to maintain their own languages during their lifetimes, continuing to speak to one another in

African tongues, and insofar as possible, using them to re-create the extended family structure they had known in Africa.

Sometimes members of a single African family found themselves still together after the African, Atlantic, and local sale conditions. Richard Jones, a South Carolina black, retelling his history in the 1930s, recalled that in the late eighteenth century: "Uncle Tom come along with Granny Judith. Two womenfolk come with dem, Aunt Chany and Daphne." In this case, as in others, notwithstanding the early difficulty of traveling between slave plantations, the family relations were maintained until the twentieth century. Even if seen but once a year, old kinship relationships were, if at all possible, kept intact; moreover, new kinship relationships were rapidly established, as is substantiated by the research of Herbert Gutman.

On arrival in America some slaves conspicuously enforced African ideas of kinship and communal responsibility. Julia Sparks of Columbus, Mississippi, recalls that when "a slave . . . married a girl from a group of Africans just received on the plantation . . . the young man was forced to obtain the consent of every member of the girl's group before he was allowed to marry her."[16]

What was the history of Africans' mores? The marriage of slaves from varying backgrounds, and their joint raising of children, intermingled the various African values. This process was hastened by the sale and dispersal of blacks. It would appear that as plantations grew, they became, to some extent, new tribal establishments with the whole "family" sharing one new name and one location. The blacks' relationship to this new family name is symbolic of their relationship to their new plantation "people" and their new society. The original slaveowner's name was not given in pride of accomplishment or as a gift, but as a brand indicating ownership, much as actual brands that were put on slaves in Africa and the Americas. Nevertheless, the plantation family did begin to function as a new kin group; in many cases some relatives were in it at the outset and it certainly built its own blood-relatedness in time. Even when slaves were sold away from their first plantations, they often kept these original owners' names as their very own family names. (Fortune, who originally was owned by Mr. Minnich, became Fortune Minnich when sold to Nelson Bang.)[17]

The means of social control adopted on early plantations helped forge the newly emerging quasi-African world view. It is very likely that on larger plantations the control of newly arrived Africans had to be delegated to black men who served as both linguists and lieutenants, supervising the black population and teaching them as well. The evidence from the Sea Islands, which may stand as an ideal type exhibiting elements that had more generally occurred, indicates that the crucial control over the newest arrivals was in the hands of slave deputies, part of a black elite known as *swonga*:

When a gang of fresh Africans were purchased, they were assigned in groups to certain reliable slaves who initiated them
into the ways of the plantation. These drivers, as they were
called, had the right of issuing or withholding rations to the
raw recruits and of inflicting minor punishments. They taught
the new slaves to speak the broken English which they knew.

The term *swonga* means African magic or power, and is still used in
this sense today. The *swonga* must have been men of power of both a
sacred and a political type, serving as holy men for Africans and foremen
for the whites. Not only did blacks control other blacks in the work
experience, but their social life was essentially their own, so long as it was
not recognized as endangering the whites. As late as 1827, a Charleston
planter claimed that as long as the work assigned was done, he in no way
interested himself in controlling slave life: "We don't care what they do
when their tasks are over—we lose sight of them till the next day."[18] This
was probably the ruling idea among most of the planters and slaveowners.
Their goal was production, and their "strange" work force could "amuse"
themselves as they saw fit, provided it did not reduce their productivity or
cause problems for whites. The result of this arrangement was that
spiritual space was left for blacks to forge the new neo-African world view.
     Many other comments about the continued use of African languages
can be put together to strengthen the contention that a quasi-African
identity was maintained. Some blacks refused to talk English. Congo-born
"Clark," speaking "very bad English," ran away from a Louisiana
plantation in 1816. He was "in the habit of answering in Congo the question put to him." He seemingly understood the questions, but his masters
could not master his responses.
     Many slaves maintained their African names, the clearest symbol of
their African identity. Footbea, who was called John by his owner,
maintained his Mandingo name by "more readily" responding to it. It is
true that many slaves were literally forced to use new English names. Their
owners also recognized the symbolic power of words, but many slaves
never learned to "speak good." Learning English was not necessarily a
function of the length of their residence in America, as Mullin suggests.
While he may be right in positing a model, in that most slaves may indeed
have learned workmanlike English after some three years in the country,
the minority that did not is equally significant. Richard Jones'
grandmother and aunt, both of whom were brought over from Africa prior
to 1830, lived long lives in America but never spoke English properly.
"When dey talk, nobody didn't know what dey was talking about. My
granny never could speak good like I can. She talk half African, and all
African when she got bothered."[19]

Many important comments on early black language usage and identity can be found in the reports sent to the bishop of London by men serving Anglican parishes in Virginia and Maryland. It must be remembered that these men were attempting to justify the small numbers of blacks they had converted. However, repeatedly the chief reason they cite for their failure is "the variety and strangeness of the languages" spoken by the Africans. This evidence not only indicates that the slaves spoke African tongues but that, even when they could understand English, they often rejected the white religion. This, in itself, is a sign of their spiritual strength.

In 1724, John Bell, pastor of Christ Church Parish in Virginia, reported that there were "a great many Black bond men and women infields [within his Parish] that understand not our Language nor me theirs." James Falconer, minister at Elizabeth City, Virginia, claimed "it is impossible to instruct these that are grown up before they are carried from their own Country *they never being able either to speak or understand our language perfectly.*"

Many of the Anglican churchmen suggested that only "the young slaves that are born among us" should be appealed to or that only infant slaves should be baptized (as many were doing) because "the old ones that are imported into the country by reason of their not understanding the Language being much more *indocile.*" "In truth [our Negroe Slaves] have *so little Docility* in them they scarce ever become capable of Instruction."[20] The use of African languages and the exhibition of what was regarded as the negative character traits of "indocility" were clearly associated in these churchmen's minds.

Recent research suggests that the illegal importation of slaves in the 1830s and 1840s may have been as high as between 1760 and 1780, indicating a larger number of Africans in the later population than once thought.

As late as the Civil War, some recent African arrivals could not speak English. Charley Barber's parents, brought in illegally in the nineteenth century, "never did talk lak de other slaves, could just say a few words, use deir hands, and make signs." But they told Charley their history of enslavement and transhipment. "Dat what they tell me," Charley said. They talked to him in their language and he understood.

It would appear that from the outset of slavery until its end there were, at all times, Africans speaking African tongues in America. Their number and importance varied greatly, but throughout the period of direct legal importation (through 1807) African languages remained important in all slave areas. The earliest newspapers in South Carolina (1730s) carried advertisements for runaways speaking "little," "bad," or "broken" English—or "none at all," which is not at all surprising given the South Carolina import statistics. During the height of Georgia's slave importation, 1760 to 1770, the advertisements there echoed South Carolina's. For example, over 25 percent of the advertisements for runaways in Savannah's *Georgia Gazette* of 1765 specified that the slaves spoke "no English" at all.[21]

Most slaves came to speak and understand at least a limited amount of English. What is significant is that there is evidence that African languages were used in America in situations other than among first arrivals. Social gatherings, both white approved and clandestine, provided opportunities for such exchange. In 1797 a visitor to the plantation area north of Charleston, South Carolina, observed a large group of slaves meeting together for owner-approved Christmas festivities: They "reverted" to their various African tongues and engaged in African "gambles."

One of the most singular suggestions in regard to African language use is found in reference to the Denmark Vesey rebellion in Charleston, South Carolina, in 1822. It is believed that Vesey was born in either Africa or the West Indies, circa 1767; that he was a skilled worker who knew English as well as several African languages; that he constantly quoted the Bible, which he knew in great detail; and that he was acquainted with abolitionist literature. Although Vesey appears to have been acculturated (he bought himself out of slavery around 1800, but he rejected emigration to Africa), when it came to organizing his followers he divided them into what were apparently still meaningful tribal groupings: "The Angolas, the Eboes and Carolina-born were separately organized under appropriate commanders." This apparently unusual occurrence has manifold implications. (Some church societies may well have been organized along similar lines, as will be discussed below.) Legal importation had ended by 1808, but here we see that as late as 1822 many South Carolina blacks identified with their mother tongue and African origins. African languages were evidently still important, structuring social life; otherwise, why was such a division made? The fact that "Carolina-born" was a separate subgroup is also significant. Clearly, some sort of English was this group's mother tongue, and they probably did not understand the languages used by the other two groups.

The leader of the Angolan group in the Vesey rebellion, Gullah Jack, was a recognized conjurer or witch doctor, who brought the promise of invulnerability and mystic power to the rebel's side. (He was often referred to as "the little man," a phrase echoing one used in black tales of mystic power.) This type of magic-working figure was prominent in many black plots and rebellions. As the official trial record indicates, whites recognized Gullah Jack's charisma as based on African values:

> Gullah Jack [Pritchard] was regarded as a Sorcerer, and as such feared by the natives of Africa, who believe in witchcraft.

He was not only considered invulnerable, but that he could make others so by his charms; and that he could and certainly would provide all his followers with arms. He was artful, cruel, bloody; his disposition in short was diabolical. His influence amongst the Africans was inconceivable.

Jack advocated specifically African customs. He "advised his followers to eat only parched corn and ground nuts before the battle and to put a crab's claw in their mouths to prevent being wounded."[22] His Afro-American followers had faith in his methods and power.

III

African languages survived the passage to North America, but, as Mullin maintains, most Africans began to talk some sort of English. The first limited English spoken widely by blacks in America was, by definition, a pidgin tongue. (Pidgin is defined as an auxiliary language which is not the first language of the people involved.) J. L. Dillard believes it highly likely that the roots of this black Pidgin English go back to Africa and that, in part, it was brought to America by some of the early arrivals. We know that African linguists or translators, and no doubt other Africans, spoke some English. It would be very interesting to know what language was spoken by Finda Lawrence, a Gambian slave trader in Africa, who in 1772 actually visited the American South as a black African tourist! Seventeenth-century North American slaves, a minority in a white society, had to learn a language of communication quickly, and their constant contact with white indentured servants facilitated that development. Based on slim evidence, as many of the relevant theses must be, Dillard is convinced that "by 1715 there clearly was an African Pidgin English known on a worldwide scale." What Dillard means here is that a separate and recognizable auxiliary English existed, having, as suggested above, a strong internal tie to African languages and reflecting the world view of Africans. When the American-born children of these slaves who spoke Pidgin English began to speak English as their first or mother tongue, its nature was essentially changed. A pidgin tongue, spoken by the next generation as its mother tongue, is called a creole language. The Gullah English of the Sea Islands is, therefore, defined as a creole language as is the French patois spoken in Louisiana and known as Creole. It is likely that second-generation Afro-Americans all over the South spoke a comparable Creole language and that Creole English also retained African nominizing categories.

Dillard suggests that by the mideighteenth century blacks were speaking on at least four or perhaps five different levels, with the same black often moving from one level to the other. Many slaves were still speaking African languages; Pidgin English was widely used, especially on plantations; Creole English had become a live and viable language, also widely used; while black English, developed out of Pidgin and Creole, was a new Negro English that sounded most like poor standard English, but was actually quite different, in great part because it, too, embodied African usages and thought patterns. Some blacks, especially in the Northeast, spoke standard English. This pattern was not an outgrowth of the others, but rather was learned without the integration of African nominizing order ór tone.

Regional and class differences had great influence on these patterns. Dillard posits that Pidgin and Creole were once used in all the colonies. However, in areas of high and late direct African importation, as in the Charleston area of the midnineteenth century, or in isolated areas, as on the Sea Islands, Pidgin and Creole were in use over longer periods. (Gullah is still spoken on the Islands and elsewhere.) In areas of high work contact with whites, as in the Northern urban centers, near-standard English spread most rapidly. Social status affected language learning similarly. The mass of field workers born in America spoke plantation Creole, while those in closer contact with whites, often regarded as the slave elite, were far more likely to have undergone de-creolization and probably spoke black English or near-standard English.[23]

All of these statements on language are provisional and based on fragmentary evidence, but further research along the lines set out should prove fruitful. It is possible that more evidence of pidgin and creole developments will yet be found to substantiate the suggestions of Dillard and others to a greater degree. Apparently, a quasi-African world view stood behind the creation of these languages and shaped their inner logic and nominizing structure. This inner logic, in turn, influenced black English and gave it a significant African content.

Black world views probably developed in tandem with these language developments, and, as suggested, a tentative typology can be posed:

1. Blacks arriving from Africa spoke African languages and found others with whom to share discourse, either in their own tongue or in a second African tongue they had known in Africa. In the process of interrelationship with different African cultures, the various African world views rapidly began to coalesce. The need for a *lingua franca* led to the rapid growth of Pidgin English (which may have begun in Africa) and of the single quasi-African world view. As new polyglot marriages and families grew, children socialized by parents speaking Pidgin English learned this language as their mother tongue. The world view of this first generation of Creole English speakers reflected a new, relatively integrated, quasi-African world view.

2. Perhaps from the outset, and certainly over time, this quasi-African world view began to assimilate white or Euro-American values that were contradictory or significantly different from the African views. This world view began to incorporate inconsistencies and confusions, especially as related to power and its source and control. The second generation spoke a tongue that reflected these noncoherencies, a creole that was in the process of becoming black English, but that to all appearances was simply a poor English. The fact that it was a combination of African and English patterns and usages was not recognized.

3. At the same time as black English was becoming a language, the black Sacred Cosmos was coming into meaningful contact with a white Sacred Cosmos. For the first time, blacks and whites began to share spiritual experiences. As a result of these encounters, blacks, speaking black English, forged a new Afro-Christian world view.

The fulfillment of the last phase was not envisioned in the first phase of black life in America, but the nature of the later developments was, in great part, determined by the rich African culture brought into North America in the earlier period. During that time, Africans, speaking African tongues and understanding the nature of God and man in African terms, were reestablishing families and institutions in America. African religious practitioners continued to practice. African parents brought children into the world and, through language, movement, and ritual, socialized them with a quasi-African understanding of the sacred.

IV

What were the beliefs and religious activities of the first-generation Afro-Americans? Assuming that the various Sacred Cosmos came into America and began to coalesce, nevertheless, under the impact of enslavement the new Sacred Cosmos was not identical with any one of the African views, tied as they had been to African soil in African time with African social structure as their strongest support. The past remained the most important period, but this was normative. What was abnormal was the fact that the divinities and the living dead were not presumed to have come across the grandywater with the slaves. How could they have when their extended families remained in Africa? The spirits would be there with them. When an African people moved as a group (in Africa), they took soil and bones and altars and moved these sacred items as well. The spirits had to make their move, too, but it was recognized that it was practically impossible for spirits to cross large bodies of water. What would happen to these Africans whose ancestral spirits were left behind over the sea? This certainly did not bode well.[24] At a time when their physical survival was threatened, they were without their spiritual protection. Their faith was intrinsically tied to Africa, and it had to suffer deeply under the conditions of such forced removal. Blacks longed to return to the spirits in Africa, sending the souls of their dead on a journey "home," even burying symbolic miniature canoes and paddles with their bodies. Some early arrivals believed that they would be able to return to Africa while alive; their attempts to escape, often in groups, may have reflected this belief. (These group efforts do suggest that they could understand one another.) There is at least one documented case of a black attempt to re-create an African settlement in America, and other maroon communities may actually have succeeded, although we do not know their history. For this small number, the African Cosmos was clearly maintained.[25]

For most blacks, however, such a re-creation of African societies was impossible. While owners might allow blacks to control their lives from sundown to sunup, as Rawick and Blassingame have emphasized, slavery imposed cultural limitations that led to a great change in the black world view. Gutman, in picking up his view of slave family structure from about 1750, sees it as already black and very different from the African. However, while marriage and family patterns are related to the Sacred Cosmos, they do not define it, and Gutman has not placed them in their broader cultural context. He is also very cautious as to what these patterns might prove about the African-ness of slave culture. The black practice of naming children after the father or grandparent, which was apparently different from Southern white practice, as well as early promiscuity but long-term marriage after the first child, suggest the different roots of black culture. Gutman cautions: "That does not mean, however, that a straight line can be drawn between eighteenth-century West African kin networks and those existing among Afro-American slaves a century later." Although it cannot be demonstrated that the black marriage and kin networks of 1750 developed directly out of any one African pattern, it can be shown—based on considerable direct evidence as well as on the nature of later developments—that quasi-African world views were brought directly into slavery.[26]

The new slave's ability, despite enormous pressure, to laugh at the ways of his oppressor is one of the significant signs that the African world view continued in America. At the outset of interreligious contact in North America, the African had a basic disrespect for white religion and the white, for African religion. The white reaction has been recognized and evaluated. Certainly, a people that was building a new identity on the basis of the genocide of Indians and the slavery of blacks could not respect the otherness of its black chattels or view black religions with anything but derision. What is surprising, however, is the already suggested negative slave response to Anglicanism. Through special efforts, white ministers did win a limited number of converts, but the Afro-Americans by and large rejected Anglicanism. Moreover, blacks "laught" at the devotions of new black Christians. Blacks, reading "their Bibles in the field and in their Quarters in the hearing of those who could not read," were disdained. Their behavior was viewed as a humorous act, an aping of the white man's peculiar ways, that was not to be taken seriously in anger but rather laughed off.[27]

The chief evidence that African world views came into America and that they coalesced into a more or less singular cosmos is the fact that belief in Voodoo actively permeated all of slave life. (I have adopted the spelling Voudou to refer to the New Orleans-based organized religious system and Voodoo or Hoodoo for the more generally held beliefs.) The world of spirits and the practices surrounding their supplication and control remained an overarching reality throughout the slave era. The changes that occurred were great, but American blacks retained the basic concept of spirit and its power, and of the soul as a participating spirit, a concept shared by most West African peoples. No slave area was without spirit-workers, and virtually no slave was without contact with spirits. Except for the later development of Voudou as a religious institution in Louisiana (which found a response based on the already prevalent quasi-African tradition), American spirit worship or Voodoo existed as a function of the practitioner rather than as an independent system or cult that could replace practitioners at will. Innumerable priests, mediums, witch doctors, herb doctors, and diviners functioned from the outset of slavery through its close, as well as afterwards. A large number accepted disciples and taught them their range of wisdom (as they often taught their own children), but in no case outside of the Haitian-influenced areas do we know of a self-perpetuating institutional framework. (We do have hints of similar rites in Missouri.)[28]

The blacks and whites alike recognized Voodoo practitioners as both special and dangerous people. Most blacks retained their belief that these people were holy. While later the black Protestant preacher occasionally merged the roles of Christian leader and Voodoo diviner, multiplying the holiness of his office, at first this step was not necessary nor was it likely. For the whites, and later for Christian blacks, the conjurer was often associated with the witch, one who had made a pact with the devil and could be powerful and dangerous. The two traditions were mutually interactive and, over time, the conjurer emerged a more frightening figure, losing much of the healthy normative role he had had in African society.

The conjurer Dinkie (a Dinka tribesman?) is pictured in the narrative of William Wells Brown as having owned a snake skin rather than a live snake (as he would have in Africa or in Louisiana Voudou) and, having no permanent or protected altar, he wore it round his neck. Brown reports that Dinkie was both feared and yet petitioned by whites and blacks; did not work; and was not punished. When his owner sold him to a slave trader, trying to pass him off as a "regular" slave, the trader returned him, having learned of his occupation. The original owner was forced to take him back, inasmuch as it was recognized as a misrepresentation to sell a conjurer without acknowledging it. Such a one was "big trouble."

As the blacks defined it, a Voodoo professional had to be "strong in de haid." This strength enabled him to confront spirit and spirits, and to use deadly "conjure power," the practitioner knowing full well that theoretically any trick could be turned back to work its evil on its originator. Such men and women had strong personalities, and the interaction with their respectful communities strengthened them further. No wonder they emerged as the slave managers or drivers in the Sea Islands. In the first phases of plantation slavery the *swonga* were likely used more widely elsewhere as well. In Louisiana, Voudou doctors are still called *wangateurs*, and the respect for their power remains formidable. In the antebellum period, slaves would not inform on them; even now, blacks will not testify against them in court cases. The conjurers' power to do evil or bring harm was the key to this fear, which was realistic. Cases of poisoning occurred in the slave period. However, it was black faith in "conjure" that gave conjurers their extensive power. Many men and women who had not actually swallowed any poison or foreign matter were in great pain and some died solely as a result of the belief that they had been crossed. In 1936, Clara Barton still felt the snake that had been put in her leg when she was a slave:

> I've had an ole snake in my laig all my life. It's been better these last years, but at first it like to drove me crazy. I can still feel that thing, though. Had a bad woman come after my man back on the plantation. One night she snuck in my room and stuck that snake in my laig. I felt it and I screamed, but it was too late. The room was dark and I couldn't see her, but I heard her paddin' over the floor, going through the door. She left that door creakin' and swingin'. When my man woke up and run in the room I was jest layin' on the floor yellin' in the dark and that door was still creakin' and swingin', creakin' and swingin'.[29]

These same conjurers were also called on to perform good works. They were appealed to, to help bring health (by removing "crosses"); to attract lovers (by "tricking" them); to bring success in a large range of ventures; to protect individuals, especially against owners' wrath; and above all to protect slaves and their families from sale. It was recognized that conjurers had the power to do these good acts, but their power was not wielded out of a desire to be good or do good. Conjurers could use their power for whatever ends they chose, which made them all the more dangerous. Their powers were not limited by a judgmental system that established good and evil. The slave social structure did not have the social controls that the African community had. It would appear that in America discretion was in the conjurer's hands.

The term *doctor* or *conjurer* was used to cover a wide range of possibilities which over the years became confused. The practitioner might be a priest of a Voudou cult; a person in contact with a divinity (a medium); a root doctor; or a diviner. Some men and women would only perform one separate role, especially as "good root doctors," while others combined several.

In the early years of slavery, conjurers were used to control slaves, but it may have proved dangerous to delegate authority to them. They were too strong in and of themselves and too independent; when these traits were combined with delegated owner authority, they may well have tricked the master as well. As suggested (and as will be discussed below), many conjurers were associated with rebellions, and official attempts were made to outlaw Negro doctoring.[30]

Slaveowners occasionally approved of the use of black doctors. Although we have little written documentation of such practices, there is extant a letter of William Dawson to his neighbor Robert Carter of Nomoni Hall, offering to hire the services of Carter's coachman, Brother Tom, to treat a sick child: "The black people at this place hath more faith in him as a doctor than any white doctor; and as I wrote you in a former letter I cannot expect you to lose your man's time, etc., for nothing, but am quite willing to pay for same."

In other circumstances, owners made use of the blacks' belief in "conjure" for their own purposes, attempting to sidestep the dangerous relationship to conjurers. The blacks' belief that harm would come to them if they lied when they swore on a charm could give owners a hold over the guilty that no threat of white power (whippings or reduction of privileges) would have. Such "swearing" could involve drinking water and graveyard dust, or handling a magic jack (an amulet) known to punish those who lied. On rare occasions, whites openly challenged black conjurers, as did an Alabama slaveowner who handed out "pills" of bread reputedly stronger than the local conjurer's medicine.[31]

Folktales describe the competition for power, of whites sometimes having the "bigger" magic, and other times of black conjurers ultimately doing in whites. Some of the ex-slaves who remembered "old conjurers" from the last years of slavery noted that they were African-born, as was "Uncle Poosa" on an Alabama plantation. On a Georgia plantation,

Emmaline Heard's family had experiences with such men and women. Mrs. Heard recounts one experience, probably from the postslavery period, in which the conjurer emerges as the counterpart to the African diviner in private practice, with a ritual that is reminiscent as well. First, Mrs. Heard "had to" drink whiskey with this conjurer (female). Through the reading of cards, the conjurer knew exactly what was wrong with her sick child and prescribed a potion of special roots, which was effective. Afterwards, the client was to bury the prescribed poltice "lak dead folks is buried," lying east to west. While the conjurer's African forebear might have read rocks or bones, the structure of the visit, the ritual libations, and the divining seem directly related to African practices, just as it is likely that this conjurer was directly related to an African practitioner.

In some cases in America, as in Africa, events rather than ancestry determined the holy role. Birthmarks or birth-associated events were seen as portents of the path an individual should take. This was the case with Nat Turner whose birthmarks and seeming knowledge of events that occurred before his birth marked him for life.[32]

The vitality of the African-related tradition is indicated by its continuation into the twentieth century. In the 1920s, Puckett (a white man) pretended to be a conjure-doctor in order to study the practice of Voodoo. He succeeded to the extent that he was regarded as a man of power, and black patients came to him. He did not hesitate to prescribe potions and charms for the sick, and he exchanged wisdom with black doctors. Puckett justified his deception on the grounds that it was the faith of the believer that healed, as witnessed by the fact that he asked for fees only if and when his prescription worked, and he was generally paid. Through Puckett's deception (and questionnaires and informants), an extraordinarily rich collection of black folk beliefs was preserved. It is interesting, however, that he was not made privy to the Voudou snake cult in New Orleans. He believed it no longer existed. But in the very same period Zora Hurston (a black woman) was being initiated into it and was attending group "ecstasa." Perhaps some Voudouists had recognized Puckett's duplicity.

While the slavery and postslavery existence of Voodoo is widely acknowledged, the African roots of the tradition have come into some question. Puckett himself came to feel that where there was conflict with white ideas of magic, either the white or the black ideas had emerged as dominant, but in the wider variety of areas where syncretism could take place (among similar ideas), white customs dominated. This is essentially the view of Norman E. Whitten, Jr., as well, who in a study of North Carolina Negroes concludes that black "occult beliefs and practices . . . exist within a broader belief system or world view quite similar to that of seventeenth and eighteenth century Europeans." Whitten maintains that blacks adopted European occultism inasmuch as he believes that they communicated with a European language and that they had adapted to the European church. He concludes that the European world view was, therefore, their inheritance.

If blacks had been European Christians speaking white English, perhaps Whitten's thesis would be correct. However, it now seems much more likely that blacks created their own style of English and their own style of Christianity and that both preserved the African ethos to a significant degree. Their understanding of occultism was, no doubt, greatly influenced by the white understanding, which in part it paralleled, but what emerged is again clearly part of an Afro-American world view.[33]

Folklorists are certain that there was a melding of folk traditions, and there seems every reason to concur. When a black on the plantation feared "Raw Head and Bloody Bones" and "was allus skeered to play in de thicket nigh de hause cause" of them, she was using English terms that had entered English literature as early as 1565. There were white sources of "Jack Ma'Lanterns" and witches and haunts, and methods of protecting oneself against them. Turning one's pockets inside out as a protection against spirits was assuredly not an African remedy, although Afro-Americans widely adopted it. Indeed, European terms and practices were widely used by blacks. What is of concern is the world view or Sacred Cosmos of which they were a part. It is important to look for African meanings given to European terms because this type of analysis tells us something important about the identity of the black.

Folklorist Richard M. Dorson maintains with great accuracy that "the Negro lives within American civilization rather than on its borders." In reevaluating the African elements in the Afro-American folk tradition, he concludes that

> the emphasis on animal tales, presumably originating in Africa, and the concentration on Gullah Negroes of the Carolina and Georgia coasts, where African retentions are highest, distort the picture. Most of the Brer Rabbit tales come from Europe and many Negro beliefs are pure British. A whole body of traditions has grown up on American soil.
> . . . Taking their raw material from a variety of sources, European, British, African, Caribbean and white American, the colored folk have selected, squeezed and shaped this dough into their very own folk property.

This last point is most important, for it alters the significance of the fact that black folk themes and usages are traceable to Europe and England: blacks "selected, squeezed and shaped" European and English folk themes with an African ethos and within an African world view. It is not racist, in the sense that Dorson fears, to maintain that to a great extent the African Sacred Cosmos continued to determine the pattern of selectivity, evaluation, and use of "white" tales and symbols.

The essence of black occult beliefs in America remained African, notwithstanding English and European content. However, the encounter with white occultism had profound ramifications, most of them negative. The African concept of soul, as distinct and separable from body, permeates all of black Voodoo or Hoodoo. Belief in dual souls, souls that can go into objects, animals, people, and things such as axes, trains, houses, clouds, and streams, was very widespread. The souls of both the living and the dead were recognized as separable, and blacks in America told innumerable stories of their encounters with these spirits. Dorson does recognize a few of the folktales as "purely" or primarily African, as in this parallel to the Nupe tale wherein the chieftain becomes the white master and the warrior a slave:

> They [the planters and overseers] used to carry the slaves out in the woods and leave them there, if they killed them—just like dead animals. There wasn't any burying them. It used to be a secret, between one plantation and another, when they beat up their hands and carried them off.
>
> So John was walking out in the woods and seed a skeleton. He says: "This looks like a human. I wonder what he's doing out here." And the skeleton said, "Tongue is the cause of my being here." So John ran back to Old Marster and said, "The skeleton at the edge of the woods is talking." Old Marster didn't believe him and went to see. And a great many people came too. They said, "Make the bones talk." But the skeleton wouldn't talk. So they beat John to death and left him there. And then the bones talked. They said, "Tongue brought us here and tongue brought you here."*

The ubiquitous spirits of the dead inform much of black lore. Spirits rustle leaves, bother animals, cause the loss of material goods, and change into familiar objects such as wash pots, bundles, a whole house, or a ghost train. "Haunts kin te'k enny fo'm, w'ite folks, even a brickbat clock, chair er ennything."[34] Southern blacks believingly recounted their encounters with these spirits both during and after slavery. Jesse Collins "knew" that:

---

*From Richard M. Dorson, *American Negro Folktales* (Fawcett: Greenwich, Conn., 1967, pp. 147-48.)

> Ghosts is liable to look like anything. Some comes back just like they was when they died, but others turns into animals and balls of fire or things with long teeth and hairy arms. You can just walk around all your life lookin' at things and you don't never know when you is lookin' at a ghost.

Collins was convinced that her grandfather had been accosted by a dog—alias a fifteen-foot tall, two-headed, twelve-armed ghost of a person that had once known her grandma. She, herself, knew spirits.

> When my husband died I give him a fine funeral. I went in deep mourning and wore me a long widow's veil. Every day I go to the cemetery and cry all day by his grave. But his spirit started to haunt me somethin' terrible. I had chickens and every night he'd come back wearin' a white apron and shoo my chickens. Every mornin' some of 'em would be dead. We had a horse and that haunt done drove me and him both crazy. Then I got mad and I quit goin' to the cemetery and I took off my widow's veil. I put black pepper 'round the sills of all my doors. That stopped him; that always chases ghostses.

Georgia Baker, an ex-slave in Georgia, was certain of their reality: "I've seed plenty of ha'nts right here in Athens." In fact, they could not be avoided:

> I had been in bed jus' a little while one night and was jus' dozin' off to sleep when I woke up and sat right spang up in bed. I seed a white man, dressed in white, standin' before me. I sho didn't say nothin' to him for I was too skeered.[35]

There was a very widespread African belief that souls are often thirsty and might desert one in search of water. Blacks in America maintained that "a bucket of water should be left in the room so that one's spirit may drink." In African terms, spirits were recognized as the cause of disease, misfortune, and death. Blacks in America were admonished: "Never answer a strange voice in the night; a spirit (of some relative) is calling you, and to answer it means death."

American blacks believed that souls could be damaged through the sympathetic wounding of dolls and images by those who had the proper knowledge of spiritual power. Dreams were regarded as soul talk, real experiences in which the soul traveled. Taken together, these beliefs indicate that meaningful ties to African concepts of soul were maintained. Soul was still seen as having a life before and after death, and professionals were recognized as having power to affect the actions of souls, especially through use of objects invested with spirit power.

This is not to say that changes had not taken place in America. One of the most important alterations involved the radical increase in the negative or loathsome aspect of souls and spirits. While they were still occasionally protective of their children or were believed to be able to show the location of hidden treasure, or to bring justice to bear by harming the guilty, spirits were generally viewed as being literally in cahoots with the devil. Here is where the influence of the white ethos can be seen to have played a most significant role. Clearly, the change came gradually and is difficult to document accurately in that so many ex-slave narratives on which we rely were recorded long after the slave period. Nevertheless, both Christian and non-Christian blacks came to emphasize the negative role of haunts, witches, wizards, and Voodoo in general. It was accepted that Voodoo practitioners "done sold deir soul ter de debbil, . . . an ole Satin gi'dem de pow'r ter change ter anything dey wants." As works of the devil, use of soul power was a negative art and not a power to be approved of. Feared, yes; believed in, of course, but the question of its virtue was seriously in doubt. The core belief and understanding of the African Sacred Cosmos remained. Spirit was still regarded as real. But the power over spirit, the ability to handle it, became an evil ability associated with a pact with the devil.

Even after much time in America, remnants of the African concept of dual souls remained. Now, however, they were often associated with the Christian duality of good versus evil rather than with the African awareness of the mixed potential of each individual spirit to be both good *and* bad, male *and* female. In the American South, the black often differentiated between man's two souls or ghosts; one was an evil ghost associated with the body, and the other a "Holy Ghost," the spirit "from de insides," a Christian distinction.[36]

V

One clearly neo-African faith system came into America almost intact and found a receptive milieu in the Voodoo-permeated world of blacks. Louisiana Voudou, which had already developed as a quasi-African slave religion prior to its arrival in North America, came to New Orleans at the end of the eighteenth century and in the first decades of the nineteenth. It was then a fully developed Afro-Haitian religion, exported as a result of the revolution of Toussaint L'Ouverture and the resulting slaveowner emigration and slave removal. When combined with the French and Spanish Catholic milieu of Louisiana, its Haitian origins gave Voudou a very special history. Zora Hurston suggests that the relatively homogeneous Haitian plantation communities had been isolated and undisturbed over time, and that Haitian Africans maintained African languages, traditions, and social institutions in a less violated fashion than any North American black community. This, taken together with Curtin's import statistics, in great part explains the emergence of a Voudou sect in Haiti and its relative rarity in a known institutional form in North America.

The Louisiana Voudou religion remained a neo-African belief system overlaid with some extrinsic Christian symbols. Even after many years there was little integration of world views, and there were few internalized contradictions since quasi-African values were the dominant, if not the only, values operative. For example, good Catholic Voudou practitioners felt no guilt when they sought to bring about the death of a human being. It was, as they saw it, within their power, and they expressed no apprehension about using their powers to the fullest. In contrast, when the Baptist integration of the African and Christian ethos took place, a new Christian-Voodoo ethic emerged which forbade using spirit for evil purposes—but this was a later development.

The demographic data developed by Curtin substantiate these suggestions. Until the revolt of 1791 (on St. Dominique), Haiti was "the pinnacle of achievement" and the "most valuable" European colony, absorbing one-third to one-half of all slaves sold in the late 1780s. At that time, there were about 480,000 slaves on the island. While there was a natural increase in population during the very last period of slavery, over the course of slavetrading some 894,000 slaves had been "absorbed" on the island. This indicates a constant repopulation with African-born slaves and their numerical dominance in the local population. The slave population of Haiti was also of proportionately different origins than the North American black community. A single ethnic group, Angolans, accounted for almost half the population, while another quarter came from another single source, the Bight of Benin, making for a much more homogeneous population. All the other African sources supplied a little over a quarter of the population.[37] (Compare this distribution with the relatively heterogeneous origins of North American slaves shown in Table 1 above.)

Marie Leveau was a Haitian Voudou practitioner who arrived in Louisiana around 1800 as the slave of an owner fleeing the black revolution. Her life story is known through local oral history, maintained by her daughter and granddaughter, both of whom were her namesakes and Voudou priestesses. The first Marie Leveau is remembered as "a small black Congo woman"; her wisdom was attributed directly to African sources and was handed down as such to her descendants. The third Marie Leveau, born on February 27, 1827, became the most important Voudou practitioner in North America, the "Voudou Queen" of New Orleans. Later, most New Orleans practitioners were to claim relatedness to this last Marie Leveau, calling themselves her grandnephews. As heir to the tradition and with the additional training she received from Alexander, another renowned New Orleans practitioner, she reigned supreme among the Voudou practitioners. Her word was regarded as God's word and as dangerous to reject—and yet she regarded herself as a good Catholic.

The Voudou that came to New Orleans was in some ways a distillation of that of Haiti, which in turn was a distillation of the religion of Dahomey with some Angolan and Congolese accretions; in each case the panoply of divinities was reduced. All three, even the simplest New Orleans form, rested on a verbalized recognition of the power of spirit. However, so far as it is known only one of the important Dahomean divinities was brought to North America. This was Damballa-wedo, a powerful spirit symbolized by the snake, who made his will known through a "King and Queen, master or mistress or even papa or maman." These titles, used in Haiti in the late eighteenth century, were in use in New Orleans in the nineteenth. A contemporary description of Haitian ritual as it was practiced in the 1790s, Saint-Mery's, parallels what we know of the later Louisiana practices. The king and queen were regarded as all-powerful mediums of God's will as to initiates, tasks, and gifts. Saint-Mery reported that at a secret nocturnal meeting, the caged snake was placed on an altar which was mounted by the queen. There "she is penetrated by the god; she writhes; her whole body is convulsed and the oracle speaks from her mouth." When a goat was subsequently sacrificed, all the participants shared in its blood to seal their pact of secrecy. Novices then began trance-like ecstatic dances, followed by "collective delirium."

> Some are subject to fainting fits, others to a sort of fury; but with all there is a nervous trembling which apparently cannot be controlled. They turn round and round. And while there are some who tear their clothes in this bacchanal and even bite their own flesh, others merely lose consciousness and falling down are carried into a neighboring room where in the darkness a disgusting form of prostitution holds hideous sway.[38]

Metraux maintains that, contrary to what Saint-Mery thought, Damballa-wedo was (and is) not the sole god worshiped in Haitian Voudou, although he is a very important one. The worship of Legba, Zaka, Ogu, Ezili, Agwe, Guede, and Loco was brought from Africa, and these gods are still worshiped on the island. It does appear, however, that the snake-god was the chief, or perhaps the only, deity brought to New Orleans. He is the only one reported in the literature, and he was the

New York Public Library Collection

Views of Variant Voudou Traditions

Courtesy The Bettman Archive

Voudou Dancing

source of Marie Leveau's power as well as that of every subsequent New Orleans practitioner.

Marie Leveau, queen, also had a king, or papa, but his authority was secondary. She, too, worshiped a live snake, climbing onto its cage and going into a trance or speaking in tongues. Oaths were taken, blood drunk, and ecstatic dances were part of the ritual (see illustration). Both in New Orleans and at her country home at Lake Ponchatrain, the ritualized services were also closed by general ecstasy, including orgies and self-flagellation.

The vitality of this tradition is demonstrated by the fact that in the 1920s Zora Hurston, a black initiate, was introduced to these rites in an only somewhat attentuated form. At that time, Samuel Thompson, a Catholic man in his seventies who claimed to use the skin of the great snake that had served Marie Leveau's altar, accepted Hurston as a neophyte. He, too, claimed "that his remote ancestors brought the power with them from the rock (Africa) and that his forbears had lived in Santo Domingo before they came to New Orleans." Thompson, and most of the Louisiana Voudou practitioners, knew a large range of ritualized Marie Leveau wisdom as memorized answers to problems. Hurston learned these as well, publishing them in the 1930s. At that time, most practitioners preferred to use their own deviant methods, but Marie Leveau's work was widely preserved. This serves as a significant mark of the respect and power it commanded as well as of the power of the oral tradition.

Hurston's initiation was with the spirit. Thompson claimed to "teach nothing." "I bring you to the Great One. If he takes you, he tell you what to do; if he don't tell you, you are nothing. The spirit don't want you." After nine days of purification, Hurston was placed on a snakeskin-covered altar:

> [N]aked as I came into the world, I was stretched face downwards with my navel to the serpent and a pitcher of water at my head that my spirit might not wander in search of it, and began my three-day search for the favor of the Great One. Three days I must lie silently, that is, my body would be there. My soul would be standing naked before Spirit to see if he would have me.
> . . . I had five psychic experiences during those three days and nights. . . . I knew that I had been accepted. . . .

The water left for the spirit was very much in the African tradition, as was the fact that Hurston was painted with a lightning symbol as her personal sign and power. Hurston drank her own blood mixed with urine and shared it with her teacher and her new colleagues. A communion celebration was held in her honor, capped by the midnight sacrifice of a goat in a local swamp, his mouth stuffed with Hurston's written supplications that in his death he might carry them to the Great One. Once accepted, Hurston was given an initiation bath or baptism by another Catholic Voudou practitioner, Albert Frechard, in which she shared her blood with him, too. He chanted "Now you are of my flesh and of the spirit and neither one of us will ever deny you." While the spirit was identified as Moccasin (a snake), Hurston was instructed to read Job "night and morning for nine days."

> I was given a little Bible that had been visited by the spirit and told the names of the spirits to call for any kind of work I might want to perform. I am to call on Great Moccasin for all kinds of power and also to have him stir up the particular spirit I may need for a specific task. I must call on Kangaroo to stop worrying; call on Jenipee spirit for Marriages; call on Death spirit for killing; and the seventeen quarters [of the Voodoo calendar] of spirit to aid me if one spirit seems insufficient.

Of the thirty "responsa" Hurston published as those of Marie Leveau, most deal with love problems, both with the same or the opposite sex; problems with the law or with enemies; problems with money or treasure, gambling, debts, or work; and problems with neighbors and friends. Power is sought to help the supplicant and harm his enemies, with the "hand" or charm or "juju" regarded as a body for an indwelling spirit. The god's answer to the supplicant "who wishes to be uncrossed," as everything and everyone seems to be against him, contains the classic elements of Marie Leveau's method:

> The God: Oh my son, be light of heart and do not let the dark clouds which surround you bear you down, for no matter how dark it looks, there is always a way that will give you help, for the god of prosperity smiles on all those who pacify him and worship at his altar.
>   It is said that if you wear around your neck a finger of the root called the Wonder of the World tied with a thread of pure linen, this will give you luck in finding work, particularly if you write the name of the headman with whom you wish to work with the blood of a white dove on it.
>   To untie yourself you will take of threads of purse silk, you will tie nine knots in it at equal distance one from the other. This you will wear upon your body for nine days and for every day of the nine days you will take of the Oriental Temple incense one drachma and burn it before a picture of the good St. Joseph and on the last day of the nine days you remove the string of silk which you have been wearing and burn it along with the temple

incense which you will burn that day. And be sure that all the
knots are burned so that you will be untied and free again.

And when you go to the head man to ask for a place to labor
you will have with you some of the Wish Beans which you will
chew as you speak to him and will spit the hulls out in and around
the field of labor wherein you wish to work. This you will do so
that your words will have weight with the head man and he
will hearken unto you and give you the task you wish for and
that he will pay you highly for your labor.

And on your raiment you will have a few drops of the oil of
Rose and Mary so that all of the evil spirits will be driven from you
and only the good spirits will commune with you and give you
good thoughts and tell you what is best for you to do. For you
must not listen to the evil spirits when you are in bad luck, only
listen to the voices of good spirits. For in the end only they
will smooth your path for you and lead you to peace and good
fortune. And at all times remember well that the good workman
is worthy of his hire and that the bad workman is not fit even to
lie down with the pigs and the cattle. That the good workman
will always find a good head man who will hearken unto him and
support him in all his efforts and that the bad workman will hear
nothing but curses and groans and will not remain long with any
head man, but will change often going from bad to worse all the
time. So do your duty well and faithfully so that you will be looked
up to and respected by the ones whom you labor with and those
whom you serve. For this way only is the true way and the wide
and free road to prosperity.

According to the oral tradition, most of Leveau's prescriptions are of
this formalistic type, involving methods of gathering and using esoteric
materials (roots, herbs, oils, and symbolic pictures), combined with
morality and good acts, all of which must be strictly adhered to if the
supplicant wishes help. Underlying the ritual acts and the creation of
potions and hands or charms was the belief system, mediated by the
queen, to whom obeisance was demanded:

But fail not to worship me and love me, for the day you cease to
worship me will be your loss. And the day you cease to love me
will be your doom, for all things I have given I will take away.
For those who never cease to love, I am a true mistress and
shower my favors on them; and for those who love me for a
while and forsake me, I am a hard mistress and cause them
deep sorrow and desolation.

The African concept of spirit pervades Voudou: the medium's spirit goes to be with the divinity and is mediator of its desires. The divinity is neither good nor bad but is powerful and can be used for all purposes. Its spirit descends on the medium during an ecstatic trance, when its wisdom and power can be sued for supplicants' purposes. The spirits of ancestors are still called on for help, while ecstatic dancing by the believers is both a system for the spirit to enter bodies and a climax or a cathartic release. (By the 1920s, ecstatic dancing was used primarily when a death was requested and was open only to Voudou practitioners, who gathered together and shared in the proceedings.)

The Catholic elements in this Sacred Cosmos are minimal, notwithstanding the ostensible Catholicism of the practitioners. Jesus is rarely called on; the Virgin Mother is appealed to somewhat more often, in that the priestess is symbolically associated with her; several of the saints are categorized as serving particular needs and are, therefore, occasionally invoked. The symbolic use of an altar, candles, and wine, which is literally mixed with blood, may have some Christian ties, but the African roots of altar, fermented brew, and blood are equally clear. The Bible, when used, is viewed in its material form as a "juju" or spirit-visited charm. In sum, the Christian symbols and ideas are hardly a veneer. They occasionally figure in what is a spirit-oriented use of ritual formula, by initiated professionals in order to occasion the transference of power by arational means.[39]

While some white people believed and participated in Voudou, others tried to put an end to organized Voudou practices. In a fascinating case in New Orleans in 1850, a free black Voudou priestess, Betsy Toledano, claimed the protection of the First Amendment to the Constitution! She acknowledged the nature of her beliefs and attributed their origin to her African grandmother. Her right to religious freedom was not denied, but she was fined for violating the law in allowing slaves to attend.[40]

Marie Leveau was also interfered with, but the curses that Leveau called forth on enemies may well have frightened even nonbelievers, both white and black. Black believers thought they had evidence that she and other initiates could do both the good they promised and the evil they threatened, invoking the deities and the spirits of recent and related dead to come to their aid. Even Zora Hurston believed the incantations she learned had brought deaths. Marie Leveau's curses were formidable:

> O Lord, I beg that this that I ask for my enemies shall come to pass.
> That the South Wind shall scorch their bodies and make them wither, and shall not be tempered to them. That the North Wind shall freeze their blood and numb their muscles, and that it shall

not be tempered to them. That the West Wind shall blow away their life's breath and will not leave their hair grow, and that their nails shall fall off and their bones shall crumble. That the East Wind shall make their minds grow dark, their sight shall fail, and their seed dry up so that they shall not multiply.

Oh Lord, *I pray that their fathers and mothers from their furtherest generation will not intercede for them before the great throne*, and the wombs of their women shall not bear fruit except for strangers, and that they shall become extinct; and pray that the children who may come shall be weak of mind and paralyzed of limb, and that they themselves shall curse them in their turn for ever turning the breath of life in their bodies. I pray that disease and death shall be forever with them and that their worldly goods shall not prosper, and that their crops shall not multiply and that their cows, their sheep and their hogs and all their living beasts and fowl will die of starvation and thirst. I pray that their house shall be un-roofed and that the rain, the thunder and the lightning shall find the innermost recess of their home, and that the foundation shall crumble and the flood tear it asunder. I pray that the sun shall not shed its rays of prosperity on them, and that instead it shall beat down on them and burn them up and destroy them. I pray that the moon shall not give them peace, but instead shall deride them and decry them and cause their minds to shrivel. I pray that their friends shall betray them and cause them loss of power and loss of their gold and silver, and that their enemies shall smite them both hip and thigh until they beg for mercy which will not be given them. I pray that their tongues shall forget how to speak in sweet words, and that it shall be paralyzed and that all about them will be desolation, pestilence and death. O Great Lord, I ask you for all these things because they have dragged me in the dust and destroyed my good name, have broken my heart and caused me to curse the day that I was born.

So Be It.[41]

VI

Louisiana Voudou initiates did not need to be from any specific people. They were accepted as members if, as evidenced by a visionary or ecstatic experience, the god had found them acceptable. Once accepted, the initiates owed their unending loyalty to the god and to his believers. In this process a new cult was created. Individual queens accepted initiates and held weekly services. There was much competition between queens, but a yearly celebration, in part a "put on" for the curious white public, brought all Voudouists together. Cosmopolitan New Orleans was a uniquely good home for this faith. Notwithstanding some persecution, there was much covert white tolerance and even direct support for the Voudouists. In this context, some black Voudouists became outspoken defenders of their faith, while some whites came out in open support and many others attended meetings secretly.[42]

Voudou was brought to this relatively unique atmosphere from Haiti, but many of the slaves attracted to it had grown up in the quasi-African culture in other areas of the American South. There are some indications that a Voudou system was known elsewhere, but this may have been a result of the sale of Louisiana believers or of their later migration. It remains possible that similar institutionalized sects functioned more widely but that they left little or no records of their existence. Other areas were not likely to have been as conducive to their "coming out."

The belief in the transference of power by arational means continued to permeate the world view of almost all blacks long after their first period of enslavement. Outside of Louisiana, this African belief was preserved in a quasi-African Sacred Cosmos. Spirit was still recognized and its servitors received much in return. The believers in Voodoo assimilated nominizing categories and learned how to evaluate reality. Positive value was given to certain choices and certain actions. The deities and spirits of the living dead still served the living; their propitiation was of value. They visited their followers and gave evidence of their support, as did fellow believers. Loyalty to this group would be repaid.

While Voudou cannot be shown to have been an institutionalized cult in most slave communities, noninstitutionalized quasi-African forms survived. The exact forms such quasi-African systems may have taken in Virginia, the Carolinas, and Georgia were different from those of Haiti and New Orleans, but so long as the Sacred Cosmos was more or less intact, the practitioner was regarded as a sacred personality whose role had a social function. Congruence between internal and external realities could, to some extent, be maintained, especially in the period when African languages were used for thought and much intimate communication.

3

THE ENSLAVED AFRICAN/AMERICAN SACRED COSMOS

I

The vast majority of the Africans brought to America found themselves in the South Atlantic section of the country where, in proximity to the Anglican church, a unified quasi-African world view was created. This initial culture contact was a crucial one. In rejecting Anglicanism and in being allowed to reject it, blacks found the psychological space to continue to shape their own world view.

To some extent, the African and the Anglican Sacred Cosmos can be seen as near the opposite termini of a continuum. In the African world view, most matter is permeated or penetrated by the holy. In the Anglican, the holy has been reduced to a moral-ethical dimension, requiring limited time and specific professional machinery; it does not penetrate every aspect of daily life in a dramatic fashion but is highly segregated. The Roman Catholic and African world views and Sacred Cosmos are closer in nature, indicating another possible basis for the high degree of syncretism that occurred in South America and the West Indies. The congruence was particularly acute in the areas of their attitude towards magic and the religious control of the arational. Although the Catholic church itself generally refuted superstitions, Catholicism had widely assimilated pagan practices: "The ancient worship of wells, trees and stones was not so much abolished as modified, by turning pagan sites into Christian ones and associating them with a saint rather than a heathen divinity." In addition, the expansion of the Catholic church's temporal power had been accompanied by an expansion of the concept of holy to include most aspects of life.[1]

One of the chief intentions of the Protestant Reformation had been to delimit the sacred. Keith Thomas convincingly argues that to a great extent the Protestant Reformation succeeded in eliminating the magical from the church's concern, but that this was accomplished by simply dechurching magic, which then went on to lead a life of its own without church control. People widely continued to believe in witches and wizards, but they began to see the church as unrelated to these powers and, therefore, as more limited in its abilities. In line with this attack on the magical in the church, the ritual (including blessings, hallowings, and exorcisms) and the symbolic decor, which had filled a once spiritually powerful church life, had all been reduced to a bare and cold fraction of what they had been when Catholic. While the sacred was severely reduced and sharply segregated from the profane, the profane remained permeated with spiritual power and nonchurch professionals were needed to deal with it. It was only during the seventeenth century that magic began to lose its power and prestige. In England, this change began rather rapidly and almost dramatically in the last half of the seventeenth century. At the same time sectarians, including the Baptists, reversed the process and reincorporated in the church's purview much that was labeled magical by the Anglicans.

It was an Anglican Sacred Cosmos (wherein magic was considered secular and generally dangerous, if not evil) that was provisionally offered to the African in America. This was the Sacred Cosmos of a people who were undergoing rather traumatic change themselves, both in their religious reformation and in their resettlement in a new world. The white Anglicans had not yet reached a full coherence in their own world view, which contained seriously contradictory messages, the magical areligious truths violating the religious antimagical truths.

Notwithstanding their stated concern with the salvation of heathens, most white Anglicans did not really want to share their faith with blacks. Their comments on the changes Christian faith wrought in their slaves indicate their sensitivity to the power still inherent in conversion. They did not want to share this spiritual power, even in its attenuated form, with their slaves.

The initial contact with the white Anglican world view was a complex one dependent upon responses of both blacks and whites. The white response involved the white's self-image, his fear of improving the black's character as well as legal status, and his deep and growing antiblack prejudice. Churchmen, pressed by the bishop of London to exhibit concern for the "infidel," almost always defended the small number of conversions on the grounds that there was no shared language. However, they were aware that the owners were unwilling both to have the blacks taught and to stand witness for them.

As is well known, the Southern colonies early reassured slaveowners that, English law and tradition to the contrary, conversion would not alter slave status. Virginia took this step in 1667, assuring slaveowners that a baptized slave remained a slave, ostensibly to encourage baptism. Despite this reassurance, by 1699 the Virginia House of Burgesses was admitting general failure to convert blacks and was again legitimating the weakness of the gospel outreach on the grounds of a basic and unbridgeable inability to communicate. Maintaining that "Negroes borne in this Country are generally baptized and brought up in the Christian Religion" the House claimed that: "for Negroes imported hither the Gros Barbarity and rudeness of their manners, *the variety and Strangeness of the languages* and the weakness and shallowness of their minds renders it in a manner impossible to attain to any progress in their conversion." But churchmen and others knew that the language barrier was not the only crucial factor:

> The truth is, there is a general indifference in churchmen, as well as in those of other sentiments, to make proselytes of their slaves; the true cause whereof is the want of zeal in Masters, and the *untoward haughty behaviour* of those Negroes who have been admitted into the fellowship of Christ's religion.[2]

"Indocile" without English or before conversion and "haughty" afterwards, the black response to the Anglican religion was not generally a positive one from either the black or white point of view. As a result, many Anglican pastors failed to convert large numbers of slaves, although quite a few pointed to numerous infant baptisms. Most, however, seemed indifferent. It must be remembered that the Anglican clergy was very weak and entirely dependent upon the desires of their parishioners as they were usually denied tenured appointments and could easily lose their positions. Local slaveowners were not pressing for slave conversion; quite the contrary. One Maryland minister, "Mr. Fletcher said his parishioners are generally so brutish they would not suffer their Negroes to be instructed, catechized or baptized." Moreover, the ignorance of whites and their need for religious education was considerable. As one pastor remarked, he could not see why he should give particular concern to the black when the white needed him so. Indeed, Mr. Lang, rector at St. Peters in New Kent, Virginia, characterized the whites as "supinely ignorant in the very principles of Religion and very debauch't in Morals." He was unique in his disapproval of parishioners who were willing to have their slaves baptized.

> Some people are fond of bringing their Negroe Servants to Baptism, how soon they are capable to rehearse the Creed, Lord's Prayer & Commandments and yet these live together after-

wards in common without marriage or any other Christian decency's as the pagan Negroes do who never were entered into the Church membership. Those who stand Godfathers and God-mothers for children at their Baptism are extremely ignorant and never mind the solemn engagements nor can they endure to be instructed or catechiz'd so as to improve in knowledge and understanding.

Mr. Lang's scruples about the depth of black conversion give us an insight into its nature and meaning under most circumstances. Slaves continued to live as before, and their sense of identity was not seriously reshaped. Lang's rejection of their conversion of this basis, however, is rare, as is the guilt that was felt by Charles Bridges, who begged for the bishop's help in rousing himself and the other ministers in the colonies from what he recognized as moral "sleep" in order that they might do "a little more good [for the blacks], while there is time and opportunity." He feared he had become morally weary.

An early eighteenth-century plan for implementing the injunction to bring the gospel to the blacks sought to play on the masters' economic motives rather than on moral issues, which were recognized as a weak basis. As a head tax was then levied on each slave fourteen years of age and over, it was proposed that the tax on those born in America (and therefore more likely to be amenable to conversion) be deferred for four years if the slaves were Christians.[3]

The Anglican ministers, under pressure from London, made in-effectual pleas for slave conversion and left it at that. "I have several times exhorted their Masters to send such of them as could speak English to Church to be catechised," claimed George Robertson, rector at Bristol Parish, James River, 1729, "but they would not." Several ministers did include blacks in their outreach, catechizing black adults together with the white children at the weekly sessions, generally held between April and June. This combination of blacks and children was, no doubt, an additional demeaning and disturbing element in the conversionary process. At least one minister, Frank Fontane, of York Hampton Parish, Virginia, set aside special Saturday afternoon classes for blacks, but the evidence given by Thomas Crawford at Kent County, Pennsylvania (1708), indicates that separate classes did not guarantee respect: "As for the Negroes I have been at pains, for I sometimes at the Church Porch teached them the principles of religion, though many are very dull, and when I am not employed, I catechise the Children."

At Pettsworth, Virginia, which was later to be the home of an interracial church with a black preacher (discussed below), an early and unusually strong start was made towards black conversion. As early as

1724, Emmanuel Jones, who worked with "such as are born in the Country," in distinction to those "brought from Africa," noted that "their masters very often bring them to read and send to the Church or Minister to be further instructed that they may be baptized and many are so." Pettsworth, together with Goochland and Accomako on the eastern shore of Virginia and with Dover and William and Mary, Delaware, were the very few churches that proudly claimed numerous black converts by the third decade of the eighteenth century. In these cases, the concern of the minister was directly responsible. William Black of Accomako made rounds and instructed slaves at their masters' houses; as a result, he could claim over 200 black baptisms in his thirteen years at this church. His unusual vigor and dedication were evidenced by "a great many negroes who came to Church" as well as by the large white congregations which filled the parish churches to overflowing—a rare occurrence in eighteenth-century Virginia. (Black reported that over 200 attended the Lord's Supper service, three times a year.) Anthony Gavin, at the frontier parish of St. James, Goochland, traveled over 400 miles a year, praying at twelve different places. In his very first year of service, 1737-1738, he baptized 229 whites and 172 blacks.[4]

These early isolated cases of Anglican efforts to reach adult blacks may well have built up a reservoir of Christian faith that provided the groundwork for some early Baptist conversions and all-black churches. At the least, those conversions created goodwill toward Christianity by reducing its strangeness.

During the 1750s, Hugh Neil, serving at Dover, Delaware, an area with a large Negro population, met with slaves "every Sunday Evening at Church, for their improvement in ye Christian Doctrines. I bless God my labour has not been lost, for these creatures give constant attendance from the different parts of the Country." By 1751, he could report:

> I have baptised 109 adults of them and 17 of their children, but as I am destitute of proper helpes for their Instruction, I would beg the favour of ye Venerable Society [for the Propagation of the Gospel] to send me a few of Lewis's Catechisms *to distribute among them*, which I make no doubt will tend greatly to their advantage.

The suggestion that blacks would read these catechisms is significant.

Hugh Jones, rector of William and Mary Church at Charles County, Maryland, proudly cited several classes of Negroes "that can give as good an account of the Faith as the white youth." By 1731, he had baptized many blacks and had initiated a practice apparently unique in the colonial church: he took "Christian Negroes for Sureties." The problem of sureties, or godparents, was a basic hurdle that the Anglican church faced in attempting to convert blacks. Whites, if willing to allow their slaves time to be catechized and if they gave permission for baptism, were not automatically ready to stand as spiritual guardians of those they might sell on the morrow. Many ministers reported serious difficulty in finding godparents, but so far as the records indicate, only Jones allowed blacks to be sureties, thereby making an important statement about their spiritual equality. Jones also published black banns and married blacks in church. This was contrary to the guidelines established by an official act of the Province of Maryland, which in 1701 specifically excluded the marriages of Negroes and "Mallatos" from the otherwise required registration rolls.[5]

Neil's plea for printed catechisms and other references to reading lessons raises the issue of the nature of the process of conversion which, in turn, is directly tied to the Anglican world view. Anglicans required that adult blacks have a brief formal knowledge of the faith. Religious experience was neither in question nor a desideratum. Generally, blacks were required to learn, by rote, the Apostle's Creed, the Lord's Prayer, and the Ten Commandments. If they could repeat these in fairly understandable English, they could be baptized and receive the sacraments, although these were often "administered with circumspection." Reading was a plus that was advisable but not required. However, it must be emphasized that many blacks learned to read as a result of the Anglican outreach. Bibles and prayer books were put in their hands, and the long-term results were very important. As suggested, several of the areas where Anglican ministers reached out to blacks later became centers of black Baptist activity.

Ministerial reports to the bishop of London generally picture parishes covering large areas with dispersed populations. Almost all the white residents were considered nominal Christians, but there was pitifully small church attendance and little evidence of white concern. While ministers or rectors generally traveled about their parishes, preaching at two or three stations, the total size of their congregations was very small and, as suggested above, often very rude. Nevertheless, laymen were in control of church polity. By the 1660s, the local vestry was a self-perpetuating and officially recognized institution. These lay committees were in full control of financial and social affairs and, through their denial of tenure, the laymen retained a crucial veto over all ministerial activity. This laicization of Anglican polity tempered ministerial opposition to local morality. The quality of the Anglican ministers in the South was also a serious problem. In part because of the unique lay control, the American pastorate was held in very low repute and it did not generally attract the most promising Anglican ministers; those who did come to the colonies were often demoralized by their status. This situation was exacerbated by the shortage of ministers during the English wars and the Commonwealth period.[6]

Anglicanism was based on infant baptism and not on conversionary experience. While most Anglican clergymen in early Virginia were committed, nonseparating Puritans, their services were not markedly emotional. As time passed, a more centrist Anglican conformity was demanded, perhaps less earnest, with the Anglican Prayer Book used even during the Commonwealth period. Communion, the high experience of the church year, was brought to the parishioners no more than three or four times—at Easter, Whit Sunday, Michaelmas, and Christmas. There was little church drama. Catechism, even for white children, was a sometime affair, being presented on summer Sundays, if at all. Overall, the evidence we have of the quality and character of this early Anglican church leads to the conclusion that it was a generally dull and dreary affair. The church music reflected this character. While Psalms were widely sung, the singing, according to contemporary reports, was of the most belabored sort. It had become a form of communal chant, limned out by a deacon and repeated in a drone by the congregation.

In the early confrontation of the Anglican Sacred Cosmos and the quasi-African Sacred Cosmos, most Africans found the Anglican religion wanting. While most historical analyses have emphasized the whites' failure to proselytize, at least one contemporary rector, William Tibbs of St. Paul's Parish in Baltimore County, Maryland, commenting in 1724, recognized that the blacks' rejection was a significant aspect of the interaction. While he claimed that some Negroes and "Mollatoes" had joined his church, he emphasized that of the Afro-Americans in his area, *"most have refused instruction."*[7]

II

The Society for the Propagation of the Gospel in Foreign Parts (SPG), the Anglican missionary organization operating out of London, was financially independent. As a result, it bypassed some of the local churches' problems and came to the slave with a relatively positive outreach. Organized in 1701, the SPG was the work of Thomas Bray (1656-1730) who in 1695 was appointed commissary in Maryland, where he functioned as a sort of associate bishop. Under his influence, the SPG became the main arm of Anglican expansion in all the colonies (save Maryland and Virginia). Together with Dr. Bray's Associates, an organization founded in his memory in 1731 specifically to educate blacks, it was primarily responsible for black conversions to Anglicanism. The over 300 missionaries of the SPG, far more secure than the local lay-controlled ministry and often well-educated and dedicated men, vigorously preached to the slaves, bringing a new emphasis on morality and ritual. They often found the local white Anglicans an impediment. Atheistic, immoral, and blasphemous, the white Anglicans provided poor examples of Christians for the slaves.

Notwithstanding their dedication, the SPG missionaries experienced only limited success in converting blacks, in part due to the white attitude toward educating blacks. A "catechizing school" was opened in New York City in 1704. It functioned well until the exposure of a black rebellion in 1712 placed the school in jeopardy, a situation indicating the white sense of the power of Christian education. At the ensuing trials, however, it was established that only one of the insurgents had actually attended missionary classes and even he was not a convert. With the support of the governor, the mission weathered this period and continued to function throughout the colonial era.

While Dr. Bray's Associates pressed for schools for both slaves and free blacks in order to bring them to the gospel, the owners who cooperated generally sent slaves to learn to read and write so that they could use these skills, and then withdrew them. This was the experience at Williamsburg, Virginia, where a school was run for some thirty students per year between 1760 and 1774. Most of the other attempts were shortlived (as at Fredericksburg, Virginia, during 1765-1770) and faced serious problems. The school in Charleston, South Carolina, Commissary Garden, attempted to circumvent one problem by buying slaves to be trained as teachers, but it too functioned no more than twenty years (1743-1763).

The SPG and the Associates were responsible for schools for blacks throughout the colonies and for the conversion of some blacks in the Carolinas, Pennsylvania, New York, and New Jersey. However, the total number that came under their influence was small.

Many black infants were baptized in parishes throughout the South, but overall the Anglican outreach to the adult African slave was not a successful one. The SPG missionaries had been admonished

> that in their instructing *Heathens* and *Infidels*, they begin with the Principles of Natural Religion, appealing to their Reason and Conscience; and thence proceed to shew them the Necessity of Revelation, and the Certainty of that contained in the Holy Scriptures, by the plainest and most obvious Arguments.[8]

Goodwill and " plain and obvious" arguments did not overcome the vast chasm between the African and Anglican world views. Most whites were loath to convert blacks, and most blacks, when offered the opportunity, "refused instruction."[9]

III

In Africa, there had been "a remarkable correspondence between the government of the universe and that of human society, between the structure of the world of gods and that of the world of men." The political organization and the social organization, the kinship and the clan, "supported and justified by a close-knit mythology, and presenting an exact reproduction of the divine pattern, provide[d] the type of all social life."⁹ In the slave society, the Sacred Cosmos could not play a comparable role in the new social processes. It could not continue what had been its normative conversation with the world. It could not expect total support and reaffirmation from the individuals that it socialized, as they became increasingly ashamed or confused about its value (but not its power). It suffered particularly because the formal institutions that had supported it in Africa could not be officially re-created in North America. The strength and wholeness of the African Sacred Cosmos had depended upon the African social structure, while at the same time the Sacred Cosmos had reflected and legitimated that very social structure.

The white world, both in its institutions and its Sacred Cosmos, was alien, antagonistic, and powerful. The white-Anglican Sacred Cosmos wrought deep damage to the new quasi-African Sacred Cosmos, in part by regarding it as nonexistent or invisible, but in greater measure by introducing contradictory social values.

As slave history developed in America, the majority of slaves rapidly became second- and third-generation Americans. At the same time as they began to speak Creole and black English, the lack of coherence in their newly forged quasi-African Cosmos became evident. Given the lack of congruence between the values of Africans and the values of slaveowners, as well as the variations between African cultures and the problem of forging a unified value system in the face of slavery, it is most likely that the world view had incorporated inconsistencies from the outset. Blacks may have become ashamed of some of their African ways and denied their meaningfulness at a very early period, or, in the classic African pattern of indirection, they may have chosen not to properly explain their practices. The result was that whites misunderstood and attributed the blacks' lack of self-explanation to stupidity, a judgment that had complicated implications for the blacks' self-image. Mullin reports that in 1773 a recent Ibo arrival, already known as Charles, whose teeth were filed and whose skin was covered with ritual scarification, "presumably tried to explain his ritual multilations in what he already perceived to be a socially acceptable manner, [and] said it was 'done by a Cow in his country.'"¹⁰ Here we have an early instance of the attack on the Sacred Cosmos. The ritual meanings of scarification are reduced to accidental mutilation to fit in with white sensibilities. Moreover, this need was recognized by a recent arrival who could hardly speak English.

The crucial onslaught on the black Sacred Cosmos did not begin with random shame but rather in relation to Nyama, the key to the African world view. Both as causal power and as goal, Nyama was put in a state of conflict in slave society. Africans first began to face the attack on Nyama in regard to its failure to consistently protect them from their owners. Perhaps, they reasoned, the blacks' power could not work on whites, or perhaps the whites had a stronger power. At times, slaves accepted both possibilities. Tales describing this new reality entered the folklore and have remained there to this day, although other tales recounted the very opposite—the power of Voodoo over the white man. These conflicting tales directly reflect that consciousness in conflict.

Some blacks held that if whites did not believe in Voodoo the lack of belief in itself reduced Voodoo's power: "W'ite folks, hoodoo cain't tech you ef you doan' believe in hit, but hit sho' lam's de gizzud out ov you ef you does believ."

These two solutions—whites had greater power or defused Voodoo through their disbelief—came in answer to the problems posed by the widespread inability of Voodoo to protect slaves. Some slaves had expected to use African spirit power to return them (or their spirits) to Africa; many looked to Voodoo to harm slaveowners and to eliminate punishments and cruel treatment. These were not simply the ideas of the first arrivals. Reports of attempts to use African power occurred throughout the slave era and indicate that slaves did not lose their faith in Voodoo. While belief in it remained strong, it did come under increasing attack. The seemingly humorous black stories of why African magic sometimes failed with whites allude to this very serious confrontation. A classic theme involves the black doctor giving the slave a magic hand (or "mojo" or charm) which he promises will allow him to sass or cuss out the master without incurring punishment. When this "mojo" fails to protect the slave, he, of course, complains to the provider. One often-repeated story ending involves the doctor worming his way out by stating "I gi' you a runnin' han! Why didn't yer run?" Here African power (which was reduced in status by the appellation magic) tricks its way out of a confrontation with whites. When it cannot trick the masters, the African becomes the butt of the black joke.[11]

The slave belief in the power of the conjurer and his "mojos" did not die; in fact, it remained one of the blacks' major strengths in adversity. However, many slaves found themselves in the predicament of believing in spirit power, or wanting to believe in spirit power, and yet recognizing again and again its particular failure with white society. In 1852, the *New Orleans Daily True Delta* told of a slave, William, who provided his beloved, also a slave, with a special charm to wear "to insure the kindness of whites" so that she might successfully steal to enable them to buy free papers and travel to Europe. This mixture of cultural means and ends was unusual, but William's sentence of fifty lashes and the fixing of an iron collar on his neck for one year was not unique. It was but a formal sign of the fact that black "conjure-power" often did not work on whites. Blacks believed they had much continuing evidence of the power of Voodoo. Yet the ever-present threat of plantation punishment and slave sale provided the most visible and most significant test and failure of black power in the white world.[12]

Whites occasionally sought to ridicule black belief and prove its falsity. (The counterclaim has also been made that whites stimulated blacks' fear of the supernatural in order to control them.) Many black folktales describe whites wearing sheets and frightening blacks by pretending to be ghosts. Sometimes, in the same tale, a "true" spirit suddenly appears, shocking the masquerading master. These tales indicate that blacks knew that they were occasionally fooled, and that awareness of this trickery did not cause them to lose faith in Voodoo. White tricksters may have been seeking to reassure themselves that black spirit power was spurious. They could far more easily laugh at the conjurer if they had tricked him into believing they were his dangerous spirits.

Several accounts of whites making hands or charms have been preserved. Puckett recounts a case of a master making a charm and hiding it in the home of an apparently dying slave. When it was found in her cabin, she recovered, believing that it had been there all along and had caused her illness. The "kind" master waited a year, but then he told her the truth as he understood it. As with ghosts, white manipulation did not end black belief in charms, but it probably sowed some seeds of doubt and confusion.[13]

The discrete beliefs and taboos of the quasi-African Sacred Cosmos continued to be operative even beyond the end of the slave period. In fact, the respect for signs, potions, and conjurers is still in evidence today. However, over time the positive aspects of the world of spirit as an ongoing reality incorporating kin and protective powers began to fade into a relatively cloudy area while the taboos and the mechanisms of propitiation remained important. Men continued to do certain acts under pain of punishment. Voodoo practitioners remained powerful but while feared, they were not as respected as they once had been. As Rias Body, an ex-slave, remembered, it would be best to give them "a wide berth." Over time, it was widely accepted that Voodoo practitioners had pacts with the devil, although some variant and more positive interpretations were offered within the black Christian setting.

It is very difficult to establish at exactly what point such changes occurred, as many ex-slaves may have projected back into the slavery period their later negative perceptions. However, at some point in time (the process actually occurring gradually and at different times in different slave areas), divinities literally became ghosts of the once powerful spirits they had been. As ghosts, ha'nts, or witches, spirits were generally not pleasant or positive images. A person did not look forward to becoming a ghost, nor did he feel that this was a satisfactory explanation of life after death. Ghosts were the frightening apparitions that inhabited cemeteries. A particularly brave or foolish man might engage one, but they were not the living dead that one joked with or argued with or sought counsel from in Africa.

When working among the Nuer during the twentieth century, Evans-Pritchard, who thought he knew a good deal about these people, was nevertheless surprised "at the familiar and off-handed way in which the prophet spoke to the spirit, calling it 'wota', 'man'—almost 'old chap'—bargaining with it about the oblation demanded, and insisting that when the sacrifice had been made it should keep its promise and leave Guluak [a sick Nuer] alone." Nineteenth-century slaves, however, were not off-handed in their treatment of ghosts, a fact that indicates the sharp shift that had taken place.[14] The African concept of the separable soul, a morally neutral idea, early became associated with the possession qualities of European witches. Thus, it was not difficult for black West Indian Tituba to feed the witch fears of Puritan children in Salem in 1692. White contemporaries recognized that "her apparition did the mischief."[15]

While African divinities were often tricksters or mixed personalities, much like human beings, for the whites witches were wholly evil fiends. In both the European and African tradition, witches were capable of riding the possessed person. In America, however, the image of being ridden implied an evil driver, cruelly using his beast, and not a potentially useful divinity who chose to speak to his people through a medium-mount. The slave tradition of being ridden by witches has very clear English antecedents, but it also involved a twisting of African beliefs. Blacks came to believe that "the hag turns the victim on his or her back. A bit (made by the witch) is then inserted in the mouth of the sleeper and he or she is turned on all-fours and ridden like a horse. Next morning the person is tired out, and finds dirt between the fingers and toes."

If this was possession it was no gift to the possessed. The African had given up the sometimes painful visits of his divinities and living dead, which had brought social rewards for medium and society, for the almost always painful visits of witches who had no positive goals in mind.

> Mr. S.: Well, I heard my grandfather tell it—. . . . He said that back in slavery times there was a woman they called a "Mammy Rye", and the boys all teased her. She was a witch. And you'd

hear her coming—zip—zip—zip. They'd say, "Where you going, Mammy Rye?" She says, "Mm boy, you better git going; I'll give you devil before day in the morning." Granddad said one would have to stay awake while the others slept; that was the only way they could get to go to sleep. I heard him tell that more times than a little.

Mrs. S.: Wasn't there no way they could move, to git out of her way?

Mr. S.: Well, they stayed there, you see. . . .

While the African had to learn taboos and propitiatory acts as a means of getting the spirits on his side, the slave who had to stay "there" (as he was not free to move on) spent much of his psychic energy protecting himself from witches and haunts. Even at this juncture, African elements were retained—notably the libation procedure of pouring a drink on the ground for the spirits and offering a gift (now of money). Generally, however, ghosts were to be avoided, tricked, or warded off, often through the use of powerful biblical words or phrases. (This, too, echoes an African usage, that of Gris-Gris, in which written Arabic phrases from the Koran were regarded as powerful. The term itself was taken into America.) Witches and hags were regarded as the evil spirits of living people. The haunt or ghost did, to some extent, preserve the character of a dead person, who might have been good. Nevertheless, he was probably out to do mischief or to cause much more serious trouble. He should therefore be dissuaded from returning, perhaps by a request for charity or through tricking him by changing the appearance of his old home.

The African belief in the spirits' ability to live in animals and things was remembered as legend or folklore, not as living belief. Children were told stories about this ability, but it was emphasized that if they ever had this power, it was only in the past. Animals could "sho talk in dem days," but "dem days" were gone. While some related African practices were retained, the ghost and the hag were not African deities or the living dead. They were "other" foreign entities that came into a hospitable world of spirit and entered as guests. They stayed, however, and as a result changed the atmosphere.

It is ironic that Puckett lamented the lack of charm or grace in the slave consciousness of the spirits.[16] He looked longingly for Irish leprechaun images or wee people, or good fairies. While with one eye he recognized the English influence on black lore, with the other he blamed the African ethos for just those unpleasant aspects that are particularly English. The African spirit world was not a fairytale land; rather, it was a mirror of the real world. Spirits were powerful and fateful personalities but not the devil's disciples.

Since it was assumed that all spirits, divinities, and living dead had great difficulty in crossing large bodies of water, and, further, that spirits were tied to place (the African spirits essentially staying in Africa and the American in America), blacks admitted white witches and hags, as well as their lore, into their sacred world. These were the local spirits. The whites they found in America attested to their presence, and there was a highly developed tradition relating their history and character. The gap in the Afro-American's Sacred Cosmos was waiting to be filled. Hence, it is not strange that witches from the white folk tradition filled it or that they were understood in partially African terms. However welcomed, lasting damage was done by the new witches' negativism and asocial behavior; they were no addition to social life. Even if they were regarded as black, they now had the character of the white witches. While they might occasionally serve a positive function (as in finding treasure), overall they were disruptive and dangerous.

While the divinities and living dead suffered irreparable harm during the long period of enslavement, the African ideas of God and man, as well as innumerable motifs surrounding them, remained intact. Again, the chief evidence is the postfacto consideration that when a new black Christian ethos eventually crystallized, it was readily apparent that the African "little me" was still there, ready to go home to be with spirit. The African understanding of man's soul survived through a long and hard period of conflicted consciousness.

IV

The new quasi-African world view began to incorporate more and more dichotomous elements, until it can be said to have become a noncoherent world view. That is, its nominizing categories were becoming confused and it no longer clearly evaluated reality. A hierarchy of values or choices was no longer apparent.

This alteration had to have a direct effect on the individuals socialized in its midst. Such individuals doubtlessly suffered value confusions. This world view was probably responsible for much black antisocial behavior, that of the so-called "no-counts," known to blacks as "bad" people, who in turn passed on an increasingly confused Sacred Cosmos.

With the growth of the second- and third-generation slave population and their sale and removal to the Deep South and the Southwest, a dichotomous African/American world view spread rapidly throughout the expanding slave community. With each generation the process accelerated. Once the system lost coherence, the individual could not be properly oriented to either past or present while the understanding of the nature of causality and purpose was increasingly brought into serious question.

Many of the first black arrivals had held on to their expectations of returning to Africa. For this group, the sense of time (its passage counted by crops and weather) remained a fully African one. The second and third slave generations, however, found their roles fixed or reified. As a consequence, the blacks' awareness of their own function in creating their world view was reduced. Concomitantly, time became intertwined with white institutions. An endless future as slaves loomed in front of them.

As the black confronted a white world view in which his person was defined as slave (forever), and nothing other than slave, he increasingly began to believe that his responsibility for developing his inner self—a task the African openly avowed—was out of his hands. Role and identity became confused. The slave continued to be a co-producer of his world view, but he was less and less aware of his own participation. He increasingly saw the institution of slavery as the sole determinant. Actually, his social role as slave was at distinct and increasing variance with part of his internalized value system, which continued to play its role in his development.[17]

Numerous taboos of African peoples, and proscriptions of divinities and spirits, remained operative in America, coalescing into a vast body of superstitions and signs. Every black child and every white child raised by or with blacks learned much of the lore, such as:

> To sneeze in the morning tells that misfortune is near. . . . To awake in the morning on the right side is a sign of good luck. . . . If a rooster crows at your window, it is a sign of death. . . . If a spider swings down on a web, company is coming. . . . If your left eye jumps, it is a sign of money. . . . When a dog stretches, he is measuring his grave. . . . If your nose burns, someone is talking about you. . . . If the sun shines when it is raining, the devil is beating his wife. . . . To see silvery money in your dream is the sign of trouble. . . . If an owl comes to your window, or you hear him in a tree, someone in your family will die. . . . If you sing before making bread, you will cry before it is eaten. . . . If someone strikes you with a broom, you will never get married. . . . If two people comb your hair, the youngest will die. . . . It is bad luck to destroy spiders. . . . It is bad to postpone a marriage. . . . It is bad luck to move into a house with an old broom. . . . Never kill a toad. Warts will develop over your body.[18]

Blacks did not doubt the truth of these beliefs. Celestia Avery, an ex-slave, knew that "when you see a dog lay on his stomach and slide it is a sign of death. *This is sho true cause it happened to me.* Annuder sign of death is ter dream of a newborn baby," a belief implying, but not acknowledging, the transmigration of souls.

The slaves' belief in signs was both deep and strong enough to govern action. Jack Atkinson, a slave in Georgia, was not sure he should marry Lucy, so he "broke off a love vine and throwed it over the fence and if it growed" he knew it would be a sign he should marry her. The vine "just growed and growed" and so he married Lucy. The slaves saw their lives as full of signs, some of which were more fateful than others: "A hootin' owl is a sho sign of rain, and a screech owl means a death for a fact." Signs or portents were connected with virtually every aspect of life, including the weather, cooking, work, love, children, health, birth, and death.

Spirit as cause or control of these signs was increasingly forgotten. The signs, in and of themselves, were seen as "true," but what made them true was no longer clear to either the black believer or the white observer. Tricks or "mojos" preserved something more of their original nature, but the difference may not have been significant enough to preserve spirit. Tricks were given names, talked to, bathed in whiskey; all of these actions were remnants of the concept of an indwelling spirit. But the trick in itself—the bag of graveyard dust or roots, animal parts, urine, wine, blood, pepper, needles, pins, hair, anvil dust, salt, and red materials—seems to have taken on an inherent power that evenutally became inexplicable. As both Puckett and Hurston found, blacks in the early twentieth century still widely believed in this power, although they might at first deny it. Slaves certainly did believe, although some had doubts. As late as the 1930s, ex-slaves were still widely recounting their early experiences with Hoodoo.

Much as conjurers became devil's disciples, the trick eventually became loosely associated with Christian power. When Ed Murphy taught Puckett to make a hand, he carefully labeled the three parts: (1) Father (the black cloth wrapping), (2) Son (the white thread), and (3) the Holy Ghost (the ubiquitous red flannel material). Bibles, biblical phrases (often said backwards), and God's name assumed special power: "When you pass a place and feels creepy and scared, you feels a ghost or a witch. If you say, 'Holy Father, don't let this thing bother me,' He ain't goona let it hurt you." This was Christian "mojo," much as Moses was understood to be a snake-controlling magic worker of great power. But this interpretation of spirit and Christianity was not integral, and both spirit and the Christian God suffered as a result.[19]

By the twentieth century, many blacks no longer understood why they followed certain practices. When queried as to why they adhered to many old-time customs and taboos, they replied, if pressed, that they did not know why. When asked why broken crockery was placed on a grave (much as it is in Africa), they made no mention of freeing the spirit in the broken vessel but simply said that this was the way it had always been done. Many other customs that had been meaningful in an African world view were continued, apparently without any understanding of their power or significance. Of what value was it to a black that the taboo against sweeping a house after dark had an African religious meaning? The act could actually be of negative value if the individual involved had "forgotten" that one must not sweep out of respect for the invisible divinities in the house.

In Sierra Leone, when Mende women used streams for bathing it was taboo for Mende men to enter these areas unannounced. "It was required of a man travelling alone and, therefore without holding a conversation by which his approach would be announced, to indicate his presence either by means of some appropriate noise—a cough or a coo—whenever he was approaching a stream." In the 1950s, Enoch Brown sang what he called a "complaint call" each time he came to a bridge over a river at Livingston, Alabama. Brown sang a long "Ohhh," followed by a song whose refrain was "I'm goin' down the road. Down the road I'm gone." While this practice may stem from an African custom involving river spirits, it may well derive from the very tradition wherein a noise was meant "to warn any women bathing near the ford of the approach of a male stranger and so give her time to cover herself." In any event, in the 1950s, Enoch Brown did not know why he sang that song when he did; he just knew he had to and he did.

When was the meaning of these rituals forgotten? Did the second- and third-generation slave still know and appreciate their meaning, or was this already forgotten lore by this early date? While this process of "forgetting" seems to have been well underway for the third slave generation, we have little hard proof and the answer must be tentative. What we do know is that black Christianity was to use many of these African forms, especially those once involved in the communal celebrations of initiation and death, investing them with new meaning and purpose.[20]

Plantation Creole English, of which we have a living example in Gullah, is the verbal counterpart to the African/American world view, and it is possible that its logic and taxonomy reflect the conflicted ethos of the speakers. Wood suggests that happenstance and white derision were the major causal factors in its creation, that "sounds and constructions comprehensible to the widest number survived," while those of the minority or those "subjected to the greatest degree of white derision were lost or suppressed." If such accident was the key, with white derision an important factor, the inner logic carried over from African languages and preserved in black Pidgin English must have been seriously weakened in Creole.

Most whites did not understand the nature of creole languages. They generally regarded the plantation slaves' use of English as ludicrous and were confirmed in their view when blacks obviously misunderstood white phrases, songs, or prayers, such as when "the annointing oil in his hand" became "de nineteen wile in his han," or when "sweet lamb" emerged as "silly yan."

The whites' negative view of blacks would not have been as harmful to blacks, notwithstanding the whites' power and prestige in the society, if the black Sacred Cosmos had not been in serious difficulty. Although blacks had rejected Anglicanism, many of the whites' values had entered their consciousness. They found themselves increasingly acting on the basis of values they or their parents had consciously rejected. (This conflict is discussed more fully on p. 99.) A Sacred Cosmos should provide a person with perspective and goals, "a sense of a wider meaning to one's existence. . . . If he lacks this sense, he is lost and miserable." As the slave's Sacred Cosmos incorporated conflicting values and ontological confusions, he increasingly lost the sense of the wider meaning of his life.[21]

part II | *God's precious dealing with their souls: the Baptist outreach to the blacks and early Afro-Christianity*

4

THE EARLY WHITE BAPTIST WORLD VIEW: REVIVALS AS AN OUTREACH TO BLACKS

During the period when the world view of many black Americans was changing from a quasi-African to an African/American ethos, the world view of the whites around them was also changing. The religions established during the early colonial period, particularly Southern Anglicanism and New England Congregationalism, had come on hard, dry days, while the members of these sects were complaining about the general lack of purpose and meaning. The broad religious excitement that came to be known as the First Great Awakening is evidence that a deep need for an encompassing and coherent ethos was felt. At the outset, the religious revivals stimulated the growth of the old churches, but they also divided them, ultimately leading to the development of two new major denominations, the Baptist and the Methodist, which became the dominant American religions.

Blacks were attracted to both of these new denominations, and black folk religion is inextricably intertwined in their history. Of the two, black Christianity has a more particular relationship to the Baptist faith. "All good niggers, as they say in Alabama, had better, by God, be nigger Baptists—or else."[1] Throughout the South, it is said that "if a nigger ain't a Baptist, someone's been tampering with his religion." This folk "wisdom" is a recognition of a very complicated and very significant social fact. Religion is extremely important for blacks, and more American blacks belong to the Baptist faith than to any other sect. (See Table 3, p. 182.) The reason is not, as is so often stated, simply because of the domination of Baptists in the South and their historical willingness to allow blacks some modicum of self-determination. While this factor is important, far more complex elements are involved. A full explanation of Baptist and black interaction must encompass the white Baptist world view, the black African/American world view, and the unique interaction between the two that resulted in a new black or Afro-Baptist Sacred Cosmos.

I

White Baptists had been in the colonies from a very early period, but it was not until the First Great Awakening that they became a numerically significant sect. It was only then that their world view, which was changing, became widely known. It was their Sacred Cosmos, the essence of their world view, that attracted converts.[2]

In contrast to the Anglicans, Baptist sectarians reextended the penetrating power of the holy, reincorporating major areas of concern that the Anglicans had eliminated from the church, although not from social life. As suggested earlier, when the Anglican church was established, it sought to eliminate the magical from the purview of the church. To a great extent it succeeded, but it did not quash interest in it, as the occult was practiced outside the church. In fact, the greatest period of witch prosecutions in England occurred between 1500 and 1675; this constitutes strong evidence of a continuing concern with witches and the occult. Keith Thomas concludes that in this period "astrology, witchcraft, magical healing, divination, ancient prophesies, ghosts and fairies" were taken very seriously by both the elite and the common people. Witches, wizards, and astrologers were very active, with the occult in some senses dominating social life, as is indicated by the fact that a high percentage of patients who consulted medical doctors were convinced of occult causes for their complaints. It was not until the last quarter of the seventeenth century that English belief in magic precipitously declined.

In the American colonies, the belief in magic was subject to the culture lag that affected many intellectual currents there, but an important contributory factor was the history of the sectarians, who as suggested above had openly concerned themselves with exactly those issues that had been labeled secular or even antireligious by the Anglican branch of the Protestant Reformation. Prophesying and healing, abjured by the Anglicans, were major concerns of the sectarians. The common people were not able to distinguish between the "magic" that was an important part of church life and the magic that had been banished from the Anglican church and that had become the private possession of professional practitioners.

> There was no difference between a sibylline prophecy and a Quaker revelation, thought one contemporary. Another reported of the Fifth Monarchy Men that in their lectures and chief con-

venticles you might have heard such raptures that you would have thought it were a reading on astrology. When the transcript of John Dee's conjuring sessions with the spirits was published in 1659, many Puritan divines suspected it as a partisan attempt to discredit religious enthusiasm. To the unsophisticated there was little to choose between a cunning man and a religious leader who healed and prophesied, or between a witch and a godly divine who predicted correctly that divine judgments would fall upon his enemies. It is not surprising that one contemporary, after seeing the cunning woman, Anne Bodenham, at work, should have concluded that she "was either a witch or a woman of God."[3]

Sectarians in America played an important role in supporting the more general belief in occult phenomena, but they had a wide base to build upon. In America, both the educated elite and the common folk continued to evidence public concern with the occult, long after such interest had declined in England. Increase Mather (1639-1723), pastor of Boston's prestigious Second Church and rector of Harvard University, was among those who specially collected "strange and true reports," such as that of "a woman living near the Salmon Falls in Berwick . . . unto whom evil spirits have sometimes visibly appeared, and she has sometimes been sorely tormented by invisible hands." Heads, tails, and other apparitions (which left visible marks on her body) were accepted as "Satanical molestations." The "facts" of known individuals having sold their souls to the devil were repeated as totally accepted truths. John Higginson (1616-1708), pastor at Salem, Massachusetts, knew (second-hand) of a man who had sold his soul in order to gain wisdom and fame, which were then given to him. When close to death, he became tormented by his future in Hell and "roared" out the truth in "a spectacle of the righteous judgments of God."

Colonial society acted on this belief in the occult. In 1648, Margaret Jones of Charlestown was hanged for witchcraft. As John Winthrop recorded in his journal, she had a "malignant touch" that caused violent illness and deafness, preknowledge, a witch's "teat," and a witch's helper or magical child who appeared and disappeared at her will. The witchcraft mania in America peaked in Salem, Massachusetts, in 1692. Cotton Mather (1663-1728), Increase's son, did not understand exactly how the Salem magic was accomplished, but he accepted its results and was sure he knew its source:

> Witchcraft seems to be the skill of applying the plastic spirit of the world into some unlawful purposes, by means of a confederacy with evil spirits.
>
> . . . .

> The Devil, exhibiting himself ordinarily as *a small black man* has decayed a fearful knot of proud, forward, ignorant, envious and malicious creatures to lift themselves in his horrid service, by entering their names in a book by him tendered unto them. . . . These monsters have associated themselves *to do no less a thing than to destroy the Kingdom of our Lord Jesus Christ in these parts of the world.*[4]

While the prosecution of witches radically declined after the Salem hysteria, belief in wizards, witches, and the devil's ability to control the spirit did not disappear. It was consciously maintained by Congregationalists, Baptists, Quakers, and individual Anglicans. Among the sectarians, the Baptists in particular returned to the biblical injunctions to heal and prophesize, and they attempted to fulfill these injunctions literally, anointing with holy oil, fasting, praying, and *casting out devils.* "Is anyone of you ill? Let him call for the elders of the church and let them pray for him and in the name of the Lord annoint him with olive oil. The prayer of faith will restore the sick one."

In returning to the words of the Bible, healing and prophecy were but two of the gifts the Baptists recognized. Christ was seen as having called some people to be apostles, some to be evangelists or pastors and teachers, some to be prophets, some to work miracles, and others simply to be the "members of the body." All the saved, both men and women, were regarded as part of the mystical body of Christ. It was this body of Christ that was the essence of the Sacred Cosmos, and the social structure was intended as a parallel and contributory form, with all gifts recognized as socially beneficial. All were to be one in Christ, equal in their partaking of His love and spirit; unequal in the gifts He called them to but equal in the need to learn to use those gifts fully and with humility and charity. Prophecy was regarded as the first and greatest gift; speaking in tongues, a sign of God's grace, was viewed as a lesser gift but more important if an interpreter could make its teaching known. Teaching, leading, and working miracles were all from God. All gifts were to be welcomed in God's community, the church, but possession of gifts did not mean spiritual inequality. In the church all members were to submit themselves to one another. The "walk" of the believer was to be open to the criticism of every other believer, and the church was to be the proper place to bring criticism. Criticism of any aspect of all other believers' lives was the responsibility of each member, important for the individual criticized and for the church as the body of Christ. The church could not continue if it contained evil. Therefore, no evil could be overlooked; it must be made public, and either the sin or the individual sinning must be eliminated.[5]

The social ramifications of this world view encompassed every aspect of life. God's constant presence and infinite concern was a key to the Sacred Cosmos and to the social consciousness worked up by the Baptists. God was seen as aware of and concerned with every act of every individual. His holy church, the covenanted body of His believers and at the same time His body, had the responsibility to evaluate and punish any and every aspect of a member's behavior. It did not wait for private confession of sins. It had the obligation to investigate wrongdoing, if any hint or sign was known to any other member. The church was the presence of God on earth and had the obligation to work with man's spirit.

Baptist churches worked out a regularized form for checking on the spirit. All members were required to attend monthly business meetings, the primary business of which was the social behavior of the members. The churches became moral courts and considered social relations between wives, husbands, children, and slaves, business dealings, gambling, stealing, tale-bearing, lying, intoxication, and sexual immorality. No area of concern was proscribed.

All Baptists shared these basic beliefs and practices but diverged in regard to the belief in redemption. Two distinct Baptist traditions emerged on this issue, and both were brought to America: The Arminian or General Baptist, which preached redemption for all (for the generality) and the Calvinistically oriented tradition known as Particular Baptist, which avowed a limited or particular atonement.[6]

Baptists of both types came to the colonies where they were soon joined by others who came out of established congregations. The few Baptist churches, established in New England beginning in the 1630s and in the South in the 1690s, were, by and large, very small and weak. A somewhat stronger group of Particular Baptist churches developed in the mid-Atlantic area.[7] It was not until the Great Awakening emphasis on adult regeneration, religious experience, and a pure church, which led individuals and whole churches to abandon infant baptism and open communion, that Arminian Baptist churches began to grow into a significant denomination.[8] Of the 98 New England Congregational churches that became Separatist during the Great Awakening (withdrawing from antirevival churches), 19 became Baptist churches; in addition, some 130 new Baptist churches were constituted. These new Separate Baptists had a great need for an active outreach and became the leading evangelicals. As Arminian Baptists, they were more concerned about every aspect of life (dress, behavior, etc.). In other words, they were stricter than the Particular Baptists but they were also freer in their approach to salvation and freer in their use of emotion and body movements. No solemn assemblies were advocated. They came to God with noise and celebration, inviting the masses and being joined by them. "The people were greatly astonished having never seen things on this wise before. Many mocked, but the power of God attending them, many also trembled."[9]

The Separatists found biblical justification for their mode of worship and celebration. As "David danced before the Lord with all his might, . . . shouting and with the sound of the trumpet" (II Samuel 6: 14-15), so movement and sound and joy were to serve the Lord in Separatist Baptist churches. God and the church had total concern for man, and man should use all his abilities to worship and praise God.

While group singing had not been an English Baptist tradition (some churches in Rhode Island actually forbade it), Baptist singing in the Americas generally developed as a healthy folk art, employing folk themes and tunes, historical events, and current speech. Baptism, the Lord's Supper, foot washings, weddings, and funerals dominated the song books in which daily life was hallowed in daily speech forms: "Baptize 'em in the awful name." Jesus came to "teach 'em," and as regards their sins, He would "sink 'em" because "Amazing is thy mercies, Lord." Christ's time and His troubles were described in very homely terms:

> Reaking with sweat and gore!
> See his side sprout a
>   stream of blood
> And water through the wound.
> His sweet and reverend face
> With spittle all profan'd.

Baptists sang "Where am I now?" and answered that only together, in and through the church, as brothers and sisters in the family of God, would they know who they were and where they were going. In New England, the Separate Baptists made extensive use of the growing Baptist song tradition. When they came to the South, they found other rich folk traditions which they incorporated into their repertoire.[10]

This Separatist family of God lived a rich communal life. Sundays were fully the Lord's day, with meetings held morning and afternoon. Midweek prayer meetings, monthly business meetings, and special extended prayer meetings, or revivals, structured the social life of members. All other forms of social life were suspect, if not actually proscribed. Itineracy was an important institution. Preachers traveled widely, stopping at Baptist homes (some of which were jokingly called Baptist taverns); occasionally, whole congregations moved together to bring the word to new areas.[11]

Shubal Stearns (1706-1771) was in this itinerant tradition. Stearns left the Presbyterian church in the wake of George Whitefield's preaching and became a Separate New Light in 1745. He was baptized in 1751 at the age of forty-five and was ordained in March of that same year by Reverend

Wait Palmer of Toland, Connecticut, after which he embarked on an evangelistic mission that carried him first through New England, then to Virginia, and finally to Sandy Creek, North Carolina. In November 1755, Stearns began a great revival that eventually spread through parts of North Carolina, South Carolina, Virginia, Georgia, and Mississippi. His emphasis was on the personal experience of regeneration and antiworldliness, accompanied by evangelical emotionalism and a rich ritual life. In Stearns' church alone, 125 ministers were ordained. Churches in this tradition were planted throughout the South. By the 1770s, Morgan Edwards could call Stearns' Sandy Creek Church "a mother church, nay a grandmother and a great grandmother." "The word went forth from this sion [Zion], and great was the company of them who published it, in so much that her converts were as drops of morning dew." As a direct result of Stearns' revival and the evangelism of the Sandy Creek Church, Separate Baptists became dominant in shaping the outreach and character of the Southern Baptists, and seriously influenced the character of much of Protestantism in the South. They were "the most active of the evangelicals and . . . the greatest factor in destroying the Establishment and securing religious liberty."[12]

This evangelical movement developed in distinct stages. In the first phase, between 1755 and 1770, the Separatist revival grew slowly, primarily attracting the poor and illiterate. In this period, Baptists in the South, both because of the social strata of their members and their world view, rapidly gained a reputation as dangerous and contemptible. Many were widely considered lawbreakers and "a menace to society." Their belief in regeneration after baptism was regarded as license to break the law without fear of damnation. A contemporary charged that by this view of baptism, "You take off all religious restraints from Men of abandoned Principles, who, having been once dipped in your happy waters, are let loose to commit upon us Murders, and every species of Injury, when they can do it secretly so as to avoid temporal Punishment."

The Baptist laymen of this period were the poor and disinherited, and, for the first time, their Christian churches uniformly included many blacks. The Baptist preachers included laymen (and even black laymen) without any special training, who widely used what outsiders termed "disgraceful" methods. Baptists violently attacked the established church and established institutions, including that of slavery; as a result, Baptist preachers were whipped, jailed, and hounded out of communities.

There was no conformity among Baptist churches. In upholding the independence of each church as the body of Christ, Baptists opposed any and all authority over the separate churches. However, they did "associate together" in regional groups which, once formed, would accept only "like" churches as members. These associations advised churches on policy and in practice imposed some conformity, but churches were free to leave associations.

The yearly associational meetings, whose records are generally dry and brief notes, were much like planned revival meetings of blacks and whites together. In the early period, strong antislavery statements came out of many of these meetings. In Virginia, Kentucky, and New York, and later in Indiana, Illinois, and Ohio, Baptist churches and associations publicly opposed slavery. Many of the more committed took as part of their church name the phrase "Friends to Humanity" to signify their antislavery stance.[13]

The well-known Baptist minister John Leland made antislavery a central part of his message. Leland, who had come from Massachusetts, was a pastor in Virginia from 1777 to 1791; his influence there was extensive. He was responsible for introducing the strong antislavery resolution passed at the 1789 meeting of the Baptist General Committee of Virginia, a voluntary association of Virginia churches:

> Resolved that slavery is a violent deprivation of the rights of nature, and inconsistent with a republican government; and we, therefore, recommend it to our brethren, to make use of every legal measure to extirpate this horrid evil from the land and pray Almighty God that our honorable legislature may have it in their power to proclaim the great Jubilee consistent with the principles of good policy.

Leland's parting act in the South was to give a highly emotional "valedictory" plea for freedom for the slaves. While he implored the whites to act, he expected the slaves to be patient and obedient and to await the time they would be free in body. However, he pointedly welcomed their worshiping "our common Lord." The fact that this sermon can be found transcribed in total in the "Day-Book" of Robert Carter's Nomini Hall plantation in Virginia is evidence of its effect. Beginning in 1791, Carter responded to Leland's plea, gradually manumitting 422 slaves, apparently in family groups. His is the most famous case of religiously stimulated manumission. Many early Baptist churches pressed their slaveowning constituents to follow this pattern, and some accepted the call. Virginia Baptist David Barrow manumitted his slaves in 1784 and left for Kentucky with a prayer for "the poor, oppressed, naked [and] hunger bitten slaves."[14]

When Leland went North in the 1790s, he continued to talk of slavery. It was one of his sermons that led the Shaftsbury Association of New York to express its "sense of that freedom which every child of Adam is entitled to by nature; and of which they cannot be deprived but by hostile usurpation." The association decried the slave trade and prayed "to Almighty God to hasten the auspicious day when the Ethiopian, with all the human race, shall enjoy all that liberty due to every good citizen of the commonwealth; and the name of *Slave* be extirpated from the Earth."

Early Baptists (along with Quakers and Methodists) widely shared these strong antislavery feelings. The Baptist appeal to and acceptance of blacks, both as equal members and as preachers, is the best evidence of the depth of their feelings about the spiritual equality of the races. Since their world view incorporated blacks as essentially equal, their "common Lord" would not approve of whites selling blacks away from husbands, wives, children, and church family.

The Anglican reaction to the new Separatist Baptist faith was very strong. The most charitable words the Anglicans could summon for it were "religious madness," and the harshest, "sham and hypocricy." Nonetheless, the Baptists were a challenge to the general sterility and coldness of Anglican church life in the South.[15]

The services of the early Separatist Baptists were geared to emotional arousal. Shubal Stearns was known for his unusual use of his voice in "a holy whine" and for his penetrating and disturbing "holy" peering at individuals, who would feel as if God's prophet has his eye on them particularly. His disciples used his methods and even exceeded them; their congregations responded warmly. In 1772, Edwards reported that the early emotionalism was already part of Baptist folklore. He had been told of "tremblings, outcries, downfalls and ecstacies of joy." Congregants fell down as "in fits" but arose reborn to recount their regeneration in emotional public gatherings, at which the congregation judged "God's precious dealing with their souls." Only those who were accepted by the congregation could be baptized and given "the right hand of fellowship." Women held an important place in this fellowship, and "an extensive ministry of women in the services" developed.

In Stearns' congregation, in line with earlier attempts to reintroduce biblical traditions, baptism was followed by the laying on of hands, during which the minister publicly prayed for the candidate. The washing of feet was practiced, sometimes at "social gatherings of Christian friends." Adult or believer baptism was, of course, central, but in place of infant baptism, babes were "devoted to God," or dry-Christened as non-Baptists put it. The infants were publicly named and blessed. Stearns used holy oil for anointing the sick and was accustomed to give the kiss of charity. Ordinances (bread and wine) were frequently brought to the people, occasionally as part of "love feasts." In instituting these methods, Stearns believed that he, too, was returning to the apostolic tradition already followed by many Baptists in Old and New England. He succeeded in making these traditions an integral part of Southern community life, and they grew along with the Separatist Baptist churches. David Benedict, a Rhode Island minister who traveled widely and who wrote several very important Baptist histories during his long life (1779 to 1874), witnessed Stearns' methods practiced as late as the first decade of the nineteenth century. Some of these traditions, such as footwashing, have survived as sectarian practices into the twentieth.

Singing was a very important part of the revival and of Southern Baptist church life after it. On the basis of the folk hymns which Baptists were already using, Southern Baptists, together with the blacks in their midst, expanded both their repertoires and the time and emphasis placed on music. "Bands went singing to meetings, sang after the preaching, went singing home and from fields, shops and houses 'made the heavens ring' with 'spiritual songs,' " many of which were original.

These rites and rituals were but part of the rich communal life that involved all the members of Stearns' churches. Everyone was a brother or sister and was expected to participate in all meetings. Ruling elders, ruling eldresses, deacons, and deaconesses were chosen from among the members and were the first among equals, preserving peace and seeking out evil. The church was a family of God.[16]

The relatively disinherited, looking for a faith that would indeed give promise that they, too, might share equally in all of God's gifts, found fulfillment in this Baptist faith and polity. The church was the community of believers. Once accepted, a man was the equal of everyone else in the church. It was his responsibility to watch and be watched, to judge and be judged, no less than any other believer. A Baptist church was both radically democratic and radically totalitarian. Every man had an equal voice, and the church as a church had total authority. Every aspect of each individual's life was subject to criticism, and expulsion from the church meant expulsion from the covenant with God. Thus, when a white or a black had experienced the death of his old sinful soul, having perhaps suffered much torment and then experienced ecstasy in his rebirth in Christ Jesus, and when he had publicly recounted this "gracious dealing" of the Lord with his soul to a congregation, he would be considered for acceptance by all in the church. If his experience and his recounting of it were found "satisfactory," he was welcomed to the congregation as a soul in Christ, baptized along with his brothers and sisters, and given the right hand of fellowship. His name was then recorded in the ledger of the redeemed. He was now a brother in the Christian family of God. God had called him by name from death to life, and his private "Christian" name was recalled at his baptism and on the rolls.

In a second wave of revivalism (beginning in 1785 and peaking between 1787 and 1789), thousands of new parishioners were added to the Baptist churches—so many that by 1790 the Baptists were the most numerous nonestablished sect. In this process, especially during this second phase, the Southern Baptists' character was somewhat altered, thereby reflecting and causing changes in their world view. During this period, Baptists became more conformist and less concerned with opposition to the establishment. As they themselves were improving their social position, they became less interested in the downtrodden and were less likely to oppose established institutions, such as slavery. In some areas, these changes came about more gradually, or at a later date.

In 1793, the General Committee of Virginia backtracked on its strong 1789 antislavery stand and decided to allow each white Baptist the freedom to decide his individual position on slavery. Slavery had become a political issue, and the Southern Baptists increasingly sought to separate it from their purview, although some remained staunch antislavery activists. That Baptists had mixed feelings on slavery is demonstrated in the response of the Dover Association of Virginia, when asked in 1797: "Would it not be good policy, as well as an act of justice, for the Baptists to form a plan, for the gradual emancipation of slavery among themselves?" Their answer was to shift the political burden to the nonreligious abolitionist organizations. At the same time, however, they advocated a thoroughgoing abolitionist plan:

> We sincerely sympathize both as Christians and citizens with those unhappy people, and although we think it a delicate matter, we would not wish to be backward in promoting their happiness and liberty. Upon cautious grounds, we would therefore recommend to our brethren, to unite with the abolition society, in proposing a petition to the general assembly, for their gradual emancipation, upon some rational and benevolent plan; but as the abolition society do [sic] not in their petition refer to slaves now in existence, we would take occasion further to testify our disappointment of that evil, by recommending them to improve every opportunity to extirpate this root of bitterness, whenever it may consist with propriety.

By the end of the eighteenth century the Separatist Baptists (who had been staunchly Arminian) were becoming less radical, as is apparent from their readiness to unite with their ideological opponents, the Particular and Regular Calvinist Baptists. While this union was posited as early as 1767, it was not possible until the Separatists achieved greater security and were more firmly established. In 1787, when the two groups joined to form the United Baptist Churches of Christ in Virginia, a general Southern Baptist rapprochement was heralded. By the early 1800s Baptist churches had healed their greatest internal divisions, had moved toward a general Baptist polity incorporating both Arminian and Calvinist elements, and had become an acceptable Southern denomination. The Separatist thrust was thus altered by its very success, but strong elements of its early world view continued to permeate all of Southern Baptist thought. With their experience in revival methods and mass crowd appeal, and with a world view that was even more widely appealing now that it had lost some of its most "peculiar" qualities, Baptists stood ready to grow into one of America's leading denominations.

In the great Western revivals growing out of Cane Ridge, Kentucky (August 1801), Baptist growth was extraordinary. Continuing to preach their strangely modified Calvinism, which allowed members to believe that "Christ tasted death for every man," the Baptists were able to absorb divergent strains. They were of the common people and grew with the common people, expanding with the American frontier. And yet, uniquely, they were also becoming the church of the American black.[17]

II

In growing from a pariah sect into a central denomination, the Baptists maintained their view of God as an all-knowing Father who was both the creator and the redeemer of man. In the traditional Christian version, man was seen as having fallen because of the first man's willful and evil acts, symbolized in the eating of a forbidden fruit. Redemption was possible through the agency of God's son and his Holy Spirit (or the Word). Even the Calvinist Baptists assumed that man should endeavor to be ready for this conversion (although it could come against his will) and that each individual had to assume responsibility for his own behavior. Predestination did not relieve man of responsibility, and the death of his old sinful soul, symbolized in immersion, did not mean he could not act immorally in the future.

Salvation, or rebirth in Christ, was the central focus of Baptist belief. Man's faith and repentance were in no way sufficient. The direct operation of the Holy Spirit, which should come to the individual in an overwhelming experience that would immediately change his basic nature, was essential. This happening would be so traumatic that he could not but know he had experienced it, and he would be able to recount it ever afterwards. Indeed, the ability to recount the occurrence was crucial, for an essential part of God's message was to tell of the Good News. One could not be a member of a Baptist congregation—a saint—without having died and having been reborn. Once reborn, it was expected that one's whole character would be different—godly, sober, rejecting the worldly or profane, and embracing the holy and sacred.

The baptism itself, the total immersion, was but a symbolic death, with the subsequent laying on of hands symbolizing the entrance of the new spirit into the soul. Here, again, the Baptist looked to the Bible for authority: "[W]e are buried with him [Christ] by Baptism into death: that like as Christ was raised up from the dead by the glory of the Father, even so we also should walk in newness of life" (Romans 6: 3-4). John clearly said that belief is equated with passing from "death unto life" (I John 3:15). "You must be born again" (John 3:5-7). "Except a man be born of water and the spirit he cannot enter the Kingdom of God." Paul characterized this rebirth as putting off the old man and putting on a new (Colossians 3:9-10).

In the basic pattern of regeneration, of ceremonial death to old ways or to childhood, and of rebirth into new responsibility or adulthood (paralleling the African pattern), early Christianity had indeed symbolically celebrated rebirth and formal commitment to a covenanted community of faith. Over the ages, many Christians had experienced this rebirth, classically described by Augustine. In the Catholic church, however, it had become ritualized in the confirmation ceremony, in which personal experience could be reduced to formal participation. While the English church had retained confirmation, the American Anglicans, having no bishops, could not celebrate this rite of passage. This change in the American ritual was in character with the colonial Anglicans' increasing distance from all emotional celebrations. They seem to have been generally unsuccessful in communicating religion as performing sacred or miraculous work in the life of man.

The Protestant Reformation in both the Lutheran and Calvinist traditions had reemphasized the need for the rebirth experience. It had returned to the Bible to analyze disciples' conversion experiences. Paul, it was noted, had seen a light and had heard a voice (Acts 9); Peter had seen visions (Acts 10). Luther explained these as "a sudden light in which he [Peter] saw the Lord Jesus," while Calvin explained baptism as a dying and rising during which man's will is bent to do God's will.[18] The English Puritans also returned to what Perry Miller called the Augustinian strain of piety. They, too, sought to experience conversion, living rich introspective spiritual lives. Most early Puritans felt they had experienced rebirth and spoke and wrote about it, for without this visible sign they were not "visible saints" and could not join their church. In America, however, many of their children did not have these experiences, and they were forced to alter their church membership requirement for direct experience with the holy, as they did formally in the Halfway Covenant of 1662.[19]

George Whitefield and the other great preachers of the First Great Awakening turned once again to the existential conversion experience.

> In the early months of the revival Calvinists defined the New Birth as something that came almost instantaneously and as a "feeling." So often did Whitefield speak of how saving faith was

"felt" that his sermons, at least according to his critics, gave rise to a popular notion that grace is a physical presence, as distinctive and as tangible as a bowel ache or a tumor.

Those who were converted had far more positive associations with their new birth, but they did indeed find the conversion experience tangible and describable. Abigail Hutchinson, a "still, quiet, reserved person," converted in the Northhampton, Massachusetts, revival by Jonathan Edwards, felt "ravished by the love of God." Phoebe Bartlet, aged four, was seen "wreathing her body to and fro, like one in anguish of spirit," and she then cried out, "Mother, the Kingdom of Heaven is come to me." By February 1742, numerous people in Northhampton were sharing this experience. "Many were not merely leaping for joy, they were falling into twenty-four hour trances, under a strong imagination that they were in heaven beholding glorious objects."

Miller would call it "a strong imagination," but it should be emphasized that when these people spoke of having been in Heaven with God they believed they had been there.[20]

David Brainerd, missionary to the Indians, was converted in a similar experience in July 1739. Depressed, as he was often to be even after conversion (and probably going through what we have come to call an identity crisis), twenty-one-year-old Brainerd went into the woods to pray in solitude. There he died and was reborn. Afterwards, he did not talk of having been in Heaven, and he recognized that what had happened took place in his soul, but he did believe he had "seen God" and was "even swallowed up in him."

> [A]s I was walking in a thick grove, unspeakable glory seemed to open to the apprehension of my soul. I do not mean any external brightness, nor any imagination of a body of light, but it was a new inward apprehension or view that I had of God, such as I never had before, nor anything which had the least resemblance to it. I had no particular apprehension of any one person in the Trinity, either the Father, the Son, or the Holy Ghost; but it appeared to be Divine glory. My soul rejoiced with joy unspeakable, to see such a God. . . . I was even swallowed up in him.

Brainerd, as Edwards, became suspicious of visions but not of the need for rebirth. Notwithstanding his skepticism, Brainerd's preaching among the Indians led to an awakening that saw his whole congregation in tears and agony. At Crossweeksung (Freehold, New Jersey) in August 1745, while preaching to some sixty-five Indians, "the power of God seemed to descend upon the assembly 'like a mighty rushing wind', and with an astonishing energy bore down all before it.'' They were all in ''mourning,'' and many died and were reborn in Christ. Among them were a leader of the people, a conjurer, and a woman who had come to mock Brainerd but fell into the hypnotic repetition of a prayer, ''Have mercy on me and help me to give you my heart.''

The trances and visions of most of those who were reborn were not random. Taken together, it is possible to discern an ideal type; although they differ to some degree, all can be seen to be related to one another. The vision typically begins with the seeker usually convinced of his worthlessness and of his inability to reach God. He prays endlessly, often alone. In this heightened state of preparation, perhaps while fasting, the seeker reports that he feels a hand touching him or hears a voice calling to him. He fears that he is dying and calls out, usually crying ''Mercy, Lord!'' or some variant of this phrase, which works in an almost magical manner. At this point, he often falls on the ground and blacks out, sometimes awakening many hours later; or he loses his sense of time. Later, he knows that during this time he had been with God (often visualized as a blazing light) and that, as a result, he has been reborn and is a new man.[21]

Sometimes only fragments of this pattern are given to us, but they seem lifted from the whole, as if the individual either cannot (if too young) or will not (if too sophisticated) share it all with us. The ideal type of trance was clearly a widely known model. At the Gasper River, Kentucky, revival of July 1800, a small child sitting on her mother's lap began to cry out:

> O he is willing, he is willing—he is come, he is come—
> O what a sweet Christ he is—O, what a precious Christ he is—
> O, what a fullness I see in him—O, what a beauty I see in him—
> O, why was it that I never could believe! That I never could come
> to Christ before when Christ was so willing to save me?

Devereau Jarratt, an Anglican, who later was primarily responsible for the Methodist phase of the Virginia Awakening (1775-1776), had a youthful conversion experience in the 1750s. He, too, gives us a fragment. His vision verges on the heavenly, but he clearly was aware he was on earth. ''Such *a bright* manifestation of the redeemer's all-sufficiency and willingness to save, and such a divine confidence to rely on him, I have never had till that moment. It was a little heaven upon earth—so ravishing, so delightful.''

Lorenzo Dow, a self-appointed Methodist missionary, was not so reticent; he reported going to Heaven in a whirlwind and talking there with God, Jesus, and Gabriel.

Henry Alline, the Rhode Island evangelist who brought the Great Awakening to Nova Scotia, had the ''full'' experience at age twenty-seven (March 1775):

> As I was about sunset wandering in the fields lamenting my miserable lost and undone condition, and almost ready to sink under my burden . . . the following impressions came into my mind like a powerful but small still voice. You have been seeking praying, reforming . . . and what have you done by it towards your salvation? . . . .

> I cried out within myself, O Lord God, I am lost, and if thou, O Lord, dost not find out some new way . . . I shall never be saved . . . O Lord, have mercy! O Lord, have mercy.

> . . . .

> [Later that day] . . . redeeming love broke into my soul with repeated scriptures, with such power that my whole soul seemed to be melted down with love; the burden of guilt and condemnation was gone, darkness was expelled.

Alline then saw "a bright blaze of light" from above. Realizing that his soul was set at "liberty," he experienced "ecstasies of joy." While the devil tempted him again, God responded to his call, and "my soul seemed awake in and with God, and surrounded by the arms of everlasting love. . . . I lost all taste for carnal pleasures, and carnal company, and was enabled to forsake them."

This pattern and these phrases are repeatedly found in conversions from the 1740s through the 1860s. In 1821, Charles Grandison Finney expectantly sought this experience. In great emotional turmoil he sat in a cold, dark room, praying. He then saw a briliant light and met Jesus "face to face":

> The Holy Spirit descended upon me in a manner that seemed to go through me, body and soul. I could feel the impression like a wave of electricity, going through and through me. Indeed it seemed to come in waves and waves of liquid love. . . . It seemed like the very breath of God. I can recollect distinctly that it seemed to fan me, with immense wings.

> I wept aloud with joy and love; and I do not know but I should say, I literally bellowed out the inutterable gushings of my heart. These waves came over me, and over me, and over me, one after the other until I recollect I cried out, "I shall die if these waves continue to pass over me." I said, "Lord, I cannot bear any more"; yet I had no fear of death.

John Humphrey Noyes (later father of the Oneida Community) fasted, prayed, and rent his soul. Finally, prepared, he lay on his bed and

> received the baptism which I desired and expected. Three times in quick succession a stream of love gushed thru my heart and rolled back again to its source. Joy unspeakable and full of glory filled my soul. All fear and doubt and condemnation passed away. I knew that my heart was clean, and that the Father and the Son had come and made it their abode.

In all of these cases, and in the myriad reports from the revivals, conversion is an act, a happening. The converted man or woman experiences it in a heightened but real way. It takes place in time and is recounted, and in the cases of important figures, it is reported. These people believed they had been with God or that God had been with or in them. The reality of this being with God and God in them was the sustaining reality of their later lives. They did change as a result. Although there were many cases of "backsliding," the majority of these individuals, even those who "fell" afterwards, fully believed they had experienced what they described.[22]

Baptists were not alone in emphasizing the conversion experience. Congregationalists, Presbyterians, and Methodists reviewed above, all shared in a similar tradition, but for the Baptist it became, for a time, a sustaining vision that was central to the Baptist experience.

Baptist Preacher Jabez Swan, who became a noted faith healer, curing people of devils and causing others to be "struck blind" in conviction, was converted at the age of twenty-one (1821). He had spent much time in self-analysis and was convinced of his "depravity" and "hopelessness." He had prepared himself for his spiritual trial. On a trip away from home (psychologically without his moorings), a violent storm began, which he took to mean "God's world was angry with me."

> [A]s the night wore on, the storm increased. The thunder was terrific and the glare of the lightning was frightful. God, I knew, rode upon the storm, which seemed of awful import to me. I prayed as though my life was well nigh exhausted, and then sunk in a despair that seemed like the deep glooms of hell. I have no power to describe the glooms of that terrible hour.
>
> While lying prostrate upon my face, hopeless and lost, I became impressed once more to pray. I fell upon my knees and besought God, for the sake of Christ, to save my soul. While prostrate before God, in midnight darkness respecting the media-

tion of the Son of God, the law of God was spread before my mind as never before. I knew I had broken it, and if I was eternally lost I could see that God was just. But how to be pardoned and saved, I could find no light, till at length Christ appeared before me in spirit, standing by the tables of the law, asserting his death as fulfilling the law, and reflecting upon me the true light—that, to them who believed, he had satisfied the law, and that thus believing I could be saved. That view brought salvation with it. Unbelief fell off like chains. Hardness of heart seemed to melt away, and Christ was revealed to my soul as precious.

I was now happy for the first time in my life. I walked the room and sang praises to God in perfect ecstasies. Morning at length came; and when the sun arose to me it dressed God's world in perfect beauty. I left for home on my way to meeting. The heavens, the lake, the forest, all put off their formidable attire; and "holiness to the Lord" seemed written on all things.

Swan confessed publicly and was baptized, but when he hesitated to preach, "God . . . attacked me with dreams, which were terrible." He finally accepted his calling, recognizing that dreams and visions were God's way of talking to men.

Baptist Elder Jacob Knapp (1799-1874) was seventeen when Christ came to him. His vision followed soon after the death of his mother, which had left him deeply depressed. He was wont to spend time alone, in the woods, in Bible reading and prayer. During such a vigil:

I felt my vileness; all my sins rose before me like mountains. . . .
. . . I saw clearly the righteousness of God in sending me to the lowest hell. At this moment the earth seemed to open beneath me, and hell appeared to be yawning for my reception. I closed my eyes, fully expecting to open them no more until I opened them in hell, and lifted them up with the rich man in torment.

But, to the joy and rapture of my soul, after a short space of time passed in this condition, my load of guilt was gone. I rose up quickly, turned my eyes towards heaven, and thought I saw Jesus descending with his arms extended for my reception. My soul leaped within me, and I broke forth into singing praises to the blessed Savior.[23]

Baptists placed ultimate emphasis on the conversion experience. It was seen as "God's gracious dealing with one's soul," and no man or woman, white or black, could become a member of a holy congregation if his soul had not been with God. White Baptists did not talk of a separable soul or of traveling in dreams, but they recognized the experiences termed visions, and even illusions by critics, as the most real and important spiritual experiences. They sought to have God know them by name, and to see and feel His presence; without the assurance of this personal acceptance, no one could ask for baptism or could join a congregation. These visions, told by each candidate and retold in Baptist group meetings, were the sustaining experiences in individual and communal life.

III

Revivals were essentially communal experiences with the dimension of the holy, or in the words of Brainerd, times when "the power of God seemed to descend upon the assembly like a mighty rushing wind." Beginning in the 1720s with the First Great Awakening and continuing through to the Civil War, waves of revivals shook the populace and led to awakenings of supposedly hardened hearts as well as the religiously sensitive. No psychological or sociological explanations have been able to deal adequately with the nature of these outpourings.

In each case, the signs and signals of spiritual presence multiplied relevant to the size of the congregation, the duration of the revival, and its place in what came to be a clearly cyclic pattern of rising and falling excitement. At the peak of the First Great Awakening (about 1742) and at the peak of the second (1801), mass hysteria was clearly reached. From Northhampton we have reports of jerking, fainting, and crying; Edwards for one wept during the whole of Whitefield's preaching at his church. From Kentucky came wilder reports of barking, shaking, running, chanting, humming, laughing, shouting, and losing cousciousness. All of these peculiarities surrounded and sometimes obscured the central goal, which was death and spiritual rebirth in Christ Jesus. Sometimes only a small minority made it "all the way through." Many stopped in fear and trembling, emotionally exhausted but not saved.

The presence of many Afro-Americans at these revivals was one of the most important happenings for the blacks in America. Their presence was noted by numerous observers, including George Whitefield and Francis Asbury. Thomas Prince cited their participation in New England (1741), and Samuel Davies and John Todd in Virginia (1742-1755). Davies held out "comfortable hope that Ethiopia will soon stretch out her hand unto God for a considerable number of Negroes have not only been proselyted to Christianity and baptized, but seem to be the genuine seed of Abraham by faith." Blacks were present at Methodist, Presbyterian, and Baptist revivals as these spread through Virginia, the Carolinas, Tennessee, and Georgia. It was only when these excitements became formalized and ritualized in the second quarter of the nineteenth century that blacks were assigned a formal area in which to sit: white women were to the right (facing the speaker's stand), white men to the left, and blacks behind the stand. Excitement often led to joint experience, and it became a tradition to pull down all barriers on the last day for a union ceremony.[24]

The most important revivals for Afro-Americans were those of the Separatist Baptists in the South, followed closely by the highly emotional Methodist revivals. These revivals were generally the blacks' first experience with an emotional dimension of white religiosity. For the first time, they saw whites responding to a religious demand with the totality of their being and participating in religious trances, shouts, mourning, and rebirth. These were totally new experiences for most whites; blacks had had experience with a similar tradition in their African/American context. The revivals opened common ground on which whites and blacks could share religious experience, and blacks immediately responded. Blacks were attracted to the revivals in great numbers.

On a surface level the methods Baptists and Methodists used at revivals were almost certain to have an appeal to blacks. But the reason for this appeal is much more complicated. Blacks began to participate in revivals in the South at a very early date and no doubt influenced the emerging so-called white patterns. It is therefore difficult to find a preblack Baptist pattern, against which the nature of the blacks' attraction can be analyzed. An important part of the attraction was this very ability to participate in and influence the character of the religious celebration. Even Ullrich Phillips recognized that whites welcomed blacks to revival meetings, for blacks clearly helped to build the emotional excitement and to bring down the spirit.[25]

Critics who maintain that all of the black Christian's practices can be traced to white Christianity are in error. They overlook the fact that blacks influenced white culture in significant ways. They err further in that a great deal of the content of black Christianity is not shared by whites.

Baptist revivals and the relatively staid church sessions (which were still quite emotional) shared an African approach to use of body and soul in religious ritual. This religious ritual called for experience, and the early invitation to the black was to come and participate. In the 1790s many blacks were ready to accept the invitation. By this time they spoke an English that was adequate for participation and in fact presented little handicap in a widely nonliterate community of believers whose emphasis was on experience rather than on the written word.

5

TRABELIN' TO
AFRO-CHRISTIANITY

I

The slave socialized with a noncoherent world view was in a double bind. To become his best self he had to follow African standards, but to attain the most freedom of action he had to become a good slave. In the process of becoming a good slave, he became ambivalent about his parents' values and their goals, but these were already part of his own inner world view.

Increasingly, blacks were growing up with contradictory norms of conduct and values. One set called on them to become self-actualizing men and women, and the second to be totally, as if by nature, slaves. One called for spiritual risk and responsibility, and the other for ultimate childlike humility. One recognized spirits and paid them homage, while the other mocked them and said spirits were primitive foolishness at best or the devil's work at worst. One Sacred Cosmos could not integrate both sets of demands coherently. This lack of coherence had profound effects on the slave personality. Luckman maintains that

> The world view is an objective system of meaning by which an individual's past and future are integrated into a coherent biography and in which the emergent person locates himself in relation to fellow men, the social order and the transcendent sacred universe. The continuity of sense in individual life is dependent on the coherence of meaning in the world view.

It became increasingly difficult for blacks to "locate themselves" socially. While the early black leader was often the African *swonga* worker, over time the magic worker became less important, although he remained a powerful and potentially dangerous man. For exactly this reason the masters would not delegate authority to him unless they had no other viable choice. Increasingly, they found alternative black leaders as the second and third generations were socialized in neo-African patterns. Thus, competitive social structures were created within the slave community, with the Voodoo worker claiming occult powers while the black driver achieved certain direct tangible controls and used his access to the master as a threat.[1]

Slave parents, attempting to prepare their children for the trials that would confront them, were faced with developing contradictory strengths and weaknesses: They tried to foster proper respect for the spirits and yet self-protective concern with white power; ability to appear dumb or foolish; strength to accept random punishments; deep attachments to the family and yet fortitude to bear the constant possibility of immediate sale away from family and home. Many children were sold and knew nothing of their sale until they were taken to their new locale; some would simply be invited for a wagon ride or a trip to town, never to return. Sojurner Truth's parents constantly recounted the last occasion on which they saw one of their many children sold away from them. At the last moment, this child, a son, realized what was happening and ran wildly seeking to hide. He did not run to his parents, for he knew they could not help. In repeatedly telling Sojurner this tale, her mother was warning both Sojurner and herself that it could happen again. Parents had the difficult task of properly socializing children who were learning that their parents did not have final authority.[2]

The order of the African Sacred Cosmos had been reflected in the social relations and social patterns of African society. The kinship structure had been an extension of the relations between spirits and living men, and the rites of passage marked the movement of an individual from birth through life to death in preparation for his continuance in this eternal order. The noncoherent world view of the slave, however, no longer gave clear promise of eternal participation in an orderly world of spirits. This ultimate disorder was both a product and a further stimulus of disorder in social life. If the Sacred Cosmos was in question, then what authority legitimated action? On what basis could ethical action be determined if the divinities were in doubt? What should a man be? And what could he be within the limits of slavery? In a normal society, the internalized world view is externalized through supportive social controls, but in this respect as in so much else, slave society was abnormal. The slave's progress in understanding and using English was probably part of this destructive process (although it later played a reconstructive role). Children began to speak better English than their parents, thereby accelerating the generation gap and alienating them further from their parents' values.

The African/American was thus uniquely ready for the Great Awakenings. First, coming from a living mystery faith in Africa, he was prepared to participate in the Christian mystery. Second, because of his noncoherent world view he deeply yearned for new coherence and a new sense of unity and purpose. The Baptist invitation came at a supremely opportune moment, when enough blacks were sufficiently comfortable with spoken English to appreciate the Baptist message and uncomfortable enough in their bifurcated Sacred Cosmos to hunger for a renewed one. In the Baptist faith the blacks found a Sacred Cosmos with which they could integrate their African values. What emerged was a new whole, a new integrity, a new coherence that was both African and Baptist. Blacks accomplished an almost impossible task, one that was not much appreciated then and has not been widely understood since. Blacks actually created a new world view that, despite their status as slaves, established order, values, and the possibility of personal development, including effectiveness, potency, achievement, and even fulfillment. In so doing, they became Baptist Americans at the same time as they made a quasi-African Sacred Cosmos at home in the New World. The new Sacred Cosmos was an Afro-Baptist one.

Blacks understood the first and basic message of the Baptist faith: "You must be born again!" African initiation experiences were rebirth experiences. While we have only fragmentary evidence that initiation ceremonies continued in North America, their use in both the Voudou system and in Voodoo practices suggests that they had probably been carried over in some form and practiced over a long period of time. In Voudou, the initiate had to prepare himself in a vigil and then undergo a trial and test; if it was passed, he shared his blood with other initiates and entered a brotherhood of believers. Voodoo practitioners followed attenuated rituals for their students, and the popular Voodoo folklore preserved the idea of blood-sharing as establishing a permanent new kinship. Blacks were anxious to be reborn, to put off their slave identities and slave names, and to find a better self, a social self truer to their internal image.

Visionary experiences also were not new to blacks. We have seen their central role in African faith systems, but in virtually every African circumstance trances were possession experiences. The divinities (and not the High God) came to speak through a medium, who was thereby enriched both in status and in spirit power but who did not keep the God within him, although he might learn to call him to come at will. The crucial difference in the Christian experience was that the believer traveled to the High God's abode, Heaven, and in knowing the High God came to have His presence in his heart forever after.

Blacks came to call this spiritual journey "trabbels" or "trabelin'," and they recognized that they had been trabelin' a long hard way before they had ever gotten to the "starting place." In retrospect, after they became Christians, the new life in America was seen as "a hard Christian journey."[3]

Blacks first became Baptists during the First Great Awakening. Their presence, noted at the revivals, led to their conversions or rebirths, and they began joining congregations. Morgan Edwards found small numbers scattered throughout the churches he visited in the South in the 1770s; early church minutes attest to their membership. Blacks early joined Baptist congregations as almost equal members. They were expected to have a personal experience of rebirth; to recount this experience publicly; to be considered by the whole congregation as candidates for baptism, and, if accepted, to be baptized in a symbolic drowning and be reborn to be called by name; to be blessed by a laying on of hands or to be given the right hand of fellowship; and to sign the covenant and join the congregation of the elect. Blacks did all of these acts together with whites in an emotional sharing of what many blacks came to view as the most crucial experience in their lives.[4]

The Separatist Baptist revival that began with Shubal Stearns in 1755 not only brought blacks into the new mixed churches, but it also led directly to the first all-black Baptist congregation. White missionaries Philip Mulkey and William Murphey gathered a black slave congregation on the plantation of William Byrd III on the Bluestone River at a point which is now called Mecklenburg, Virginia. The slaves' names and experiences were not preserved, but they entered the Baptist folklore as true and lasting Christians, even when they were sold away from this plantation. The plantation remained a center for Baptist activity. In 1772, another black church was formally constituted there, and its congregants later served as the nucleus for the Petersburg Baptist congregation of 1820. Black Baptist roots were being put down side by side with white roots, and while the evidence of the nature of rebirth among these early black Baptists is scanty, it is sufficient to outline a preliminary picture.

One of the earliest references to black meetings was an anonymous criticism lodged with the *South Carolina Gazette* of April 24, 1742, which inadvertently gives us evidence of the early "trabelin'." Alluding to the dangers inherent in bringing Christianity to slaves, the writer notes that "instead of teaching them the *Principles* of *Christianity*," irresponsible preachers were "filling their heads with a parcel of *Cant-Phrases, Trances, Dreams,* Visions and Revelations."[5]

George Whitefield, an Englishman who stormed the colonies on seven evangelical journeys from 1739 until his death in 1770, was the first of the great emotional preachers in America. Whitefield's written sermons were relatively dry, but according to all reports, his extemporaneous outpourings were electrifying. His description of Peter's emotion after publicly denying Christ allowed every sinner in his audience to empathize and walk along with Peter. Even the written version has power:

Methinks I see him wringing his hands, rending his garments, stamping on the ground and, with the self-condemned publican, smiting his breast. See how it heaves! Oh what piteous sighs and groans are those which come from the very bottom of his heart! Alas! It is too big to speak; but his tears, his briny, bitter repenting tears, plainly bespeak this to be the language of his awakened soul. Alas! where have I been? On the devil's ground. With whom have I been conversing? The devil's children. What is this that I have done? Denied the Lord of glory; with oaths and curses denied that I ever knew him. And now whither shall I go, or where shall I hide my guilty head? I have sinned against light, I have sinned against repeated tokens of his dear, distinguishing and heavenly love. I have sinned against repeated warnings, resolutions, promises, vows. I have sinned openly in the face of sun, and in the presence of my Master's enemies, and thereby have caused his name to be blasphemed. How can I think to be suffered to behold the face of, much less to be employed by, the ever-blessed Jesus any more? O Peter! Thou hast undone thyself. Justly mayest thou be thrown aside like a broken vessel. God be merciful to me a sinner.

Many blacks traveled with Peter and were reborn as a result of Whitefield's preaching. One free black man, John Marrant, provided a narrative of this spiritual journey. Marrant was born free in New York in June 1755 but after his father's death (1759) his mother took him to Georgia. He attended school there, but in 1767, by his own choice and contrary to his mother's will, he apprenticed himself to a musician and rapidly learned to play the violin and French horn. Independent by the age of fourteen, he was on his way to play at a dance when he passed a meeting at which Whitefield was "halooing." Marrant scoffed at religion. When a friend dared him to go in and play his French horn in the crowded meeting hall, Marrant accepted the dare.

I was pushing the people to make room, to get the horn off my shoulder to blow it, just as Mr. Whitefield was naming his text and looking round, and, as I thought, directly upon me, and pointing with his finger, he uttered these words, "Prepare to meet thy God, O Israel." The Lord accompanied the word with such power that I was struck to the ground and lay both speechless and senseless near half an hour. When I was come a little too, I found two men attending me, and a woman throwing water in my face and holding a smelling-bottle to my nose; and when something more recovered, every word I heard from the minister was like a parcel of swords thrust into me, and what added to my distress, I thought I saw the devil on every side of me. I was constrained in the bitterness of my spirit to halloo out in the midst of the congregation.

They carried Marrant out to the vestry, and at the close of the sermon Whitefield came to him "and the first word he said to me was, 'Jesus Christ has got thee at last.' " Marrant was again thrown down low by God, then "filled with joy," and he began to praise God publicly. His mother, family, and friends thought him insane; feeling persecuted, he went "travelling in the desert," fasting and reading his Bible. "The Lord Jesus Christ was very present and that comforted me through all." Taken captive by Cherokee Indians, he "bewitched" the king's daughter with Christ and was saved from death at the stake on the condition that he make her well. According to his account, he converted her and was allowed to leave.

After his return, Marrant eventually became spiritually lax, "cold and dead." Pressed into the service of the English, he was not awakened again until he was in London in 1781. At that time, he undertook a new mission which took him from England to Nova Scotia "that the black nations may be made white in the blood of the lamb."[6]

In 1774, approximately five years after Marrant's initial conversion, Goerge Liele came to Christ. Liele had a very different life history and yet came to the same critical impasse as Marrant. He was born a slave on a Virginia plantation and, all he knew of his parents was that his mother's name was Nancy and that his father was called Liele (the name he took as his family name). He later wrote: "I cannot ascertain much of them, as I went to several parts of America when young and at length resided in New Georgia." This traveling was apparently a euphemism for being sold or moved and not for a spiritual journey, except insofar as it toughened or hardened his spirit as a child. Under these circumstances, it is unclear how Liele learned the following intimate detail about his father. He wrote that he "was informed both by white and black people that my father was the only black person who knew the Lord in a Spiritual way in that country." Whatever Liele meant by this statement, it was clearly important to him. His father knew God, and he claimed for himself "a natural fear of God from my youth" and a belief in doing good works. However, in 1773 this "false" sense of his own goodness was shaken when he heard the sermon of a white Baptist preacher, the Reverend Matthew Moore.

[H]e unfolded all my dark views, opened my best behaviour and good works to me, which I thought I was to be saved by, and I was convinced that I was not in the way to heaven, but in the way to hell. This state I laboured under for the space of five or six months.

The more I heard or read the more I [saw that I] was condemned as a sinner before God till at length I was brought to perceive that my life hung by a slender thread, and if it was the will of God to cut me off at that time, I was sure I should be found in hell, as sure as God was in heaven. I saw my condemnation in my own heart, and I found no way wherein I could escape the damnation of hell, only through the merits of my dying Lord and Saviour Jesus Christ; which caused me to make intercession with Christ, for the salvation of my poor immortal soul; and I full well recollect, I requested of my Lord and Master to give me a work, I did not care how mean it was, only to try and see how good I would do it.

Within the year George Liele had the experience he sought: "I felt such love and joy as my tongue was not able to express. After this I declared before the congregation of believers the work which God had done for my soul."

David George, another slave in the circle of early black Christians in and around Savannah, was a second-generation American. His parents, known to him as Judith and John, were born in Africa; he himself was born on a plantation in Essex County, Virginia, around 1742. When he, too, later gave an account of his life, he felt that his parents "had not the fear of God before their eyes" and that he, himself, while he had traveled to attend the "English Church" at Nottaway some eight or nine miles from his plantation, "did not fear hell, [and] was without knowledge." Owned by a Mr. Chapel, whom he described as brutal to himself and his siblings (four sisters and four brothers), George ran away from the plantation one midnight and began traveling on his own. Extraordinary adventures took him to the Creek and "Nautchee" Indian peoples, where he was a well-treated chattel servant. He eventually became the possession of George Galphin, a "very kind" man who owned a plantation and trading station at Silver Bluff, South Carolina, some twelve miles from Augusta, Georgia.

Here I lived a bad life, and had no serious thoughts about my soul; but after my wife was delivered of our first child, a man of my own color, named Cyrus, who came from Charlestown, South Carolina, to Silver Bluff, told me one day in the woods, That if I lived so, I should never see the face of God in glory. (Whether he himself was a converted man or not, I do not know.) This was the first thing that disturbed me, and gave me much concern. I thought then that I must be saved by prayer. I used to say the Lord's prayer, that it might make be [sic] better but I feared that I grew worse; and I continued worse and worse, as long as I thought I would do some thing to make me better; till at last it seemed as if there was no possibility of relief, and that I must go to hell. I saw myself a mass of sin. I could not read and had no scriptures. I did not think of Adam and Eve's sin, but *I* was sin. I felt my *own* plague; and I was so overcome that I could not wait upon my master. I told him *I was ill*. I felt myself at the disposal of Sovereign mercy. At last in prayer to God I began to think that he would deliver me, but I did not know how. Soon after I saw that I could not be saved by any of my own doings, but that it must be by God's mercy—that my sins had crucified Christ; and now the Lord took away my distress. I was sure that the Lord took it away, because I had such pleasure and joy in my soul, that no man could give me. Soon after I heard brother George Liele preach. . . . I knew him ever since he was a boy. I am older than he. . . . His sermon was very suitable, on *Come unto me all ye that labour and are heavy laden, and I will give you rest.* When it was ended, I went to him and told him I was so; That I was weary and heavy laden; and that the grace of God had given me rest. Indeed his whole discourse seemed for me.

A Brother Palmer (perhaps Reverend Wait Palmer, the Connecticut New Light preacher), "a very powerful preacher" who frequently preached to the Silver Bluff seekers, counseled and baptized George who now had "a desire for nothing else but to talk to the brothers and sisters about the Lord."

Liele and George talked of the Lord to their black brothers and sisters for the rest of their lives. Liele founded a black church at Yama Craw, outside Savannah, in December 1777. He also preached at three or four surrounding plantation churches, including the one at Silver Bluff, singing psalms and reading scripture. Liele was freed prior to the Revolutionary War by his owner, a Baptist deacon. Nevertheless, in 1782, he decided to leave America, going to Jamaica with the English. He was the founding father of the Baptist faith in Jamaica, and, after years of severe trial, was very successful.

David George, after working with Liele in Savannah, also left the South. He fled slavery by emigrating with the British, arriving in Nova Scotia in 1782. In Canada, he was a highly successful missionary to both blacks and whites, often working at great personal risk. In 1792, he decided to lead a black hegira "back" to Africa; over 1,000 joined him in his emigration to Sierra Leone.[7]

George Liele and David George were reborn in a black Baptist faith through which they gained a new sense of their selves, a new individuality, and a new purpose. They began new lives as a result of their conversions and were able to become creative and even charismatic leaders as a result of the coherence they achieved in the black Baptist Sacred Cosmos. They were in a dialogue with this cosmos, which was peculiarly theirs. They became takers and givers, makers of themselves, and teachers to a wide posterity. Their status was comparable to that of clan leaders and the living dead, in that their work influenced myriad blacks both during and after their lifetimes. While they saw themselves as fully Christian and did not recognize the African qualities in their world view, their new cosmos had enormous appeal and particular strength just because it was an Afro-Baptist cosmos. The black Baptist's cosmos and its relationship to that of white Baptists of the period can be investigated in several ways. It is clear that both whites and blacks recounted God's precious dealing with their souls, and that both races had visionary experiences. It is clear, too, that good white Baptist preachers heard and accepted the visionary travels of blacks. Abraham Marshall, who was the son of Daniel Marshall (brother-in-law and disciple of Shubal Stearns) and who, as his father before him, was pastor at the Kiokee, Georgia, Baptist Church (a church which early welcomed blacks to a full communion, even allowing them to criticize their white owners), heard the experiences of a group of forty black or "Ethiopian" believers in Savannah in 1788. A Reverend Thomas Burton had earlier heard eighteen experiences there and had accepted them. However, neither Marshall nor Burton nor the other preachers who accepted blacks into their mixed congregations during this period left comments on the content of their visionary experiences.[8]

The basis for the thesis that the black Baptists achieved a unique and extraordinarily significant synthesis of the African and Baptist cosmos rests on a comparative analysis of their visions. A content analysis of white visions, suggested above, and of black visions (discussed below) seems to reveal both *remarkably similar and significantly different elements*. Both recounted the worthlessness of the sinner, his sense of eternal damnation, his sudden salvation, and his pure joy at having experience with God and the assurance of God in his soul. Notwithstanding this apparent similarity, black religious experiences began to be singled out as particularly ecstatic by white Baptists, signifying consciousness of a difference. Reverend Hosea Holcombe, writing in 1840, noted that "a great number of those [Negroes] who unite with our Churches, express themselves in a very visionary manner," implying a qualitative difference from white conversions. In 1842 C. C. Jones, a missionary to the slave plantations in Liberty County, Georgia, wrote that blacks were converted through "dreams, visions, trances, voices all bearing a *perfect or striking resemblance to some form or type which has been handed down for generations,* or which has been originated in the wild fancy of some religious teacher among them." Jones and others clearly viewed the black use of this "form or type" skeptically.

There are two possible explanations for these different black visions. Either black visions had always been somewhat different from white conversion experiences, or by the 1840s most whites had so changed their expression that they had forgotten the earlier patterns. Perhaps both factors were involved. While, as indicated above, some whites continued to experience the white Baptist's classic vision in the midnineteenth century, white experiential religion began to decline as the Baptists grew from sect to denomination. The vision was not eliminated, but its character was changed. Black experience remained far more emotional. While Ryland commented in 1855 that blacks in his congregation seemed to place "less reliance on dreams and visions" than they once had, he may have made this statement to demonstrate the success of his attempts to acculturate the black. The evidence from slave and ex-slave narratives, down into the twentieth century, indicates that in this specific regard Jones' analysis was cogent. The vision tradition of 1840 was already an old one, and it was retained for at least another hundred years. Analysis of the black visionary experiences indicates that they were very different from the outset, and that their uniqueness was highlighted as the whites grew less concerned with spiritual journeys.[9]

II

God Struck Me Dead, a volume of thirty-eight religious conversion experiences collected by A. P. Watson in the 1920s and edited by Clifton H. Johnson, provides the most important body of data for analyzing black conversions. While these narratives are indeed from ex-slaves and their children, several variant but similar accounts from the slave period, as well as strong internal evidence, indicate that these are traditional visions, very similar to those experienced and recounted by blacks from the 1750s on.[10]

Here too, as in the white experiences, there is an ideal type of vision with a simple structure that can be reduced to eight basic elements: The seeker is called by name, by his very own private name, signifying that God knows this name and is ready to encounter or know the soul of that person. (The terms *sinner, seeker,* and *mourner* were all used for individuals prior to conversion. All people were sinners, but the term *sinner* was often used to denote those not yet seeking the Lord. One who was trying to get "that thing" was a *seeker,* and one who felt close to salvation, who perhaps sat on the "mourner's bench" close to the pulpit where he or she could be particularly prayed over, was a *mourner.*)[11] The call by name is of ultimate significance. The individual then recounts his death, saying unambiguously: "I died." Two selves are then seen, a "little me, inside the big me."

The "little me" is brought to the brink of Hell and is almost lost, but the call of "Mercy, Mercy, Mercy, Lord" has immediate effect, and a little white man leads the "little me" eastward, sometimes through terrors, from Hell to Heaven. In Heaven, sheep are grazing in green pastures and *mourning*—singing a lowing, sad tune. God, in blazing white robes, calls the individual again; promises to be in him and with him; and sends him back to life, against his will, to proclaim the good news. Reborn, "the true me" is a totally different person than he or she was before the experience and is suffused with joy.

The white and black visions of death and rebirth share some elements but are nevertheless significantly different. In both, the individual begins in a low state and is saved by a cry for mercy to see God in His glory and to be reborn. The black visions have four unique aspects: (1) the concept of the two selves, the "little me" in the "big me" permeating the whole vision structure; (2) the detailed journey or travels of the soul from Hell to Heaven; (3) the appearance of a little (white) man as guide on this journey; and (4) the visual description of Heaven and God, with its emphasis on whiteness. In each case, these differences between white and black visions can be attributed to an African ethos which was an integral part of the black's Christian cosmos.

This is not simply to say that elements of the black ethos were incorporated into a Euro-Christian one. That such a process occurred has been recognized since the early nineteenth century. However, black Baptists reached another level of integration (generally not recognized) in which *a new cosmos was forged uniting African and Baptist elements in a new whole.* Aspects of African soul and spirit found an intrinsic role in the black Baptist rebirth experience, infusing the Christian Sacred Cosmos with an African one. The visions, which were recounted again and again in experience meetings and "love feasts," are the mythic expression of the new black Baptist Sacred Cosmos. An extended analysis of these visions, undertaken below, provides firm evidence of the Afro-Christian quality of the black faith.

The African regarded his essential being as "the little me in the big me." As Parrinder suggests, this "me" was not regarded as parenthetical but as "the true me" that had existed before life and would continue after death. The goal in Africa was for this "me" to go home to spirit. In the black Christian vision, the black "little me" went home to Jesus or to God.

Blacks prepared themselves for the Christian mystery, much as Africans had prepared themselves for initiation. Sixteen-year-old Mary fasted five days and then went to the graveyard to await a vision. Mollie fasted two weeks and then got down on her knees, staying there for several days until the vision came. Fasting and lack of sleep, which are part of both the African and white Baptist traditions, prepared many of the candidates, most of whom were between the ages of twelve and twenty-two when "struck." Many felt ill before conversion, but they recognized that theirs was a spiritual illness, and they called it "sin-sickness." They generally understood this psychological distress in an African fashion, as punishment for having broken taboos or having gone back on promises to the Lord. As they believed, God, having made one sick, should be sought in order to bring back health. A spiritual advised "Take car' de sin-sick soul." The care necessary, fasting and prayer, involved the opposite of pampering, but it was the right way to seek God.[12]

Dancing, now seen as a torment of the devil to tempt man to violate God's laws, figures as the most prominent known cause of "sin-sickness." Worldly dancing, objected to by the white Baptists, came to symbolize the strictures of the new Sacred Cosmos for blacks. It was the most significant taboo.

Nora, a slave, promised her father on his deathbed that she would not dance so that they might meet in Heaven. Later, her worldly husband objected to her vow and took her dancing. Nora was torn by contradictory demands:

> Some time later I got heavy and began to die. For days I couldn't eat, couldn't sleep: even the water I drank seemed to swell in my mouth. A voice said to me one day, "Nora, you haven't done what you promised." And again it said, "You saw the sun rise, but you shall die before it goes down". I began to pray. I was making up my bed. A light seemed to come down from heaven and it looked like it just split me open from my head to my feet. A voice said to me, "Ye are freed and free indeed. My son set you free. Behold I give you everlasting life."

Sin-sick blacks went to private "praying places," while whites often went into the woods to pray. The black's emphasis on a particular spot for praying, a place that is a God-infused location, seems to be African in character. Spirit is found in particular trees or hidden places. William, whose mother had been sold away from him when he was a little boy and for whom he grieved deeply, had heard voices from an early age. He had fasted and prayed many times and had been treated by a witch doctor to cure his "sickness," but he still heard voices and so he went to his "regular praying place." "I usually prayed behind a big beech tree a little distance from the house, and often during the night, when I would feel to pray, I would get out of bed and go to this tree. That night I said, 'Lord, if I am praying right, let me hear a dove mourn three times.'" God responded, sending him into a trance, but transmitted His own symbolic message and not the call of doves.

Of the thirty-eight cases reported by Watson only six experienced their first Christian vision in a church. While subsequent soul travelin' often took place during an ecstatic shout in the congregation, the vast majority of blacks experienced their deaths and rebirths while alone, in bed at night or in the woods or fields. For all the crucial importance of the communal revival as a stimulant, the rebirth itself was essentially an individual experience and this was symbolized by the privacy of the primal vision. Over and over again, the words "lonely," "alone," "by myself" appear. It is the "me" who has this experience apart from the group members, who then hear it as "good news" when it is recounted to them.

> I wait upon de Lord, I wait upon
> de Lord,
> I wait upon de Lord, my God, who
> take away de sin of the world.
> If you want to find Jesus,
> go in the wilderness,
> Go in the wilderness, go in the
> wilderness,
> Mourning brudder, go in de wilderness
> I wait upon de Lord.

As sung on Port Royal Island, 1862

While the experience is awaited and prepared for, the actual death and rebirth come in a shocking flash. "It hit me in the top of my head" is a most common image. "It was like lightning." "Like a flash, the power of God struck me." "It split me" and "I fell over." If God does not "hit" in a flash, it is usually His voice that is suddenly and shockingly heard, most often calling the penitent by name—"Morte," "William," "Mary," "Nora," "Mollie." The candidates are called by a voice that speaks "as plain as day" and that is clearly recognized to be "the voice of God."[13]

In Africa mediums and priests heard divinities call. They too often called them by name. Indeed, as mentioned earlier, in America this tradition became confused with the fear of witches, and it was said one should not answer a voice for fear it was a dangerous spirit. But when called by God there was no choice. One could not fool God with pins or brooms or counting tricks that might keep a ghost busy, and one could not frighten or bribe Him away. This was not an African divinity or a spirit from the living dead, nor was it a ghost or a haunt. It was the High God Himself who sent this vision, a God who had not been contacted in this intimate fashion in Africa.

Once called or "hit" there is no turning back. Up to this point the candidate had tried to prepare himself, but once called, he began "to die."

In many cases, God's voice proclaims: "You must die this day." The penitents talk of "truly" dying, of being "killed dead"; of saying farewell to life; and of traveling to Hell. It is only by God's will that during the journeys of their souls they are saved from Hell and are then reborn. AS they understand this experience, God actually struck them dead. This is not, by their reckoning, allegory or symbolism. They were sin-sick and dying, and God "killed" them.

Killed, the seeker finds himself at the jaws or brink of Hell, and it is here that he sees himself as twofold: "a man in a man." Morte saw his "old body suspended over a burning pit by a small web like a spider web." Jonathan Edwards' spider image in the Enfield sermon ("Sinners in the Hands of an Angry God") is literally experienced by many of the seekers. However, several African peoples have a folklore image of Father Spider as creator, and the spider figures widely in West African folklore, so that the web image has African roots as well. Hanging over Hell, the black seekers see the devil, a "great monster," "his face as *black* as it could be and his eyes are red as fire," or in a dark tunnel often on a black horse. Hell is full of ravenous beasts and fires, and yet it is symbolized by blackness.

It is there that God shows the penitent mourner His infinite mercy, and it comes in a revelation of the individual's true self. For the first time, the black in America formally understands himself as Africans had understood themselves; he sees that "there is a man in a man." This is the vision he is given at the brink of Hell. In a very important way, this vision is telling the black that it was the lack of recognition or acknowledgment of his true nature that brought him to death and that almost led him to eternal perdition. But at the last moment, God reveals this inner self, this true man that African wisdom had known, and leaves the old man, the old unaware, undifferentiated "nigger" self, at the brink of Hell.

> I remember looking down on my body as my soul flew away.
>
> . . .
>
> I saw myself in two parts—this body sitting over dead body.
>
> . . .
>
> There is a being in a being, a man in a man. Little Mary was standing looking down on old Mary, on this temple, my body, and it lay on the very brink of hell.
>
> . . .
>
> He showed me myself in two parts of me. He carried me off in the spirit, and showed me this old body in the ground and the new body up in the air and me singing, "Hark from the tune."
>
> . . .
>
> . . . I saw myself in two bodies. Little me was standing looking down on the old, dead me lying on a cooling board.
>
> . . .

... There was a little William and the old William.

· · ·

... Little Mary came out of old Mary and I stood looking down on old Mary lying at hell's dark door.[14]

In recognizing the African wisdom about his soul and his true nature, the black was ready to rebuild his wholeness, to find completion and purpose. There was a decided similarity to the white understanding of rebirth, which indeed made it possible for the black to work through and with the Christian experience, but *the African did not simply see his old self die and a new self born, as the white did. The Afro-American recognized that there had always been a little me inside me;* that it was irreducible spirit, his essence which had always been in him and had been his true nature and value. Whites did not give it to him; spirit was not a gift of the white man. (In fact whites did not share in the African awareness of the complexity of souls and their eternal life.) Spirit is eternal, and the black had brought it with him from Africa, not as a deity but in his own inner self. In recognizing his own internal and external worth, the black knew himself both in a new way and in an ancient way. The Baptist rebirth experience served as the catalyst to bring him in contact with his African soul: to again know it, to pay it proper respect, and to keep it alive. The "little me" did not die, but it was reborn, and it was the Great God, whom he had not known personally in Africa, that brought him back to his African heritage. This was the crucial act of integration. Out of this act emerged a new Sacred Cosmos, a new creation.

While the black candidate dies alone to go on his spirit journey, he finds that God has sent a guide to lead and accompany the soul on its travels. This guide generally is seen as a little white man, who takes the penitent from Hell to Heaven, always traveling to the east. Sometimes he wears a golden crown and a white robe, or he travels on a narrow white path. One penitent saw the guide as a spearbearer whose weapon was tipped with "a star that outshone the morning sun." For all the travelers he is small and yet has great power in his knowledge of the right way to go. Is he an African divinity? If he is, he has become Christian. He does not need propitiation. He is not untrustworthy. Unlike Legba, a messenger of African divinities, he does not trick the candidates. On the contrary, he is consistently considerate and reliable, taking them in his arms and protecting them from the terrors of the journey out of the region of Hell. He does not have the character of a man, but neither is he Christ, who most often met whites in their visions. He is unique to black visions. There is no counterpart in the white experience with dying and rebirth. He is in almost all black visions. This suggests an African source, as African divinities often had messengers, but again it indicates the integration of this African source into a black Christian cosmos. The little man brings ultimate reassurance to the candidate, for he shows the candidate that his name is written in God's book of eternal life. The name, the essence, is thus given a renewed Christian meaning, symbolizing his chosenness by God and tying the individual to his new Christian clan for eternity. In Africa, names had also served to symbolize the unique individual spirit as well as the eternal clan association. In the Christian vision, the chosen man is occasionally given "a deed" to this name or a personalized ticket. A black slave in body, he now owns his own essence, his own soul, and he shouts out "My name's written on high."[15]

The guide, the little man, leads the candidate to Jesus or God. The path leads through Heaven, which is seen as a green pasture or a golden meadow. Africans were also accustomed to using the imagery of green pastures. In the black Baptist visions, the meadows are filled with numerous sheep, all of the "same size," grazing and moaning. These are the lambs of God, the souls of the saved, all equal in God's Heaven and all praising him with African mournful music. The angels in Heaven shout and clap and rejoice, in African (and Afro-American) fashion.

And here sits God, awaiting the candidate. He is a white God, sitting on a golden throne.

> I saw the Lord in the east part of the world, and he looked like a white man. His hair was parted in the middle, and he looked like he had been dipped in the snow, and he was talking to me.
>
> . . .
>
> Then Jesus came to me just as white as dripping snow, with his hair parted in the middle just as white as snow.

Only rarely does a discordant, and perhaps African, image appear. God is envisioned with "full armor, and across his chest [is] a breast protector that shone as if it was made of bars of gold." But in most visions, pure whiteness dominates God and all the surroundings, and God is usually a solemn white man, although occasionally three heads or three suns (representing Father, Son, and Holy Ghost) are seen. The walls of the Heavenly City are white, the robes of the angels are white, and the Holy Mother is white.

The candidate, too, is robed in "a long snow-white robe," and he is carried on a white chariot or a white horse on a white path to the glowing heavens and pure God. Here the Negro becomes white too: "The first time I ever saw a vision I saw myself a little body, pure white, and flying along a beautiful stream that flowed from the east." "The next morning everything was white. My hands were like snow. They just shined. They looked like the sun was on them." In Heaven, "in a world of light, peace, and harmony . . . I didn't see anything but myself and other white images like me." They were, as the black missionary Marrant had hoped, "made white in the blood of the lamb."[16]

Given the racism of American society and the fact that we are looking at the religion of black slaves owned by white masters, one would assume that the key element in this Sacred Cosmos colored white was its reflection of the social reality. There is, however, a very important African dimension that entirely changes this evaluation. In Africa, white was symbolic of goodness, purity, and holiness, while black symbolized evil. This color consciousness and value judgment runs throughout the West African world view. The most important Yoruba God was Orishala, the creator god, who gave bodies life. He is also known as Obatala, which means the "king in white clothing," or an "essentially white object." He "likes white—albinos are sacred to him and his priests wear white clothes. His temples are white-washed, chalk and white beads are placed there as symbols," as is white material without any pattern. The Ewe god Lisa also favors white. Again, his priests and even his worshipers wear white, and albinos are sacred to him. The priests of Mawu, as those of Tanu, Lisa, and Orishala, and many other African deities, wear white, and the holiness of albinos is an important sign of the significance of whiteness throughout West Africa. The symbolism of white as pure and holy is apparently an ancient African (and Middle Eastern) tradition predating the master-slave contact with whites. Parrinder notes that West African seers claim to be able to distinguish a glow or an aura coming from each and every individual, an aura whose color symbolizes the character of the individual. "The best people have a white aura, and are full of light," while blackness stands for evil.

Black as evil has deep roots, perhaps universal in nature, and is no doubt tied to fear of night and darkness and loss of the sun. These associations may have played a role in the whites' perception of blacks, but ironically they played a role for blacks as well. The African roots of this association are indicated by the Voudouists' use of black as the color of death and deadly omens. Black cats, black dogs, black cows, and black hogs were and are evil signs.

The black in America brought these African images with him, and they were mixed up in the complex self-perception of a black slave in a white slaveowning society. The black Baptist put on white robes at his baptism and sang: "Whitah dan snow; yes, whita dan snow,/Wash me, an' I shall be whitah dan snow."[17]

Having been brought before God and having been shown his name in the Book of Life, the sojourner is "new born again." The face-to-face contact with God is a sealing of his chosenness for a new birth, for freedom, and for a calling. God gives him total assurance of his new status:

> Fear not, for you are a chosen vessel.
>
> . . .
>
> Be not afraid, for I will be on your right hand and on your left.
> I will be as a refuge and as a fortress.
>
> . . .
>
> I am with you always, even until the world shall end.
>
> . . .
>
> Fear not, for I am with you, an everlasting prop.
>
> . . .
>
> I will encamp around you like a mighty wall.

An essential part of this experience was the act by which the High God gave the candidate the vision to see his inner essence. This was a liberating act in which God freed the seeker and his soul. Nearly every reborn person spoke of three things: First, he spoke of having "come through" by which was meant having passed through death to the new life or having had "the" primal experience. Praying, mourning, and shouting, he sang, "I done done what you told me to do, Good Lord, till I come through."

Second, the saved individual spoke of having "that thing" inside him, by which he meant the essence or spirit. Here again, very significantly, it is an African phrase that is continuously used. The black knows of "that thing," and once he has it he cannot lose it. It is new, yet it is also old and simply renewed. God says "I am with you always and have taken care of you from your earliest existence." But now the convert knows he has "it," and that makes all the difference.

The saved black, the Christian, talked of a third aspect, being "free at last." This freedom was not conditional on his physical freedom. Only God could free his soul, and if God did this he was free for all eternity. Virtually every trance experience, both the primal rebirth and the later growth experiences, was concerned with this everlasting freedom.

In these visions, God clearly states that either He or His Son has granted this eternal freedom:

> I have freed your soul.
>
> . . .
>
> Ye are freed and free indeed. My son set you free.
>
> . . .
>
> You are free indeed.
>
> . . .
>
> Free, free, my Lord.
> Your Father's done set you free.

"Free! Free! Free!" converts called in ecstatic trance, and long after slavery had ended, the convicted shouted out, "I am so glad I am free." "Free at last." "Thank God a-mighty, I am free at last."[18]

The Christian rebirth set blacks free forever. They might remain slaves in body for the rest of their lives, but they were free, in ways their white masters might or might not be. Theirs was a freedom that could not be bought. This conviction provided blacks with an internal strength. It was not just an accommodation, a way in which to accept their status as slaves. It was a spiritual wisdom that became the core of their lives. External status, external appearances, aspects of personality, and the outer me did not share in eternal spirit.

Jupiter Hammon's comments on physical liberty are often quoted. Writing in February 1787, Hammon, the slave poet, pointed out the irony of white Americans fighting for liberty while closing their eyes to the slavery in their midst. But Hammon also wrote of what he considered the more important liberty, spiritual liberty. These words are not usually reprinted:

> But this, [physical liberty] my dear brethren, is by no means the greatest thing we have to be concerned about. Getting our liberty in this world is nothing to our having the liberty of the children of God. Now the Bible tells us that we are all by nature, sinners, that we are slaves to sin and Satan, and that unless we are converted or born again, we must be miserable forever. Christ says, except a man be born again, we must be miserable forever. Christ says, except a man be born again, he cannot see the Kingdom of God, and all that do not see the Kingdom of God must be in the Kingdom of darkness. There are but two places to go after death, white and black, rich and poor; those places are Heaven and Hell.

Hammon warned blacks of the eternal slavery that awaited the unsaved. If not reborn, "we shall be slaves here, and slaves forever. . . . What is forty, fifty, or sixty years, when compared to eternity?" This is not to suggest that Hammon and other Christian blacks did not want physical freedom. They did yearn for freedom and, in fact, believed it would establish a congruence between their inner and outer states. In other words, Christian freedom of soul made them certain that they were worthy of physical freedom. While some whites made strong attempts to prove that Christianity sanctioned slavery, and they called on the slave to accept his status, the basic message of the rebirth made the black know his essential freedom. The appropriation of the history of the Israelites gave them the example of God's ultimate aid to His people in slavery.[19]

The Christian rebirth and freedom brought responsibility to the reborn individual, giving him an ongoing mission that was an essential part of the new relationship between God and man. In knowing man and in showing him his soul, God showed him his duty in life. This was a Christian duty, which involved going into the world and publicly proclaiming the gospel. Thus, God made each and every convert a responsible person, who had a lifelong job of great, even eternal, importance. Perhaps he would be a slave for life, but his free soul had to choose to testify. Even if it was a hard choice to make, the black Christian, in much the same way as the white Christian, *had to publicly confess* his experience with Christ. In becoming a Christian, he had become a full person, an adult with adult responsibilities, a free soul. In undertaking these responsibilities, the Christian was sent on a difficult journey, a journey through life.

> I had waited at hell's dark door and got my order *to travel.* I have been traveling ever since, looking to my Captain for my every want and need.
>
> . . .
>
> He set my feet in the path and told me to go and I have been traveling ever since. Falling down and getting up, I keep my eye on the bright and morning star. He told me I would have hard trials and great tribulations—but I must fight on.

This image of the sacred journey entered the folk consciousness. Many spirituals tell of "traveling on":

> Well, I been travelin' all through this way
> Well, I take Jesus, he will be my friend
> Well, I been travelin' through this way
> Well, I cried out
> I take Jesus to be my friend
> He will lead me, safely through
> Whiles I'm travelin', whiles I'm stumblin' all the time
>
> . . .
>
> When I'm on my lonesome journey,
> I want Jesus Be with me.

Africans also saw life as a journey, but they wanted their minds to be "at ease" in their traveling: "Nuer speak of life as walking through pastures and they ask for a path that has no hidden danger, that is, free from evil, and for softness underfoot, that is, a mind at ease."

Since the Christian was given freedom and promised glory, his mind should have been put at ease, but the path through life was not to be easy. The Christian had a cross to bear, and black Christians could not doubt it. Heaven was their eventual home, but the journey God sent one out on at rebirth was a long and hard one.

> Lord, I'm bearin' heavy burdens,
>   Tryin' to get home.
> Lord, I'm climbin' high mountains,
>   Tryin' to get home.
> Lord, I'm standin' hard trials
>   Tryin' to get home.[20]

It was only by traveling that road, by bearing the cross and proclaiming the gospel, that Christians, white and black, could expect to make Heaven their home. Unquestionably, blacks looked forward to the time when they would be in Heaven, "at home," "in the promised land."

The black convert had something special to help him on his way. He had "that thing." When blacks used this phrase in Africa they meant their inner essence, that spirit that was their essential self and yet part of all spirit. When a black Christian got "that thing," he had himself *and Christ* in him. Jesus clearly promised to be with and in the reborn spirit.

> I command you to go in yonder world.
> Open your mouth, and *I will speak through you.*
>   . . .
> My little one, I have loved you with an everlasting love. You are this day made alive and freed from hell. You are upright before me, and I will guide you until all truth. My grace is sufficient for you. Go, and I am with you. *Preach the gospel and I will preach with you.* You are henceforth the salt of the earth.
>   . . .
> I jut said what the spirit directed me to say.

Perhaps there was a remnant of the African idea of spirit possession when the black Baptist spoke of God being in him and speaking through him. Unlike the African deity, however, this High God stayed in him always, yet did not ride him or possess him. The convert's soul and God's spirit merged to become "the thing" that was his essence.

> Folks had ter starve deys' f and' pray and seek, sometimes a month er mo', fo' dey come froo. You had ter be right good and ser'us fo' you could mak up yo' min' ter go under de deep dark waters what de Baptis's frowed you in. But den when you got *it* you had *it.*

To have "it," "the thing," was to have made it over Jordan, to have moved from mourner and seeker to a saint in glory; for God had promised the reborn soul that it would sit at His right hand for all eternity. But first the reborn spirit must return to earth and preach the gospel, enduring many hardships on this journey. The spirit had to hold out to the end; it had to go uphill to reach Heaven. To "carry on to the end" was the responsibility and the initiative-demanding task God gave the converted man. Once converted, he had a hard role to play. The road was expected to be very difficult. The high God did not promise ease, but He did promise to be "a refuge and a fortress" on the way, and a savior for all eternity. He promised the slave that after death "He will bring you out more than conquerer."[21]

It is this image of eventual release that numerous commentators have cited as turning the slave from his temporal troubles to visions of eternal glory. They suggest that Christianity invited the slave to escape from reality. It is true that many blacks sang of being "done with the trouble of this world," and they thanked God they were on their way to Heaven. It should be remembered that concern with spirit life after death reflected continuity with African concerns. Christianity did not introduce the African to the afterlife. West Africans shared a consuming interest in this "time phase"; the Dogon, for example, regarded some spirits as alive only after death.[22]

The Christian ethos emphasized Heaven and maintained that life was but a preparation for eternity. The Africans had maintained something similar in Africa: If all went well, man's spirit would go on to become one of the living dead and finally a divinity. It is wrong to evaluate the black Baptist's concern for death-time without knowledge of its African background. It is also wrong to overemphasize it without recognizing its corollary: the strength of the black Baptist faith lay in its demand that before the saint could go to glory he *had to face life*. The Baptist's God demanded wholeness of the convert. He had to "keep the faith" and "persevere," coming through trials and tests. He had to respond to good and evil. He was not simply to accept everything the white master said or did or expected as moral imperatives. While Christianity was often perverted in an attempt to make quietude its message, the new black Baptist cosmos did not incorporate any aspect of accommodation to evil. On the contrary, the black had a far more difficult task—he had to find a way to be a moral man in an immoral society.

The reborn Baptist had a new inner strength to cope with this immoral world. He knew himself and he knew God, and these experiences with spirit were renewed in new vision travels. This new inner knowledge was strengthening and expressed itself in a new outward appearance. Much as the white Baptist, the black Baptist convert became a new man, showing a total personality change.

> Ever since the Lord freed my soul I have been a new man.
>
> . . .
>
> I rose to my feet a new creature and went spreading the news.
>
> . . .
>
> I am a new creature in Jesus, the workmanship of his hand saved from the foundation of the world. I was a chosen vessel before the wind ever blew or before the sun ever shined.

The most obvious aspect of this newness was the turning away from what were defined as worldly things. "The things I used to enjoy don't interest me now." Profane music and dancing (much of which had religious African roots) were the two most overt symbols of worldliness, and their rejection was an important symbolic act. Abandoned banjos hung on myriad cabin walls, their renunciation a visible cross being borne by converted blacks. But the moral turning demanded was very significant. The new coherent Sacred Cosmos made distinct demands on the believers and led them to reject many of their old ways, including some African patterns of social interaction.

> God's goin' to get you 'bout your low-down ways.
> You talk about yo' elder when he's tryin' to preach the word.
> You talk about yo' neighbor when he's tryin' to praise the Lord.
> You talk about yo' sister when she's on her knees prayin'.
> God' goin' to get you 'bout your low-down ways.

Love is one of the chief elements of God's wisdom given to seekers in glory. In ecstatic wonder, a convert asks "What is this, God, that you're giving me?" And the answer is simply "It is love." The gift of God is "love and union," or "peace and joy and calmness." This joy given by God makes the seeker "love everybody": "I just wanted to kiss the very ground. I had never felt such a love before." "I rejoice in the love of God. The love of God is beyond understanding. It makes you love everybody." Many converts talk of having been fighters and haters before God's love "turned" them. They emerge from the visionary experience with a love in their hearts such as they had never felt before. Charlie, an ex-slave, recounts that when he met his ex-master after emancipation, the white man asked if Charlie forgave him the whippings he had given him. Charlie answered: "I love you as though you never hit me a lick, for the God I serve is a God of love and I can't go to his Kingdom with hate in my heart." In itself this statement would seem to support the general view that the black Baptist faith forced the slave to love or at least to embrace slavery. But Charlie said other things as well, things indicating that he knew himself to be superior to his master and knew that his ability to love the evil white man or forgive him was part of this superiority. Charlie told his ex-master that, notwithstanding his cheating him and whipping him, "I used to serve, work for you, almost nurse you, and if anything had happened to you I would have fought for you, *for I am a man among men. What is in me,* though *is not in you.*" By this, Charlie clearly meant "the thing," the spiritual essence. It was in Charlie, but Charlie knew it was not in the white man. "I used to drive you to church and peep through the door to see you all worship, but you ain't right yet, Marster."

The counterpart to the fullness of love in the heart was the elimination of fear. Fear of death and of life's terrors receded as the new whole man emerged. God specifically made this promise as well: "I will drive all fears away." "If I call you through fire and water, come on, follow me." "My little one, be not afraid, for lo! many wonderous works will I perform through thee." "I will take away your fear." This promise is tested in the vision experience itself. Devils attack seekers, but they "sail on unafraid." Dogs search for the mourner but cannot get him. Snakes, snares, and angry beasts cannot hurt a seeker; dangerous snows are crossed; "traveling, trusting in the Lord," the convert is safe.[23]

III

The black in America could understand the spirit or God the Baptists knew as being his own High God or Creator God. If there is but one High God and he created everything, then Nyama and Nana Nyankopon and Odoman Koma and Eloheem and Adonai must all be one and the same: different words for different attributes of spirit. Slaves expressed an awareness of this unity in song:

> God is a God! God don't never
>   change!
> God is a God, An' He always
>   will be God!
> He made the sun to shine by day,
> He made the sun to show the way,
> He made the stars to show their light,
> He made the moon to shine by night,
>   sayin'
>
> God is a God! . . . .
> The earth, his footstool an' heav'n his
>   throne,
> The whole creation all his own,

His love an' power will prevail,
His promises will never fail,
                    sayin'
God is a God!

Africans, as suggested earlier, did not generally try to come in direct contact with God. They accepted His withdrawal as permanent, and they believed that their contacts with his surrogates, the divinities, were sufficient. But they had prayed to God, and some of their prayers are amazingly parallel to biblical prayers.

Africans had understood divinities as God's sons. Jesus presented no difficulty in this sense, and his closeness to man was similar to the divinities' closeness. In fact, the third aspect of the Akan trinity was "the One on whom men lean and do not fall." Jesus was certainly such a One. As early as 1660, Spanish Capuchin missionaries in Dahomey had translated the name Jesus by using one of the African deity's names, Lisa. They recognized that Dahomeans would thereby understand Christ's Sonship.[24]

The Holy Ghost as spirit incarnate was certainly understandable to Africans. The power of spirit to be in anything or to be, by itself, was fully accepted. The Holy Ghost and the Sonship of Jesus can be viewed as a reduction of African ideas rather than as new concepts. Even the Platonic-New Testament idea of the word as spirit and power was known in Africa. The Dogon defined words as force and their loss as a loss of power. (The evil power of "bad words" was symbolized as a bad smell.)

The concept of virgin birth was not unknown in Africa. The Akamba believed in "spirit husbands" who could cause pregnancy without physical contact. The Dogon believed words "assisted procreation," entering the woman's body and making it "possible for her to be impregnated in the normal way."[25]

The African symbolism of spirit as water was carried to America and may have been brought into the Baptist cosmos. The death and rebirth in the watery grave may have incorporated African memories of spirit as water. Later, Baptists would sing:

I've just come from the fountain, Lord,
I've just come from the fountain, His name's so sweet.
O brothers I love Jesus, His name's so sweet.
O sisters I love Jesus, His name's so sweet.
Been drinking from the fountain,
His name's so sweet.

One black convert experienced God's love as "a shower of rain [that] came down on the top of my head and went to the toes."

By and large, Jesus was not spirit, water, or power, but he was known as a man, a very special, pure, and perfect man. Turning to Jesus was the primary strength in the black Baptist way. Jesus was a friend to gab with, to cry with, to shout to, to give joy, and to provide love. "A little talk with Jesus makes it all right."

Jesus became the rock and the salvation of the black man. The role the living dead had played in being concerned for their kin was taken over by Jesus, who was a far more reliable spirit. Blacks turned to him in joy and in sorrow:

> For Jesus said at one time, "Come unto me, all ye that labors, and are heavy laden, and I would give you rest."
> . . . And whenever the way is hard, we goes to Him and tell Him about it.
>
> . . .
>
> Nobody knows de trouble I see
> Nobody knows but Jesus.

Blacks truly took their troubles to Jesus as they took him to their hearts. They knew him as they knew their contemporaries, and they envisioned his life as the lives around them.

> They crucified my Lord.
> An' he never said a mumbalin' word;
> They crucified my Lord,
> An' he never said a mumbalin' word,
> Not a word, not a word, not a word.
>
> They nailed him to the tree, . . .
>
> They pierced him in the side, ...
>
> The blood came twinklin' down, ...
>
> He bow'd His head an' died,
> An' He never said a mumbalin' word, ... [26]

This existential contact with Jesus, as with Noah, Gabriel, Joshua, Daniel, Moses, and other biblical personalities, was made possible by the nature of the vision experience. The African did not have a sense of time future, but he had an extraordinary sense of time past in which the character traits of the living dead figured as important knowledge. Each individual was to become an integral part of time past, and the character of each individual while living was, therefore, of great significance. This sense of time and individuality had been intertwined with sense of place. The divinities and living dead lived in Africa and in some way needed space after death.

The blacks in America, coming from many peoples, did not have a single redeemable oral history nor a single recountable character analysis of their living dead. Their Sacred Cosmos could meld in America, but its myriad personalities had not emigrated. Bible history—the history of Israel, of the Hebrew slaves and their redemption—became the black Baptist's sacred past. They themselves felt as if they were of the seed of Abraham, and biblical "space" became their sacred topography. They would go home to Heaven, as African spirits went home to Africa ("Gonna make heaven my home"), and they would find mother, father, and kinfolk there, waiting.

It was the time transposition of visions that made this redemption possible. In the vision experience, time future became time past. The convert would go to Heaven when he died, but he had already been there. He knew Heaven, as he knew God, Christ, the angels, and the lambs of God. He had already been there. He had already traveled there, and, therefore, knew he could travel there again. The black made a change towards accepting time future but only because he knew it as time past as well.

Patience was an African virtue. Time was the natural time of sun and moon and seasons; one could not speed it up. The Twi said, "In your patience is your soul," and they knew that one had to work in and with the natural rhythms of time to be fulfilled. The Christian vision was a sudden rebirth that came outside of the natural order; it was not part of an initiation ceremony that occurred at a set age, even though most seekers seem to have been preparing for adulthood. Therefore, one needed unusual patience to wait for it. Some seekers sought their visions all their lives and were never given the assurance. A slave master wrote of his own "mammy" who had been baptized at birth, and who

> went sorrowing all her days. Whole nights have I known her to pass on her knees. As she staid in her room with us, I would often see her in the attitude of prayer; and her unpressed bed would prove that she had been all night trying to "seek" acceptably. That she was a child of God, though thus walking in darkness, none who knew her ever doubted; . . . but as she never experienced what is known as "conversion" by her class, she never became a Baptist.

Most slaves did not know how to use white people's time; they could not "count the clock." Did their experience with God's sudden conversions outside of set celebration times bring them a new time consciousness? On the contrary, it seems to have confirmed their African patience. God was seen as a "time-God," but this meant that he did everything in His own good time and not according to the clocks or desires of men. In the visions, God spoke of time, saying:

> I am a time-God working after the counsel of my own will.
> In due time I will bring all things to you. Remember and cause your heart to sing.
>
> . . .
>
> I am a time-God. Behold, I work after the counsel of my own will, and in due time I will visit whomsoever I will.

The black Baptist accepted this wisdom. It explained who he was and where he was going.

> In the very beginning every race and every creature was in the mind of God and we are here, not ahead of time, not behind time, but just on time. It was time that brought us here, and time will carry us away.
>
> . . .
>
> . . . The God I serve is a time-God. He don't come before time; he don't come after time. He comes just on time.

In the black vision, Jacob's ladder is not used to rush to Heaven. A black vision seeker describes herself as "on the bottom rung, and somebody was on every rung, climbing upward, but no one seemed to be in a hurry." Rushing through life would not get blacks to Heaven any quicker, and even the last man or woman on the ladder, the lowest in the social order, would share in God's promise in God's own time.[27]

In these visions or "trabels," the lonely journeys of blacks signified liberation. These journeys brought great spiritual growth, renewed knowledge of self and of death and of the great and compassionate God. The voices heard were of the true self and the true God, and they could not be disputed. As a result of these dreams, the individuals' ways of life changed and a new Sacred Cosmos emerged. True to the new Afro-American, this cosmos was both African and Baptist.[28]

Timothy Smith, in one of the finest appreciations of nineteenth-century black religion, has concluded that the "unique" aspect of the blacks' religious consciousness "was their ready absorption of the radical views of man's duty and destiny which characterized primitive Christian thought." Smith accepts as "a sufficient explanation" for the nature of black Christianity the influences of evangelical Protestantism. He sees the blacks' theology of hope, forgiveness, and reconciliation as being formed by their successful experiences in coping with slavery through use of biblical morality which "supported their moral revulsion toward it [slavery] and promised eventual deliverance from it without demanding that they risk their lives in immediate resistance." However fine Smith's analysis, he makes at least one very serious error in judgment that undermines his entire argument. In assuming that nineteenth-century Protestantism is a "sufficient" background for black religion in America, he has ultimately treated the moral and theological consciousness of the blacks as though it were newly born in the nineteenth century. Blacks did not begin to have moral perceptions when they heard Bible stories, as he intimates. Rather, they began to use Bible stories in place of, and in conjunction with, their earlier mythologies. Their traditional values and ways of thought determined which stories were meaningful and under what conditions they could be used.

Smith sees the Christian experience as "expand[ing] the capacity of the more sensitive Africans to experience awe." Had Smith assessed the capacity of Africans to experience awe prior to their contact with Christianity, he would not have made this statement. But he did not feel it necessary to analyze the African experience, as he assumed that the Christian and the slave experience explained the matter satisfactorily.[29]

Smith means no disrespect. On the contrary, he finds black Christians far better Christians than whites. In his view, they truly learned what Christian love and forgiveness and existential irony were all about. Given this evaluation, he simply is not aware of the disrespect he shows their past and of his ethnocentric mistake in maintaining that nineteenth-century Protestantism sufficiently explains black religion. Black Christian awe, ecstasy, self-respect, and hope (which Smith credits to Protestantism) are all based on African traditions that the blacks brought with them to America and maintained in some fashion. Moreover, it was the African view of man and divinities as both good and evil that gave the African an existentialist's pain and hope. The African man had to seek to fulfill himself in a dangerous and difficult world (where even divinities were untrustworthy), but he knew that he could expect to return to spirit. His religion was a hopeful and even joyful one that affirmed life and death in the midst of ambiguities and trials.

The Protestant ethos provided the experience of personal forgiveness and ethical earnestness, but it did this as a counterbalance to its provision of a sense of primal sin and damnation. The African viewed his failings as proceeding from avoidance of duty or contravention of taboos. While he had the responsibility to develop himself through rebirth and spiritual growth, he did not regard himself as "fallen" or in need of salvation.

Africans explained evil in the world as resulting from a primal act, but their souls were not lost in that process. It was their bodies that would die as a result, but soul, which was spirit, would return to spirit.

Christianity gave the black a sense of sin as well as an experience of personal forgiveness to redeem him. Africans had been moral men without a sense of sin, and Afro-Americans used the experience of personal forgiveness as an ideal opportunity for a spirit journey. They became extraordinary Christians, but it was their African Sacred Cosmos that led them to deeply appreciate and existentially appropriate Christian symbols and Christian meaning.

When George Liele wrote: ''I agree to election, redemption, the fall of Adam, regeneration and perserverence, knowing the promise is to all who endure, in grace, faith and good works, to the end, shall be saved,'' he believed every word with his heart and soul, and he staked his life on it. He himself did not necessarily realize the African quality of his Christianity, but he was an Afro-Christian and one of the fathers of a continuing Afro-Baptist tradition.[30]

IV

Prior to the Civil War, the Christian world views of blacks in America varied widely. A small number, such as Phillis Wheatley, Jupiter Hammon, and Lemuel Haynes, came to hold a Christian world view that was very similar to the white view and expressed it in the whites' English. A larger number came to view the world via an African/Christian dichotomous Sacred Cosmos, encapsulated in Creole English. (This was the world view of many black Christians in the early plantation period, such as the Gullah.) Only in the Afro-Christian world view, the world view of most black Baptists and Methodists whose language of expression was black English, was there a new creation, a new supportive and enveloping whole that could aid the individual in relating to his past, present, and future in a coherent spiritual and social sense. African roots and Christian consciousness, spirit and Christ, soul growth and redemption, were all intertwined in a living whole.

In respecting the unique nature of each church as a covenanted body, the Baptists provided particularly fertile ground for Afro-Christianity to develop. Methodists always had to adjust to limits set from without, and while they managed to stretch these limits considerably, they could not break them. The individual Methodist church was part of the body of Christ and had to function in response to messages from the head and heart.

> Methodism from the first had been very stricly governed. . . . In the independent American church, the superintendent (or bishop,

as he came to be called) wielded more actual authority than any other Protestant official. Once elected, he could define the circuits which the traveling preachers were to cover and assign men to these circuits or to local charges as he saw fit. He appointed the presiding elders who in turn supervised the several districts into which the circuits were arranged. Thus he could marshal his men and resources in such a way as to make maximum gains.

In contrast, the Baptist associations were technically no more than mutual aid societies, with absolutely no formal control over the beliefs or practices of member churches. Each church was the body of Christ in itself, and each held to "the liberty wherein Christ has made you free" as the basic tenet of independent church life. In practice, group pressure might have a great deal of influence, but churches broke away from associations with impunity; division and divisiveness were part and parcel of Baptist life. No uniformity could be demanded. Six Principle, Nine Principle, Particular, General, Regular, Free Will, Hard Shell, Two Seed Predestination, Primitive, and Landmarkian were only some of the divisions that marked this denomination. There had been tendencies for centralization, centering around both the (Particular) Philadelphia Association and the (Arminian) Sandy Creek Association, but while the association structure eventually became normative, in most cases individual churches retained their independence. Independent black churches were members of white associations and yet functioned with much self-determination. This Baptist tradition, as Ahlstrom suggests, was at the "opposite pole" from Methodist practice in regard to order and authority. Even when blacks formed a separate African Methodist Episcopal (AME) Church Organization (Philadelphia, 1816), its structure and order were basically white-Methodist in character. Centralized control by Philadelphia blacks led to the breakaway of the New York-based AME Zion in 1821.[31]

Both the Baptist and Methodist faiths emphasized personal experience and required its recounting. Blacks were attracted to the Methodists because of this aspect. However, Methodist theology, while Arminian and maintaining that God's grace was available to all, emphasized the fallen nature of man. With the depravity of man as its primary message and its call for Christian perfection as the major goal, Methodism was more alien to the African understanding of man's mixed nature than was the Baptist faith. Baptists generally believed that the saved man can fall and be saved again and again. Continuing experience and traveling, in visions and in daily life, were expected. A man could move to "the backbench" if he sinned and could come back to the "Amen corner" in return. Perfection was not as significant an aspect of the Baptist faith as it was in Methodism. The African Sacred Cosmos was thus more likely to find congruences in Baptist theology.

The Baptist faith not only emphasized experience, but it also ritualized it in the most meaningful way possible. Most blacks felt such a great need to be baptized, to be immersed in the living waters, that it is virtually certain that they were responding to this ritual as an initiating rite—a rebirth into a new community that the Methodists could not provide.

Israel Campbell, a slave in Tennessee, had a visionary experience in which Christ told him he had "found *it.*" But he was not all the way over. He had not "passed through," and a free-will Baptist preacher told him: "Go on, baby, go on to the goal." He prayed for a further sign daily, beginning around December 1, 1837, and continuing to pray through the end of January 1838. Suddenly, one night, while in bed he "was shown a vision":

> I was conducted to a large pond of water. There were many people standing on the border of the pond, and in the midst of it were several dead trees. While I was standing there, I heard a voice say—
> "When you are baptized, your progress shall be renewed."
> The vision departed, and my natural feelings returned, and I found myself still in the bed. I lay there some time, turning the things I had witnessed over and over in my mind. I did not remember of ever having seen the pond and the people were nearly all strangers to me. Then I thought I had been asleep and dreamed what I had seen; but I did not feel as if it had been so, as I was not rested in body like sleep leaves you, and the scenes were too forcibly impressed on my mind for a dream.

Acting on this vision, Campbell (and his wife) joined a new Baptist church in his area and were taken to be baptized at a pond he claimed never to have visited before. However,

> I was surprised, on coming to this pond, to find it the very one which I saw in my vision; and as I lifted my eyes there I beheld the people standing on the shores and there were the dead trees, all of which I saw so plain, and yet I have no recollection of ever seeing them before.
> . . . Then could I sing that beautiful song of Zion:
> "How lost was my condition, till Jesus made me whole!
> There is but one Physician that can cure a sin-sick soul"

Many blacks who were nominally Roman Catholics or Methodists were "practicing" Baptists who followed rituals they adapted on the plantations. Elizabeth Ross Hite was a secret Baptist on a Catholic plantation:

> See, our master didn't like to have too much 'ligion, said it made us lag in our work. He jest wanted us to be Catholicses on Sunday and go to mass and not study 'bout nothin like that on week days. He didn't want us shoutin' and moanin' all day long, but you gotta shout and you gotta moan if you wants to be saved.
>
> . . . We used to have baptisms in a pond by the sugar house. Everybody was anxious to get baptized and be saved. The preacher would yell, "Halleluyah! Halleluyah"!, and the niggers would sing,
>> "I baptize you in the ribber Jordan, (2)
>> Hallelujah, Hallelujah, Hallelujah, Lord!
>> Children, come a-running', (2)
>> I baptize you in the ribber Jordan"
>
> You know, when we saved a sister there was glory in our hearts. When she was baptized the crowd would shout, "Thank Gawd! There goes Sister Amy! I been prayin' for this night on to two years now! Bless Gawd! She is saved at last. Her sins are washed away."[32]

Beginning in the last quarter of the eighteenth century, numerous blacks hungered for this rebirth and began to experience it.

It is important to try to reconstruct black Baptist development over time. The rich materials available about the last years of slavery, especially the ex-slave narratives, as well as the wealth of abolitionist and proslavery descriptions of the South "as it was" have too often led to a shallow time dimension in studies of slavery.[33] The realities of 1830 to 1865 were not the realities of 1800 or of 1750. In each period from the 1750s on, several, if not all, of the possible levels of development were present. In fact, in some ways it was easier for some of the earliest black Americans seemingly to abandon their African world view and immediately adopt a white one without any transition through the black Christian cosmos. They were a minority in a white world, often working together with white indentured servants. Phillis Wheatley might well serve as a typical Christian of the first type— an English speaker with an almost white world view. Wheatley, born perhaps in Senegal, was brought to Massachusetts in 1761, at the age of seven. She was purchased by the John Wheatley family and treated "as a loved member." She was an extraordinary person and was soon reading the Bible, classical literature, and mythology. At the age of seventeen, after ten years in the country, she was baptized at the Old South Meeting

House. Seemingly, she was a black functioning with a white world view. She traveled to England, published poetry, and, to all appearances, was becoming successful in the white world. But in 1778 she chose to marry John Peters, a black with strong problack feelings and "a proud man who insisted she estrange herself from her white friends."

Wheatley became a washerwoman living in dire poverty in the black community where she died in childbirth at age thirty (1784). Looking back, even her early poetry shows her ambivalence and disquiet in the white world. Her now famous 1771 poem, "On Being Brought from Africa to America," already contained a barbed attack on white Christians. It suggests there were deep roots for her later choice to move out of the white world that she had seemed to adopt.

> Twas Mercy brought me from my *Pagan* land,
> Taught my benighted soul to understand
> That there's a God, that there's a *Saviour* too:
> Once I redemption neither sought nor knew.
> Some view our sable race with scornful eye,
> "Their colour is diabolic die."
> Remember, *Christians, Negroes,* black as *Cain,*
> May be refin'd and join th' angelic train.[34]

Jupiter Hammon also appears to have been a black Christian with a white world view. His "Penetential Cries" (1760) was particularly intended for slaves, but his message, at least as published, suggests his world view was close to the white one, or as Timothy Smith would have it, the apostolic (white) view. Hints of African indirection and irony do emerge in his poetry. A charming wordplay between a master and his dutiful servant begins with the master calling on the slave to follow him first and Christ second. The slave, in response, begins by "praying" for the master. To "pray for" one is a classic double-edged phrase—one could "pray for" the death of the individual involved and still be praying for him.

Afro-Americans clearly translated the African witch doctor curse into Christian terms. Voudouists accepted petitions to bring about evil and death, and good black Christians prayed for evil to befall their enemies. They found biblical justification for their understanding. (Sojourner Truth was certain her "prayer" had caused the murder of a member of the family that had taken her son Peter South to slavery.) To pray was also part of the "magical" phrase by which a slave was supposed to signify his submission when being beaten. If he or she would shout out "Pray, master," it was expected that the white master would stop the beating. In Hammon's poem the slave has the last word, putting Christ before his earthly master: "Let every soul obey his word/And seek the joy of heav'n. Finis." In body Hammon remained a slave, but in spirit he was free.[35]

Several Northern blacks were prominent preachers "to whites," and it can be posited that they essentially shared their parishioners' white world view. The black Congregationalist Lemuel Haynes, 1753-1833 (see illustration) was very successful in New England and was widely perceived as a preacher first and as a black second. Fathered by an African, he was bound out by his white mother to a pious white deacon named Haynes. Lemuel Haynes studied, preached, served in the Revolution, and returned to marry a white woman whom he had converted. He served congregations in Torrington, Connecticut, Rutland and Manchester, Vermont, and was invited to preach from many other pulpits in white churches. Haynes was known for his learning and for his anti-Universalism; neither blacks nor slavery seems to have been of special concern to him in his ministry. On the one occasion he is known to have mentioned Africans and their tribulations in America, he spoke of Afro-Americans as if he were not one of them.

Several of the most prominent blacks who were known to preach to whites moved back and forth between world views and generally settled with a black view in apparent recognition of their roots and destiny.

Black Reverend Haynes Preaching to a White Congregation,
Early Nineteenth-Century American Tray
Source: Museum of Art, Rhode Island School of Design,
Gift of Miss Lucy Truman Aldrich.

Richard Allen, Samuel Ringgold Ward, and Henry Highland Garnet were all accepted to some degree in the white world but found their home in the black.[36]

Southern blacks also moved into the white world. The example of the black Presbyterian John Chavis, who was both a preacher to white adults and a teacher to the children of leading South Carolina white families, is perhaps the most famous. Chavis was born free circa 1763, lived in Virginia, served in the Revolutionary War, was tutored in Princeton, New Jersey, and was licensed by the Lexington, Virginia, Presbytery in November 1800 on his presentation of a Latin biblical exegesis. He was a popular circuit preacher in North Carolina during 1801-1809, and numerous whites and blacks were converted at his meetings. By 1808, Chavis was running both a day school for prominent upper-class white students, who boarded with his family in Raleigh, and a separate evening school for blacks. Repressive North Carolina legislation passed in 1831 (in the wake of the Nat Turner revolt) silenced Chavis, and he ended his life in dire poverty. Nevertheless, he seemed to have retained a white world view, for he continued to oppose immediate emancipation and regarded slavery as God's means of bringing the African to Christianity.[37]

The black Henry Evans established a Methodist church in Fayetteville, North Carolina, around 1785. The whites who came to observe were so impressed that they joined the church in increasing numbers and eventually pushed the blacks into a side shed. Evans, a free itinerant preacher (a shoemaker by trade) who was born in Virginia, had taken on the mission in Fayetteville as his God-given task. When he became very successful, he was willing to take a subservient second place and to allow whites to take over the institution he had established. His public demeanor was self-effacing in the extreme, and whites always found him "properly respectful."

The white world view was even approximated among Southern black Baptists. Several Southern black Baptist churches would not allow slaves into their fellowship, and even after the war they would not allow ex-slaves to join. The distinction was clearly not based on color but on world view. Elam Church in Charles City, Virginia, was a church for free blacks only and was distinguished by both blacks and whites as very different from slave or mixed churches.[38]

Several black Baptist preachers in the South—William Lemon, Jacob Bishop, and especially Joseph Willis—played important roles in white circles. Either they were functioning with white world views, or the black Baptist Sacred Cosmos sufficiently overlapped with the white Baptist Sacred Cosmos to enable some charismatic figures to function in and with both communities.[39]

While only a small group of black Baptist preachers led whites on a permanent basis, many Southern black preachers preached to white congregations and converted white seekers. Moreover, blacks dominated joint revival meetings as well as joint church services. Black vision experiences, or travels, often dominated mixed church meetings, and black dialogue and singing often filled mixed churches.

The Baptist Sacred Cosmos of the Southern whites reached coherence while in close contact with blacks so that it, too, incorporated African elements. These elements can be seen chiefly in the dialogue structure of the Southern sermon and in the emotional tone of the ritual life. It is possible, however, that African ideas of spirit, its reality and its visible presence, also influenced whites.[40] With evidence of Christ visiting blacks all around them—Christ talking with blacks and leading blacks in their journeys—believing whites who accepted these converts had to be affected.

part III | *Nobody knows but Jesus: the coherent Afro-Christian world view*

6

THE NEW AFRO-BAPTIST SACRED COSMOS

I

Blacks began joining Baptist congregations as they spread through the South and soon formed their own black congregations as well. As suggested earlier, they were welcomed into an almost equal fellowship with the whites. They were not judged on their ability to memorize a simple catechism such as the Anglicans required; they had *to be* something. The challenge and the rewards were much greater. They had to be Christians reborn through the love of Jesus Christ. They had to retell their spirit travels and symbolize their death and rebirth in "drowning" and yet live again. While many feared this act, they nevertheless had ecstatic experiences during and as a result of baptism in the "living waters." They were rewarded by knowing that God was with them.[1]

An extraordinary recording of a contemporary black baptismal ecstasy can be heard on Allen Lomax's *Sounds of the South.* Reverend W. A. Donaldson of the St. James Baptist Church in Huntsville, Alabama, in baptizing his own teenage daughter, calls on God: "Lord, I need you, right now, I need you." Together with the deacons and the congregation, he works up the spirit. They are in a high state of excitement, shouting without set words but with great form and rhythm. Then there is sudden laughter, which breaks the tension, and the girl is bowed down and baptized in the name of the Father, Son, and Holy Ghost. She emerges from her total submersion shouting "Blessed Jesus, thank you Jesus" over and over and over. Her voice rises to near hysteria, and there is rhythmic beating and singing to back her up. She is "coming through" with a spiritual experience prepared for and expected but real and overwhelming nevertheless.[2]

There was a somewhat similar traditional initiation bath for mediums in Africa, but in keeping with the different expectation of a dominating spirit, the African herbal bath was intended to "render one lethargic" so that the divinity might come into the initiate's mind. Donaldson was anything but lethargic; perhaps manic would be the most proper descriptive term![3]

The ecstatic "shouts" of blacks, such as Donaldson's, were not unknown to whites. Davenport and his followers in the First Great Awakening were known for their "screamings, crying, swooning, and fits." According to his critics in Boston, they went "singing all the way thro' the streets, he with his hands extended, his head thrown back, and his eyes staring up to Heaven, attended with so much disorder that they look'd more like a Company of Bacchanalians after a mad frolick, than sober Christians who had been worshipping God."[4]

At revivals, white shouts became the norm. At Gasper River, Kentucky (1799), "many fell to the ground and lay powerless, groaning, praying, and crying for mercy." Reverend James McCready remembered that he ran among the log benches "shouting and exhorting with all possible energy and ecstasy." Many observers remembered shouting, laughing, weeping, and shaking. There was clearly a white shout, although it was occasionally called the "singing exercise" "in which the worshipper chanted melodiously to the captivation of those nearby, and in which the sound issued entirely from the breast, and not the nose or throat." This white shout may have been related to the black practice; it is likely that American whites developed their attenuated form, which had European roots, under the unconscious influence of black practices. The black form of the shout is far more ritualized and, taken together with the evidence of the role of music and dance in African religion, it is clearly an African form which was brought to America and penetrated by Christian meaning.

Africans recognized the drum beat as a form of symbolic language. The Dogon call the drums the ears of the spirit and believe their sound was given to man by God as the "third word." The rhythm of the primal smithy, hammering out consciousness, shook and reverberated in the earth, transforming being. Africans respect this rhythm of being and celebrate it in dance.

Rhythmic drumming, dancing, and singing are known to directly stimulate altered states of consciousness. Unlike the first call of God which generally came when the seeker was alone, subsequent travels of the soul would usually take place in the congregation during these shouts, stimulated by rhythmic beating.

It was on the South Carolina Sea Islands that the ring-shout found an integral place in black Baptist ritual. This amalgam of African and Christian ritual can be posited to have had far wider application in an earlier period. Remnants of ring-shouts found in Virginia, Alabama, Florida, and Georgia demonstrate the widespread, if not ubiquitous, use of this ritualized preparation for the frenzy which was variously known as the Flower Dance, the Rope Dance, Rocking Daniel, or simply "the shout." Thomas Higginson's 1862 description was of an old practice that had been sheltered on the isolated islands but was moving with the black soldiers into the Civil War army camps:

> [F]rom a neighboring cook-fire comes the monotonous sound of that strange festival, half pow-pow, half prayer-meeting, which they know only as a "shout". These fires are usually enclosed in a little booth, made neatly of palm leaves and covered in at top, a regular native African hut, in short, such as is pictured in books, and such as I once got up from dried palm leaves for a fair at home. This hut is now crammed with men, singing at the top of their voices, in one of their quaint, monotonous, endless, negro-Methodist chants, with obscure syllables recurring constantly and slight variations interwoven, all accompanied with a regular drumming of the feet and clapping of the hands, like castanets. Then the excitement spreads: inside and outside the enclosure men begin to quiver and dance, others join, a circle forms, winding monotonously round some one in the centre; some "heel and toe" tumultuously, others merely tremble and stagger on, others stoop and rise, others whirl, others caper sideways, all keep steadily circling like dervishes; spectators applaud special strokes of skill; my approach only enlivens the scene; the circle enlarges, louder grows the singing, rousing shouts of encouragement come in, half bacchanalian, half devout, "wake 'em, brudder!" "Stan' up to 'em, brudder!"— and still the ceaseless drumming and clapping, in perfect cadence, goes steadily on. Suddenly there comes a sort of snap and the spell breaks, amid general sighing and laughter. And this not rarely and occasionally, but night after night, while in other parts of the camp the soberest prayers and exhortations are proceeding sedately.

In moving into the army camps a slight popularization or change in the shout occurred. On the islands more direct prayers and hymns were included, as we can visualize from Allen's 1865 description:

> The true "shout" takes place on Sundays or on "praise" nights through the week, and either in the praise-house or in some cabin in which a regular religious meeting has been held. Very

likely more than half the population of the plantation is gathered together. Let it be the evening, and a lightwood fire burns red before the door of the house and on the hearth. For some time one can hear, though at good distance, the vociferous exhorta- · tion or prayer of the presiding elder or of the brother who has a gift that way, and who is not "on the back seat,"—a phrase, the interpretation of which is "under the censure of the church authorities for bad behavior;"—and at regular intervals one hears the elder "deaconing" a hymnbook hymn, which is sung two lines at a time, and whose wailing cadences, borne on the night air, are indescribably melancholy. But the benches are pushed back to the wall when the formal meeting is over, and old and young, men and women, sprucely-dressed young men, grotesquely half-clad fieldhands—the women generally with gay hankerchiefs twisted about their heads and with short skirts— boys with tattered shirts and men's trousers, young girls bare-footed, all stand up in the middle of the floor, and when the "sperichil" is struck up, begin first walking and by-and-by shuffling round, one after the other, in a ring. The foot is hardly taken from the floor and the progression is mainly due to a jerking hitching motion, which agitates the entire shouter, and soon brings out streams of perspiration. Sometimes they dance silently, sometimes as they shuffle they sing the chorus of the spiritual, and sometimes the song itself is also sung by the dancers. But more frequently a band, composed of some of the best singers and of tired shouters, stand at the side of the room to "base" the others, singing the body of the song and clapping their hands together or on the knees. Song and dance are alike extremely energetic, and often, when the shout lasts into the middle of the night, the monotonous thud, the thud of feet prevents sleep within half a mile of the praise-house.

The black Baptists kept the holy dance in their tradition, even though they accepted the Baptist injunction against dancing. So long as the mover did not cross his feet he was not dancing! Shuffling, stamping, even jumping and running, were all right. Even in the middle of ecstatic experiences, believers were expected to maintain the discipline. Lomax states that deacons were given the responsibility of being watchmen. If shouters crossed their feet, the deacon was to call out: "Look out, sister, how you walk on the Cross,/Your foot might slip and your soul get lost."

In Georgia, it was reported that the traditional African drum was used for shouters' ring-dances until the Stono Rebellion (South Carolina, 1739) when its association with black violence led to its banning. Thereafter, a broomstick or simply heel tapping took its place.

Shouting, involving movement and ecstatic yells, was a carryover from the ritual surrounding the ecstasy of the possessed medium. Black Baptists maintained that, much as every believer had to have direct experience with Jesus, everyone could shout. W. E. B. DuBois grouped all these vocal aspects of black religious celebration together and called them "the frenzy": "It varied in expression from the silent rapt countenance or the low murmur and moan to the mad abandon of physical fervor—the stamping, shrieking, and shouting, the rushing to and fro and wild waving of arms, the weeping and laughing, the vision and the trance." However, under the pressure of white values and practices the unity of the frenzy was broken, and vocal aspects of shouting were sometimes separated from the dancing.[5]

In the folklore of the Cincinatti blacks, it was told that a black brother, striving to contain his shouts in deference to the white members of his mixed congregation, burst a blood vessel. As a result, the blacks decided they had to have a private black church where they would feel free to shout.

Even though they themselves employed a shout at revivals, many whites found the frenzy both frightening and revolting. White preacher Robert Ryland proudly reported in 1855 that the blacks in his large all-black Virginia congregation had adopted decorous "scientific singing," "learning to avoid habits of *whining, snuffling, grunting, drawling, repeating,* hicoughing, and other vulgarities." It can be assumed that he was describing shout practices and that such ecstatic behavior was uncivilized in his eyes.

In 1819, John F. Watson published a strong attack on "extravagant" practices among Methodists. He singled out the African-Methodist shout and ring-dance practices (which he claimed had "already visibly affected the religious manners of some whites") as particularly distasteful.

The whites were not the only ones appalled by black frenzy. African Methodist Bishop Daniel Payne attended a black "bush meeting" where there was a "Prayer and Singing Band." He objected to their activity and forcibly tried to stop their "Fist and Heel Worshipping." "After the sermon they formed a ring, and with coats off, sung, clapped their hands and stamped their feet in a most ridiculous and heathenish way." The group was very sullen when Payne demanded they desist. Payne later talked to the leader of the ring, who insisted that "the Spirit of God works upon people in different ways. At camp-meeting there must be a ring here, a ring there, a ring over yonder, or sinners will not get converted." Payne met such bands in many places and always objected to their "disgusting" practices.

The black Methodist Richard Allen was equally critical of what he recognized as African carryovers in Christian worship. He rejected groaning, shouting, clapping, ring-dancing, and all such activity. Music itself became suspect. When, in the 1840s, "decorous music" was brought into the AME church, many older "sanctified" members could not tolerate it and left.[6]

In stark contrast, the Baptists approved the use of the ring-dance and the shout for Christian purposes. One should shout for Christian joy here on earth as one will shout in Heaven. "Getting happy!" was taken as a description of religious ecstasy, and it was expected to manifest itself in "shouting" and "mourning"—a special form of humming that probably had an African origin as well. Frederick Douglass thought these sounds came out of the slavery experience. They had a special meaning for him as for most blacks: "The hearing of those wild notes always depressed my spirit, and filled me with ineffable sadness. I have frequently found myself in tears while hearing them."

White Baptist preacher and historian David Benedict had only praise for black music. He preached at black Reverend Jacob Walker's Springfield African Church "a number of times" and "with much satisfaction." He found "the most interesting part of their *modus operandi* was, to see the exhorters, or lay preachers, and their excellent band of singers, carry on a conference meeting, after the preaching services were closed." Here, as on the Sea Islands, the shout was a second separate part of the religious ritual, symbolically separating the Baptist and African aspects and yet exhibiting the interpenetration of the two aspects.

The ring-shout "Rock Daniel" closed the services at St. Ann's Primitive Baptist Church in Delano, Florida, as recently as at the turn of the twentieth century. After washing each other's feet, the members formed a circle, with a leader in the center, and began to sing "Rock Daniel":

> Gradually they move round in a circle, single file, then begin to clap hands and fall into a regular step or motion, which is hard to describe. Finally when they have come worked up to a high state of excitement, and almost exhausted, the leader gives a signal and they disperse.[7]

In vision travels, blacks "began to shout and praise God with the rest of the angels," and after visions believer after believer went about "shouting and happy." In fact, black Baptists believed that "whenever the spirit begins to play on the main altar of your heart, you will cry out no matter where you are or what people say."

Black Methodists continued to do "the holy dance," although they were "forbidden by the preachers." Insofar as possible, they hid the practice from white eyes. Frederika Bremer witnessed the letting go and the pain of attempted containment in Georgia in 1850. Blacks in ecstatic dance stopped as she came in. A black hoarsely exclaimed "O! I wish I could Hollo'," and a black congregation "all dressed in white [were] striking themselves on the breast and crying out with the greatest pathos."

In the old days, the shouters easily responded to sensitive associations. The Baptists did not restrain themselves; they moved so violently in trances that others in the congregation would have to try to hold them down:

> It took some good ones to hold [Aunt Kate] down when she got started. Anytime Uncle Link [the Preacher] or any other preacher *touched along the path she had traveled* she would jump and holler. . . . The old ones in them times walked over benches and boxes with their eyes fixed on heaven. God was in the midst of them.

The "spirit would begin to move on the inside" and the body would move on the outside. While the old ring-dance was not preserved by most congregations (although some continued it in secret), the ecstatic shout that had been worked up in its midst was perpetuated, and the blacks sang out: "you will feel this ol' earth rock an' reel."

> I wonder where's my dear mother
> She's been gone so long
> I think I hear her shouting
> Around the Throne of God.
>   . . .
> Know you shoutin' happy, so sit down.[8]

The black Baptist experiences with shouting reported by Lomax in the twentieth century echo those of the nineteenth century:

> Reverend: When the ole spirit hit you, honey, I'm gonna tell you the truth, you're not of yourself. I've knowed it to trip people, send um to the floor.
>
> His wife: I've hollered myself—Oh' it hurt me so.
>
> Reverend: Once I had to help pick up a woman that had the spirit and it hit me—"Wham!"—like that, so I couldn't help but holler out "Glory!"
>
> His wife: But you never really hurt nobody if you got the spirit, no matter how much you shout.
>
> Reverend: I don't know about that. I grabbed my first wife one time when she was shoutin'. Then I didn't have no religion. That

woman jerk me across every bench in church. I turnt her loose.
I said I'll never grab that fool again.

His wife: That's cause you didn't have religion. You didn't know
how to handle her. Or let her be. Now I have a friend, when she
gets happy at church, she runs. Run and laugh. Did you ever hear
the Holy Spirit laughin'? And Lord, she'll run up and down the
aisle till she feel satisfied, just *laughin'* hard as she can.
Diggy-diggy-diggety-dig! She'll have her own way over everyone
and everything. And don't you touch her. She don't like that.
Just let her be—to shout. . . .

Reverend: Better let her alone! I 'member one time old Deacon
Jones got to shoutin' so that he actually flew around the altar,
not a hand or foot touchin'.⁹

While the churches on the Sea Islands had set days for ring-shouts,
the more generalized excitements of the less isolated Baptist churches
might occur at any meeting—regular Sunday, weekday prayer, or monthly
"business" or "experience" meetings.

As has been suggested it is likely that the practice of the Sea Islands
preserved forms generally followed in an earlier period, giving these
practices, and the analysis of them, particular importance. Church
members on the Islands regularly prayed to Jesus to harm enemies:

Me Jedus (Jesus) help me ful fool de man! Uh put me finguh een
de man' eye, en' 'e nebbuh ketch me.

W'en de man ketch me een 'e house 'en 'e hab 'e razor een 'e
han', Gawd, tangle' de man' foot, en' help me foh git 'way.

Besides their central church building, the Baptists of the Sea Islands used
local plantation meeting houses several evenings a week for ring-shouts.
The usual name given them is Praise Houses, but in a careful study of
religion on the Sea Islands Lawton concluded they should properly be
called "de Pray's house," the place "way oner go fur pray." At these
houses, prayers to God were very personal, and it was expected that God
would respond to every request made by "his chillun." Harriet Ware
described a Pray's house on Port Royal in the 1860s as "a little
chapel . . . made very roughly of boards whitewashed, covered with straw,
rough wooden benches, the pulpit and altar made in the same way, but
covered entirely with the grey moss." At Pray's house meetings,
"seekin' " and "trabelin' " were very important, and the aura supposedly

given off by visions was crucial: black meant the devil's work and white God's.

On the Islands, 83 percent of the 1861 population was black (11,000 blacks). For generations they had lived in an unusual state of isolation (for black Americans), and they clearly preserved earlier practices. The rapid change during the war, however, indicates how significantly social patterns could be altered in a short period of time. During the war, blacks on the Islands began to adopt white concepts of singing hymns; instituted a choir; closed their communion to non-Baptists; and tried in general to rapidly alter their "backward" ways, becoming somewhat ashamed of ring-shouts. When Northern teachers and preachers made their first contact with these blacks during the war, they found them to be remarkably spiritual, "favored with the Master's special smiles." Even the children stayed "out in the wilderness" all night long "seeking" God.

As in Africa, the elders of the community, who were literally the oldest members, were given special respect. The Baptist title "elder," given to chosen leaders in the church, paralleled the African meaning, and the two were combined on the Islands. One African-born woman, "Maum Katie," who remembered "her own gods," was over 100 years old in 1861, but she was still an active spiritual leader. African respect for age and African patterns of polite behavior were generally carried over into plantation life and were particularly well preserved on the Sea Islands. Frederick Douglass commented on plantation manners that "a young slave must approach the company of the older with hat in hand and woe betide him, if he fails to acknowledge favor of any sort with the accustomed "tank ee'. etc." The many African kin relationship groupings had been transformed into (1) aunts and uncles for elders (or "Daddy and Maum" in South Carolina) and (2) cousin or brother and sister for equals. These marks of status, respect, and relationship in the slave community strongly preserved an African quality, although brother and sister were also Baptist usages.[10]

As might be expected, Hoodoo or Voodoo was more purely African on the Sea Islands than on the mainland. Charms were called blind gods and were respected; witch doctors were called "guffer doctors" (perhaps after goobers or groundnuts) and were very active. Children, in an African pattern, were not named until the ninth day; and the ability of souls to travel was fully accepted. Babies' spirits were called to follow when on trips and at crossroads, for fear they would leave their young bodies. Troublesomeness in children was seen as resulting from bad spirits, and doors were left open at night so as not to lock spirits out. However, these slaves on the Sea Islands were Christians. They knew Christ and believed he had accepted them personally, as they expressed so beautifully in their spirituals:

> O me no weary yet,
> O me no weary yet.
> I have a witness in my heart
> O me no weary yet.

In the following stanzas, "O me no weary yet":

> Since I been in de field to fight . . .
> I have a heaven to maintain . . .
> De bond of faith are on my soul . . .
> Old Satan toss a ball at me . . .
> Him tink de ball would hit my soul . . .
> De ball for hell and I for heaven . . .
> O me no weary yet.

Some of the African patterns which the Sea Islanders retained functioned as separate entities. The rapid change that occurred during and after the Civil War consisted essentially in the dropping of these African carryovers, which is evidence of their extrinsic nature. They could be shed like an old skin.[11]

The key African understanding which they retained was a spiritual one. In the melding of the African and Baptist Sacred Cosmos that occurred both in plantation congregations and in more acculturated urban areas, the core of the African and of the Baptist world views united to form a new whole. Blacks became Baptists. This union of the two world views was occasionally delayed, in part because of the many African folkways retained. The key retention and the key melding were spiritual phenomena: In the interpenetration of Sacred Cosmos, African concepts were merged with those of white Baptists. As suggested, the African High God and the Christian God became one—a God close to man, but one who still sent messengers to lead his black people home. Spirit force or power was still recognized, but it was exerted by God, Christ, and the Holy Ghost, as well as by holy men. The African idea of separable souls, of the eternal "little me," found a proper place in the Afro-Christian cosmos, and the African goal of resolution and growth could be reached through a Christian life. The only formal African patterns whose retention was significant were those which supported this interpenetration of Sacred Cosmos. Among them were the shout and the moan, the dream and the vision. With the shout and the vision, the black knew his future and he appropriated an African past. His African soul, with its essential inner self, found the means to travel to the Christian heaven while time past became the future.

While the African trance, shout, and vision patterns helped bring the blacks to a Baptist faith, after they created a new black Baptist ethos their need for even these patterns changed. The crucial union of African and Christian world views, which was at a spiritual level, was maintained while many African customs were abandoned. The whites did not realize what was happening, however. They saw the task of missionizing as one of turning blacks "away from their dance around the Devil Bush" and of dispelling superstitions. When blacks accepted Christ, whites assumed they would share the white world view. Although the blacks did become *"clear in the grand doctrines of the Gospel"* (as a white commented about an early black preacher), they reflected their melding of the two cosmos in their prayers, songs, and practices.[12]

In plantation Creole, a black said to a white owner, "You no holy" but "We be holy. You in no state o salvation." Dillard comments that here Pauline theology finds adequate expression in Creole, the use of the *be* meaning the convert was in a permanent state of grace, while "You no holy" implied the white owner could yet *be* holy or "conversion is not permanently withheld." Plantation slaves prayed: "Make he good, like he say/Make he say, like he good,/Make he say, like he good, like he God," which is interpreted as "Make him, good as his doctrine, make his doctrine as pure as his life, and may both be in the likeness of his God."[13]

II

There is a Twi maxim that if you want to talk to God "Tell it to the wind." In Africa, God is certainly not seen as the wind, but His spirit is recognized as being in it, all around us. The Afro-American spiritual "Hold the Wind" suggests that the black Christian saw himself as having a new hold on this God. This was a new relationship in which the spiritually free black had great power, although the familiarity with God echoes the African familiarity with the divinities:

> When I get to Heaven, gwine be at ease
> Me and my God gonna do as we please.
> Gonna chatter with the Father, argue with the Son,
> Tell un 'bout the world I just come from.
> Hold the wind, hold the wind,
> Hold the wind, don't let it blow,
> Hold the wind, hold the wind,
> Hold the wind, don't let it blow.[14]

A most extraordinary black church covenant from one of the earliest all-black churches in the eighteenth century has been preserved. The covenant of George Liele's Yama Craw (Georgia) church, constituted in December 1777, provides a concise introduction to the gamut of black Baptist beliefs and practices and an approach to the black cosmos through the words of blacks. It is, therefore, reprinted in full; the salient points it raises are discussed below in relation to their wider ramifications in the black community.

The COVENANT OF THE ANABAPTIST CHURCH, begun in America, December 1777, and in Jamaica, December 1783.

I.   We are of the Anabaptist persuasion, because we believe it agreeable to the scriptures. Matth. iii, 1,2,3,—2 Cor. vi, 14-18.

II.   We hold to keep the Lord's day throughout the year, in a place appointed for Public Worship, in singing psalms, hymns, and spiritual songs, and preaching the Gospel of Jesus Christ. Mark xvi. 2-6, Coll. iii, 16.

III.   We hold to be baptised in a river, or in a place where there is much water, in the name of the Father, and of the Son, and of the Holy Ghost. Matth. iii, 13-17 Mark xvi, 15, 16. Matth. xxviii, 19.

IV.   We hold to receiving the Lord's Supper in obedience according to his commands. Mark xiv, 22-24. John vi, 53-57.

V.   We hold to the ordinance of washing one another's feet. John xiii, 2-17.

VI.   We hold to receive and admit young children into the Church, according to the word of God. Luke ii, 27, 28. Mark x, 35-16.

VII.   We hold to pray over the Sick, anointing them with oil in the name of the Lord. James v. 54, 15.

VIII.   We hold to labouring one with another according to the word of God. Matth. xviii, 15-18.

IX.   We hold to appoint Judges and such other Officers among us to settle any matter according to the word of God. Acts vi, 1-3.

X.   We hold not to the shedding of blood. Genesis ix. 6. Matth. xxvi, 51, 52.

XI.   We are forbidden to go to law one with another before the unjust, but to settle any matter we have before the Saints. I. Cor. vi, 1-3.

XII.   We are forbidden to swear not at all. Matth. v, 33-37. James v, 12.

XIII.   We are forbidden to eat blood, for it is the life of a creature, and from things strangled, and from meat offered to idols. Acts. xv, 29.

XIV.   We are forbidden to wear any costly raiment, such as superfluity. I. Peter, iii, 3,4.

XV.   We permit no slaves to join the church without first having a few lines from their owners of their good behaviour. I. Peter, ii, 13-16. I. Thess. iii, 13.

XVI.   To avoid Fornication, we permit none to keep each other, except they be married according to the word of God. I Cor. vii, 2. Heb. xiii, 4.

XVII.   If a slave or servant misbehave to their owners they are to be dealt with according to the word of God. I. Tim. i, 6. Eph. vi, 5. I. Pet. ii, 18-21. Titus ii, 9-11.

XVIII.   If any one of this Religion should transgress and walk disorderly, and not according to the Commands which we have received in this covenant, he will be censured according to the word of God. Luke xii, 47, 48.

XIX.   We hold, if a brother or sister should transgress any of these articles, written in this covenant, so as to become a swearer, a fornicator, or adulterer; a covetous person, an idolator, a railer, a drunkard, an extortioner, or whoremonger; or should commit any abominable sin, and do not give satisfaction to the Church, according to the word of God, he or she, shall be put away from among us, not to keep Company, nor to eat with him. I. Cor. v, 11-13.

XX.   We hold if a Brother or Sister should transgress, and abideth not in the doctrine of Christ, and he or she, after being justly dealt with, agreeable to the 8th article, and be put out of the Church, that they shall have no right or claim whatsoever to be interred into the Burying-ground during the time they are put out, should they depart life but should they return in peace, and make a concession, so as to give satisfaction, according to the word of God, they shall be received into the Church again and have all privileges as before granted. 2 John. i, 9,10. Gal. vi, 1-2. Luke xvii, 3-4.

XXI.   We hold to all other Commandments, Articles, Covenants, and Ordinances, recorded in the Holy Scriptures, as are set forth by our Lord and Master, Jesus Christ, and his Apostles, which are not written in this Covenant, and to live to them as nigh as we possible can, agreeable to the word of God. John xv, 7-14.[15]

These "Ethiopian Anabaptists," as they saw themselves, understood their Christianity as a complete break with idol worship. As the scriptural basis for their faith, they cited 2 Corinthians, vi: 14-18:

Be yet not unequally yoked together with unbelievers: for what fellowship has righteousness with unrighteousness? And what communion hath light with darkness?
And what concord hath Christ with Belial? or what part hath he that believeth with an infidel?
And what agreement hath the temple of God with idols?
For ye are the temple of the living God; as God hath said,
I will dwell in them, and walk in *them;* and I will be their God, and they shall be my people.
Wherefore come out from among them and be you separate, saith the Lord, and touch not the unclean *thing;* and I will receive you.
And will be a Father unto you, and ye shall be my sons and daughters, saith the Lord Almighty.

Black Baptists knew that their faith separated them from other blacks. They specifically barred the drinking of blood and the eating of strangled creatures or meat offered to idols (item XIII) because these were still prevalent black practices. Voudouists shared blood at initiations and offered food to idols, even into the twentieth century.

The black Baptists were visibly cut off from other Afro-Americans by their initiation into an almost "secret Christian society" by means of river baptism. "I heard the voice of Jesus say,/Behold I freely give/the Living water; thirsty one,/Stoop down and drink and live." Once separated from other blacks, they marked their communion with water and light by "singing psalms, hymns, and spiritual songs, and preaching the Gospel of Jesus Christ." We have seen that the singing incorporated the African moan or groan, and that even the sheep in heaven were heard to echo this sound. This moan was not a sorrowful one but a "kind of blissful or ecstatic rendition of a song or prayer, often interlaced with humming and spontaneous melodic variations and improvisation": "When you feel like moanin',/It ain't nothin' but love. . . ./When you feel like groanin', It ain't nothin' but love."[16]

The extraordinary singing of blacks has been widely analyzed. While Jackson and others have concluded that both the music and words in black songs can be traced to whites, nearly every white person who heard slaves sing commented on their unique quality. The unique quality was an African one, brought into the hymn and into the Christian experience, influencing whites as well. In 1775, Samuel Davies termed black singing "a seraphic exercise" and "a kind of ecstatic Delight in Psalmody." Nearly 100 years later, the perceptive Frederika Bremer concluded that "one must see these people singing if one is rightly to understand their life." Isaac Watts' hymns, as well as popular Baptist and Methodist folk hymns, were all "blackened," which radically altered their character. Jackson's exceptionally thorough study of black and white music, which is intended to show the parallelism and dependence of black songs on white songs, inadvertently indicates their radical difference. In addition to altering the essential character of white music, blacks added a whole new range of hymns. Their subjects were the key black Baptist experiences—the stealing away to pray, the baptism in the River Jordan, the appropriation of the history of Israel and its heroes and the close climax-relationship with Jesus.[17]

As has been well documented and much analyzed, a West African pattern of dialogue permeated the song and the sermon and had great affect on the culture of both black and white Baptists. The response and involvement of both parties are essential to the "conversation," and the holy dialogue with Christ shared in this tradition, influencing speech, the telling of folktales, singing, and sermons. Constant response enlivened and affected the character of them all. This black style was not unrelated to content: truth was arrived at in dialogue, and in a dialectical development, which had a rhythm that built to a climax and then came down. In the sermon as in the singing, the leader set the tone but allowed for group participation and innovation. Only if the group responded could leader and group have a meaningful experience.

Black Baptist sermons used the life and experiences of blacks to understand the gospel. They talked in terms that were not unlike those used by Jesus and that became the popular Baptist sermon style. Popular white Baptist Jacob Knapp preached of God as the father of many children; of the "Lesson taught by the Ox" and of the other homely everyday lessons that should bring one to a new birth. He, too, called for the Christian to be consumed by his love for Christ; to appear "beside himself" with enthusiasm and excitement; to "brave the ridicule of the world." His homely example was the tale of Noah. What did the local people, who knew Noah, think of him? Knapp suggests that a contemporary of Noah's, an innkeeper, might say:

> Well, there are different opinions about him. Some think him crazy, others say he is a downright hypocrite, desirous of making a stir in the world. Others surmise that he has some great speculation in view; but most people give him the credit of being sincere, but laboring under a delusion. He certainly warns the people of the approaching flood, sometimes with tears; and I know that he has expended a fortune in the enterprise, and is up early and late.

Blacks used a similar style to bring the Bible into the lives of their congregations. When the Baptist slave preacher John Jasper talked of Adam, he, too, became the man next door. When the devil tempted Eve,

> Adam worn't wid her; doan know whar he wuz,—gorn bogin' orf sumwhars. He better bin at home tendin' ter his fambly. Dat ain' de only time, by a long shot, dat dar haz bin de debbul ter pay at home wen de man hev gorn gaddin' eroun', instid uv stayin' at home an' lookin' arter his fambly.[18]

Black sermons and spirituals placed Christianity in the present. Adam was next door, Jezebel was a present danger, Jesus a friend to share burdens with, and Moses the ever-expected emancipator. How did this living Christianity affect the life of a slave? Did it alter his values and life choices? Was he to wait patiently for Moses? Was Christianity a major support of slave accommodation?

The Covenant of Leile's 1777 black Baptist church, which gives the church the power and duty to discipline slaves whose behavior toward owners is improper (Article XVII), suggests that either this black church was accommodationist or that it was seeking to placate potentially antagonistic whites by promising to be a bulwark of the slave system.

The most widely publicized white sermons to slaves cited Ephesians 6:5-8.

> Servants, be obedient to them that are *your* masters according to the flesh, with fear and trembling, in singleness of your heart,

> as unto Christ; Not with eye service, as men pleasers; but as the
> servants of Christ, doing the will of God from the heart;
> With good will doing service, as to the Lord and not to men:
> Knowing that whatsoever good thing any man doeth, the same
> shall he receive of the Lord, whether he be bond or free.

There is much evidence that slaves deeply resented this attempt to justify
slavery as service to God; the white sermons that dwelt on this theme were
the basis for much anti-Christian feeling. Black Christians rarely addressed
themselves to this passage. When the 1777 Liele congregation did cite it,
they added a biblical reference to suffering that suggests that the blacks'
patience is Christlike and their punishment unjust (I Peter 2:20). While
Christianity gave ultimate meaning and purpose to human suffering, the
strength or hope given the Baptist was not simply a hope for life after
death! It was a strength to face a hard life, to know oneself as a free spirit,
and to develop and function to the limit of one's possibilities.[19]

Did the black Baptist world view legitimate antislavery action as
Christian action? As suggested above, most of the religiously awakened
whites of the early period (1740-1800) held strong antislavery views.
Black Christians did not ignore these attitudes, nor did they fail
to reach conclusions of their own.[20] While the Liele church of 1777, and, so
far as is known, all formal black churches in the South, ostensibly accepted
slavery and some even asked for formal owner approval of slave
membership (item XV of the covenant), many blacks repeated the Pauline
message: "Stand fast in the liberty in which God has made you free."
Their understanding of this message has been much debated. Wilmore, for
example, maintains that they assumed that the Pauline message meant
spiritual *and* temporal freedom. It is certain that black Christians
recognized themselves as free already, that is, in soul. This message may
have been a stimulus for some to achieve physical freedom and for others
to accept their slave status. Owners recognized both of these possibilities,
as did the slaves. Henry Bibb recounts that a slave dealer "tried to make it
appear that I was so pious and honest that I would not run away for ill
treatment, which was a gross mistake, for I never had religion enough to
keep me from running away from slavery in my life." Slave preachers who
ran away concurred with Bibbs' statement. Others who stayed slaves had,
as they saw it, "the last laugh" in that they believed whites might be
masters here on earth but "servants" for eternity.[21]

Certainly, some blacks openly equated physical freedom and spiritual
freedom. In the 1770s, a slave preacher, David, educated in England, was
hastily returned there under threat of lynching when he used "unguarded
expressions" in regard to physical liberty in preaching to slaves in
Charleston. In 1807, a Kentucky Baptist church excluded a black woman
who denounced slavery, even though many white Baptists were condemn-

ing the institution. When black Lott Carey was ordained to carry the word of God to Africa (January 1821), his ordination sermon at the Richmond, Virginia, First Baptist Church was a powerful exposition on the liberty of the believer in Christ. As such it was acceptable.[22] If he was intimating that Christians should oppose physical slavery, as I strongly suspect, it was left for the listener to draw this conclusion.

In the North, black churches became open abolitionist platforms, and blacks cited Christian morality as the basis for their antislavery statements in petitions and public papers. Slavery was a painful subject for Northern black Christians, particularly for Northern black Baptists, an increasing percentage of whom were "up from slavery." (Northern black Baptists were generally from the lower class ex-slave population). Northern churches celebrated the end of the slave trade (1808) and the separate abolitions in the Northern states. By 1834, the Albany African Baptist Church had instituted a formal monthly prayer meeting in behalf of "our Southern brethren," and it is likely that other black Baptist churches in the North followed this practice. Reverends Nathaniel Paul of the Albany Baptist Church and Leonard A. Grimes, a Virginia-born free man serving in Boston, became the most famous black Baptist abolitionists, but slavery was a crucial issue for every black Christian. Nathaniel Paul went as far as to stake his soul on abolition. If slavery were to last forever:

> I would deny the superintending power of divine Providence in the affairs of this life; I would ridicule the religion of the Saviour of the World, and treat as the worst of men the ministers of the everlasting gospel; I would consider my bible as a book of false and elusive fables, and commit it to flame; Nay, I would still go further: I would at once confess myself an atheist, and deny the existence of God.[23]

Baptist preacher Israel Campbell, who had himself fled from slavery, made antislavery the core of his Christian message. His erudite abolitionist sermons, given in the Midwest and Canada, were concerned with white prejudice in the North as well. (He recounts that while welcomed by whites as a Baptist minister, he was fed at separate tables and expected to sleep on the floor.) He preached fervently, sang his own abolitionist songs, and was certain God was on his side: The voice of right is crying, is crying,/ The voice of right is crying from above,/Oh, set the captives free!"

By far the most powerful black Christian antislavery statement came from a free Methodist layman, David Walker, who had been able to leave North Carolina because his mother was a free black woman, but whose slave father remained there. In his famous "Appeal" of 1829, Walker warned the white man that God would not tolerate slavery much longer. The Bible was his proof text:

> I tell you Americans!! that unless you speedily alter your course, *you* and your Country are gone!!!!! For God Almighty will tear up the very face of the earth!!! Will not that very remarkable passage of Scripture be fulfilled on Christian Americans? Here it Americans!! He that is unjust, let him be unjust still: and he which is filthy, let him be filthy still: and he that is righteous, let him be righteous still: and he that is holy, let him be holy still.
>
> . . .
>
> I warn you in the name of the Lord (whether you will hear or forbear,) to repent and reform, or you be ruined!!! Do you think that our blood is hiding from the Lord . . . ?

Walker was also hard on his black brothers. Certain that God was at his side, he called them to manhood through battle:

> Are we MEN!! I ask you, O my brethren! are we MEN? Did our creator make us to be slaves to dust and ashes like ourselves? Are they not dying worms as well as we? Have they not to make their appearance before the tribunal of Heaven, to answer for the deeds done in the body, as well as we? Have we any other master but Jesus Christ alone?
>
> . . .
>
> Look upon your mother, wife and children, and answer God Almighty; and believe this, that it is no more harm for you to kill a man, who is trying to kill you than it is for you to take a drink of water when thirsty; in fact, the man who will stand still and let another murder him is worse than an infidel, and, if he has common sense, ought not to be pitied.[24]

Blacks in the South could not take such a stand against physical slavery without risking their lives. Even in Boston, Walker died under suspicious circumstances less than a year after the publication of the "Appeal." Moreover, Southern black leadership was pushed into a far more compromising situation than were their Northern counterparts. In order to continue functioning and to prosper, it was essential that a working relationship be effected with the increasingly defensive proslavery establishment. In this process, many blacks adopted the values of the white society and emerged as supporters of the slave society, and occasionally as slaveholders themselves.[25]

In many cases, Southern whites called upon black Baptist preachers to impose order in the black community. In one respect, this call was a privilege, for the blacks wanted to be self-policing. Moreover, they succeeded in creating essentially the same type of church discipline imposed by and on white Baptist churches. It was an important Baptist tenet that they did not go to law (item XI of 1777 covenant); the church was their court and all matters should be settled within it. When white slaveowners asked the Baptist preachers to "preserve order" among the blacks, however, the social reality was a unique one. If a white was disciplined by a church, he expected it to end at that. If the black did not do what was expected of him, he might, in addition to church disciplining, expect punishment by his owner or the civil authorities. However, the issue was generally not one of seeking to control or punish a particular act, but rather of establishing values that the whites believed in.

John Jones, a free man and an ordained minister to the "colored people" at the First African Baptist Church of Shreveport, Louisiana, between 1856 and 1877, "exercised great influence over his race, and did more to preserve order among them than all the police of the city." When legislation passed during the Civil War against free blacks not born in Alabama led him to leave the state, "it was found that the influence of his example was so essential in preserving order among the blacks that the Legislature . . . passed a special act recalling him."

Uncle Jack in Virginia, who died in 1843 at a very advanced age, was an African-born slave preacher who built a successful Baptist church and large congregation. He was reputed to have such influence that owners referred recalcitrant slaves to him, in that he was more feared than they were. Similarly, Loudon Ferrill, a black Baptist preacher in Lexington, Kentucky, from 1821 until his death in 1854, was "more potent" than the police and the city recognized his worth by subsidizing his salary.

Andrew Bryan of Savannah, ordained in 1788 and a pastor until his death in 1812, was also employed to support the owner's "rightful" position. "Bryan was often sent for by the mistress to correct an offending maid or by a master for a servant. . . . Being threatened with a debarring of their Christian privileges insured their faithfulness to the household duties better than the older harsher means." In his comment on Bryan, Simms suggests the complex role of the black leader. He was not simply a "handkerchief head" or an Uncle Tom trying to placate the owner; a compromise or an act of contrition might save an individual from sale or punishment. Many of the leading black preachers, as well as the whites who preached to blacks, tried to serve both communities. Theirs was a very difficult task under any conditions, and, as Genovese reminds us, the interrelationship that was worked out affected the character of both sides.[26]

The charge that Christianity abetted social conformism made by Benjamin Mays, Gold Refined Wilson, and others, did contain an element of truth. Nevertheless, in the slave period whites feared the revolutionary equality preached by Baptists and Methodists, as well as the opportunity for fellowship and conspiracy afforded by religious meetings. Contemporaries claimed that recruiting for the "near insurrection" led by Gabriel Prosser in Richmond in 1800 took place at Sunday meetings, and the Bible was cited as his sourcebook in regard to freedom. Indeed, Ben Woolfolk, a coconspirator, spoke of his cause as "similar to [that of the] Israelites." Mullin, however, concludes that the planned insurrection failed precisely because it did not have a sufficiently religious dimension.[27]

Denmark Vesey and almost all of his principal associates in planning a rebellion in Charleston in 1822 were members of the African (Methodist) Church, and two were even class leaders. The church was used for recruitment, and its meetings were a place for passing the "news." Vesey, a West Indian or African-born ex-slave carpenter of good reputation, was known as a Bible-quoter, but, as a young white neighbor testified, "all his religious remarks were mingled with slavery." He was cited as quoting Zachariah 14:1-3 and Joshua 4:21, both of which are concerned with the utter destruction of the city of Jerusalem when "the day of the Lord cometh." Vesey and his associates used the Bible as proof texts at meetings of supporters, with Vesey reading "how the children of Israel were delivered out of Egypt from Bondage." This use of the holy word particularly galled whites. It was singled out in the court's death sentence for Vesey. He was accused of "attempting to pervert the sacred words of God into a sanction for crimes of the blackest hue," and he was reminded of Paul's admonition to serve earthly masters "in singleness of your heart." He and his associates were, in part, convicted for their "grossest impiety." As a result of this experience, the white community concluded that no meeting of blacks should thenceforth take place without whites in attendance. The church was closed and black religious activities throughout the region came under increased scrutiny.[28]

While Christianity played an important role in the development of the Vesey plot, the most integral use of Christian imagery and meaning in a slave rebellion occurred in the revolt led by Nat Turner. Nat Turner was a black Baptist, an exhorter and prophet who had heard a call and was responding to it.[29] While he was not a preacher called by a congregation, he did preach. In order to evaluate his role, it is necessary to consider the Baptist preaching tradition.

Lay preaching among the Baptists was not unusual. White and black Baptists believed that all Christians should tell of their experiences and, if called by the Lord, preach His word. The black folklore was rich in comical stories which satirized false calls (such as responding to a mule's braying), and clearly many poor preachers tried to make a place for themselves as church leaders.[30] But many respected and powerful preachers were not ordained or even licensed. The formal church organization recognized floor preachers, licensed preachers, and ordained preachers. In order to be an official preacher, a man needed a license from a church, which could be given for a limited time and specific area, or for a far more extensive outreach. Black preachers were licensed by mixed churches as well as by black churches all over the South. They were given the "Liberty to improve their gifts wherever Providence shall open a door." If called by a church to be their presiding elder or minister, a preacher, upon examination by a board of ordained preachers, could be ordained in that church, a status he then gained for life. He was thereby considered part of the apostolic chain, descending from Christ.[31] At least 106 black Baptist preachers were ordained prior to the Civil War. The earliest known ordination of a black took place in 1788 when Andrew Bryan was ordained by white Abraham Marshall. (There is a possibility that four slave preachers—Moses, Benjamin and Thomas Gardiner, and Farrell— were ordained in 1774 by white John Michaels at their church on the Byrd plantation in Virginia.) White Baptists generally held that slaves should not be ordained, but whenever the question was formally raised they decided that free blacks had every right to ordination. In 1821, the First Baptist Church of Lexington, Kentucky, asked the Elkhorn Association meeting: "Is it admissible by the Association to ordain free men of colour ministers of the Gospel?" In 1822, a committee of five ministers unequivocally replied: "They know of no reason why free men of colour may not be ordained ministers of the Gospel, the Gospel qualifications being possessed by them." The question was not academic. It had arisen in relation to Loudin Ferrill, a black preacher, who was subsequently ordained by the First Baptist Church of Lexington to serve at the First African Church in that city.[32]

Many white and black Baptists preached without ordination, and even without the formal license of a local church. This lay preaching, generally called *exhorting,* became quasi-institutionalized among blacks, partly because formal black preachers were legally banned in several states in the period after the Nat Turner revolt. (Miles Fisher, a slave, was a lay preacher for the black congregation at LaGrange, Georgia, which met in the white church after the whites left or in the summer in a "brush arbor" in the graveyard. He was never allowed in the pulpit, but he was the preacher.) "Chairbacker" (a preacher whose pulpit was a common chair in a slave cabin) and "floor preacher" became common appellations in the last years of slavery, but the custom of lay preaching predates the legal restrictions. Reborn Baptists generally felt the call to preach. There were numerous white and black Baptist exhorters who used "imagination and invention"—metaphors, parables, and allegories based on life rather than on book learning. Both white and black exhorters were reputed to be very emotional, often "even warmer" than licensed preachers, and they were known to have moved many to accept salvation.

Ex-slaves remembered these preachers with great nostalgia. Arrie Binns, born on a plantation in Georgia and about fifteen years old at the end of the war, recalled that "the Chairback fellows went er round preachin' an' singin' in the cabins down in the Quarters and dey use to have the bes' meetin's, folks would be converted an' change dey way. . . . Dem days of real feelin' and keerin' is gone."[33]

Nat Turner, a member of this large group of lay preachers, had an uncommon ability to communicate his convictions to others. Turner's neo-African understanding of spirit power provides an insight into the plantation African/Baptist faith at its most powerful level. Through this faith Turner developed into a charismatic leader, and he and his followers derived the strength to be ready to sacrifice their lives.

The primary source of information on Turner's spiritual development is *The Confession of Nat Turner* . . . , published in 1831 and advertised as a confession "fully and voluntarily made to Thomas R. Gray." This highly interesting document raises many questions, the first of which concerns its reliability. Gray was a Jerusalem, Virginia, lawyer who was appointed by the court to defend several other slaves in the insurrection, but he had no official attachment to Turner himself. On his own initiative, he visited with Turner in his jail cell on November 1-3, 1831. Gray claimed that Turner spoke at length and that "during his statement . . . unnoticed by him, [I had] taken note of some of the particular circumstances" and then cross-examined him. Gray did not claim that *The Confession* was a stenographic copy of Turner's statement, although he later read the statement to Turner in front of witnesses and asserted "that Nat acknowledged the same to be full, free and voluntary."[34]

The language reportedly used by Turner raises difficult problems. The *Richmond Enquirer* of November 22, 1831, was doubtful that the "superior" language of *The Confession* could have been spoken by a slave. But why would Gray want to elevate Turner's image? Why would he want to make him seem more intelligent or "eloquent" than he really was? We must conclude that Turner *was* eloquent. It is probable that Turner used a different rhythm and language than Gray used and, in trying to faithfully portray Turner's visions and power, Gray superimposed his own style.

At one significant point in the narrative, a different English is suddenly introduced, which may well be Turner's authentic language. This passage occurs in the discussion of the voice that Turner heard in the midst of his most important vision (discussed below). However, notwithstanding this evidence of a different English within *The Confession,* the suggestion that Gray substituted his own English may be in error. The language in the rest of *The Confession* may also be authentic. Perhaps Turner did talk of verbal "intercourse with his fellow servants," of "cutaneous eruptions" of "zeal," "austerity," and "studiousness." He knew how to read and write, and he had a Bible and knew it well. The language of the King James version is very eloquent, and he may well have used it as a second language for sermons and for a final confession to a white lawyer.

Turner had contact with both white and black Christians. His childhood master, Benjamin Turner, belonged to the Methodist church; church people visited Benjamin Turner's home and Nat Turner saw them at prayer. They impressed him greatly, for he remembered them vividly many years later. Equally important, his grandmother, to whom he was "much attached," was "very religious."[35] Turner was marked from birth as a person of spiritual potential. This was in a very African tradition, a tradition his mother Nancy, who had been taken from Africa only some five years before his birth, was not very distant from. (His father may also have been born in Africa.) Nat Turner had birthmarks on his head and chest, which both of his parents described as signs of greatness, noting also that at the age of three or four he seemed to have knowledge of events that had occurred prior to his birth. They concluded that spirit was shown to be working through him. Turner grew up with this conviction. Those around him responded to his growing sense of uniqueness, further supporting and stimulating it. Austere, secretive, and a loner, he consciously played a role: "[I] wrapped myself in mystery, devoting my time to fasting and prayer." But clearly he was in contact with Baptist meetings, either on the plantation or at the local Barnes' Baptist Church, and it was the Bible that served to spark a visionary experience:

> Hearing the scriptures commented on at meetings, I was struck with that particular passage which says: "Seek ye the Kingdom of Heaven and all things shall be added unto you." I reflected much on this passage, and prayed daily for light on this subject —As I was praying one day at my plough, the spirit spoke to me, saying "See ye the Kingdom of Heaven and all things shall be added unto you."

When asked in jail what he meant by spirit, Turner responded: "The Spirit that spoke to the prophet in former days." Significantly, Turner used the term *spirit*. In other contexts, Turner spoke of Christ and of trying to take on his yoke, but Christ did not appear to him, as he appeared to many other black Baptists. Nor did he recount any contact with a spirit guide. Pure spirit came to Nat Turner, calling him and giving him "full confirmation" that God had chosen him for "some great purpose."

Turner consciously rejected Voodoo. (He "always spoke of such things with contempt.") However, he communicated with spirit, served it, and learned mysteries from it in a traditional African fashion. While the slaves to whom he spoke of his visions "believed and said my wisdom came from God," they respected him as one who knew how to use spirit-power.

According to *The Confession,* perhaps in 1821 Turner lost his standing with his followers. He had run away and succeeded in staying hidden some thirty days. When he voluntarily returned, his fellow slaves ridiculed him and his powers. Turner explained himsef as a Jonah. He had been seeking to run away from his God-given call to special leadership. He had been thinking of his selfish desires, but he returned to slavery to do his Heavenly Master's will by preparing for insurrection.

Apparently, while alone and away from all he had known, Turner had a vision in which spirit told him to return, to take his punishment, but to do His will. Additional visions came to him: he traveled, seeing the future and hearing his destiny:

> I saw white spirits and black spirits engaged in battle, and the sun was darkened—the thunder rolled in the Heavens, and blood flowed in streams—and I heard a voice saying, *"Such is your luck, such you are called to see, and let it come rough or smooth, you must surely bear it!"*

It is in this decisive revelation of the racial violence to come that his own voice (or his inner voice) seems to break into Gray's narrative. In Gray's account, Turner states that he then increased his social withdrawal as much as the "situation would permit" (although the other slaves may have imposed it upon him):

> for the avowed purpose of *serving the Spirit more fully—and it appeared to me,* and reminded me of the things it had already shown me, and that it would then reveal to me the knowledge of the elements, the revolution of the planets, the operation of the tides, and changes of the seasons.

Turner now walked with spirit; he was given the "true knowledge of faith" and was "made perfect." (His new wisdom recalls that of the Dogon, for whom spirit provided a full knowledge of all natural phenomena.) In his completion, the spirit came to Turner as the Holy Ghost, closer to Christ, but not Christ himself, although he saw the stars as Christ's hands stretched out for the redemption of sinners.

Turner's vision experiences brought him a surety of purpose. Nonetheless, he asked for physical signs for himself and for those around him. Drops of blood like "dew from heaven" appeared to him on the corn, and he showed these to both whites and blacks. "Hieroglyphic characters and numbers" and "forms of men in different attitudes, portrayed in blood'' confirmed his heavenly visions.[36] After the rebellion, Turner's wife was apparently forced to relinquish copies he had made of these signs. The white man who took them wrote that they were ''filled with hieroglyphical characters, conveying no definite meaning. The characters on the oldest paper, apparently appear to have been traced with blood; and on each paper, a crucifix and the sun, is distinctly visible.'' This white man, whom we know only as the contributor of an anonymous letter from Jerusalem dated September 26, 1831, in which he calls himself a busy ''professional man,'' confirmed that Turner was an exhorter who ''had acquired the character of a prophet.'' He himself attributed Turner's signs to trickery:

> Like a Roman Sybil, he traced his divination in characters of blood, on leaves alone in the woods, he would arrange them in some conspicuous place, have a dream telling him of the circumstance; and then send some ignorant black to bring them to him, to whom he would interpret their meaning.

This white informant, who does indeed seem to have known the local situation, acknowledged that Turner ''acquired an immense influence over such persons as he took into his confidence,'' as the events had proved.[37] His followers believed his claim to spirit contact and approval.

The drops of blood were explained to Turner as the blood of Christ ''now returning to earth again in the form of dew.'' The Day of Judgment was at hand. A spirit vision now called on Turner to be baptized. This was probably in 1825, when Turner was twenty-five years old and four years after the visionary experience he had had while a runaway. He had been in contact with spirit many years before he was called on to be baptized. His was not the usual Baptist dialogue with God.

Notwithstanding this idiosyncratic behavior, the unbaptized Turner brought about the conversion of Ethelred T. Brantley, a white man, who began to bleed from his skin. This was seen as another significant sign of Turner's power. After fasting and praying for nine days (the same number used by Voudouists prior to initiation), Brantley was cured. Only then were Turner and Brantley baptized, but again not in the usual way:

> Spirit appeared to me again and said, as the Savior had been baptized so should we be also—and when the white people would not let us be baptized by the church, we went down into the water together, in the sight of many who reviled us, and were baptized by the Spirit.

The local Baptist churches baptized blacks if ''God's precious dealing with their souls'' was found acceptable. Very often it was the blacks, in separate session, who advised on the acceptance or rejection of a black seeker; in other cases, the black deacons functioned in this advisory role, although whites could generally veto a black recommendation. Clearly, in not accepting Turner for Baptism, the church did not consider his soul-travels a proper conversion experience. Local Baptists did not accept his baptism of himself. It was said locally that Turner had claimed that God would show His approval: "A dove would be seen to descend from Heaven and perch on his head" while he was baptizing himself.

Turner's Baptist faith was of a most unorthodox type, unconsciously reflecting influences of the Voodoo that Turner consciously rejected. Visions of spirit, and not of Christ, brought him the truth. With spirit, he could cure disease and prophesy the future. Although the Baptists accepted faith healing and prophecy as God-given roles, they believed Turner used individual power beyond permissible limits. As a result, the church played a negative role in the working out of his destiny. Had he been absorbed within the black Baptist church, his visionary travels might have taken him in another direction. As it was, he came to see himself as the savior of all black men.

On May 12, 1828, Turner had his most fateful vision:

> I heard a loud noise in the heavens and the Spirit instantly appeared to me and said the Serpent was loosened, and Christ had laid down the yoke he had borne for the sins of men, and that I should take it on and fight against the Serpent, for the time was fast approaching when the first should be the last and the last should be first.

It may have been at this juncture that he began to publicly proclaim that it was his destiny to take up Christ's yoke. The white man who later reported having Turner's papers wrote: "I have been credibly informed that something like three years ago, [i.e. 1828] Nat received a whipping from his master for saying that the blacks ought to be free, and that they would be free one day or another." After this vision of when "the last should be first," Turner procrastinated, waiting for signs, and could not draw up a satisfying plan to "fight against the Serpent." Nevertheless, he was on his journey. Much as had his African spirit-knowing forebears, he, too, apparently claimed invulnerability.

After the rebellion, in the weeks during which Turner was in hiding, the whites remembered his claim of invulnerability: "He . . . pretended to have conversations with the Holy Spirit; and was assured by it, that he was invulnerable, His escape, as he laboured under that opinion, is much to be regretted." This factor added even more impetus to the whites' desire to apprehend Turner, for in capturing him they would prove to his fellow slaves that he was not indestructible.

Turner was finally taken captive, shackled, and imprisoned. While awaiting a certain death, he was asked if he did not then recognize that his visions had been but his imaginings. His famous answer confirmed his identity: "Was not Christ crucified?" Turner saw himself as a black Christ dying for his black brothers and sisters, "the last who would be first." At his examination by the local magistrates, he spoke calmly and forthrightly "of the signs he saw; the spirits he conversed with; of his prayers, fastings and watchings, and of his supernatural powers and gifts, in curing diseases, controlling the weather, etc."[38]

At his trial, a white man, Samuel Trezevant, the justice before whom Turner was examined, reported "that he [Turner] pretended to have had intimations by signed omens from God that he should embark in the desperate attempt." Turner did not speak in his own behalf. Trezevant stated that Turner and his followers believed Turner "could by the imposition of his hands cure disease" and that he had "command over the clouds." Trezevant further reported that Turner had given a "medly of incoherent and confused opinions about his communications with God." In earlier times, Turner had talked freely of spirit and its message; now at the trial his visions were described as his "confusions and pretensions." When called on to speak, his only response was that he had nothing to say "but what he had before said." He pleaded "Not Guilty."

Turner had seen himself as Christ baptized by the spirit; carrying his yoke; awaiting crucifixion. He had had a vision of a fight between white and black spirits and of blood flowing in streams. The dark appearance of the sun on August 13, 1831, had been his final sign: "Nat encouraged his company on their route, by telling them, that as the black spot had passed over the sun, so would the blacks pass over the earth." In the end, the blood covered him and his men, and as Jesus before him, he went to his death in a city called Jerusalem.[39]

In the slave revolts, there was generally a nonorganic combination of the African and Christian ethos. Quasi-African Voodoo existed side by side with Christian promise. Nat Turner (who claimed not to believe in Voodoo) did believe in his own invulnerability, and this matter of invulnerability runs through all the major revolts. In the New York City plot of 1712, it was reported that Coromantee and Paw Paw Africans "had procured the services of a conjurer to make them invulnerable."[40] Ben Woolfolk, an associate of Gabriel Prosser in 1800, reported that a third leader, George Smith, proposed to enlist the African-born on plantations as they were "supposed to deal with witches and wizards and thus [would be] useful in armies to tell when any calamity was about to befall them." Smith planned to make African crossbows as weapons, much as Gullah Jack actually did make African-style pikes or spears for his "Gullah band" in preparation for the planned revolution in Charleston in 1822. (Jack had taught blacksmith Tom Russel conjuring, and it was Russel who prepared the spears.)

The official account of the Denmark Vesey conspiracy, published by the City Council of Charleston, took note of Jack's claim to invulnerability:

> Gullah Jack was regarded as a sorcerer, and as such feared by the natives of Africa, who believe in witchcraft. He was not only considered invulnerable, but that he could make others so by his charms; and that he could and certainly would provide all his followers with arms. He was artful, cruel, bloody.

The account suggests that Jack's "influence among the Africans was inconceivable," but the trial record gives a good indication of its effect. A state's witness, a slave named George Vanderhorst, who had been in Jack's Gullah company, found it very difficult to give his evidence for fear of Jack. "It was not without considerable difficulty that the court satisfied him that he need no longer fear Jack's *conjurations* (as he called them)." Gullah Jack had given his followers charms (crab claws) and special food (parched corn and ground nuts) that were reputed to have positive magical properties, thus obviously continuing African traditions. However, one testimony, censored in the original trial record, may well have suggested that Jack distributed poison. Black Harry Haig reported: "Jack was going to give me. . . . [censored]." It is Haig's reaction that leads to the conclusion that the item proffered was potent and "immoral": "I refused to do this as I considered it murder, *and that God would never pardon me for it;* it was not like fair fighting." This black Christian could accept that he should revolt; he could accept belonging to a company of fighters grouped around a witch doctor; he could accept the doctor's charms and magical food; but it appears that he could not accept the morality of poisoning, although a Voodooist would have. Harry Haig apparently regarded this as "unfair," and his Christian God demanded fairness.

Vesey's potential rebels were, as already suggested, organized in ethnic bands: the Gullah were under Jack (and their language was spoken); the Ebo under Monday, an Ebo who had been brought to America fifteen to twenty years earlier; and the American-born under Vesey and other leaders. (Vesey was not American-born but was highly skilled in English and other languages.) A fourth ethnic group was the French Creole band; these French-speaking blacks were reputed to be "very skillful in making swords and spears such as they used in Africa." These ethnic divisions for the planned revolt may have developed out of similar divisions in the class meetings of the Methodist church, as is vaguely hinted at in the trial record.

African-born participants, many of them members of the African Methodist Church, clearly kept traditions from both worlds alive.[41] Conspirators were ready to share an almost raw fowl with Gullah Jack, "as an evidence of union.'' This African tradition, recalling the ritual sacrifice, was long remembered in a Christian context when blacks sang: "Ef yer wants ter hear er preacher sing,/Jes' cut up er chicken an' gib him er wing.'' Notwithstanding the strong Africanisms, it was the Bible and the example of Israel that provided both the past and future orientation for these revolutionaries. These blacks planned to repeat the sacred history in a new exodus from slavery. God would lead them with a strong right hand and bring destruction to their enemies.

Nat Turner, too, apparently thought himself indestructible. While he was eventually killed, he brought his vision of the flowing blood of whites and blacks to a gory completion. While harsher immediate repression resulted, the blacks attained a greater sense of the distance between free souls and slave bodies.

In the white community, one of the results of the Nat Turner rebellion was a strong Baptist sense of betrayal, stronger than that of the nonreligious whites in that Baptists had extended a special hand to blacks. Southampton had been the Virginia home of the antislavery white Baptist David Barrow and of many black Baptists. The local Baptists did not acknowledge that any of the revolutionaries had been church members, but they did make known their deep depression over the happenings. The local Portsmouth Baptist Association, noting little church vitality in 1832, explained:

> The insurrection in Southampton, which exhibited scenes of murder and carnage unparalleled in the history of our country, had produced a most lamentable effect upon the religious feelings of many of our churches, and especially those in the immediate vicinity of the dreadful tragedy. The high character of godliness, claimed by many of the insurgents, and the extensive religious influence they actually possessed (though we believe none of them were Baptists) have destroyed with many of our brethren all confidence in the professions of that class of persons.[42]

Black religion was in for particular trouble after the revolt. All preachers and all "conjure-doctors" were suspect as conspirators, and all societies and congregations as hotbeds of rebellion. Early reports on the Turner revolt had associated it with a revival or a Sunday meeting. In the public mind these were logical possibilities. The black church was singled out for particular attack in post-1831 Virginia where the attendance of white ministers and white observers was legally required at all black religious gatherings. The black churches found it rough going for a period, but they were able to maintain themselves. Over time, they even began to expand again, having developed sub-rosa forms through which they countervened the intentions of the laws.[43]

Many Southern blacks had found it difficult to be Baptists long before the Nat Turner revolt. In the early period when Baptists were regarded as a subversive sect, black preachers and black laymen suffered whippings and other severe punishments as a direct result of their religious activity. When the early white followers of Shubal Stearns were abused and imprisoned, the blacks who came to hear his preaching were "flogged." Moses and Gowan Pamphlet in Williamsburg and Joseph Abrams in Richmond, Virginia; George Liele, Andrew Marshall, and Andrew Bryan in Savannah, Georgia; Israel Campbell in Tennessee; and Nelson D. Sanders in New Orleans, Louisiana, were some of the black Baptist preachers who suffered for their faith. Reverend Joseph Abrams recognized the historic and psychological significance of his beatings: "Even I can say with Paul, I bear in my body the marks of the Lord Jesus."

Early black Baptist preachers were whipped not only because of general anti-Baptist feeling but also because of a particular animus for blacks who talked of "freedom of the soul." In the later years, from about 1830, blacks going home from late night meetings were often beaten in order to reduce their secret and feared association. Again, blacks used this suffering to reinforce their sense of identity. Israel Campbell, a slave convert to the Baptist faith in Tennessee in 1837, reported that

> at night I would walk several miles to attend prayer meetings. We would sing and pray there until near midnight.
>
> Sometime the patrols would come in upon us and if any of us were found without passes, they would give us a few stripes. *We freely rejoiced that we were called upon to suffer for Jesus' sake.*[44]

After the First Great Awakening, all-black and mixed black and white churches existed throughout the South, increasing in number in each decade. Nevertheless, slaves from every area of the South have left records of secret services. It was frequently necessary for a slave to have written permission, a "ticket," in order to attend a church service off his plantation, and many could not always get this permission. However, local plantation churches or meeting houses were very common in the last period of slavery. Yet, it is from that very period that we have innumerable reports of secret services and of owners or overseers denying slaves the privilege of attending church. The fact that many reports of hidden meetings come from the very same plantations where slaves were allowed to go to church or where there were meetings attended by whites suggests one of the reasons for this seeming inconsistency. In part blacks *wanted secret meetings.* They wanted to continue the tradition of secret societies and to preserve their privacy and proprietary interest in their own practices. They could not do this in overseer or owner-supervised meetings.[45]

Secrecy and illegality in themselves added a very special dimension to black meetings. However, while a certain level of slave religion could have been maintained without secrecy, the slaves would not have been given permission to stay up all night when the following day was a workday, or to engage in what appeared to be African "devil dances." It was only by taking the risk of forbidden meetings that they could freely continue certain quasi-African traditions. The great numbers who took the risk and who were punished for it indicate how important a function these meetings played. The risk-taking itself was important. Elizabeth Ross Hite, nominally a Catholic, remembered the black Baptist services on a Louisiana plantation:

> Sometimes we held church all night long, 'til way in the morning'. We burned some grease in a can for the preacher to see the Bible by, and one time the preacher caught fire. That sure caused some commotion. Bible started burnin', and the preacher's coat caught. That was ole Mingo. And ole Mingo's favorite text was "Pure God tried by fire". I always say that Mingo must've had to be tried hisself, else the Lawd wouldn't made him be catched on fire quick like that.
>
> Next day everybody was late to work and everybody who was got whipped by the drivers.

The fondest memories of many ex-slaves centered on these secret meetings. They were the highpoint of communal as well as individual emotional life: they were the scene of spirit travels.

> De most fun we had was at our meetin's. We had dem most every Sunday and dey lasted way into de night. De preacher I liked de best was named Matthew Ewing. He was a comely nigger, black as night, and he sure could read out of his hand. He never learned no real readin' and writin' but he sure knowed his Bible and would hold his hand out and make like he was readin' and preach de purtiest preachin' you ever heard. De meetin's last from early in de mornin' till late at night. When dark come, de men folks would hang up a wash pot, bottom upwards, in de little brush church house us had, so's it would catch de noise and de overseer wouldn't hear us singin' and shoutin'. Dey didn't mind us meetin' in de daytime, but dey thought iffen we stayed up half de night we wouldn't work so hard de next day—and dat was de truth.
>
> You shoulda seen some of de niggers get religion. De best way was to carry 'em to de cemetery and let 'em stand over a grave.

> Dey would start singin' and shoutin' about seein' fire and brim-
> stone. Den dey would sing some more and look plumb sanctified.

The formal black churches established missions or societies on many
of the plantations; these societies paralleled and often absorbed the more
spontaneous plantation developments. William Campbell organized
fourteen such societies in the area surrounding Savannah; the Springfield
African Church in Augusta, Georgia, had a large corps of exhorters and
preachers who were sent into the countryside; and C. C. Jones recognized
that his plantation missions were often used as a legitimating structure for
indigenous leaders and meetings. Black Baptists in Georgia were
apparently bringing the ordinances of baptism and communion to the
plantations. The white preachers, running their "joint" association in the
1840s, forbade them to continue the practice, because they were cognizant
of the more overtly African character of the separate plantation meetings.[46]

Secret services became an important black institution. Many were
early sunrise meetings, in part because patrols went to sleep before sunrise
and meetings were then somewhat safer. But they were essentially
after-dark meetings, held around the famous pots or overturned tubs
whose African origins as sacred water pots or drums have been much
debated. Baptist preacher Peter Randolph, born a slave in Virginia and
freed in 1847 by the will of his late master, wrote an excellent description of
the pattern of the meeting he knew, a pattern that was not very different
from those of many known or formal black churches. Randolph reported
that in his experience the slaves met in cabins, with a "watch" outside, or

> in the swamps, out of reach of the patrols. They have an under-
> standing among themselves as to the time and place of getting
> together. This is often done by the first one arriving breaking
> boughs from the trees and bending them in the direction of the
> selected spot. Arrangements are then made for conducting the
> exercises. They first ask each other how they feel, the state of
> their minds, etc. The male members then select a certain space,
> in separate groups, for their division of the meeting. Preaching
> in order, by the brethren; then praying and singing all round
> until they generally feel quite happy. The speaker usually com-
> mences by calling himself unworthy, and talks very slowly, until,
> feeling the spirit, he grows excited, and in a short time, there
> fall to the ground twenty or thirty men and women under its
> influence. Enlightened people call it excitement; but I wish the
> same was felt by everybody, so far as they are sincere.
>   The slave forgets all his sufferings except to remind others of
> the trials during the past week, exclaiming: "Thank God, I shall

not live here always!'' Then they pass from one to another, shaking hands, and bidding each other farewell, promising, should they meet no more on earth, to strive and meet in heaven, where all is joy, happiness and liberty. As they separate, they sing a parting hymn of praise.

Revival Scene. Courtesy The Bettman Archive.

While these meetings were similar in structure to nonsecret weekday meetings, slaves regarded them as *"the* real meetings'' with ''real preaching'' ''and real experience.''[47]

In many areas, slaves were allowed to hold protracted revival meetings on a formal basis once or twice a year. In prewar Virginia, both a postharvest and a Christmas-New Year revival period were common, while in the Deep South an annual meeting was more likely. At these meetings, there was ''real preaching'' as well and the blacks used forms that seemed African: brush arbors, shouts, dances, and trance excitements. Although whites used all of these methods, for whites they had a different character and tone, especially after 1830 when white revivalism became routinized and almost professionalized. White Baptists moved to a routinized pattern of revival meetings that had, by and large, lost the heat and excitement of the early days. Most whites preferred the newer and more decorous ways and did not look back with great nostalgia on the lack of education and lower class patterns of the first period. Occasionally an old preacher, such as David Benedict, would pine for the close family feelings of the early days. (In 1860 Benedict wrote a volume nostalgically recalling the warm Baptist family of 1810.) Those feelings had embraced blacks as well as whites, and in the nurturing support of the early Baptist outreach blacks had found something very important. While the white and black cosmos moved apart again, during their brief period of interaction,[48] blacks had come to know a freedom of spirit and a life in Christ; they had used this knowledge to support themselves in the routine tribulations of life in slavery and in their attempts to rebel and achieve physical freedom. The cleansing in blood had Christian as well as African meaning.

III

The strong emphasis on Baptist sexual morality in the 1777 covenant of Liele's church indicates that blacks were working strongly and consciously to become Baptists. "To avoid Fornication, we permit none to keep each other, except they be married according to the word of God" (item XVI). Herbert Gutman's recently published study establishes that, by 1750, the black family existed as a distinct institution. This conclusion dovetails with this study's finding that a new black Sacred Cosmos and a black church institution began in that period. Gutman, studying black communities in both the upper and lower South, with varying economies and of varying size, finds that in all these circumstances "similar domestic arrangements, kin networks, sexual behavior, marital rules and naming practices existed." This he views as definite evidence of "a distinctive Afro-American slave culture," although, as noted above, he does not analyze his evidence in a cultural matrix. While Gutman estimates that "one in six (or seven) slave marriages were ended by force or sale," he maintains and documents the fact that "the characteristic, or typical domestic arrangement" was a long-lasting male-present or double-headed household established at the black parents' own choice and supported by extended kin networks.[49]

Gutman's work shatters the widely held theories of weak slave family structure, theories based in good part on contemporary observations and comments. How is it possible that white contemporaries did not recognize the pervasiveness and strengths of the institution of marriage among blacks? Part of the answer lies in the invisibility of blacks. Much as the black church was not really "seen," while it, too, was pervasive and strong, so the black family was invisible. Second, it served white purposes best to see slave morality in a negative light. It placed the black in an inferior position, legitimating both slavery and the sale of fathers and mothers who were not "legally" wed. Indeed, slaves separated by sale or forced migration tended to establish new families, fulfilling the contemporary white image of the black as immoral, but in Gutman's terms actually evidencing the strength of the family ethic.

Part of the answer to the question of the invisibility of black culture lies in the very fact that the sex and marriage customs of slaves developed very differently from those of the Southern whites and, as a result, whites did not recognize them as mores. Gutman's data confirm the accepted view that blacks widely accepted premarital promiscuity and that in the case of the woman this promiscuity could last until after the birth of her first child. However, she was then expected to marry and establish a long-term union. His data further confirm that alongside the normative double-headed households were single, woman-headed households and that many women had children with several different partners. Whites did not recognize such practices as acceptable social mores and simply labeled them as resulting from promiscuous "fornication."

Baptists placed a high value on sexual abstinence until marriage and on sexual purity thereafter. It was one of their abiding concerns, as is shown in the fact that white church records are filled with charges of fornication and adultery and expulsions of white members for violations of the sexual ethic. Black Baptists were expected to share this ethic; as blacks became Baptists they, too, demanded that members adhere to this "white" ethic. Premarital and extramarital sex could not be accepted. Perhaps as a result, black women in the African/Christian dichotomous communities often joined the church when they were ready to change their sexual activities. Initiation into the church became the rite of passage into Christian adulthood. Preconversion fornication was forgiven, and postconversion fidelity to one's spouse was expected. The 1863 testimony of Robert Smalls, reporting on the religious life of black women on the Sea Islands (cited by Gutman), bears this out:

> QUESTION: What proportion of the colored girls join the church?
>
> ANSWER: Most all girls join the church, generally between fifteen and sixteen years of age. They go through a certain probation and are admitted as members. No matter how bad a girl may have been, as soon as she joins the church she is made respectable.
>
> QUESTION: Does joining the church make a difference in her behavior?
>
> ANSWER: Yes, sir, the change is very great—as great as between sunshine and a hail storm. She stops all this promiscuous intercourse with men. The rules of the church are very strict about that.[50]

While Baptists demanded marriage unions, marriage was not an ordinance in Baptist practice; only baptism and communion were church ordinances. As a result, the churches did not officially record marriages. Free blacks, increasingly over time, had binding legal and church marriages, but marriage for slaves, even if performed by a white minister, had no standing before the law and was violated by sale, putting the church demand and practice into question.[51]

African marriage practices had run a wide gamut. Monogamy was known but polygamy was widely practiced, and the range of proper premarital and postmarital behavior was very broad. However, while behavioral patterns in the different societies varied, each of the West African peoples had rigid and traditional sexual and marital patterns. Violations of mores and laws were punished both informally and formally.

Africans did not bring one single marriage pattern to North America, but virtually all West African patterns involved contractual relationships between kin groups—the transfer of property in the form of a bride price and great emphasis on progeny as the proper fulfillment of both partners individually and of marriage as an institution.

The mixing of Africans in North America, the breakdown of the traditional social structures, and enslavement made it imperative for blacks to create a new pattern of marriage and kinship. Gutman's data showing that black families had established new kin networks by 1750 open up wholly new areas of concern. Did the plantation family take over the African kin group functions of sanctioning or disallowing unions? Did the new plantation families retain concern with the contractual aspects of marital relationships and with children as fulfillment?

Both carryover and significant change are apparent. Perhaps non-tangible exchange of aid and support replaced the exchange of material goods. Emphasis on children was retained, and it would appear that as blacks became Christians, they began to use the institutions of the Baptist and Methodist churches much as the community convocations and tribal courts were used in Africa. This suggests another significant area of melded values.

The Baptist and Methodist churches eventually served functions fulfilled by the social group in Africa, where if a person commits a serious crime within a group to which he belongs, strong group action is generally taken through its leaders. This is particularly true in cases of theft or adultery, both of which are almost universally considered extremely serious crimes in Africa. The individual may be fined, ostracized, or even banished from the group, particularly for repetition of theft or of adultery. Christian and African marriage patterns differed, but adultery was not a new crime nor were group control and punishment new to Africans. On the contrary, they had a very strong traditional emphasis on these areas and found the black church a fine institution for revitalizing community control.

Most slave unions were not controlled by whites, although on rare occasions there was direct white intervention. There is frequent reference to the practice of requesting the owner's consent, especially if the partner was on another plantation, so that the woman might be provided with a cabin for the family and the man with the occasional opportunity to visit. This practice raises some question of white interference in black unions but does not suggest white control.

While blacks created their own kin patterns, "white" values may have influenced black practices in both subtle and basic ways. As blacks incorporated white values into their new Christian ethic, they themselves absorbed (and changed) these values and passed them on. Black Baptist churches demanded that their members have Christian marriages and Christian families. In doing so, they were evidencing the new melded ethic, which did depend on the interaction of black and white values. Slaves responded to this black demand, but it did bear a direct relationship to white culture.[52]

As blacks became Baptists and Methodists, it became common for them to ask a preacher, black or white, whenever he might visit, to "sanction" already established unions "in one way or another by offering a prayer." In some cases, slave marriages became elaborate and joyous affairs. When Tempie Herndon was married to Exter Durham, in a marriage "abroad" (i.e., to a slave on another plantation), she had a glorious and long-remembered celebration. In her description, she explains the significance (although not the origin) of the much remembered custom of "jumping the broom" at weddings:

> We had a big weddin'. We was married on de front porch of de Big House. Marse George killed a shoat and Mis' Betsy had Georgianna, de cook, to bake a big weddin' cake all iced up white as snow with a bride and groom standin' in de middle holdin' hands. De table was set out in de yard under de trees, and you ain't never seed de like of eats. All de niggers come to de feast and Marse George had a dram for everybody. Dat was some weddin'. I had on a white dress, white shoes, and long white gloves dat come to my elbow, and Mis' Betsy done made me a weddin' veil out of a white net window curtain. When she played de weddin march on de piano, me and Exter marched down de walk and upon de porch to de alter Mis' Betsy done fixed. Dat de prettiest altar I ever seed. Back against de rose vine dat was full of red roses, Mis' Betsy done put tables filled with flowers and white candles. She done spread down a bed sheet, sure 'nough linen sheet, for us to stand on, and dey was a white pillow to kneel down on. Exter done made me a weddin' ring. He made

it out of a big red button with his pocket knife. He cut it so round and polished it so smooth dat it looked like a red satin ribbon tied round my finger. Dat sure was a pretty ring. I wore it about fifty years. Den it got so thin dat I lost it one day in de wash tub when I was washin' clothes.

Uncle Edmond Kirby married us. He was de nigger preacher dat preached at de plantation church. After Uncle Edmond said de last words over me and Exter, Marse George got to have his little fun. He say, "Come on, Exter, you and Tempie got to jump over de broom stick backwards. You got to do dat to see which one gwine be boss of your household." Everybody come stand round to watch. Marse George hold de broom about a foot high off de floor. De one dat jump over it backwards, and never touch handle, gwine boss de house. If both of dem jump over without touchin' it, dey won't gwine be no bossin', dey just gwine be congenial. I jumped first, and you ought to seed me. I sailed right over dat broom stick same as a cricket. But when Exter jump he done had a big dram and his feets was so big and clumsy dat they got all tangled up in dat broom and he fell head-long. Marse George he laugh and laugh, and told Exter he gwine be bossed 'twell he scared to speak lessen I told him to speak. After de weddin' we went down to de cabin Mis' Betsy done all dressed up, but Exter couldn't stay no longer den dat night 'cause he belonged to Marse Snipes Durham and he had to go back home. He left de next day for his plantation, but he come back every Saturday night and stay 'twell Sunday night.

They were married long enough before the Civil War to have nine slave children (and two afterwards, free-born). It was not until freedom came, however, that the Durhams could live together during the week, but they had certainly been married all that time.

Many blacks, much as whites in the slave period, continued to establish permanent unions without any sanction. In the 1930s, ex-slave Georgia Baker maintained that "Niggers don't pay so much 'tention to gittin' married dem days as dey does now." She herself "aint' never been married, but I did live wid Major Baker 18 years and us had five chillun."[53] For both white and black Christians, making a change in this pattern was a most important moral goal, although this meant encouraging slave marriage at a time when it was under increasing threat through growing sales and forced migrations.

An increasing conflict for Baptists, both black and white, as for other Christians in the South, was to determine how far their responsibility extended in regard to the dilemma of married slaves permanently separated through sale. The problem led to lengthy and spirited debates in many churches. The solutions were generally ambiguous, as in this *responsa* from the all-black Illinois Wood River Association in 1858:

> QUERY—If a slave man is married to a slave woman, and should they be separated by the master, or by making their escape into a free state, and marry another, is he or she guilty of bigamy.
> RESOLVED, That we believe the marriage of slaves to be morally binding, yet we do not believe it to be legal. We would, however, caution the churches to look well into the matter before they act.

White Baptist churches settled on various provisional solutions. The Nashville Baptist Church, for example, seemed to regard the city limits as the "universe" for blacks, and others viewed sale of a spouse as tantamount to death.[54] Clearly, formal doctrine could not promulgate these practices. Most churches, black and white, sought to have blacks solemnize their marriages. They disciplined those who obviously violated the Christian ethic by leaving a still "available" spouse for another person or by having children out of wedlock. Such actions were equivalent to "treating the Church with Contempt," and if the individual would not leave the second partner or marry, he or she would be excommunicated. Some mixed Baptist churches lived with a dual standard; others refused, although it was clear that it was the blacks who would suffer for this moral purity. At Rome, Georgia, in April 1852, George, a slave, asked if he might marry a woman who had been "another man's wife." When refused the approval of the church, he chose to continue living with her and accepted the church's censure and exclusion. The white members of the church were divided, but the majority formally decided on the "equality" of the blacks before the moral law.

The two black Baptist record-books in Virginia available from the slave period both record church concern and action in regard to adultery and marriage among blacks dating from as early as 1819. The records left by the 1777 Yama Craw Baptist Church, Georgia, and by its successor, the Savannah Baptist Church, led by Bryan, indicate that a marriage candidate would not be accepted for baptism unless he or she could prove proper marriage. Christian marriage had become a black value.[55]

Black preachers performed formal marriages both in the cities and on the plantations. Tempie Herndon's wedding, for example, was performed by black "Uncle" Edmond Kirby, and it was her white owner who insisted on the broom ritual. Baptist preacher, Israel Campbell, used a Methodist service to marry slaves since the Methodist service was available in printed form. While he himself was then illiterate, some white children read it aloud and he memorized it. Slaves made their marriages into true celebrations, notwithstanding this reliance on "odds and ends" of available culture and the seemingly inorganic assimilation of white patterns. Campbell, whose own marriage was performed by a justice of the peace and celebrated by his master and fellow slaves, recounts his policy in regard to officiating at marriages:

> They [slaves] most choose the Christmas holidays, while they have an opportunity to enjoy themselves, before going to hard work, when there is very little time given for a honeymoon. They often have a very lively time, having a large dinner or supper, and invite all their friends to participate. For a slave man to marry a slave woman out of the family* it is necessary for him to get the consent of the girl's master and mistress and of his own master and mistress, and they are very often the witnesses to the marriage. When celebrating the ceremony, the company stand around; the groom and bride walk out into the floor. After addressing the throne of grace, I address the company and say—
>
> "We are gathered together in the sight of God, and in the presence of these witnesses, in order to join together this man and this woman in the holy estate of matrimony, which is an honorable estate in the sight of God, and instituted in the time of man's ignorance. If there are any person or persons who can show any just cause or lawful right wherefore this couple should not be lawfully joined together in the holy estate of matrimony, please speak now, or hold your peace for ever hereafter."
>
> I here pause long enough to allow any one to make any objections they may have. There being none, I proceed by asking the waiters to join their right hands. I then say, "Mr. A., will you take Miss B., whom you hold by the right hand, forsaking all others, cleave unto her only; love her, honor her, obey her so long as you both shall live, even until death parts you?"
>
> If he answers, "I will," I then ask the woman, "Miss B., will you take Mr. A., whom you hold by the right hand forsaking all others, cleave unto him only; love him, serve him, honor and obey him so long as you both shall live, even unto death part you."
>
> I then ask a blessing on the parties and dismiss the company.[56]

In mixed churches, the whites originally called blacks (and whites) to task for sexual immorality. As black congregations and subcongregations

---

*Note the use of the term "the family" for the plantation community.

developed, black deacons and black business meetings took over this function and seemingly carried it out with equal diligence. Black Baptists formally accepted the ideal of Christian marriage as the signification of their new world view. Their practices could not match their ideals, however, because even good Christians were sold away from their families and because the differences between black African and white Baptist traditions were subtle and complicated.[57]

The new Baptist cosmos maintained the white goal of monogamy without any syncretism with African polygamy. Formally, the concept would not allow any stretching or change, but, informally, the black Baptist churches lived with a range of marriage practices because of the "complications" of slavery and conflicting pre-Christian values that affected both individual and communal life.

Despite internal and external pressures, the new black Baptist world view held together, uniting the African and the Baptist cosmos both perfectly and imperfectly. Its existence was proven in the lives of black Christians and in the social institutions they built.

7

COHERENT LIVES AND VISIBLE INSTITUTIONS

I

The spiritual coherence that the black Baptists achieved was reflected in an institutional structure of broad dimensions that was in no way hidden, although its visibility was often obscured. Prior to the Civil War, there was a vast network of large and small urban churches, plantation cabin-churches, "Pray's houses," and brush arbors; associations, missionary societies, and burial societies; and ordained or licensed preachers, exhorters, or chairbackers. Blacks functioned as full members in the early mixed churches and in the generally separate and nearly independent congregations of the later period. From 1758 to 1864, however, blacks had a growing number of black churches and black preachers that they could call their own.

Black Baptist churches began to be established in the pre-Revolutionary War period and continued to grow throughout the antebellum era. At least ten formal black churches were established prior to 1800 (all in the South), and by 1864 some 205 formal churches can be documented—75 in the North and 130 in the slave South. (See Table 2, Table 3 and Appendix I.) With perhaps 400,000 black Baptists, many other churches functioned, but they have left few, if any, formal records.[1]

The numerous Baptist plantation churches should have been the equal of urban churches. Traditionally, a Baptist church could be constituted wherever two or three baptized believers gathered, but the American churches had come to a formal and controlled conception of church establishment. A church was not deemed a proper one unless a presbytery of at least two ordained ministers had approved and formally constituted it. This came to mean that without association approval (the associations

TABLE 2

Formally Constituted Black Baptist Churches

Period	North	South	Total
I 1758-1822	7	30	37
II 1823-1844	30	32	62
III 1845-1864	38	68	106
Total	**75**	**130**	**205**

See Appendix I for details.

TABLE 3

Estimated Black Membership in Recognized Baptist and Methodist
Churches, North and South*

Year	Black population	Total of blacks in churches	% of blacks churched	% of whites churched	Baptists		Methodists	
					Black	Total	Black	Total
1790	757,181				18,500 [a]	73,471 [b]	3,900 [c]	12,884 [b]
1797		65,000 [c]	7 [c]	6.9 [c]			12,218 [c]	
1810	1,377,808				40,000 [d] in South	90,000 [d] in South		34,724 [k]
1816							42,304 [e] 30,000 in South 1,067 AME [k]	39,800 [k]
1840	2,873,648							94,532 [k]
1845					100,000 [f]	700,000 [f] 365,346 in South [g]	17,500 AME [k]	150,120 [k] (ME & MES)
1849					120,000 [h]			135,000 [k] (MES)
1860	4,441,830	634,000 [k]	14.3	22 [c]	400,000 [i]	645,218 in South [g]	170,000 MES [j] 19,914 AME [k]	207,000 [k] (MES)

*Black population statistics are based on U.S. census data. Other "total" figures are generally the officially recorded church membership figures, which include some of the black members. The black church membership is generally estimated and very far from accurate.

AME = African Methodist Episcopal; MES = Methodist Episcopal Church, South.

(Table 3 Notes Continued)

Baptists were the dominant black church group in Virginia and Georgia, while black Methodists were the majority among churched blacks in South and North Carolina. The major centers of black Catholic activity were Baltimore and New Orleans, although many Louisiana black Catholics were secret Baptists and made this their open affiliation after the Civil War.

Estimates of black church membership are very tentative, but their relative size indicates the importance of each church's outreach. In addition to the Baptist and Methodist estimates in the table, the following have been suggested for c. 1860:

AME Zion	6,000	Disciples of Christ	10,000
AME	20,000	Episcopal	6,000
Presbyterian	34,000 (slaves 1859)	Lutheran	1,500
Catholic	6,000		

a. W. E. Burghardt DuBois, *The Negro Church* (Atlanta, Ga.: Atlanta University Press, 1903), 19-20.

b. W. P. Harrison, *The Gospel Among the Slaves* (Nashville, Tenn.: Methodist Episcopal Church, South, 1893), 61-148.

c. Kenneth Scott LaTourette, *A History of the Expansion of Christianity,* Vol. IV, *The Great Century . . . 1800-1914* (New York: Harper & Row, 1941), 341-342.

d. David Benedict, *A General History of the Baptist Denomination in America and Other Parts of the World* (New York: Lewis Colby & Co., 1848), 207.

e. Dwight W. Culver, *Negro Segregation in the Methodist Church* (New Haven, Conn.: Yale University Press, 1953), 42.

f. C. C. Jones, in the 10th Annual Report of the Association for the Religious Instruction of the Negroes in Liberty County, Georgia (Charleston, S.C.: Observer Office Press, 1845), 69.

g. Robert A. Baker, *The Southern Baptist Convention and Its People, 1607-1972* (Nashville, Tenn.: Broadman Press, 1974), 144, 219.

h. Lewis G. Jordan, *Negro Baptist History, USA, 1750-1930* (Nashville, Tenn.: Sunday School Publishing Board, 1930), 112.

(Continued)

(Table 3 Notes Continued)

i. N. H. Pius, *An Outline of Baptist History* (Nashville, Tenn.: National Baptist Publishing Board, 1911), 62. In 1859 the Southern Baptist Convention listed only 150,000 blacks as members, but many congregations had not reported their racial breakdown, and Northern congregations were not affiliated. *Proceedings* (1859), 60-61.

j. *Minutes of the Annual Conference of the Methodist Episcopal Church, South, for the Year 1860* (Nashville, Tenn., 1861), 293.

k. Communication from John H. Ness, Jr., Commission on Archives and History, The United Methodist Church, Lake Janaluska, North Carolina, February 1977.

---

delegated ordained preachers to carry out the task) a new church could not achieve recognition. This provision gave the associations power far beyond their legal prerogatives.[2]

Black churches sought and gained association legitimation. Prior to the war, some eighty-three black churches (sixty-six in the South) were members of mixed, or as they were known, "white" associations, while sixty-eight (primarily Northern and Western churches) were in six all-black church associations. These were generally urban or village churches. Plantation slaves were often members, coming in for communion services but also meeting separately in their societies. By and large, the white associations did not grant recognition to their meetings (it was not generally solicited), nor would they allow the black churches to formally incorporate these more obviously African societies into their structure. Informally, the large churches sent deacons, lay exhorters, and elders into the countryside and did continue a more than casual conversation with the more traditional rural population.[3]

Many of the urban black churches never achieved the status of formal or white-supervised constitution, or if they were so (re)constituted it was many years after they were originally established. This explains part of the myth of the invisible institution. The Stone Street or African Church of Mobile, Alabama, was probably begun as early as 1806 but did not appear on the books until 1840 when it helped out a weak, new white Baptist church and formally became a branch of this new church.[4] Louisville African, begun as a white missionary operation in 1815, was functioning as an independent black church for many years prior to 1842 when it was finally recognized. The fact that an ordained free-born mulatto then became its pastor probably was the crucial factor moving the 513-member congregation from invisibility to visibility.[5]

Many large black churches never made the move onto paper; the formal records of churches kept by associations only hinted at their existence. For example, in 1843 white Reverend Thomas Malcolm (in a letter printed by David Benedict) noted that Lexington, Louisville, Georgetown, Frankfort, and Shelbyville, Kentucky, "among other towns," all had well-established black Baptist churches. In 1842, Louisville and, in 1944, Lexington were officially (and for the first time) recorded as churches. In 1855, Georgetown's black Baptist church suddenly appeared in the record book, but afterwards it again disappeared back into the official records of the Georgetown white church. After the war, all of these churches, and many others, appeared in the very first postwar black Baptist associations as though new-born. There is much evidence that many of these black churches, which had from 200 to 950 members at their postwar "births," had a separate prewar status.

For example, we know about a black church in Simpsonville, Kentucky, because Elijah P. Marrs, a slave in the area, wrote of his experiences. He had attended the church while it was pastored by black Reverend Charles Wells. Marrs heard a farewell sermon preached there at the war's outset by a Reverend Sandy Bullitt, and during the war he saw the church used as a haven by blacks and searched by Southern whites. It is evident that the whole community recognized this black church, but it never appeared in any official tabulation. Simpsonville is recorded as having had one church with 160 whites and 177 blacks as of 1860.

Zion Church in Hampton, Virginia, was probably one of these "unnoticed" churches. After the war, at the First Virginia Baptist State Convention Colored, Zion Church reported that its Sunday School had been "reorganized" in 1866 and that by 1867 it had 1,161 members. Prior to the war, it was never listed separately, neither as a mission nor as a branch, but it is fairly certain that it had some form of quasi-independent existence. In 1849, a black pastor from Hampton, W. B. Taylor, joined the Northern (black) American Baptist Missionary Convention and attended the annual meeting held at Philadelphia. This suggests an initiative-taking black subcongregation, one of a very few that sent representatives North to work together with other blacks. By 1860, Zion, and most churches with a majority of blacks, had separate services for blacks (in addition to mixed services). Such black subcongregations were often really separate churches in operation, if not in status.

Many known independent black churches never joined any association. These ranged from "private churches" where chapels were owned by black pastors, and which were as idiosyncratic as their owners chose to be, to very "regular" Baptist churches such as Lott Carey's Providence Baptist Church (January 1821). This church was constituted solely as a missionary arm, so that Carey might be ordained to carry the good news to black Africans. However, Carey was ordained, and his church was constituted at a white, Baptist church in Richmond, Virginia, and he preached his ordination sermon to a mixed audience in this church. It is significant that in that setting, as suggested above, he chose to talk about the *liberty* in Christ that sets the believer free. The sermon was powerful and was recognized as such by white and black parishioners who could not have disregarded the social implications of his words.

Other formal black churches were never affiliated with associations. Ordained slave preacher "Uncle" Harry Cowan constituted five churches in North Carolina in 1830 and 1831. The repercussions of the Nat Turner rebellion negatively affected his mission, and no evidence of these churches can be found other than Cowan's own testimony. In fact, so far as is known, none of the churches affiliated with white associations (as they were known) were formally constituted by black preachers. Many were organized by blacks, but when they chose to join associations they called in whites to (re)constitute the churches and ordain their preachers. Blacks simply did not "count" in this regard. When white Abraham Marshall constituted the Savannah First Colored Church and ordained black Andrew Bryan pastor (January 1788), black Pastor Jesse Peter was present. Nevertheless, Marshall felt he had abrogated the law by "acting alone," since at least two white pastors normally constituted churches and ordained pastors. The black church itself asked the association to legitimize this irregular act.

Many black Baptist churches in the North chose not to affiliate with regional associations. Little information as to how they constituted themselves or ordained their pastors has come to light. Several of these churches, however, did hire pastors who had been ordained at white-constituted black churches, and many affiliated with a black missionary association, leaving us some record of their life history.[6]

In the above cases, the black churches were essentially ignored by the white associations. There was another range of cases, primarily after 1830, in which whites went out of their way to obscure the independence of blacks. In New Orleans, as is well illustrated in Benjamin Quarles' study of that city, the white churches "covered" for the black churches so that they might conform to the letter, if not the intent, of the restrictive laws. In the 1850s, the Coliseum Place Baptist Church became the legal guardian of several black churches in New Orleans. The blacks, however, were allowed to retain internal control of their church life, notwithstanding their legal subservience. They could not have defended their internal freedom, for it was not theirs legally. However, the white Baptists wanted them to function. They sought to placate public fears by acting as their masters, and at the same time they allowed them a great measure of independence. Apparently, much the same pattern evolved in Virginia after the Nat Turner revolt, as well as in several other more isolated instances in the South (discussed below).

Both blacks and whites often regarded a low profile as a healthy profile. As Ellison phrased it, blacks "walked softly, so as not to awaken the sleeping ones." As for whites, some thought black churches of little consequence and therefore often disregarded them, while others sincerely sought to protect black churches by reducing their visibility. Still others saw black churches with one eye, and denied their existence with the other. As a result of these factors, together with the black churches' general failure to preserve records, it became accepted as fact that while the prewar black church had existed, it was a "hidden institution" that could not be revealed.[7]

II

Three broad periods of black church growth can be outlined, although considerable change took place within each period.

1. The 1740-1822 period was originally one of radical white Baptist outreach. Baptist revivals began with an appeal to the disinherited and an almost equal concern with the black. Blacks and whites shared church life; blacks preached to whites; and blacks began to establish separate churches. This situation was gradually altered as the Baptists became established and as the black population grew. Blacks' rights were reduced and their inequality gradually institutionalized. The Vesey revolt of 1822, while associated with the black Methodists, put all black religious expression into question and can be seen as finally closing this era. During this period, some thirty-seven Baptist churches were constituted—thirty in the South and seven in the North.

2. Between 1823 and 1844, theological and practical retrenchment took place among whites, along with numerical growth and geo-graphical dispersion among both races. White Baptist class status rose as did slave membership, leading the whites to become less willing to share church life. At the same time, separate black churches became highly suspect as a source of dangerous independence, especially after the Nat Turner uprising (1831) which was the central event of this period, influencing all black religious organization to some extent. During this period, thirty-two separate black Baptist churches were established in the South (many more quasi-independent or branch churches actually functioned separately), and thirty churches were constituted in the North and Midwest.

3. The 1845-1865 period was one of renewed white Baptist outreach to the blacks, but now on an unequal basis that was, in part, a legitimation of slavery. Nevertheless, there was continued interaction as well as a growing black membership in many new all-black churches. This period is defined by the formation of the separate Southern Baptist Convention in May 1845, which marks the recognition of a separate Southern denomination with its special attitude towards slavery. It is closed by the formal or legal end of slavery at the conclusion of the Civil War.[8] Some sixty-eight formal churches were established in slave areas and thirty-eight north of slavery. (See Table 2 and Appendix I.)

The development of the black Baptist Sacred Cosmos was intertwined with this institutional history. Blacks socialized in the new world view made new life choices and sought to build new institutions. To the extent that they succeeded, they reinforced elements of the cosmos, and in their failures they altered other elements. The cosmos was in the process of change and, at any one time, it was at many different points of development in the black communities, each changing and interacting with one another.

The earliest Southern black churches generally began not as outgrowths of mixed churches but as independent black churches. Blacks, generally converted at revivals, met together (very often in areas in which there were no white Baptist churches) and sought to become the body of Christ. By 1801, ten black Baptist churches had been formally established in Virginia, South Carolina, Georgia, and Kentucky.[9]

The Silver Bluff, South Carolina, revival was a seminal development, whose role among blacks rivaled that played by the Sandy Creek revival of the Separate Baptists, to which it was indirectly related. It was probably the same Wait Palmer who had baptized Shubal Stearns in 1751 who came to Silver Bluff in 1775, baptizing and constituting a church. Abraham Marshall, who encouraged the later offshoots, was a Separate Baptist of the Sandy Creek school. The revival at the Silver Bluff plantation of George Galphin (some twelve miles from Augusta, Georgia) had brought David George to the Afro-Baptist faith and had provided a ministry for George Liele.

George Liele, baptized around 1774, preached in the area of Silver Bluff and at the revival and afterwards included the black plantation congregation in his outreach. During the war, many of the Silver Bluff slaves, abandoned by their prorebellion owner in the wake of English advances, followed Liele to form a new congregation at Yama Craw, outside Savannah. Liele served the church at Yama Craw from 1777 to 1782. Even though he had been freed by Baptist Deacon Sharpe prior to the war, Liele chose to emigrate with the evacuating British and played a very active and eventually successful role as a Baptist leader in Jamaica. (The articles of constitution, discussed at length above, were the basic charter of both the Yama Craw and Jamaica black Baptist churches.)

Among the members of the black congregation of Yama Craw (or Savannah) who returned to slavery was itinerant Pastor Jesse Peter, sometimes known as Jesse Gaulfin (or Galphin or Golfin or Gaulsing) after his (and David George's) owner. Jesse Peter had been baptized at Silver Bluff in 1775 along with David George. He, too, was one of the original members of the church constituted by white Reverend Palmer, and he listened to black Preacher George Liele and black Elder David George. Along with George and forty-eight other slaves, he fled to Savannah, but he did not leave the United States in 1782. Unlike George, he remained a slave and was still a member of the black church at Savannah in 1788 when he associated with white Reverend Abraham Marshall, the Separate Baptist pastor of the Kiokie Georgia church, in reconstituting the Savannah church. Perhaps because he had remained a slave when he could have been evacuated, he was given "uncommon liberties" and traveled widely, ministering to three or four fixed black congregations, among them the remnant back at Silver Bluff. Sometime around 1791, Peter pastored a group of Silver Bluff blacks who had come to Augusta, Georgia. By 1793, this group was formally constituted as the Springfield African Church (Augusta) with white Reverend Abraham Marshall again officiating at the investiture. Marshall then described Peter as "grave, his voice charming, his delivery good, nor is he a novice in the mysteries of the kingdom."

The largest black church at the turn of the eighteenth century was the Savannah Georgia First Colored, the successor to Liele's Yama Craw congregation, reestablished by Liele's convert Andrew Bryan and formally constituted by Abraham Marshall. By 1800, Bryan's congregation numbered over 700, and Bryan, who had been whipped for his early Baptist preaching, could then write "we enjoy the rights of conscience to a valuable extent."

Andrew Bryan's biography is one of the few black Baptist biographies widely reported, owing in part to his high visibility in Savannah. Born a slave in Goose Creek, South Carolina, in 1737, he was converted by George Liele just prior to Liele's emigration in 1782. Some nine months later, Bryan began his ministry, primarily to blacks, although a few whites attended his services. Bryan was whipped, imprisoned twice, but finally protected by his owner and provided with a place to worship at Brampton. By the time Abraham Marshall ordained him and constituted (or reconstituted) a Savannah church (January 19, 1788), Bryan had purchased his own freedom. His church prospered (575 members in 1788 and 850 in 1802, at which point two daughter churches were formed). He himself became the owner of property and of eight black slaves, although his daughter and seven grandchildren were still enslaved. He was widely known and respected, and at his death in October 1812 he was memorialized by the leading white preachers of his community.[10]

Bryan's congregation and other large black churches of the period met several times during the week. Their Sunday service, as in white Baptist churches, was an all-day affair, punctuated by a picnic lunch. Their use of the song, shout, and vision travel was in the old tradition, even when the churches grew large. Deacons then took responsibility for classes or groups, becoming assistant ministers in practice.

At the same time as the separate black churches were growing, the black populations of mixed churches continued to grow, with separate black deacons generally responsible for advising on black admission, discipline, and dismissal. These black deacons began to preach to the blacks in the mixed congregations, who continued to attend both open and secret meetings. The pattern of separate black meetings, under the aegis of mixed churches, was to become general in the second or postradical period (circa 1823 to 1844), but its roots go back to the very first period of radical Baptist outreach. By the 1770s, many Southern black lay preachers were regularly preaching to blacks.[11] The black Baptist population was, as suggested, growing at the very time that white Baptists were moving away from their early radicalism, which had included an antislavery stance. An important result of the new conformist tendencies in Baptist circles was the growing desire of whites in mixed churches to separate from their black brothers and sisters. This was effected both by actual separation and by the creation of semiseparate congregations under one roof.

The Gillfield Baptist Church of Petersburg, Virginia, is representative of this second trend in black church history. In 1788, a mixed black and white congregation constituted the Davenport Baptist Church in Petersburg. White Reverend P. Black was the pastor of this congregation in which blacks outnumbered whites. A leading black member, Israel Decoudry, a free man of West Indian origin, represented the church at the white Portsmouth Association meetings of 1797, 1800, and 1801. Around 1802, the Davenport Church was disbanded. No documentation of the internal dynamics has survived. However, racial "imbalance" seems to have been the issue, as the races then separated. The whites joined various rural churches, but they did not establish a Petersburg church until 1817; the blacks were reconstituted in a separate church in 1803. At Sandy Beach in 1809 and finally in Petersburg proper, by 1818, they became known as the Gill's Field Church, an all-black church, with blacks in full control and among them, Israel Decudra [sic] who was an active preaching deacon. The black church did not remain united. By 1810, a group of free blacks had broken away from Gillfield to form the Elam Baptist Church in Charles City, a church for free blacks only. Many free blacks, however, remained in Gillfield, and the positions of leadership were formally divided between slaves and free men.[12]

Class differentiation in black church organization was a very significant factor. Church divisions were along class lines both in Petersburg and in Savannah where the Second Colored (1802) was composed of free blacks and the enslaved elite, while the Great Ogechee Church (1802) was the plantation slave church. In many cases, the distinction between slave and free-born congregations was very strict and was maintained by some even into the post-Civil War period.[13]

The better known Northern black Baptist churches developed very differently, growing out of open black dissatisfaction with unequal treatment in mixed churches. This was probably the case at Joy in Boston (1805), Abyssinian in New York City (1807-1808), the First African Baptist in Philadelphia (1808-1809), and in many other Northern churches. The whites did not leave nor did they push the blacks out. The origin of the Abyssinian Church in New York City illustrates the bind Northern blacks were in and the ways in which circumstances forced interaction. In 1807, when a small number of blacks wanted to opt out of their mixed church so that they might exercise equal rights, the Gold Street Baptist Church unequivocally refused to give them letters of dismission. In the North, free blacks in a separate church, which might claim full equality, were threatening, and whites generally preferred to maintain the status quo; in the South, blacks in a separate church were clearly inferior and could be legally controlled, outside of the Baptist polity. In the face of the Northern response, the blacks in New York City decided on a political tack. They called in the popular and highly acculturated Reverend Thomas Paul from Joy Street in Boston to mediate. Paul, born in Exeter, New Hampshire, in 1773, had been educated under the aegis of a white church in Limerick, Maine. His preaching at several New York City churches won him enough white respect to gain letters of dismission for four black men and twelve black women who then organized Abyssinian.

These blacks could have simply begun their own unrecognized church, but they wanted full recognition from other Baptists and from the New York Association. They desired and received equal status. As a recognized Baptist church, Abyssinian grew to be the largest Baptist church in New York City, with some 400 members by the late 1830s. This would not have been an unusually large church in the South and indicates the very different role played by Baptists in the North.[14] (See Table 4.)

III

In the South, alongside independent activities, blacks continued to worship with whites in mixed churches. They converted whites at many revival meetings and on many plantations, and as the black Baptist population grew, many whites found themselves surrounded by blacks in their churches. Under normal, nonrevivalistic, congregational circumstances, as suggested above, blacks served as pastors of mixed black and white congregations, which is an important reflection of the relationship of their world views.

Jacob or Josiah Bishop was official pastor of the mixed Court Street Baptist Church in Portsmouth, Virginia, serving from about 1792 or 1795 through 1802. Bishop, a slave member of the Magotty Bay Baptist Church in Northampton County, moved to Portsmouth and joined Court Street, which was then a mixed church in a declining state. Begun in 1789, with some sixty-eight congregants, it had been served by a white pastor, Thomas Armistead, until it was disrupted by the free-will preaching of a Reverend Frost. It was in "a cold and inactive condition" when Bishop came. His emotional exhorting began to revitalize the community, and he was very well received. With the aid of the congregation, Bishop purchased himself, his wife and his son and, as a free man, became official pastor of the now prospering Court Street Church. However, by 1802 Bishop had left the community, perhaps because the whites became dissatisfied with a black minister, or because he himself felt the need to leave. All we really know is that he left the South and mixed congregations, moving first to Baltimore and then to New York City where he was called to the important pastorate of the all-black Abyssinian Baptist Church (circa 1810-1813). As for Court Street, although some blacks later withdrew from it, it remained a mixed church under white leadership.

Black William Lemon was a pastor at a Gloucester County, Virginia, mixed church, a church known variously as Gloucester, Pettsworth, or Ware. Lemon served between 1797 and 1801, during which time there was an important revival in the area. Pettsworth had been established by a white preacher, I. Lewis, and was pastored before Lemon by white Robert Hudgin and some time after by white Thomas Taliaferro. Lemon was the only black leader. The church had begun with eighty-eight members and was "moderately prosperous" under Hudgin, but declined after his death. Indeed, from the point of view of a white Southern Baptist in 1850, this decline explained Lemon's choice: "In this destitution, the members of the Church, after a time, chose as their pastor Wm. Lemon, a man of color." Little is known of Lemon's life, but his contemporary, church historian Robert B. Semple, has left a very mixed memorial: "He, though not white as to his natural complexion, had been washed in the laver of regeneration; he had been purified and made white in a better sense. As a preacher, though weak, he was lively and affecting." Lemon represented the church at the white Dover Association in 1797, 1798, and again in 1801. There is further confirming evidence of his role at the church in the minutes of the First Baptist Church, Washington, D.C., which record that a new member's letter of dismission from Gloucester Church was signed by "the pastor, William Lemon," with no indication of race. Lemon died in either late 1801 or early

1802, and while little more is known of his ministry, just the simple fact of its existence is significant. William Leigh, a white man who had accompanied Lemon to the Dover Association, occasionally preached at Pettsworth after Lemon's death. Even without a permanent pastor, the church maintained a membership of over 280. Despite the return to white control, many blacks continued to join the church while whites left to form daughter churches, the first in 1801 (perhaps in response to Lemon's role) and the second in 1826. When in 1852 Pettsworth had become virtually all black, it was dissolved and its membership absorbed into the Ebenezer Baptist Church, a daughter church with a white population.[16]

Mulatto Joseph Willis was a pioneer Baptist missionary in Louisiana and accomplished more than any other black who preached to whites. As a missionary "on his own account" he established the first Baptist church ever constituted in the area, Calvary Church, planted at Bayou Chicot. Although he had suffered and risked much to missionize, his church was not readily recognized by established white Baptist organizations. By the second decade of the nineteenth century, Southern Baptists had strong doubts about black preachers as leaders of biracial groups. While a great deal has been written about Willis, much of it has been polemical and his early life story is still in some doubt. Willis was born around 1770 in North Carolina. As a young man, he emigrated to the northwestern part of South Carolina joining the mixed Main Saluda River Church, where he achieved recognition. He was licensed to preach and represented the mixed church at the Bethel Association meetings during 1793-1796. With the decline of this church, Willis, together with three other pastors, incorporated the Head of Enoree Baptist Society in 1799. Clearly a leader and determined to become a missionary, Willis went West, paying his own way, preaching in Mississippi and arriving in Louisiana in 1804. "In November of that year, at the risk of his life, he preached at Virmilion—now Lafayette, some forty or fifty miles southwest of Baton Rouge—the first sermon known to have been preached by a Baptist minister in Louisiana west of the Mississippi River." Together with a small group of Baptists, Willis decided to make a permanent settlement at Bayou Chicot, some thirty-five miles south of Alexandria. Local records show that by 1810 he was well established—in 1805, he sold some slaves and in 1809, he purchased land. Even though his values were those of upwardly mobile white Baptists, his Bayou Chicot congregation experienced marked difficulty in gaining association recognition. The Mississippi Association (formed in 1806) was closest, and in 1810 the congregants petitioned that group to ordain Willis. The association decided to act with discretion and sent two investigators to see if such an act would be "expedient." Apparently it was not, as in 1811 Willis had to attend the meetings and personally ask for ordination and official constitution of his congregation. It was only in 1812 that two ordained white Baptist ministers, Moses Hadley and Lawrence Scarborough, were finally appointed to go to Willis' area, ordain him, and constitute a church. On November 13, 1812, five men and one woman were constituted into Calvary Church, yet it took another four years until Willis's church was formally accepted into the Mississippi Association.

This lengthy delay was quite unusual. Greene, writing in 1973, makes no textual mention of Willis's color (although an appendix considers the "issue"). However, he comments that the long wait for ordination and constitution was Willis's own fault in that he was not "aggressive" or "innovative" but rather "traditional" and "deferential." No doubt he found deference the best means for a mulatto working within the traditional white system. However, once ordained and recognized, Willis did opt for self-determination and freedom from the Mississippi Association. Having been instrumental in the founding of five Louisiana Baptist churches between 1805 and 1818, he organized them into a separate Louisiana Baptist Association. He continued working at Calvary some twenty years and then moved to more pioneering territory, pastoring Occupy Church, in Cheneyville, Louisiana, between 1833 and 1849. Neither church was large, but the work started by Willis was the basis for a thriving Baptist community in Louisiana.

Willis worked until "enfeebled by age." When he died in 1854 he was memorialized as "Apostle to the Opelousas" and recognized as a pioneer father figure. His stature has grown in historical assessments, but his color has been revised: Many Louisiana Baptists, proudly claiming his ancestry, now deny his blackness and suggest that "at most" he was part Indian.[17]

Baptist preacher "Uncle Jack" of Nottaway County, Virginia, had his own small church in which he preached to blacks and whites. Born in Africa, circa 1758, he was brought to America at the age of seven. He learned to speak excellent English, was converted by an erudite white Presbyterian preacher (the president of Hampden-Sydney College, Reverend John Blair Smith), and learned to read in order to study the Bible. Jack chose to become a Baptist and became widely known for both his piety and preaching. On the petition of whites he was licensed by his mixed church and a subscription was raised to emancipate him.

The personality of Jack emerges as that of an extraordinary human being: brilliant and yet self-effacing, black and yet thankful for slavery as the means of bringing him to Christianity. An eminent white churchman, John H. Rice, then editor of the *Virginia Literary and Evangelical Magazine,* wrote that Jack's knowledge of the scriptures was "wonderful. Many of his interpretations of obscure passages are singularly just and striking. In many respects, indeed, he is one of the most remarkable men I have ever known." Other whites appreciated Jack's many-faceted personality: He maintained order among slaves and was allowed to preach on plantations at the same time as he achieved rapport with educated whites. Dr. James Jones, a rich and educated slaveowner in his area, wrote of his "enthusiastic admiration" for Jack and valued him "as a burning and shining light" of "moral purity seldom equalled and never exceeded in any country." Jones wrote that his feelings for Jack were "seldom felt by me for any member of the human family, of any rank or station." Jack preached to whites, converting several, including his former master's son.

While Jack had rapport with both blacks and whites, he did not move between world views. He brought the white world view with him when he went to blacks. He opposed emotion and vision travels, hasty conversions, and revival "disorder." Black noise appalled him: "You noisy Christians remind me of the little branches (of streams) after a heavy rain. They are soon full, then noisy, and as soon empty. I would much rather see you like the broad, deep river, which is quiet, because it is broad and deep."

Jack was very strict with both white and black converts. He himself practiced "Christian submission," accepting public denigration without anger but quietly comparing himself to the Apostle Paul. Thus, without comment, he accepted the closing of his church in 1832 following the Nat Turner revolt. His public demeanor was so "proper" that, in 1859, a white Presbyterian preacher, William White, published an appreciative biography of Jack, no doubt intended to show how well slavery worked but inadvertently revealing a black man of great stature who bore a cross in silence.

When Jack spoke of sin, he might well have been speaking of the African world view that he had "grubbed" out of his own soul:

> If a farmer in clearing and preparing a piece of ground for cultivation, should do no more than to cut down the trees, and remove the bodies and branches of those trees, whilst all the stumps were left undisturbed, he would very soon find that around every one of these stumps a considerable number of sprouts, of the very nature of the old tree, had *put up,* and he would have even more clearing to do than he had at first. Now, to get his land in a proper condition, he must not only cut down the trees, but he must *grub up* the stumps. . . . Just so with sin in a man's heart and life. He must not only forsake open sin, he must look to the heart, where the roots of this open sin are, and these roots must be grubbed up. And this grubbing he must keep at, as long as life lasts, or he will never bring forth the peaceable fruits of righteousness to the praise of God's free grace.[18]

During the antebellum period, many other black Baptists preached to whites on a fairly regular basis: Charles Bowles in New England, Lewis (Brockenbrough) in Virginia, Thomas Blacknall in North Carolina, Tom Clements, James Staryman, and Thomas Lemly in Arkansas, George Bently and Cyrus Chin in Tennessee, and John Jones and Henry Adams in Louisiana. Bently was a Giles County, Tennessee, slave. Yet, he had a congregation that included the "best whites," and his position was such that he could debate a white minister and be considered "victorious." A black Baptist "runaway," Joe Strater, was responsible for founding the mixed First Baptist Church in Kansas City, Kansas. Strater, having made himself physically free, took on the perilous mission of preaching freedom of the soul to the Wyandotte Indians and then settled in Kansas City to establish a mixed, rather than a black, Baptist church.

Some of these preachers, notably Bently, Lewis, and Staryman, remained slaves all their lives. Yet, it is probable that all of them, including ex-slave Blacknall, who became a slaveowner, did not function with a black Baptist world view. This likelihood is exemplified by Bowles's experience. He preached successfully in a white area (New England) and in a period when white Baptists were not particularly popular. Notwithstanding their black experiences and the early closeness of the black and white Baptist Sacred Cosmos, all of these preachers, especially those of the later periods when white and black Baptists had moved further apart, likely had near-white world views.[19]

IV

Most of the popular black Baptist preachers shared the black Sacred Cosmos of the black masses, but they were able to share some experiences with white Baptists as well, or seemingly to move back and forth between styles of expression. Many of these preachers, responding to both inner and outer calls, frequently changed congregations and locations, moving many times and over a wide area. In adopting this white Baptist tradition, black leaders developed skills and wide experience, and a large mobile leadership class early emerged.

The missionary life-style adopted by George, Liele, and Willis was followed by mulatto Henry Adams, who led a group of Baptist pioneers from Edgefield, South Carolina, to Louisiana in the 1830s. Ordained at Mt. Lebanon, Louisiana, Adams pastored a white congregation that served as a center for Baptist missionizing. Adams then chose to return to an all-black church, Louisville, Kentucky's African Church, and he was the man who led this church into a white association. Adams stayed at Louisville for over twenty-five years, gaining an "excellent" reputation and running a "flourishing" church that grew to some 900 prior to the war. As in the other large churches, the congregation met for preaching three times weekly, held two additional prayer meetings, and ran a large Sunday School. Adams continued to work successfully with the black congregation and, at the same time, he handled political relationships with whites. He accepted the fact that his church was represented by the white Walnut Street Church at the white Long Run Association meetings. Immediately after the war, however, Adams led the blacks out of the white organization and was instrumental in organizing, and later chaired, the Kentucky Colored Baptist Convention.[20]

Even slave preachers were mobile. Between 1815 and 1823, a slave preacher regularly came over from Kentucky to pastor a black church in Cincinnati, and in 1832 Samuel and John Bivins, free blacks, stood security for their minister, slave James Burrows, so that he might leave Northampton County, Virginia, to go to Philadelphia to pastor the First African Church. From Philadelphia, Burrows sent back money to pay for his own freedom, releasing the Bivins family from the bond for which their bodies had been collateral.[21]

Slave Tom Clements played an interesting role at Mt. Zion Church in Green County, Arkansas, although in Arkansas Clements traveled only in the general area of his home. Clements' owner was a pastor who had taken Clements West. Slave preachers were often owned by pastors, elders, or deacons, and Benedict early commented on a slave preacher who was more popular than his owner. The influence of this close contact was generally significant. In this case, Clements was very active in his mixed church, filling in for his white master on many occasions. A white contemporary considered him:

> an outstanding soldier of the Cross. He was always present at every meeting of his church. He was always ready for every good work. He could lead in singing; he could conduct a prayer service; he could bury the dead. He could pray with more spirit and fervor than anyone I ever heard, white or colored. . . . It is said that he officiated at the funerals of over one hundred white people in the faith.[22]

Whites usually came to preach at black funerals and not vice-versa. Blacks, of course, had fine reputations as funeral orators, and many established their names through their graveside performances. Both white Baptists and Africans had a strong tradition of funeral drama. At the white Baptist funerals, lay exhorters and the grieving family were expected to sing their testimony, occasionally in a new and personal way. By the first decade of the nineteenth century, Baptist song books included lengthy personal laments for lost wives and husbands, for the bride gone "With Jesus, my bridegroom to be" and for the husband "took away and gone": "Hark, from the skies what's this I hear?/A loud and dreadful sound!"

The blacks' rich African traditions of first and second funerals were merged with white traditions. While the body might be buried soon after death, an elaborate "second burial" or commemoration service was held at a later date. "Hark, from the skies" usually became "Hark, from the Tombs a doleful sound"; occasionally the borrowing was more creative as in "Harps from the Tomb." The black Baptist excitement, shout, and vision travel found their place in the second funeral, orchestrated by the central figures, the funeral orator or preacher.[23]

At death, bodies were laid on cooling boards, the women bound in winding sheets and the men in black shrouds; all the bodies were attended by congregants until burial in a formal "settin'-up" ceremony. It was generally believed that the soul was still in the body until it was buried and that it would remain around its old house and its grave for some three days afterwards. The first task was to make the soul "lie-easy" so that it would not return to haunt family and friends. Mourners talked to the soul (i.e., the dead body) on the assumption that it could hear them; said their farewells and touched the body at the actual burial; and spoke directly to the soul of the person at the second funeral. This was in the form of dialogue in that it was assumed spirits could respond. At this time, signs and portents were carefully observed: Mishaps on the way to a burial were considered indications of the disquiet of the departing soul, and storms very ominous.

The grave was generally dug in an east to west direction with the head laid to the west, "so de daid won't hab ter tu'n iroun' when Gabr'l blows de risin' trumpet in de east." In medieval England a similar belief had been maintained, although bodies had been buried facing east. The tradition was also an African one. In both cases, it probably related to the ancient association of goodness with the rising sun.

At the grave, the African pattern of breaking pots was often followed, at least in Georgia and on the Sea Islands where broken pottery can still be seen in graveyards. (See illustration 6.) For Africans, it symbolized the loss in death and the freeing of the man's spirit to leave his possessions and to find unity. Even though the Afro-Americans may have forgotten the meaning of these rituals, they continued the practice. The far more elaborate second funeral had the trappings of a pageant. Preparations were lengthy, and while they began at the time of death and burial, they might not be consummated in the second service for many weeks afterwards. Large numbers were generally invited; slaves from surrounding plantations and/or free people from a wide area, and whites who knew the dead person often attended.[24]

Black Cemetery, Liberty County, Georgia. Photograph by Orrin Sage Wightman. Margaret Davis Gate Collection, Fort Frederica National Monument.

John Jasper is one of the best examples of the funeral orator of the late prewar period. He began his preaching as a slave in 1839 and gradually built a considerable reputation as the leading funeral speaker in the area around Richmond and Petersburg, Virginia, traveling considerable distances to officiate. William E. Hatcher, who knew him, describes him as the black funeral "director" (in the sense of a dramatic director) par excellence:

> A negro funeral without an uproar, without shouts and groans, without fainting women and shouting men, without pictures of triumphant deathbeds and judgment day, and without the gates of heaven wide open and the subjects of the funeral dressed white

and rejoicing around the throne of the Lamb, was no funeral at all. Jasper was a master from the outset at this work. One of his favourite texts, as a young preacher, was that which was recorded in Revelations, sixth chapter, and second verse: "And I saw and beheld a white horse; and he that sat upon him had a bow, and a crown was given unto him, and he went forth conquering and to conquer." Before the torrent of his florid and spectacular eloquence the people were swept down to the ground, and sometimes for hours many seemed to be in trances, not a few lying as if they were dead.

In the dying and the travels, the believers often saw the dead: they visited mothers and fathers and other kin in Heaven, knew them to be well situated, and promised to join them when called to finish their journeys. Jasper helped them reach these states of excitement and gave them legitimation, and in return blacks elevated Jasper into one of the most important black preachers. He did not achieve full stature until the postwar period, but he had been preaching for twenty-two years prior to the war and was well established as a Petersburg preacher. Throughout this period, he was a slave and had to live in Richmond.[25]

The dramatic celebration of death and the attempt to contact spirit are ancient and perhaps universal practices. In fact, Ernest Kirby holds that these very practices are the origin of all drama and communal catharsis. In contacting spirit, the living are reassured of the meaning of life and death. The body is buried, but the spirit goes on to live a spiritual life in which the living can participate. Black funerals were orchestrated to reach this catharsis. They were often held at night, and myriad pinewood torches and fires were important elements in the drama and pageantry. As late as 1887, fires and graveside dancing were reported from Mississippi in what was interpreted as an attempt to reincarnate a black preacher. However, what was then seen was probably one of the ceremonies geared to generate ecstatic experience and spirit contact, such as were used throughout the slavery period.

Formal funerals were marks of respect for the dead and status for the living; accordingly, they were elaborate and expensive affairs. As blacks created formal Christian organizations, burial became one of the central tasks. Baptist preachers took on this job from the outset. Formal Christian burial societies were ultimately created which paralleled African societies and similarly assured proper respect and pageantry. The Burying Ground Society of the Free People of Color of Richmond was established in 1815, and other free communities followed their example. Slaves had land provided, generally a separate black cemetery, but they too had organizations which were ready to take proper care of funerals.[26]

V

Once blacks began to achieve the black Baptist synthesis of African and Christian world views, the new faith spread very quickly, with ever larger numbers seeking baptism. As suggested above, whites began to react far more negatively to the blacks in their midst than they had at the outset of the Baptist revivals as the population of both blacks and black Baptists grew. On the one hand, they were increasingly worried about blacks using separate meetings to formulate "plots." After the Vesey scare, they did not need the report of the City Council of Charleston to recognize "the great impropriety of allowing meetings of any kind to be held solely by slaves." Yet, whites increasingly preferred to separate themselves from blacks. For example, in 1816, the twenty-five white members of the First Baptist Church of Norfolk, Virginia, left their church to found a separate congregation. The church building, name, and white pastor were left to the 252 blacks.

Whites sought to influence the choice of leaders for blacks, although blacks often opposed the whites' desires and, protected by their Christian freedom, succeeded in maintaining their independence. For example, the Norfolk black church, which the whites abandoned, survived despite heavy pressure, as did Andrew Marshall's Savannah congregation and the relatively weak White Bluff Church in Georgia (discussed below).

The Norfolk First Baptist Church functioned as an independent black church without open opposition from 1816 to 1838. Suddenly, in 1839, when the church had over 400 black members, its white pastor, James Mitchell, was brought up before the white Portsmouth Association on undisclosed charges. The association demanded that the blacks choose a new white pastor, but the black church quietly defied the ruling and continued to meet with Mitchell for another nine years.[27]

Reverend Andrew Marshall, nephew and successor to Andrew Bryan, was pastor at the important black church, Savannah First, from 1813 to 1856. Born a slave, he had become free, rich, and powerful, buying his wife and children and owning other blacks. Attracted by the antinomian "heresy" of Alexander Campbell, Marshall invited Campbell to preach at his church in 1831. The association to which he belonged, the Sunbury Association (with an almost all-black membership but under white control), reacted very strongly. Recommending Marshall's dismissal and silencing, they officially declared his church dissolved. Marshall defied the association and set up a new First Colored Church with some 2,640 of his old parishioners. Only 150 congregants initially conformed to the association demands. Over time, the blacks willing to stay with Marshall dwindled to 700, and it is likely that they were under severe pressure to leave. Nevertheless, Marshall successfully maintained his opposition for six years. In 1837, Marshall, admitting his error, asked for readmission to the regular Baptist fold and, when he was granted fellowship, he emerged stronger than he had been prior to the conflict. His was a victory in defeat, in that he had stood up to the whites for a long period. Blacks again flocked to his church, which had 2,296 members by 1841. At his death, the whites eulogized him as "a Father in Israel." While denied a vote in the Sunbury Association while alive, the white Baptists did not deny Marshall a place in Heaven: "Full of years . . . and full of honors, he has obeyed the welcome summons 'come up higher.' "[28]

When the Sunbury Association was formed in 1818, the great majority of its 4,000 members were blacks in separate black churches. At the outset, all churches had equal voting rights, but in the mid-1840s blacks were denied this right and a small white minority took over the running of the association. Whites in Georgia (in contrast to the upper South) tried to turn black churches into mixed churches and thereby control them; or to send white missionaries to officiate at otherwise black churches. They voiced their disapproval of the African quality of the black Baptist faith and specifically forbade the black "innovation" of sending bread and wine for communion to the plantations through the deacons. The whites wanted the blacks to centralize their worship, away from the plantation meetings and under the watch-care of whites. Short-handed, for a brief period they were even willing to allow white Presbyterians to help in the supervision of black Baptists, but they came to have guilt feelings about this practice and ended it.[29]

Despite the white domination of the Sunbury Association and its campaign to oversee black behavior, *all black churches in the association were independent and essentially inviolable.* A brief item in the report of white missionary A. Harmon reveals this extraordinary contradiction in Baptist polity and the Christian liberty that could not be denied blacks. In 1852, Harmon (who was a missionary with over twenty-five years of service) was preaching to the all-black congregation at White Bluff Church in Chatham County, Georgia. While he could preach to the congregation, he was not a member nor was he privy to their business or discipline meetings. When local whites complained to him about some black Baptist's alleged misbehavior, Harmon went to the church with an ultimatum: He would leave the church entirely, he said, "unless I had supervision over their discipline and could be present at all their business meetings." Harmon "desired to know the opinion of the Church . . . [and] received for answer from one of the Deacons, *that they would not consent to it.*"[30]

Here we have a slave church in Georgia in 1852 refusing to consent to a white preacher's participation in their business sessions. The white preacher and the white-controlled association accepted this decision.

Harmon "withdrew . . . and discontinued [his] appointment." Although the association was very displeased, it recognized that "the Bible gives no sanction to any controlling power above the churches, save that of God." Had the black church agreed to white control, it would have been legitimate, but under the circumstances of church refusal, the association had to accept the situation. It was "the liberty wherewith Christ hath made you free." Ironically, one of the last acts performed by the Sunbury Association, which dissolved itself after the war, was to ordain White Bluff's new black preacher, Harley Housten. Sunbury had been created essentially to "serve" blacks. While it segregated them and sought to control them, Christian service to blacks was its first and last task. (See Appendix II.)

VI

The practices of both black and white Baptists changed over time, and the changes were to some extent interrelated. The Lexington, Kentucky, developments illustrate the generation gap between early black Baptists and their children, and the role whites played in legitimating new black leadership. Sometime around 1786, a black man known only as "Old Captain" began preaching in Lexington. His name alone says a great deal about his status and identity. He was known by neither a Christian nor a family name and has come down to us with nothing more to define him. All that is recorded is that he had a large black following and baptized many, but as he had not been ordained his practice did not meet the formal white requirements. By the next generation, a very different black was ready to assume leadership in the black community. Loudon Ferrill was an ex-slave who had once been willing to baptize believers without white permission to do so. But by 1817, after having been manumitted and having traveled from Virginia to Kentucky, he chose to join the white First Baptist Church rather than Old Captain's irregular black church. Married and working as a skilled house-joiner, Ferrill, through floor preaching at the First Baptist Church, established a reputation among younger blacks that rivaled Old Captain's status with the older community. His followers did not simply set up a church with Ferrill at its head; they appealed to the white church, which in turn sought sanction from the local association. When, in 1821, the Elkhorn Association approved the idea of ordaining a free black man, the First Baptist Church helped organize the First African Church, whose membership grew to over 2,200. Ferrill's church became the largest church in the Elkhorn Association and, in fact, the largest church in Kentucky, although it remained technically an auxiliary of the smaller, white First Baptist Church.

Ferrill was one of that large group of black preachers appreciated by whites for his role in preserving order in the black community. He became a man of wealth, power, and standing, and the black community seemingly appreciated him all the more for the respect whites showed him. At the same time, however, his church proudly claimed that "he was descended from a royal line of Africans."[31]

References to a royal African background are not uncommon in the descriptions of black preachers. For example, Lott Carey is described as "a typical Negro, six feet in height, of massive and erect frame with the sinews of a Titan. He had a square face, keen eyes and a grave countenance. His movements were measured; in short, he had all the bearings and dignity of *a prince of the blood.*" Nat Turner's mother is remembered as "of Royal African blood."[32]

A definite strain of black ethnocentrism can be found through black faith. Notwithstanding the holiness of whiteness in Africa, there were Afro-American folktales suggesting that all men had once been black and that only when Cain killed Abel had whiteness been introduced: Cain "turned white from fear." Alexander Young's "Ethiopian Manifesto" of 1829 openly forecast a black Messiah, while black Baptist Nathaniel Paul, writing in a more hesitating fashion in 1827, prophesied the coming of a black Moses:

> The God of nature had endowed our children with intellectual powers surpassed by none; . . . And may we not, without becoming vain in our imaginations, indulge the pleasing anticipation that within the little circle of those connected with our families may hereafter be found the scholar, the statesman, or the herald of the cross of Christ. Is it too much to say, that among that little number there shall yet be one found like to the wise legislator of Israel, who shall take his brethren by the hand and lead them forth from worse than Egyptian bondage to the happy Canaan of civil and religious liberty . . . [or who might lead them to Africa] to plant the standard of the cross upon every hill.[33]

The black Christian Sacred Cosmos of the pre-Civil War period informed the black that he was God's chosen. As J. H. Hensen later wrote, "my heart burned within me and I was in a state of great excitement . . . that such a being [Christ] . . . should have died for me . . . a poor slave." Henson had no doubt that he would go to Heaven; he had already been there. Many blacks still envisioned themselves when in Heaven as white "in the laver of regeneration." Lily Cohen puts these words in the mouth of her old black retainer, Andrew:

> Oh, leel missy, Andrew sholy do lub heems! Dey mek eem feel
> as dough de Lord was a-hangin' ob de snow-w'ite robe ob de
> purifiction on ee po' black pusson. Does yo' know, honey dat
> bemeby de Lord gwine do dat t'ing? An' w'en de Lord done do
> eet. *Andrew soul ee gwine git jes' as w'ite as yo own skin.* Now,
> mebbe yo don't beliebe dat, honey-chile; but eet's so. Dey's one
> place een de Book,—I speek eet's de place whey Paul p'ints
> ee pistol at de Romans,—whey de Lord say dat Andrew shall be
> w'iter'n de snow,—yes' w'iter'n de snow. Does you min' dat,
> honey?

"Honey" did mind! How would she recognize her servant in Heaven if he
too were white? In response to her tears, Andrew agreed to ask the Lord
to "mek me a nigger again, an' let me stay de only black t'ing een dis
snowy white place; please, please, good Lord, do dis, jes to please my leel
missy; 'cause Heaben ain' Heaben ef my honeychile dunno her old
Andrew." If this was indeed Andrew's response, he was certainly
magnanimous by white standards. He had good reason to sing: "Howdy
Lord. I neber turn back no mo."[34]

VII

Whereas white Baptists in Georgia sought to infiltrate and dominate
black churches, those in Virginia strove to demarcate their differences from
black and to reduce interracial contacts. Virginia Baptists generally chose
to maintain black churches as branches or to provide official pastors, as
was required by the post-Nat Turner laws, but above all to maintain or
increase their functional separation.

As a result of the Turner uprising, no new black church was formally
constituted in Virginia until after 1840, but nine pre-1831 black Baptist
churches functioned throughout the 1830s, and they were joined by
thirteen new black churches established after 1841. The ability of Virginia
blacks to overcome the harsh restrictions born of white fears is further
evidence of the coherence of their world view and the strength it provided
in adversity. While, after 1831, whites were the formal or legal ministers in
Virginia's black churches, blacks served as lay preachers or prayed from
the floor. Blacks continued to hold their own business meetings, often
without the presence of whites, as is indicated by the extant minutes of the
all-black Gillfield Church of Petersburg. This church elected two separate
groups of deacons—one free and one slave—and a black moderator. For
almost all of the period after the Nat Turner revolt, their official preachers
were white, but unofficially blacks maintained control over finances,
discipline, membership, and prayer.

For one year, in defiance of the Virginia law, the Gillfield Church actually chose a black man as official pastor. Black Sampson White became *the* preacher in 1837. We know very little about Sampson White in Virginia, other than that simply by standing as official preacher he risked a great deal, as did his church. He took a stand as an equal leader, even where the law expressly forbade it. In his later life, White joined the black branch of the First Baptist Church in Washington, D.C., and, despite the opposition of white Baptists, he was instrumental in moving this group towards independence, no doubt pressuring blacks to make use of the possibilities he appreciated because he had not had them in Virginia. In September 1839, he pastored a new breakaway First Colored Church in Washington, D.C., and he was very active in the American Baptist Missionary Convention, an important black interstate leadership group founded in 1840. He left Washington to take the pulpit of the prestigious Abyssinian Church in New York City, and when he left there, he founded the Concord Street Church in Brooklyn (1848). White was one of the large group of mobile black Baptist preachers who moved about between the urban communities, exerting new influences and stimulating community development. Through their interaction, these preachers helped unite communities whose world views were at different levels of development, bringing both the richness of Southern practice to the North and the full integration of black and Baptist practices to a wider forum. After the war, many of these black preachers returned to the South. Sampson White was among them, returning to Virginia and pastoring the African Church at Lynchburg. It is likely that there, as among the Sea Islanders before them, black Baptists were anxious to eliminate what came to be seen as slave practices. White, having served in the North for thirty years and having achieved recognition and a leadership role (symbolized in his presidency of the American Baptist Missionary Convention), brought an extraordinarily rich experience with him when he returned to the South. He was particularly suited to lead others to make the leap he had made in his own life.[35]

Although White was the only official black preacher at Gillfield, Gillfield always had black exhorters and unofficial black preachers. It was the black deacons' duty to "select from its Brethurin such as in there opinion Posest qualification for Public Teaching." The church would then decide if they should "exercise thare Gift." The men so chosen were very much part of the community and under community scrutiny. Occasionally they, too, were brought up on charges, expelled, and accepted again if they were penitent and attempted to "conform to the Doctrines of the Bible."

Gillfield, which for a short time called itself the Church of the Lord Jesus of Petersburg, was a church with rich and old traditions. Candlelight and sunrise services were dramatic participatory experiences there. Business meetings were community courts, and the issues of personal morality and interrelations were central concerns. Members brought their "objections" to this forum, charging their neighbors with fighting, adultery, harsh words, lying, and stealing. Committees were appointed to look into each matter. Generally, men looked into issues involving men, women formed committees to investigate other women, free men concerned themselves with the free, and slaves ran affairs for the slaves. The slave and the free members elected two separate groups of deacons and deaconesses. Black members opened their meetings with "prayer," "used words of Exortation," and even "preached the gospel." Blacks generally ran both the business and prayer meetings. The white (Sunday) preacher might be the official moderator, but he would usually turn the meetings over to a black to "chair" them. The blacks paid the official white minister's salary and, when allowed, sent black delegates to the local Portsmouth Association. The blacks were clearly running their church, notwithstanding the white "overseeing."

While in the earlier years, "fighting" was the major cause of excommunication, in the later period sexual mores seem to have taken up more of church time. Members were expelled for "living with an on lawful woman"; "for living not Christian like in his family"; "for not marrying his wife"; for marrying "a married man knowing him to be married"; for visiting "a certain house through which a report is in circulation injurious to the cause of God"; for "having a woman in his private room after hours night after night"; and simply for "adultery" or the "sin of fornication." The church pressed blacks to marry and at the same time "searched the word of God" in an attempt to find some text that could justify the relationships blacks worked out, oftimes in the face of the sale of a partner. If a remarriage could be justified, as by the adultery of a former partner, the church would gladly concur. If it could not find a just cause, the "remarriage" would have to be dissolved or the new partners excommunicated.[36]

The social concerns and the pattern of internal control worked out in Gillfield were common practices in the black Baptist churches of Virginia. The 1832 civil laws and the restrictive regulations of white Baptists which predated the Nat Turner uprising were generally abided by, as is well documented by Harrison Daniel. However, the inner life of these black churches was run by blacks and essentially independent of white interference. The source materials confirm the analysis of Luther P. Jackson: While white churches approved black membership and dismission, the blacks actually made these decisions and submitted them to the white business meetings. While whites were formal ministers, in virtually every case blacks were preaching. In addition to Sampson White, black Lewis Tucker was preaching at Norfolk's First Baptist Church; ordained black Reverend William E. Walker was preaching at Fredericksburg; black W. B. Taylor was preaching at Zion Church, Hampton; ordained black pastor William Evans preached in Alexandria; and ordained Reverend Joseph Abrams preached at Richmond's First African. By the 1850s all of Virginia's black churches were meeting separately and privately during the week, they "exercised their own choice in the selection of a pastor, paid him his salary, conducted their own finances, and appointed all of their own church officers." They built new churches, Sunday schools, and missionary societies. Above all, they grew in numbers. They weathered the dangerous thirties and prospered in the forties and fifties.[37]

This achievement of sub-rosa autonomy in Virginia is demonstrated by the best-known black church of the post-1840 period, the First African Baptist Church of Richmond, which ostensibly had a Presbyterian form of government with a white pastor and a white review board in authority. Blacks in Richmond had been affiliated with a mixed Baptist church since the 1770s. In fact, their numbers were soon greater than those of the white Baptists, and by 1800, there were 150 black and 50 white congregants. Over the following years this trend was accelerated, and by 1838, 1,600 blacks were on the rolls as compared with 350 whites. Blacks longed for a separate church. By 1823, they had formulated a plan that they thought would succeed in that it paid homage to white approval. However, that was an unfortuitous time to ask for separation, given its closeness to the Vesey uprising; not surprisingly the State Legislature rejected the request for an independent organization. By 1838, both whites and blacks were "satisfied" with a new plan—the whites pleased to be relieved of "a heavy burden" and the blacks content to have far more opportunity to express themselves and to run their own affairs.

White Reverend J. B. Jeter (of the First Baptist Church) and Robert Ryland (then president of Richmond College) worked out a unique Presbyterian form of government for the new black church that was not required by the law and was not in keeping with Baptist policy. Church independence and direct congregant participation were abrogated. The new black church was assigned a pastor (Ryland) as well as a form of republican government. Thirty black deacons, chosen by the blacks, were given regional responsibilities. Together with Ryland, these black deacons ran the church, but a committee of white overseers had final jurisdiction in disputed cases. The congregation itself could not vote on any issue, although they chose the deacons.

The Richmond black church was immense and would have provided difficulties for any administration. (By 1845, there were 2,167 congregants and by 1859, 3,160.) Other black churches also gave deacons wide-ranging authority. In Virginia, all "branch" churches had to submit their rulings for final approval to their mother (white) churches. Despite these similarities, the independent First African was significantly different. Whites considered it a separate church inasmuch as it was represented and voted at the Dover Association meetings (although it was represented by whites). Yet, this "independent" church had to act without direct congregational involvement and with the knowledge that its rulings could be overturned by nonmembers. This extreme overseeing action was taken only twice, however, and, by and large, the black deacons were running the huge black church, with blacks functioning as preachers, although "praying from the floor."[38]

The involvement of black Reverend Joseph Abrams in the life of this Richmond church provides a good example of the extent to which the law was circumvented. Born in 1791, Abrams joined the First Baptist Church (mixed) in 1817 and was licensed by this congregation prior to 1832. Officially silenced by the 1832 law and whipped for preaching, he nevertheless continued to "aid" Ryland until his death on June 4, 1854. At his funeral, he was honored as befitted a major preacher. White Reverend John Bryce preached a funeral sermon before some 8,000 blacks, many of whom were from distant parts of Virginia. Ryland, too, praised Abrams, but possibly with mixed feelings, inasmuch as he noted that Abrams "was heard with far more interest than I was."

Abrams and other blacks "prayed" (or preached) and ran all the church's business committees. Blacks controlled many facets of the congregants' lives, as witnessed by the special committee "on the private debts of members." A black representative was even sent to the Northern black missionary association, the American Baptist Missionary Convention. Clearly, this was a black-run church, but its independence was definitely limited by the caveat that it had to be to the whites' liking as represented by Ryland, who was the official overseer. Ryland's role as white preacher and overseer was not exercised without strong pressures from the white community. He had to overcome white denigration of his function as well as serious doubts as to his entire "loyalty" to his race. Ryland wanted to retain the trust of the blacks but, of course, he had certain primary obligations to the whites. Involved in a serious case of black-white confrontation, he claimed to have refused "to degrade my office to a police [sic] to detect and to apprehend *runaways!*" Ryland came under suspicion when he forwarded the mail for his immense congregation. It was alleged that some of the letters he distributed to the slaves were either invitations to run away or reports of runaways' whereabouts. In order not to "disturb the legalized usages of society," Ryland stopped serving as mailman.

In July 1852, after two of Richmond's slave congregants were convicted of murdering their owner, the church got into very serious difficulty. The very idea of a black church was harshly attacked as a stimulus to black rebellion. In response, the pastors and deacons of the three white Baptist churches in Richmond publicly rallied behind both Ryland and the black church, issuing a strong supporting statement which, at the same time, totally upheld the institution of slavery. They felt called upon to issue a lengthy explanation of baptism as well, clarifying that in no way would it protect or preserve a sinner. It was apparently again being charged that the slaves were deluded into thinking that once baptized they were free to sin.

Ryland and his congregants came into conflict over their visions and spirit guidance. Ryland was suspicious of the blacks' "dreams" and strongly rejected their respect for spirit "as independent of or opposed to the word of God." He found the noisy patterns of black services abhorrent and claimed he had brought blacks to a new appreciation of order. Nevertheless, it was the black Abrams and other black floor preachers to whom the blacks responded fully, and it was without hesitation that they called an official black pastor, Reverend James Holmes, at war's end. Ryland may indeed have altered some patterns and may have helped create increased ambivalence about spirit travels. That they continued to exist and to be significant, however, is documented by his persistent attempts to control them.[39]

VIII

Interaction between white and black Baptists continued throughout the prewar period, but in modified form. Both blacks and whites had achieved the coherence of their new world views in close proximity to one another. That proximity and interaction had been important for both races. While black membership in mixed churches continued to grow, white Baptists reduced their rights. Over the years, blacks lost their voting rights in mixed business meetings, while the symbolically important titles of brother and sister, used in the earlier period, were generally dropped.

When blacks became the majority of mixed churches, their recountings of religious experiences, their baptisms and criticisms, would, of necessity, dominate church life. Whites increasingly welcomed the opportunity to separate themselves from black "domination" of church time. On the other hand, blacks, given their loss of equality in Baptist congregations, welcomed the increased freedom of quasi-separate congregations. While the Richmond Presbyterian-style structure was not repeated elsewhere, black subcongregations, ostensibly subservient to white churches, became the typical development in the 1830s.[40]

Generally, Southern churches moved slowly towards separate meetings. Blacks might ask for such a privilege over a period of years before it was granted (as the group grew larger), or they might ask for church approval of a "custom" of separate meetings already initiated. For example, by 1849, the slave majority at the First Baptist Church in Charleston, South Carolina, was meeting separately as well as occupying the gallery at white services. While still being baptized together with whites, the blacks' testimony was being heard at separate sessions. In addition, a special white Committee on Colored Members was making final decisions, although it acted on the advice of the leading blacks. The Charleston blacks maintained a separate Sunday School, owned their own church lot and burial ground, and ran their own poor fund. In 1851, two black congregants, Jacob Legase and Thomas Bell, were licensed to preach. At least one white man was expected to attend each black meeting, but it was difficult to get whites to accept this responsibility. Therefore, whether by omission or commission, the whites abetted the development of extensive black autonomy.

The second major step towards black independence was marked by the creation of an independent black business meeting, although decisions still had to be submitted to the whites. At Charleston, the blacks had all of the above-listed privileges *without* an independent business meeting. Even without separate business meetings, black deacons generally had great influence over decisions regarding black membership, such as acceptance, criticism, or expulsion, but with this second major step the black deacon's role was sanctioned and expanded in that he functioned more like a minister.

It was at this juncture that most white churches wanted to call a halt. However, either under pressure from blacks (as in Washington, D.C.) or because once begun the creation of a quasi-independent church had its own momentum (as in Nashville, Tennessee), this process often led to independent black churches or churches that were independent in all respects save in name.[41]

Blacks were members of the First Baptist Church of Washington, D.C., within a year of its founding in 1802. They were accepted as full and equal members, signing the covenant; black males exercised their right to vote at church business meetings. Witnessing, baptism, and criticism sessions were biracial, and the types of problems encountered by both races were much the same. Of the 173 blacks who joined between 1802 and 1830, 66 were slaves and they, too, were given an almost equal welcome to church life.

This church made a serious attempt to have Baptist slaveowners manumit their slaves, as we know from a case in which the owner reneged on such a promise to the church. One Samuel Smoot was expelled in August of 1817 "for selling two of his slaves contrary to his voluntary stipulation with the Church to emancipate them; after they should serve him a reasonable time to remunerate him for their cost, [and] expenses, (which time was by his request to be at the judgment of the Church)." Within two years, Smoot's "sorrow" over his sale of these slaves led to his restoration, and he was unanimously welcomed back to the Washington church, as was his new slave. His sin had been in breaking his promise. The old slaves remained someone else's property. Smoot made no such promises again, nor did the church solicit them. Slavery had become an accepted institution, and slaves were increasingly regarded as less equal in the Washington church.

By 1819, blacks in the Washington, D.C., church were functioning as a definite subgroup. Rhoda Hampton (or Rhoday Hamilton), the first black member of the church, was "sanctioned" as a "leader among the colored members." He was not given a title of honor, but as a sanctioned leader he officially led black assemblies. The blacks as a "body" began to submit their opinions on matters relating to their brethren. When a new church was built in 1824, the growing racial separation was formally marked by a separate black gallery. By 1830, the Washington blacks announced that they had secured the services of black William Butler who had been a preacher prior to his admission to the Washington church, and that they were meeting separately except on communion days. At this time, tentative black moves towards separation were stimulated by white attempts to disenfranchise blacks. In March 1832, two white deacons proposed that blacks be allowed to vote on black issues only, while whites would vote on all issues. However, the blacks, still having voting rights, refused to sanction this reduction in their status.

Having lost through a vote, white members pushed through a reorganization of the white church and by declaration established a new covenant in which all authority was vested in whites. This decision of November 1834, led directly to a parting of the ways. Led by black Brother Sampson White (from Gillfield, Virginia) "desirous . . . of enjoying the privileges which pertain to the people of God," thirty-one blacks (seven men and twenty-four women) sought letters of dismission from the First Baptist Church so that they might create a separate black church.

This decision split the black community and alienated the whites. Blacks became highly "agitated." Those blacks in favor of accommodation and subservience to white demands were excommunicated by the separate black meeting but were reinstated by the whites. Emotions ran very high.

Black brothers White and Butler pushed the blacks to decide for separation, and Black brothers Philip See, John Edward, and Armistead Long pressed for moderation. The two groups almost came to blows over this issue. Butler did not hesitate to call the opposition "slaves" willing to stay with those who "will not drink out of the same cup with them at communion."

Sampson White and his thirty-one followers (including Fanny Hampton, daughter of the first black member) were excommunicated from the First Baptist Church for "disorderly and unchristianlike conduct," which amounted to demanding letters of dismission. Forming an independent church, they risked illegitimacy, but the Philadelphia Baptist Association chose to disregard their dispute with their white mother church and legitimated their constitution.[42]

Thirty-nine blacks remained in the old mixed church, still functioning as a quasi-independent arm. They were determined to be orthodox Baptists and did not risk excommunication, nor would they harbor idiosyncratic practices. In October 1847, they excluded Synch Wormly, one of their members, for his behavior. Wormly had "been in the habit of talking much in the street . . . about his having the Keys to Heaven . . . having unlocked the Saviour's breast . . . and being as great a man as the Apostle Paul." Wormly's "spiritual pride" was an extension of normative black vision travel. The more conservative white-oriented "stayers" in the old First Baptist Church were more likely to be ashamed of such behavior than were the "radicals" who left to form their own possibly unacceptable independent church.

The risk of leaving under these uncertain conditions had caused many of White's followers to have second thoughts. While a majority of blacks had rallied behind White and Butler in the all-black meeting in the vote to exclude the moderates See and Long, when it came time to make the ultimate decision about leaving, the majority, including the great majority of males, remained in the mixed church. However, when the new black church succeeded in gaining recognition and proved itself over time, calling the distinguished black preacher Chauncy Leonard (1859), blacks increasingly rallied to the all-black church. By 1862, the black membership in the mixed church had declined to 8 while over 300 blacks were in the First Colored Church.[43]

IX

It was not uncommon for Southern black Baptist churches to grow to immense size. Both of necessity and by choice, separate societies and prayer groups or bands would meet several times during the week. On

Sundays and holidays, far larger numbers would congregate, but it was communion services, generally held once a month, that brought the largest numbers together. Many black churches had over 500 members, and at least eight had over 1,000 congregants. (See Table 4 and Appendix IB.)

The situation was very different in the North, where only the rare black Baptist church numbered over 300. The older, long established churches were the largest, but even the Abyssinian in New York City, the largest in its (mixed) association, had only 400 members in 1860. In the last twenty years prior to the war, many new churches were established in the North and Midwest. Most were very small and struggled to exist, and many had hardly appeared before they were disbanded. They were not generally organic offshoots of white churches, nor did they arise out of direct opposition to white discrimination. Small groups of ex-slaves, whose main concern was security north of slavery, planted the new black churches. Between 1845 and 1864, at least forty-five black Baptist churches were established north of slavery. Unlike the Northern black churches of the first two periods, these churches seem to have preferred all-black associations or no association affiliation at all to joining white groups. Already in general need of economic and social support, they suffered greatly as a result of the Fugitive Slave Act of 1850 and the subsequent Canadian exodus of blacks. (See Table 5.) Although the Fugitive Slave Act and the change in climate that it heralded led some Northern Baptist preachers and churches to a new black activism, the black churches still suffered.[44]

X

In the climate of near equality that marked the early period of Baptist church growth, black churches chose to join mixed or white associations rather than form separate organizations. Even in that period, however, some churches, such as the Williamsburg, Virginia, and the Bayou Chicot, Louisiana, black churches faced serious difficulties in gaining association approval. The Savannah church, however, was welcomed into the Georgia Association in 1790, and when the Savannah River Association was organized in 1802, the new Savannah Baptist Church (1800) and the Newington Church (1793) worked together with the Savannah First Colored. The Savannah First Colored was the oldest and by far the largest church in the Association (with 850 members), and blacks were the majority of this association. This was often true in Southern "white" associations. In 1818, in view of the changing racial climate, the Savannah

River Association agreed to divide along almost purely racial lines, creating the predominantly black Sunbury Association. In the 1840s, the blacks in the Sunbury Association, as in many other Southern associations, lost their right to vote and found themselves members of a white-run organization. (See Appendix II.) In many other Southern associations, black churches came to be "represented" by local white churches.

Black churches in the North affiliated with and voted in mixed or white associations. It was not until 1835 that several new weak churches in the old Northwest first attempted a separate black organization. In September

TABLE 4

The Largest Black Baptist Churches, North and South

Church	Year	Membership
North:		
African, Boston, Massachusetts	1851	110
Abysinnian, New York City, New York	1860	440
Ebenezer, New York City, New York	1855	108
Zion, New York City, New York	1851	378
First African, Philadelphia, Pennsylvania	1859	268
Shilo, Philadelphia, Pennsylvania	1859	303
Union, Philadelphia, Pennsylvania	1859	359
Chillicothe Baptist, Chillicothe, Ohio	1845	181
Total		2,144
South:		
First African, Petersburg, Virginia	1851	1635
Gillfield, Petersburg, Virginia	1851	1361
First African, Richmond, Virginia	1859	3160
Second African, Richmond, Virginia	1859	1029
Springfield, Augusta, Georgia	1863	1711
First African, Savannah, Georgia	1862	1815
Second Colored, Savannah, Georgia	1862	1146
First African, Lexington, Kentucky	1861	2223
Total		14,080

SOURCE: Appendix I.

TABLE 5

A Sample of Church Membership in the Period of the
Fugitive Slave Act

North (decline)	1848 Membership	1851 Membership
Joy, Boston	136	110
Hamilton Street, Albany	88	51
Abysinnian, New York City	424	373
Ebenezer, New York City	113	98
Zion, New York City	444	378
First African Church, Philadelphia[a]	252 (1844)	197

South (increase)	Pre-1850	Post-1850
First Baptist Church, Norfolk, Virginia	199 (1840)	250 (1851)
First African Church, Richmond, Virginia	2,167 (1845)	2,729 (1853)
Second African Church, Richmond, Virginia	312 (1849)	615 (1851)
Williamsburg African, Virginia	230 (1849)	305 (1852)
First Colored, Washington, D.C.	62 (1841)	216 (1851)
First African, Lexington, Kentucky	1,143 (1846)	1,548 (1851)
First African Church, Savannah, Georgia	1,202 (1846)	1,369 (1851)

a. However, the other Philadelphia black Baptist churches—Blockley, Shiloh, the Third Colored, and Union African—grew in this period, and the total black Baptist population of Philadelphia increased.

SOURCE: Appendix I.

1835, six Ohio churches, whose 178 congregants were primarily ex-slaves, formed the Providence Association. This example was followed by an Illinois group in 1839 and, inasmuch as both groups divided and a new group formed in Indiana, by 1857 there were five separate black associations functioning. (See Appendix III.) These new black institutions were formally much like the white associations, but most of their congregants were ex-slaves whose faith was Afro-Christian. When they spoke of "standing fast in the liberty wherein God has made you free," they knew that they had to "contend for the faith" in ways in which whites did not. These black associations chose education as the principal means to achieve their goals, thereby rejecting violence and revolt. Establishing educational institutions became their "holy endeavor," the means to "hasten the time when 'Etheopia shall stretch forth her hand to God' and as a people become unto 'God a royal priesthood, a chosen generation, a holy nation, a peculiar people.' "[45]

One quasi-national black organization was formed in the prewar period. The American Baptist Missionary Convention of 1840, formed around the safe issue of missionary activity, grew into a unique forum for interaction between Northern and Southern black Baptist leadership, and the annual meetings provided a context for creating and strengthening a national black Baptist community. While Northerners predominated, black Southerners attended the annual meetings (held in various Northern churches) and remained members as late as 1860. (See Appendix III.)

Although a wide-ranging group of blacks attended, the formal results of the yearly meetings seem meager. The convention helped a small number of pastors serving young and struggling churches on a missionary basis; it supported the widows of a few deceased members; and it sent and supported several missionaries to Sierra Leone. The formal statements issued by the convention were muted, and the references to slavery very few and far between. The strongest statement, issued in 1859, declared "slavery is against the progress of the gospel at home and abroad. *Resolved,* that we use all laudable means to abrogate it."

The significance of the American Baptist Missionary Convention lay elsewhere. This organization provided the only Baptist forum for blacks from Africa, New England, the South, and Midwest to meet together. By 1860, twenty-nine churches, forty-one ordained ministers, eighteen licentiates, thirteen societies, and sixty-eight individuals were all members, among them many leaders well known for their outspokenness, if not militancy. With Jeremiah Asher, Leonard A. Grimes, and Sampson White as active members, and with the yearly movement from one major population center to another, the American Baptist Missionary Convention was an important forum for contacts and discussions between black Baptists. The need to protect the Southern participants probably muted public utterances, but the very existence of this interstate annual meeting is significant. Black Baptists had developed important separate institutions long before the Civil War.[46]

Conclusions:
THE WAY OF THE WORLD

"If you are soaked by rain and then scorched by sun you see the
way of the world."

Twi Maxim[1]

By 1865, blacks in America had known much rain and much sun. They
had experienced great hardships and had passed through severe trials over
many years of changing seasons, and over those seasons they had changed
as well. They had not come with one language or one culture, but the
majority had shared a belief in a supreme preexistent power, in subordinate divinities and in the nature of being. The understanding of
being was the central element of the West African world view: there was
being with intelligence, being without intelligence, and being tied
concomitantly to time and place. All being shared in spirit: it was spirit and
could be controlled by the delegates of the supreme spirit. A person's
spirit, existent before birth, continued after death and could then be
contacted by those yet living to aid them.[2]

These understandings were common to most West African world
views, although the cultural matrix that was built upon these core views
varied considerably. Deities and their interrelationships varied as did the
parallel social structures, but virtually all West African societies believed
in God, spirit power, and eternally existent souls and divinities, and each
society had traditionally established ecstatic means for contacting and

consulting these deities. West African languages reflected these basic shared concepts and values. Categories of being structured language use and form, while time was intimately connected to the essence or being-quality of people and things.

Africans brought their many cultures to North America. Although it was once generally accepted that the promiscuous mixing of slaves and "seasoning" in the islands effectively eliminated West African culture, these assumptions have been brought into serious question. Slaveowners in different areas had very strong (and very different) prejudices as regards choice slaves, while changing conditions in Africa altered the available range of peoples. In addition, during the height of the slave trade to North America, a very large percentage of slaves were brought into a relatively limited area directly from Africa.[3]

African languages may very well have been preserved by many first-generation Afro-Americans. However, the thesis that African world views came into North America can and does stand without the support of this language argument. That argument will, if further evidence is found, strengthen and partly explain this development. That African world views came into America and coalesced into one black world view is based on the evidence that basic African values and understandings persisted throughout the slave period. This phenomenon is, in part, evidenced in the development of Pidgin English, Creole English, and black English, all of which to some extent preserved African concern with being and the African view of time. African verb structures indicate "whether the action . . . is habitual or completed or conditional or obligatory . . . rather than whether it is in the past, present or future." Black English preserves the concern with habitual, completed, or ongoing action—"He praying" describes the simple present, while "He be praying" is an "act along a continuum of time." (The Baptists promised that each baptized man and woman would *be* saved now and forever.)[4]

The development of a common black English is evidence of a common black culture. But this development occurred relatively late and was preceded by some variant creole and pidgin forms. It would appear that different African cultures (or mixtures of cultures) had dominated different areas, while the differing ratio of blacks to whites had variously affected the development of language. Resale, the forced migration of blacks, and "intermarriage" led to a common culture, although to this day pockets of language singularity remain.

I have suggested that, in a simplified fashion, the Afro-American Sacred Cosmos can be seen as having developed in three phases:

    (1) The period of mass arrival when African languages and Pidgin English were spoken and African world views more or less coalesced.

(2) The period dominated by second generation Afro-Americans when Creole English was the dominant language and when an increasing number of white culture values were absorbed into an increasingly dichotomous African Christian world view.

(3) The period of primarily third-generation Afro-Americans, who spoke black English and traveled toward an Afro-Christian world view. This was a period of mass forced migration and kinship restructuring, leading to further cultural homogeneity.

While such a formulation has heuristic value, it must be noted that actual developments were more complex than this, or any outline, can suggest. Blacks who came to America in the seventeenth century found themselves in a white world. Their daily interrelationships were more with whites than with blacks, and their world views altered relatively rapidly, giving some among them a quasi-white outlook. The mass purchase of slaves between 1740 and 1760 rapidly altered the racial composition of the South and gave each new arrival a far more African community to adjust to. It is in that period that African languages were most likely spoken and that a shared quasi-African world view emerged. At the same time, some blacks were already second- and third-generation Americans, and dichotomies were apparent while the search for a new coherence was already underway.

Gutman's data suggest elements of a common black culture by the 1750s, particularly in relation to marriage, kin networks, and naming traditions. The Baptist church data indicate the beginnings of a new black Christian culture during that same period. However, it was not until the 1770s that significant numbers of blacks were recorded as being Baptists. (Others may have been Christians on their own terms prior to this time.)

By 1800, black Christian churches were scattered over the South, and blacks were becoming Baptists and Methodists in increasing numbers. This trend continued until 1865, when it was estimated that one in four or six blacks belonged to a church.[5] (See Tables 3 and 6.) However, as the white South increased its defenses, an increasing number of black churches were forced to remain formally subservient to white mother churches. Informally, the situation was far more complex, with plantation Christianity a very significant phenomenon.

African tribal structure did not come into America, but to some extent the new plantations came to play a comparable role. Some early slaves called their first owners "father," and we know that many slaves took their first owners' names as their own. Marriages with individuals from other plantations, which were very common, were considered marriages "outside the family" or "abroad."[6]

African religious practitioners continued to practice in America. Eventually, many large plantations had one chief Voodoo practitioner; other

TABLE 6

Totals of Known Formal All-Black Churches[a]
in the Antebellum Period

Denomination	South	North	Total
Baptist	130*	75*	205*
Methodist Missions (white supervised)[b]	329		329
AME Zion[c]	3	46	49
AME[d]	89	192	281
African Union (Methodist Protestant)[e]	1	29	30
Presbyterian[f]	1	21	22
Catholic[g]	3		3
Disciples of Christ[h]	4		4
Friends (Quakers)[i]	1	3*	4*
Episcopal[j]	2*	2*	4*
Total	563*	368*	931*

*The number of churches is known to have been higher, but the accurate figures are unavailable.

a. Many of these churches were supervised by whites, but all were black congregations.

b. See W. P. Harrison, *The Gospel Among the Slaves* (Nashville, Tenn.: Methodist Episcopal Church, South, 1893), 325, and Joseph C. Hartzell, "Methodism and the Negro in the United States," *Journal of Negro History* 8 (1923): 301-315.

c. See Emory S. Bucke, *The History of American Methodism* (Nashville, Tenn.: Abingdon Press, 1964), Vol. I, 609ff., and James F. Shaw, *The Negro in the History of Methodism* (Nashville, Tenn.: Parthenon Press, 1954), 72.

d. See Bucke, *The History,* 601ff.; George A. Singleton, *The Romance of African Methodism: A Study of the African Methodist Episcopal Church* (New York: Exposition Press, 1952), 28-37; and Daniel A. Payne, *History of the African Methodist Episcopal Church* (New York: Johnson Reprint Co., [1891] 1968), 414-417.

e. See Bucke, *The History,* 616.

f. See Andrew E. Murray, *Presbyterians and the Negro—A History* (Philadelphia: Presbyterian Historical Society, 1966), 33-60.

g. See John T. Gillard, *The Catholic Church and the American Negro* (Baltimore, Md.: St. Joseph's Society Press, 1929), 16-30.

h. See Robert O. Fife, *Teeth on Edge* (Grand Rapids, Mich.: Baker Book House, 1971), 5-8.

i. See Henry Joel Cadbury, "Negro Membership in the Society of Friends," *Journal of Negro History* 21 (1926): 151-213.

j. See Theodore D. Bratton, *Wanted: Leaders* (New York: Department of Missions . . . Episcopal Church, 1922), 181-185.

---

plantations evidently had several (rival) Voodoo conjurers and perhaps other "good" root doctors as well. These roles were sometimes separate and sometimes combined, and as a new Christian leadership developed, they too became intertwined with this quasi-African leadership group.

Some Christians abjured Voodoo and yet respected spirit in an overtly African manner. Nat Turner was such a Baptist exhorter, rejecting Voodoo and yet embracing spirit; and it may well explain his remaining outside the church structure. Other churched black Christians, including preachers, were occasionally root doctors or near-conjurers. The Vesey trial record tells of a blind preacher "said to have been born with *a caul* . . . [who] was supposed to foresee events." It was an African belief that such a caul (a membrane sometimes enveloping the head of a child at birth) indicated spiritual powers. The court recorder recognized that the preacher's "influence over the minds of his followers was no doubt therefore very considerable."[7]

In 1851, a "minister of the gospel" reported that

> on almost every large plantation of Negroes there is one among them who holds a kind of magical sway over the minds and opin- ions of the rest; to him they took as their oracle—and this same oracle . . . [is] most generally a *preacher*. . . . It is more likely that he has seen sundry miraculous visions, equal to those of John on the Isle of Patmas; Angels have talked to him, etc., etc. The influence of such a negro on the quarter is incalculable.

The line between African powers and Christian visions was difficult to draw. This white preacher viewed most such magic-working men as "thieves, villains and hypocrites" and as particular obstacles to white missionary endeavors, unless the white theology happened to be that of the black.[8]

Blacks, however, certainly honored these men. Slaves on the Sea Islands called their preachers *Fathers*, and the respect they showed them was shared by other blacks. The terms uncle, aunt, sister, and brother, referred to as "fictive kin" by Gutman, established an age group structuring, involving prescribed polite forms and obligations comparable to those in West African cultures, as did the secret societies, which often became Christian secret societies.[9]

The evidence of changed African forms is but part of the proof that African values survived in America. The key evidence is found in spiritual matters. African deities were not generally believed to have crossed over the "grandywater." There was a deep and poignant sense of loss—of deities, tribe, family, prophets, priests, diviners, and medicine men. Blacks in America set out, in an unorganized and unpremeditated way, to remedy this loss. Their newly developing patterns were, perhaps, as dependent on their common African background as on their common slave history.

Within the framework of chattel slavery, much was left open for blacks to work out for themselves. Owners objected to anything that interfered with work, but most "didn't care what they did when their tasks were over." However, all-night ecstatic dancing and singing would interfere with work the next day; secret societies did provoke fear of antiwhite activity; and plantation promiscuity or polygamy might well lead to rivalry or violence that would interfere with the plantation as an economic unit. Belief in Voodoo did give the blacks a sense of power and secret control. All these aspects could and did arouse white concern. Nevertheless, aside from the limited interference of strongly committed Christians who attempted to enforce a different behavior pattern, blacks found the time and the psychological space to develop their own black culture with its own inner dynamic and outward form. This culture built upon the shared core of African understandings of man, spirit, and the world. Man's spirit was still seen as dual. Spirit was viewed as pervasive and approachable, and the world as the present merging with the past. Man's soul was to join spirit after death.

Sometimes whites interfered in ways that made the journey to Christianity more difficult. Many ex-slaves remembered having been beaten for praying or attending meetings. This interference may have had a reverse effect in that it made the choice of Christianity a decision, painful but significant, by means of which the slave could achieve much psychic reward. He was not doing the easy or white-approved action. Ironically, if most slaves had accepted the Christian view of marriage, it would have complicated the slave economy considerably. Sales and the resulting family disruption would have severely reduced procreation.

Whites may have had an unconscious awareness of this inherent contradiction. Occasionally, an indication of some white opposition to the growing black Christian leadership and the new Christian values was recorded. The Plantation Manual of James H. Hammond notes: "Church members are privileged to dance on all holyday occasions; and the class leader or deacon who may report them shall be reprimanded or punished at the discretion of the master.'' Hammond was ready to punish black Baptist leaders for their new Christian ethic if they attempted to interfere with the well-established (a-Christian) social order on his plantation.

Old black values often continued functioning unbeknownst to whites. Naming and the use of names were important in this regard. Gutman has identified widespread black necronymic naming patterns that white contemporaries were apparently unaware of. He suggests that these naming practices were related to those of West Africa and that they ''reveal an attachment to a familial 'line' and suggest the symbolic renewal in birth of intimate familial experiences identified with a parent or grandparent.'' Although West African naming practices vary, it is a widely held belief that spirits return to bodies named to welcome them. Jomo Kenyatta explains that among the Gikuyu:

> tribal custom requires that a married couple should have at least four children, two male and two female. The first male is regarded as perpetuating the existence of the man's father, the second as perpetuating that of the woman's father. The first and second female children fulfill the same ritual duty to the souls of their grandmothers on both sides. The children are given names of the persons whose souls they represent.

Bringing a child into the world is thus a personal, family, and clan responsibility. Kenyatta recognizes that marriage and childbirth are ''the most powerful means of maintaining the cohesion of Gikuyu society and of enforcing conformity.''

Naming continued to be important to Afro-Americans. Christian conversion, where God called to the ''traveler'' *by name;* baptism, where the preacher called the convert *by name;* and admission to the church, where the *name* of the black was recorded, all provided new avenues to celebrate the significance of black names and provide a welcome to reborn spirits. Christian marriage was a more problematic slave institution, but church records substantiate the existence and use of slave family names that differed from their owners and indicate that these names were honored by the churches, both white and black.[10]

As suggested above, the understandings and practices of whites affected black consciousness. If blacks who arrived during the first peak of importation (1740-60) were able to preserve an African sense of self, their children and grandchildren experienced greater and greater difficulty as well as an increasingly reduced consciousness of the African content in their world views.

This is not to say that Africa was ever lost from their vision. Even larger numbers of Africans came between 1790 and 1810, and blacks continued to come directly from Africa until the last period of slavery. Africans, and particularly African-born Voodooists, were known to slaves through the Civil War. However, American born blacks were then dominant in the black community. Africa figured as a fixed symbol of their past but a confused sign for the future. A small incident in Georgia in 1843 suggests how Africa was used to express black identity in the South. When a white representative of the mixed Sunbury Association proposed that each church member be tithed 12.5 cents a year for foreign missionaries' salaries, five all-black churches (representing a majority of the association's members, but with a voting power unequal to their numbers) voted against this proposition. They were defeated. In order to emerge with some sense of control or to make their mark, as it were, the First African Church of Savannah (with some 2,250 black members) "requested that their contribution for Foreign Missions be appropriated to the Liberia African Mission." This was not an isolated case. Black Georgia churches continued to contribute to African missions through 1860, and there is evidence of similar black contributions in Charleston, South Carolina (1852), and in Matagorda, Texas (1848), where the whites sent $11.50 for China and the blacks matched that sum for Africa. It is very likely that many of the funds raised for this purpose by mixed Southern churches all over the South actually came from blacks, although whites did support missions in Africa and the sending of (free) black Christians "home."[11]

Both blacks and whites worked to organize missionary societies to send the good word to Africa. The interracial African Baptist Missionary Society organized at Richmond, Virginia, in 1815 was officially led by white William Crane, but black Collin Teague was vice-president and Lott Carey, also black, was recording secretary. Blacks in both Petersburg and Richmond supported the organization as well as the emigration of Carey, Teague, and their families in 1821 and the later emigration of Colston Waring, John Lewis, and other groups of black laymen and preachers.[12]

There is little evidence that Southern blacks objected to the Colonization movement, in the way that Northerners did, but it is difficult to accept Miles Mark Fisher's contention that large numbers of second- and third-generation antebellum blacks wanted to go to Africa (which he believes is shown by the many spirituals referring to "home"). It is true that Carey saw himself as both returning home and carrying out a new phase of the blacks' sacred history. He compared himself to a biblical Jew, returning to Zion to build the Temple, but he called himself an African:

> I am an African and in this country, however meritorious my conduct and respectable my character, I cannot receive the credit due to either. I wish to go to a country where I shall be estimated by my merits—not by my complexion; and I feel bound to labour for my suffering race.

Southern black Baptists, as well as those more politically active in the North, sometimes objected to the appellation African, an objection that suggests the confusions or conflicting values of the blacks. Preacher Jacob Walker of the Augusta, Georgia, black Springfield Church regarded himself as a nonhyphenated American:

> Most of us were born in this country, and of course we claim to be *Americans:* our ancestors, it is true, came from Africa; those of the white people came from *England, Germany, France, &* c., and it would be just as proper to call their descendants, *Englishmen, Germans, Frenchmen &* c.

Others expressed a desire to be called "colored Americans," but only a very few, such as Phillis Wheatley and "Uncle Jack," actually expressed thankfulness for having become American slaves. Generally, whites put words of thankfuness into "good" retainers' mouths. A tract from the early nineteenth century described a "simple and pure" Christian slave as saying: "me mean God let be made slave by white men to do me good. . . . He take me from the land of darkness and bring me to the land of light."[13]

Life in the "land of light" led blacks to absorb contradictory mores and grave doubts as to the value and efficacy of African ways. New immigrants were often haughty and able to laugh in the face of the Christian outreach. Could second- and third-generation slaves do as much? I have suggested that blacks lived with a bifurcated conscience. This is not the bicultural socialization posited by Charles A. Valentine, but rather a socialization in a single ambivalent world view, where contradictory values from both cultures existed side by side, where blacks could go to church on Sunday and visit the conjurer on the morrow. (There was also the white culture as an "outside" culture, and in this sense the blacks did come in contact with two cultures.)[14]

Slaves continued to believe in Voodoo. Blacks in America continued to have ecstatic trances and to accept esoteric wisdom and herbal medicine. Blacks used this power among themselves and in their relationships with whites. Slaves told tales of success as well as of failure:

His master beat him so sevare, so de man went to a witch. De witch said, "Never min'! you go home. Tomorrow you will see me." When de man got up in de mornin', de white man was jus' as happy as happy can be; but de more de sun goes down, he commence ter sleep. At de same time he call to his Negro, "Tomorrow you go an' do such and such a tas'." Giving out his orders kyan hardly hol' up his head. As soon as de sun was down, he down too, he down yet. De witch done dat. He [witch] came, but he stay in his home an' done dat.

Henry Bibb, born a slave in Kentucky in 1815, later suggested that it was witchcraft's failure to protect him against whites that led him to think of running away from slavery. Facing punishment for going off his plantation at night, he went to a conjurer:

He said if I would pay him a small sum, he would prevent my being flogged. After I had paid him, he mixed up some alum, salt and other stuff into a powder, and said I must sprinkle it about my master, if he should offer to strike me; this would prevent him. He also gave me some kind of bitter root to chew, and spit towards him, which would certainly prevent my being flogged. According to order, I used his remedy, and for some cause I was let pass without being flogged that time.

I then had great faith in conjuration and witchcraft. I was led to believe that I could do almost as I pleased without being flogged.

Bibb then purposely flouted his owner, staying away over the Sabbath, and "talking saucy" on his return. This time, however, he was harshly punished and, as a result, was convinced that these particular roots had no power. Nevertheless, he directly went off to a second conjurer (who called the first a quack) and paid for his recipe: cow manure, red pepper, and white people's hair, all dried and ground up and spread over the owner's bedroom, boots, and hat. A second failure still did not lead Bibb to abjure conjurers (he continued to turn to them to help him in love problems with black women), but perhaps it led him to doubt their efficacy with white power.[15]

Africans had traditions of ecstatic dancing and singing, often "working up the spirit" until a medium would go into a trance, be mounted by a divinity, and transmit the divinity's commands or advice. Ecstatic dancing and singing were brought into North America. The North American blacks were peripherally exposed to a very different white religious tradition, one of relative decorum and order. Among the Anglicans, there was little evidence that the white God visited his followers or that they could consult him in a public fashion. It was only in the First Great Awakening that whites at revivals gave public expression to their ecstasy. As stated earlier, for the very first time, blacks saw whites experiencing symbolic death and rebirth, "mourning" and redemption, religious joy and spiritual pain. They recognized these signs of initiation into the life of the spirit and were ready to participate when invited to the Baptist and Methodist "love feasts." Blacks began to go on new spiritual journeys which led them individually to Christ and to God. They were no longer "mounted" by other spirits nor did they have to rely on mediums, but they were individually led, perhaps by African-style messengers, to go down to Hell and then, if saved, to travel to Heaven to know Jesus and God. Their dual souls participated and their eternal "little me" was saved. God was "that thing"—and once He was in their hearts, He was there to stay: "Couldn't fin' dat leetle tin—hunt for 'em—huntin' fur 'em all de time—las' foun' 'em."

At an early stage of development, it was difficult for African/ Christians to coherently integrate their African and Christian values. Catholic Voudouists regarded the Bible as "the greatest conjure book in the world," and Moses was "honored as the greatest conjurer."[16] Christians on the Sea Islands maintained what were obviously neo-African initiation customs and neo-African ecstatic song and dance practices. These practices could certainly be syncretically integrated into Christianity. More problematically, they maintained a neo-African sex ethic side by side with a Christian one. Prior to initiation, one could be (and perhaps should be?) promiscuous; afterwards, as a Christian, one should reserve sex for a single lifetime marital relationship. While premarital promiscuity was accepted among some African peoples, others advocated sexual abstinence until marriage and most regarded adultery as a very grave crime. The range of patterns was wide. While most Africans knew a polygamous form of marriage, some did accept serial marriages for women as well and the bearing of children for the grandfather's household by unmarried daughters. Some societies such as the Gikuyu accepted certain well-defined extramarital relationships as honorable, while other extramarital relationships were considered very dishonorable crimes. The distinctions (such as if the husband approved or not, or if the liaison was in the homestead and, therefore, acceptable, or outside and taboo) could not appear proper in white Christian eyes. Gutman's data indicate the widespread existence and modal status of black families as well as the myriad relationships outside of this norm, but he does not explore the deeply conflicting black attitudes on this matter. Many black Christians continued to be promiscuous or to establish serial unions or several relatively permanent connections at one time, causing difficult problems that had to be confronted in some overt way. Concern with sexual "purity" had been dominant in white Baptist congregations in the early period of relatively shared experience. As whites moved away from the ecstatic involvement of the early revival period, they also reduced the watch-care exercised by the church. By the 1860s, most white Baptist churches were far less involved in the daily lives of their congregants than they had been in 1800. Thus, the reduced emphasis on white "immorality" is not necessarily a reflection of changes in white sexual behavior, although it may be.[17]

Black Baptists and Methodists continued to regard the sexual behavior of blacks as a central concern; in fact, its centrality grew over time. Again, this does not reflect a "deterioration" in black behavior (as judged by Christian standards). On the contrary, it probably indicates an increasing acceptance of Christian institutions as the means for policing social behavior. The Baptist church assembly was carrying out what had been the functions of the African social community. Blacks widely accepted this development. What remained as a source of conflict was the definition of proper social behavior—adultery was wrong, but one simple definition of adultery had not become socially accepted.

Rhoday Hampton (or Rhoda Hamilton), who in 1803 was the first black man to join the one-year-old First Baptist Church of Washington, D.C., faced such a dilemma. From his first attachment to this "white" church, Hampton was an active participant. Unanimously accepted, he signed the common role book and attended and voted at business meetings. He was part of a self-disciplining Christian community that had vowed "to bear, reproof and reprove each other in love, in case of visible fault in Christian charity and humility." Hamilton showed visible fault and was reproved! He was suspended in February 1807 and charged with having married without "the advice of this Church." Nevertheless, in September 1810, he was invited to return.

> Rhoda Hamilton . . . has been for a length of time in state of suspension for having married another woman while one was still living with whom he had been connected as a wife. After due investigation, it appears to the satisfaction of the Church, that the woman with whom he was formerly connected confessed to him, before he had formed his present marriage covenant, that she received another man to her bed during his absence; which, according to Matthew 5: 32 . . . we deem a perfect dissolution of a compact with her—. Therefore, resolved that

Rhoda Hamilton be restored to his former standing and full
fellowship with this church and in token there of that the right
hand of fellowship be given to him, which was done accordingly.

We have no way of knowing whether the church sought this manner of
sanctioning Hamilton's action or whether this was his own (and perhaps a
more common) tactic. Hamilton was emerging as a leader of the growing
black membership in the mixed Washington, D.C., church, and perhaps
his presence had been missed by all. Hamilton was welcomed back and by
June 1811 his new wife, Fanny, had testified and was baptized and
unanimously received into the church. Much later, in May 1830, their
daughter Fanny Hampton joined the same congregation.

Black and white Baptist churches did pressure blacks to accept a
Christian sexual ethic. Formal marriage was suggested to applicants
seeking admittance (and performed by the minister), and "untowared"
relationships publicly discussed. When Spencer Johnson was found to be
living in "scandalous intimacy" with a white woman in Washington, D.C.,
it was the church's responsibility to investigate and labor with and (having
failed to change him) exclude the sinner. When James Monroe's
"servant" Kitty was found guilty of "intoxication and fornication," she too
was excluded.[18]

As discussed above, adultery and "remarriage" (while the first
partner was still alive) were serious charges in independent black
churches, in subchurches where black deacons and black committees
generally handled such issues, and in mixed churches where whites
retained direct involvement in black discipline. Blacks were working at
becoming Christians. Their African history, where polygamy was modal
and serial marriage often accepted, was an impediment in this particular
area, and integration of the two sets of values was very difficult. Blacks did
not usually feel "Christian" shame over children born "outside" of
marriage or of unwed mothers. Nevertheless, the discrepancy between
their new values and their continuing behavior often led to unresolvable
conflicts.[19]

In using the churches as their "courts," blacks found a new institution
that was as concerned with adultery and other transgressions as the
African communities had been. Concern with adultery was not an
imposition of white values, although the definition of adultery was. Blacks
were not only "charged" with social transgressions; they also turned to the
churches for guidance and approval. In November 1808, a black woman in
the First Baptist Church of Washington, D.C., asked the mixed business
meeting (attended by at least several free black male members) for marital
advice. The church spent much time on her case and, in the end, became

more concerned with the faith of her partner than with his marital status, as he was not yet a Christian:

> November 7, 1808:
> Brother Fox having mentioned the circumstances of one of our coloured sisters who wishes to be married to a man who was separated from a woman with whom he was formerly connected (as his wife)—this Sister desired to know the opinion of the Church (she having related all the circumstances relative to herself and the man to Brother Fox) on the propriety of her marrying him.
>
> The question on that subject being taken into consideration it was Resolved that Brethren Brown and Gaines be appointed to inquire particularly into the circumstances of the case, and report thereon to the Church at a meeting especially to be held for that purpose on next Monday.

> November 14, 1808:
> Resolved that the woman be permitted to marry, but the Church recommend it to her, to take into consideration the expediency of marrying a man that is an unbeliever.

The church was not completely satisfied with this decision, and the issue was raised again in September 1809. Since an unbeliever could not be expected to respect Christian ideas of marriage, the crucial issue was, "Is it consistent with the Word of God for a believer to marry an unbeliever?"

As Genovese's perceptive analysis reminds us, Africans did not have a sense of original sin. Their understanding of misfortune was that it was indeed a punishment, but its cause was the breaking of a taboo or negligence in regard to proper ritual conduct, seen as an offense to elders, spirits, the living dead, or the live rulers of the society; or the use of sorcery by an enemy. Conduct, and not thought, was to be judged, and immorality came to be anything that hindered the development of the community. Long after the slave period, black Christians continued thinking in these terms, still understanding sin as the breaking of the new Christian taboos or that which hindered the development of the new Christian community.

> God has done get angry on his Throne. He got tired of all his chillun dancin', drinkin' and fiddlin' themselves on the road to hell. He decided he gonna wipe the human race off the earth. But Lil Jesus, he ask for time. He beg his Father for time to walk the earth and find the folks who ought to be saved.

Black Baptists were well within the white Baptist tradition when they emphasized sumptuary sins. At the revivals of the 1800s, gambling, drinking, horse racing, and cockfighting were the sins whites testified to as given up after the new birth. However, it would be very wrong to assume that black Christianity demanded adherence to new mores without ethical concern, any more than African religions had. Both the African and the black Baptist Sacred Cosmos made wide-ranging ethical demands. The Christian was called upon to have love in his heart; to eliminate strife; and to care for his brothers and sisters.

> God's goin' to get yo' 'bout yo'
>   low down ways.
> You talk about yo' elder when he's
>   tryin' to preach the word.
> You talk about yo' neighbour when he's
>   tryin' to praise the Lord.
> You talk about yo' sister when she's
>   on her knees a prayin'
> God's goin' to get yo' 'bout yo' low down ways.[20]

Black families played a very important role in the development and continuity of Afro-Christian morality and faith. Black women found much room for involvement, expression, and leadership in the Baptist churches, which was in keeping with both the Southern Separatist tradition and earlier African traditions. Each and every woman was expected to have as full an experience as each man; to recount it; to shout and have joy; to be baptized and to continue to witness. Women were given formal roles as deaconesses and served on committees to work with women who had violated Baptist ethics. They helped run missionary and fraternal societies, and they traveled about organizing projects. Southern black women even attended the meetings of the American Baptist Missionary Convention in the North.[21]

Black women played a prominent role in revivals where their ecstatic travels were perhaps even more evident than those of men. In this, there was continuity with the West African tradition in which so many women had been mediums.

Religious women, as mothers, had great effect on their children:

> The old folks used to slip out in the fields and thickets to have prayer meetings, and my mother always took me along for fear something would happen to me if left behind. They would all get around a kettle on their hands and knees and sing and pray and shout and cry.

> My mother was a great prayer, and she always asked God to take
> care of her son—meaning me. I would look and listen; sometimes
> I would cry. I didn't known what I was crying for, but the
> meaning [moaning?] and singing was so stirring that I couldn't
> help it. Now, as I look back, I know that these things sunk
> deep in my heart.

Fathers also figure in such childhood memories, even if they were
from "abroad" and saw their children only at intervals: "Every
Wednesday night when he [father] came to see us, as soon as it was time
for us to go to bed, he always called me to him and made me kneel down
between his knees and say my prayers."

Slave children experienced religion in the family circle. They saw their
mothers, fathers, grandparents, aunts, and uncles die and be reborn. They
heard shouts and "mourns" as part of their daily family lives. They were
prayed over as children, and they "knew" their own religious commitment
would play a central role in shaping their life-style and the evaluation
others made of them. A mother's parting words to her thirteen-year-old
son, being sold South in 1858 were: "Meet me in glory." He knew he could
do that only if he, too, were saved. Thus, baptism became the "ticket" to
the blacks' (new) ancestral home. The blacks believed that they would
meet their families in Heaven with God, as Africans had believed their
spirits would join spirit. Abream Scriven, being sold away from his wife in
1858, wrote

> Give my love to my father & mother and tell them good Bye for
> me. And if we Shall not meet in this world I hope to meet in
> heaven. My dear wife for you and my children my pen cannot
> express the griffe I feel to be parted from you all.

This theme of Heaven as the ancestral home figures in many black
songs:

> I'm just a goin' over Jordan
> I'm just a goin' over home
> I'm just a goin' over Jordan
> I'm goin' there no more to roam.
> I'm goin' there to see my mothr'n
> I'm goin' there no more to roam
> I'm goin' there to see my fathr'n
> I'm just a goin' over home.[22]

Many prominent preachers, such as George Liele, remembered their fathers' religious concerns. The religious activities of black fathers directly influenced the life choices made by sons. By the last period many could remember their fathers as Baptist ministers, and many sons chose to follow these role models. As with the white clergy, sons of preachers were more likely to be preachers than others. However, this pattern too may exhibit a continuity with both African and white traditions. As suggested above, preachers were occasionally cited as of "Royal African *blood*," and they may have been viewed as inheritors of traditional authority.[23]

Of 284 antebellum black Baptist preachers for whom some biographical data are available, at least 106 were known to have been ordained, 57 of these in the South.[24] This is another strong indication of the reality of the institutionalized church and, as most were ordained by whites, of its interrelationship with the white Baptist polity. The range of personalities and life experiences among these preachers was very diverse, yet only two Baptist preachers were known to have been born in Africa. This fact indicates the generational and cultural distance between African religions and the Afro-Baptist faith. One, Uncle Jack (d. 1843), is discussed at length above. Known for both his wisdom and his humility, he was opposed to African ways, especially the frenzy which he regarded as primitive and unworthy. Job Davis, the second, was brought to Charleston, South Carolina, in 1806 and purchased by a Mr. E. Davis, who brought him to Alabama. There he converted, joining the Bethel Baptist Church in 1812. He rapidly learned to read and was soon teaching Sunday School. Regarded as a saintly man, he was licensed to preach in 1818. Hosea Holcombe, writing in the 1830s, suggested that "few better preachers were found in Alabama in those days." Davis died in November 1835, a widely known and "loved" slave.[25]

John Berry Meachem, whose father was a black Baptist minister, was born a slave in Virginia. Through his own efforts, Meachem bought himself and his father and moved on to Kentucky where he married an enslaved woman. When she was "moved" to Missouri, Meachem followed (1815) and once again earned enough as a carpenter to purchase her outright. He joined the St. Louis Mission Church established by the Baptist General Convention in 1816. When the mission became an independent black church in 1827, Meachem was called to be its pastor. Father to a largely slave congregation (200 out of 220 in 1837), Meachem bought twenty slaves and allowed them to buy their freedom from him. By 1835, he was a wealthy man; he owned a "Temperance Steamboat" and was reputedly worth over $25,000. Meachem remained active in the St. Louis First African until the Civil War. He was a powerful and respected free black man, leading a "mixed" church of freemen and slaves.[26]

Many black Baptist preachers remained slaves—hundreds more than the forty-seven recorded as having served constituted churches. Slave plantation preachers ("chairbackers") were not likely to have had their names and vital statistics recorded. Names such as Uncle Link and Brother George occasionally surface in the narratives and the white church records, but little more is known of them. Brothers Moses Gift (South Carolina, 1794), Titus (South Carolina, 1804), and Black Bill (South Carolina, 1804) were all disciplined for preaching contrary to church orders, and so we know of their existence. Albert (South Carolina, 1859) could preach at funerals if his master permitted it. Anderson was licensed by the First Baptist Church (Nashville, circa 1840) while "Black Harry" is recorded as preaching on the Carter estate (Virginia, 1805) and Simon, slave of John Davis, was purchased by the Roanoke Association in 1792.[27] Of the thirty Baptist slave preachers known to have become free, eleven bought themselves, four were purchased by a Baptist Association and one by a Baptist church, and four were known runaways. Religious owners occasionally manumitted preachers (as Deacon Sharp had given George Liele his freedom); others gave them freedom to preach the gospel while their bodies remained enslaved.[28]

We have a fuller biography of "Uncle Harry Cowan" than for most, although no records of his prewar churches can be found. Cowan was born a slave in Davie County, North Carolina. Converted in 1825 and licensed to preach in 1828, he was ordained by the Reverend Harry Powers in 1830. He remained a slave and yet served as an itinerant pastor, organizing five churches in Rowan and Davidson Counties, South Carolina, during 1830 and 1831. His first owner, Thomas L. Cowan, gave him great freedom of movement, but his mobility was curtailed after the Nat Turner rebellion and his sale to a new owner. His new overseer "mocked my baptizing, clubbed me and fed me on half rations." It was only when Cowan converted his new master, who then often attended his meetings, that he was again given freedom to preach. An active preacher during the war, Cowan is credited with constituting thirty-seven freedmen's churches, many of which may have had unofficial prewar status.

Many ex-slave preachers achieved prominence, notably Liele, George, Bryan, and Marshall. Moses Clayton, born a slave on a plantation near Richmond in 1783, was a carpenter who achieved his freedom. In 1834, a religious white friend, William Crane, asked him to come north to Baltimore to lead black Baptists there. Given this opportunity, Clayton emerged as a charismatic leader, organizing the First Baptist Church, Colored, in 1837, and becoming active in the American Baptist Missionary Convention. Clayton's church, however, was beset by unrest and monetary problems, and in May 1852, twenty-six members, led by congregant John Carey, left to form the Union Baptist Church.[29]

Rivalry between black preachers and congregational divisions were not uncommon. Baptist churches, both black and white, often divided over theological and/or leadership issues or along class lines.[30] But preachers and churches also extended a strong arm of support to one another. For example, after Moses Clayton moved to the North, he convinced the mixed Maryland Union Association and the Southern Baptist Missionary Convention to purchase Noah Davis, a slave preacher in Fredericksburg, Virginia. Davis had been North before, when his owner had allowed him to travel to Boston seeking aid to purchase himself. He failed and returned to slavery as he had a wife and family in Virginia. When freed through Clayton's efforts, he gradually purchased his wife and five of his seven children.

In 1847, Davis began missionary work in Baltimore. Working together with white William Crane, he organized the Second African Church (later called the Saratoga Street African Baptist Church). Davis continued to work together with white people, who dominated his board of trustees (6 to 3), and in 1854, the white Maryland Union Association joined Davis in sponsoring a four-year high school for blacks which functioned for some ten years.[31]

Black Baptist biographies are the best illustration of how the new Afro-Baptist values affected individual blacks and helped them to find purpose and direction and to establish priorities. Daniel Scott, according to the manuscript minutes of the Gillfield Church, Petersburg, was licensed in about 1815. He was allowed "to exercise his gift anywhere the Lord might cast his lot." By 1832, he had cast his lot with the Union African in Philadelphia, remaining there until his death in 1850. During the last year of his life he was also president of the American Baptist Missionary Convention, and active on a national scale.[32]

Reverends Sampson White (discussed above) and William Butler led the blacks who rebelled in Washington's First Baptist Church. Butler, regarded as "the prime mover and principal instigator of it," had been admitted to the church in August 1828, presenting a letter from the United Baptist Church, Whiteoak Meeting House. "The letter . . . states that he had been indulged to exercise his gift in the ministry, whereupon it was agreed that he be permitted the same privilege." By this means, Butler became the first official black preacher at the Washington church. Elected moderator by the blacks in October 1833, Butler pushed the group toward independence, attacking blacks See, Edwards, and Long as "Mr. Brown's slaves." (White Reverend Obadiah B. Brown was pastor at the First Baptist Church. An active manager of the American Colonization Society, he had helped Lott Carey to emigrate.) Butler was incensed over what he regarded as public insults, especially the fact that "the white members will not drink out of the

Pages of the Manuscript Minutes of the First Baptist Church of Washington, D.C.

same cup with them at communion," and over the blacks' acceptances of formal second-class status including lack of voting parity. Fulfilling Butler's expectations, black Brother See publicly announced the loyalty (or complacency) of the conservative group through a declaration (see illustration) signed by fifteen men and four women:

> We are satisfied that in our present situation we enjoy enough privileges as our Heavenly Father sees good for us to enjoy, and that it will be better for us and for the cause of Christ to have the fellowship and council of our white brethren in Church matters than to forego them by separation.

White and Butler led the rebels out of the white church and as a result were formally suspended in March of 1839. At that critical juncture Butler drops out of sight. He did not join the new Washington black church that he had helped to create. Perhaps he returned South, as did so many of the members of this congregation.[33]

Many blacks who were born free and had relatively good educations achieved prominence in the black Baptist denomination. There are more published data on this second group than on the slave preachers, although they tended to work in the North and Midwest and, therefore, led smaller congregations. Jeremiah Asher (or Ashur), born free and a grandson of a black soldier in the Revolutionary War, was licensed in Hartford's mixed church in 1839. Appalled at the segregated seating, Asher led the blacks out of the mixed church and with several other individuals was responsible for the black Meeting Street Church becoming a black Baptist church. (It had been an interdenominational black meeting house, set up by white Quaker Moses Brown.) Asher pastored missions and churches in Hartford, Providence, Baltimore, Washington, D.C., and Philadelphia, and served the American Baptist Missionary Convention. He visited England on a tour to collect funds for the Philadelphia church. There he met with white Baptist leaders and laymen, and returned, as did many other black preachers, with an expanded sense of his abilities. Back in Philadelphia, he found his church, Shiloh, in a "low state." In the black church, much was dependent on the charismatic leadership of the preacher; as a result, churches both grew and declined rapidly.[34]

Charismatic leaders were not lacking in the North. Duke William Anderson (1812-1873), a free-born "mullatto" schoolteacher in Indiana and Illinois, was ordained in 1844. Anderson purchased eighty acres of land in Wood River, Illinois, and invited black families to join him in a new black community. He established a school, a church, and eventually the Wood River Association. Active in abolitionism and in the Underground Railroad, he was also employed by the white State Missionary

Society. When the Missionary Institute burned, Anderson moved to a pulpit in Buffalo, New York (1854), and then to the Groghan Street Church in Detroit, Michigan (1857), where he led a highly successful revival.[35]

After the war, Anderson and many other preachers, many of whom had come "up" from slavery, went South. Anderson went to teach at the new black Theological Institute in Nashville, Tennessee; Sampson White to the African Church in Lynchburg, Virginia; Jesse Boulden (of Philadelphia and Chicago) to Natchez, Mississippi; Thomas Hensen (of New York and Boston) to Norfolk, Virginia; Peter Randolph (of Prince Georges County, Virginia, New Haven, Connecticut, and Newburgh, New York) to Richmond; and William Williams (of Washington, D.C.) to the Gillfield Church in Petersburg, Virginia.[36]

Protestant preachers from the North had an immediate influence on plantation African/Christianity, as can be seen by evidence from the Sea Islands. Prior to the war, there were twenty-seven Baptist, twenty-three Methodist, eleven Episcopal, and two Presbyterian churches on the Islands, and it is estimated that close to one-half of the black population belonged to a church. These same blacks (and perhaps others) were also members of quasi-secret black societies which met in Pray's houses. The "white" churches also ran black missions. At least one of these missions was granted independence prior to the war: In April 1841, Huspah, a branch of the Beaufort Baptist Church, was constituted a separate church, with an official white minister, and 251 black congregants were transferred to its books. In 1861, Beaufort Baptist Church had 3,557 black and 166 white congregants, and it was supervising four black missions, each with black "deacons" who were, no doubt, preachers. After the arrival of Union forces, all but four of the blacks left the Beaufort white church to organize two separate black churches: (1) Tabernacle, with a Northern white missionary preacher, Reverend A. B. Woodsworth, which met in what had been the white lecture room, and (2) the African Baptist Church, with black Reverend Arthur Waddel as preacher. This second church met in an old Pray's house, thus symbolizing its more African orientation. These two congregations probably divided along class lines, although the slave elite, still called *swonga* people, generally attended the Episcopal church.

Black Baptists on the Sea Islands began to judge their own practices according to what they understood of the evaluations made by the new Northern clergy. Local blacks were beginning to resent (or fear) white Northern influences on their churches and at the same time were starting to imitate their ways. The decision of the important black Baptist Brick Church on St. Helena Island to form a choir was a symbolically important attempt to move away from ecstatic congregational involvement and to adopt the order and decorum that the white missionaries desired.

African/Christians of the Sea Islands at first excluded the unsaved; that is, anyone who did not have that "thing" could not be a member of the church community. Through the persuasion of a new arrival, white Baptist Minister Horton, they began to bar saved Protestants who were not of their denomination from attending their church. Thus, they expelled, among others, the white Unitarian teachers. Notwithstanding Union Army disapproval, at least one congregation maintained this new sign of their purity and their parity with Northern churches.[37]

Ex-plantation blacks who went North before, during, and after the war faced a more jarring confrontation with a black Baptist world view that had moved closer to the contemporary white one. This was apparent in Chicago, where the first black Baptist church, the Zoar Church, dating from April 1853, was constituted by old Chicago families that had been free for many years. When a large number of Southern Baptists recently up from slavery joined, very serious and disruptive problems resulted. Under the pastorate of H. H. Hawkins (1855-1857), twenty-one of these migrants were accepted and then rejected. One of the key issues was marriage and remarriage: the ex-slaves' more pragmatic attitude towards remarriage caused the Chicago church embarrassment. (When Miles Mark Fisher wrote a history of the church in 1922, he shared the 1857 emotion: "Some few of the recent immigrants from the South were neither good citizens nor useful church members. The Zoar Church had a few of this class. They had brought with them their own ideas of church worship and government which retarded the progress of the Zoar Congregation.") In 1858 the congregation called Pastor David C. Lett who promptly readmitted the twenty-one Southerners. (Fisher judged him a popularity seeker and was very critical of his "unwise handling of discipline.") The congregation was not unified. Lett remained pastor only seven months, and the church began a decline that led to a formal division in March 1860. The breakaway group of thirty-three members (who formed the Mount Zion Church) was probably made up of the older, more acculturated members, as is suggested by the fact that the church chose to join the white (abolitionist) Fox River Baptist Association rather than the all-black Wood River Association that supported the Zoar Church. (The Wood River Association was demanding that member churches reintroduce the practice of footwashing, an important indication of renewed Southern influence.)

The new Mount Zion Church called an important black preacher to its pulpit, the Reverend Jesse Freeman Boulden, D.D. Born in Delaware, educated in Delaware public schools and Philadelphia Quaker schools, Boulden was called to and ordained in the pulpit of the Philadelphia

Union Baptist Church in 1854. His call to Chicago came after a seven-year stay in Philadelphia during which Boulden had been very active: he had helped the congregation grow from 254 members to over 359, and he had served as vice-president of the American Baptist Missionary Convention. Boulden had a good deal of experience in handling the complex problems of a mixed Southern ex-slave and Northern free-born congregation. Philadelphia was a haven for those coming up from slavery, and the greatest number of newcomers joined the Baptist churches. Boulden's Union Church probably had a Virginia "connection," as its first two pastors were Daniel Scott and Sampson White, both of whom had preached at Gillfield in Petersburg. In Chicago in December 1861, Reverend Boulden succeeded in reuniting Zoar and Mount Zion, and the renewed church took a new name, Olivet.[38]

In an attempt to establish harmony between these two groups, Olivet made compromises symbolized by its eventual joining of both the white Fox River Association and the black Wood River Association. A new preacher, Richard DeBaptiste, made this move, as Boulden had gone South early in 1863. DeBaptiste, far more than Quaker-educated Boulden, was a man of both Southern and Northern traditions. Born in Fredericksburg, Virginia, in 1831, his early formative years were spent in the South, but in 1846, his free and fairly prosperous family moved to Detroit, Michigan. Both his mother and his father, who was a builder, were known as religious people; given his name, the Baptist tradition may have gone back even further. Baptized in 1852, DeBaptiste soon emerged as a powerful preacher. In April 1860, he was called to and ordained at the black Baptist church in Mt. Pleasant, Ohio. There, and at Olivet in Chicago, he drew large numbers to his preaching, and many became baptized congregants. DeBaptiste was able to bridge the Northern and Southern traditions successfully, and he remained at Olivet until 1882, by which time it had grown to 800 members.[39]

The way in which free-born and ex-slave black Baptists began to work out their problems in separate and joint congregations calls for a new in-depth study of religious developments during reconstruction. It is clear that there was a confrontation between African/Christianity (where African elements were discrete) and the highly integrated Afro-Christianity. Down through the Civil War, there were still very different black communities exhibiting a broad range of integration. Black Baptists of the Sea Islands' Brick Church, for example, practiced a faith somewhat different from that of the black Baptist church of Nashville, Tennessee. However, it was also different from neighboring Beaufort's African Baptist Church while still more distant from the black Baptist Joy Church of Boston. Later, as a normative black Baptist faith developed and became more orderly, the range of difference would be expressed in black cults and breakaway sects, where ecstasy and frenzy remained the most potent components.[40]

But many elements, both good and bad, changed forever with the end of slavery. The black plantation community had indeed taken over some of the tribal functions. It had become a new black society with structure and form and with normative behavior and social sanctions for nonconformity. The black church had been an integral part of that society, punishing wrongdoers and rewarding leaders with formal status, and it was to serve as a bridge to a new period of black life. When many blacks looked back nostalgically at slave life, it was not generally the slaveowners' paternalism that they missed, but the warmth and fullness of the "world the slaves made."[41] Black postwar churches sought to provide that warmth, fullness, and joy based on an existential security that was both African and Christian at its roots.

An African maxim taught that "where you have had joy excels where you have been born." Joy had come to Afro-Baptists in antebellum America. To die in Christ was to know Christian joy, and to live attempting to fulfill oneself was to know African joy. The tears of the black Baptist, often running freely during the joyful vision experience, were tears of happiness from God's well of holy water, but in crying the black American knew only a joyful homecoming in which he did not differentiate between black or white roots: his soul was one and his experience was of joyful love.

> O make-a-me ho holy
>   I do love, I do love,
> O make-a-me ho holy,
>   I do love the Lord.
>
> Feel the spirit moving.
> Now I'm getting happy.

To get happy was a euphemism for having a visionary experience: to be with the Lord was to be happy.[42] But the slaves sang "Religion make you happy," which in black English means it makes you happy for a limited time. (If religion would make you "be happy," it would be permanent.) Black joy, through tears, was a very mixed emotion. A slave, visiting God, knew he would "conquer," and yet he had to return to his unfree life and "persevere to the end." He had to hate the sin of slavery and yet love the sinner, the slaveowner. Solomon Bayley was almost broken by this dilemma. He shared his church life with his wife's owner and was close to despair over his inability to love this man. When the white slaveowner suddenly agreed to sell Mrs. Bayley to her husband, Bayley believed Christ had "appeared" to help him and he retained his faith and found love. But what of all those slaves whose owners were not affected by Christ? All men suffer in life, and perhaps wisdom is born only of trials and suffering. If so, the blacks had a "peculiar" advantage in this regard. Indeed, it would appear that a high percentage of slaves achieved wisdom and dignity. Their Afro-Christian faith was the matrix in which their identities were forged.

Black Baptists talked and sang of being "born in sin," and they spoke in Calvinistic terms of God having a chosen people and calling "whosoever he wills." However, in practice every individual was appealed to: all sinners were expected to be seekers and mourners. "Rascals" and "evildoers" could repent and be reborn; the saved could fall and fall again. Leaders in virtue, deacons, preachers, and even ordained ministers fell, confessed their sins, testified to their repentance, and were returned to good standing. The goals were clear, and the means to redemption were ostensibly available to all at any time.

Abraham Smith, "property of John Lyon," is an example of the sinning and repenting Baptist. Although he was not a preacher, there are more separate entries about him in the handwritten church minutes of the First Baptist Church of Washington, D.C., than about almost any other individual. Much church time was spent hearing his case. He joined the church in December 1813 already a Baptist, having in hand a letter of dismission from the Baptist Church of Zoar, Jefferson County, Virginia. (Mixed churches often went to great pains to trace slaves suddenly "sent away," so that they might have the proper Baptist credentials.) In September 1819, Smith was excluded from the Washington, D.C., church for causing "divisions and dissentions among the col'd. brethren, [and] that he forsook their assemblies," but in less than one year he was restored to membership. He was in trouble again four years later, in February 1824, when he was excluded for giving "much dissatisfaction to the col'd. brethren," having taken a coat from a congregant and not having returned it. In September 1825, Smith came before the black assembly and "stated to their satisfaction, his sorrow for his conduct, and a wish to be restored to fellowship with the Church." Upon investigation, a white committee accepted the black recommendation to restore Smith to fellowship. When Smith was excluded again in December 1832, he did not return until eight years later. By that time, there was an independent black church in Washington, D.C., but Smith chose to come back to the mixed First Baptist Church, his old home. When Smith died in April 1843, notwithstanding his three previous exclusions, he was a fully restored brother, one of the unconditionally elect, a saint vouchsafed "Perserverence to Glory."[43]

With the acceptance of Christianity, much of the evil in the black community was laid at the devil's doorstep; it was widely believed that Hoodoos "done sold deir soul ter de debbil." As such devil-servers, they were aligned against God, but this did not mean that the spirits they knew were not real and powerful.

Healing and divination had been important aspects of African ritual practices. The spirits had helped men with practical advice and actual physical transformations. In the new world view, Jesus became *the* intermediary, *the* messenger, *the* doctor, and *the* spirit with whom blacks had contact. He could advise, understand, foretell, and cure: "Doctor Jesus tells me what to do. I always take Doctor Jesus with me (when I treat sick patients) and put him in front, and if there is any hope he lets me know."[44]

In the last years of slavery, there was both conflict and syncretism between Voodoo and Christianity. Blacks were expelled from churches for conjuring, and other black Christians turned to Jesus to protect them from conjurers, indicating thereby their respect for "conjure power" but their belief in God as a spirit proven stronger:

> I remember one time when I was almost conjured by a hoodoo, and I prayed to the Lord and asked him to save me from him. I promised him if he would protect me and save me from being destroyed that way I would serve him the balance of my days. This he did, and I mean it has been a blessing.

Puckett relates that in a black congregation near Columbus, Mississippi, the congregants' reliance on charms or jacks forced many preachers to leave the church, until one preacher claimed to have a "daddy-jack" more powerful than the "mojos" of any of his congregation and, thereby, controlled them successfully.

Unquestionably, throughout the slavery era, spirit workers and their wisdom were still widely respected and feared among the Christian community. Those who claimed not to believe in Hoodoo were often the very ones who wore amulets or who sprinkled their houses with special concoctions. "I believe, Help me in my unbelief" had special meaning for those with a bifurcated world view.[45]

In the new black Baptist Sacred Cosmos, belief was replaced by knowledge. The converted black had been to Heaven, and *knew* God and *knew* Jesus and *knew* himself saved. African time had become Afro-Christian time; past had become future! "The soul that trusts in God need never stumble nor fall, because God, being all-wise and seeing and knowing all things, having looked down through time before time, foresaw every creeping thing and poured out his spirit on the earth."

In this new time and new place, God gave people a renewed purpose and a renewed way in which to achieve it. Black Baptist faith provided a new pattern of priorities that could lead to a new identity. Each individual knew where he was going, and he knew God was going with him. The sacred history of the Old Testament and its heroes had become the common black sacred history, the common past with its living dead; the New Testament promise of redemption had become the core of all visions of the future. Without consciousness of its source, the new sense of self helped the black return to the African sense of self. He now viewed the "thing in itself," "the man in a man," as the inner essence that Christ knew and appreciated. Africans knew "real life is spent in touch with the Supreme Spirit," and black Baptists experienced this real life. They were no longer dependent on African mediums, nor were they possessed by deities. Each "little man" traveled to be with God and returned with God in him to sing his joyous song.

After the war, the old traditions underwent much development and change, but there was also much continuity. In 1954, Richard Jolla, born in 1878 on the Claremont Plantation in Pond, Mississippi, sang a dream song very much in the prewar tradition. Guided by a dead preacher to see his dead mother, he heard her sing what sounded very much like an African call meant to guide him on his way to her. He knew that after many fateful turnings he would travel up "that road" one day.

> This pastor . . . he was dead . . . he's dead now, but I heard him in a dream. It seemed to have had association, and I was standing near the door, on the outside, an' he walking up with his grip in his hand, and he marched right on into that do', an' I went in behind him. And as we started in, he started a song. All right, after this song was over, I found myself in another place on a highway. An' I got to a place where the highway forked. An' this left-hand fork went down through a beautiful grove. A very small road, pretty road go through 'round there, but I looked, an' here was a big highway layin' out up there, an' didn't see any body gonn' that way much, an' when I looked up that highway, I saw a woman standin', 'way up that highway. It was my mother. An' after I sing what the pastor sing, this verse, then I'm goin'. . . .

> When the way is dark and dreary
> There's no star to light the way
> Just keep on—, oh toiling
> Till the dawn and the day . . .

(That's what he sang. Travelin' down this road,)

I saw this woman standin' . . .
I heard a call
I heard my old mother ooo, calling, saying
Come on, son, this is the way . . .
(That was my dream.)[46]

NOTES

The Works Project Administration collection of the reminiscences of ex-slaves has been published in George P. Rawick, ed., *The American Slave: A Composite Autobiography,* 17 vols. (Westport, Conn.: Greenwood Press, 1973). The references below, however, are generally to the original Federal Writers' Project typescript, housed in the Library of Congress and available on microfilm under the title "Slave Narratives: A Folk History of Slavery in the U.S. from Interviews with Former Slaves, 1936-38" (Washington, D.C.: Library of Congress, 1941). This reference is abbreviated "Slave Narratives." Other abbreviations in the notes are: *Journal of Negro History = JNH; Journal of Southern History = JSH; Mississippi Valley Historical Review = MVHR; Journal of American Folklore = JAF;* American Baptist Missionary Convention (1840-1860) = ABMC; and Historical Commission of the Southern Baptist Convention in Nashville, Tennessee = HCSBC.

Acknowledgments

1. Ralph Ellison, "Conference Transcript," *Daedalus* 95 (1966): 435.

Introduction

1. All of the classic studies of the black church in America (those of DuBois, Woodson, Frazier, Mays, and Washington) are based on relatively limited church data. The one historian who has perhaps the widest acquaintance with the original sources, in particular with the data on blacks in mixed churches in Virginia, is Harrison Daniel, but he approaches black church reality as limited by what those primarily white sources reveal. He has not analyzed the psychosocial nature of black church life. The same is true of Milton Sernett and other capable analysts of black and white religious interaction. Luther Jackson comes closer to the heart of the matter, but his fine work is too brief and too specialized (primarily on Virginia) to give us a full picture.

Almost all of the recent books on slavery have considered black religion in some depth. George Rawick, John Blassingame, Ira Berlin and, particularly, Eugene Genovese have made significant contributions to this discussion, but they, too, have not given a broad enough picture of developments. Genovese's spectrum is so broad and his contribution so important that this comment seems specious, but he, as the others, did not know of the existence of most of the formal black churches. More importantly, I believe he found it difficult to take religious excitement seriously. In none of the many pages of *Roll, Jordan, Roll* is the crucial trance or vision travel analyzed.

One of the most serious considerations of black religious consciousness can be found in Lawrence Levine's work. However, his excellent book on black culture, dealing with the last period of slavery and the first century of freedom, appeared in print too late for use in the preparation of this book.

A good statement of revisionist views can be found in a recent article by Kenneth K. Bailey, "Protestantism and Afro-Americans in the Old South: Another Look." Bailey shifts emphasis to the evidence of black participation in antebellum church life. However, his view is closer to the old position than to what I believe was the reality. Bailey places new emphasis on the respect shown black souls by whites, but he states that black pastors and congregations were tolerated "here and there" and that "a few blacks were . . . ordained as . . . ministers." He regards the examples he presents of strong black churches and independent black individuals as essentially extraordinary. As this book will endeavor to document, the reality was far different.

The documents used for this study are cited in these notes. In addition, a list of the manuscript church minutes studied is appended to A Note on Sources. The classic studies mentioned above are: W.E.B. DuBois, *The Negro Church* (Atlanta, Ga.: Atlanta Press, 1903); Carter G. Woodson, *The History of the Negro Church,* 2d ed. (Washington, D.C.: Associated Publishers, 1921); E. Franklin Frazier, *The Negro Church in America* (New York: Schocken Books, 1964); Benjamin E. Mays and Joseph W. Nicholson, *The Negro's Church* (New York: Institute of Social and Religious Research, 1933); and Joseph R. Washington, *Black Religion* (Boston: Beacon Press, 1964). Among the articles by Harrison W. Daniel, see "Virginia Baptists and the Negro in the Early Republic," *Virginia Magazine of History* 80 (1972): 60-70; "Virginia Baptists, 1861-1865," *Virginia Magazine of History* 72 (1964): 94-130; "Virginia Baptists and the Negro in the Antebellum Era," *JNH* 56 (1971): 1-16; and "Southern Protestantism and the Negro, 1860-1865," *North Carolina Historical Review* 41 (1964): 338-359. Milton C. Sernett, *Black Religion and American Evangelism* (Metuchen, N.J.: Scarecrow Press, 1975). Luther P. Jackson, "Religious Development of the Negroes in Virginia from 1870 to 1860," *JNH* 16 (1931): 168-239; Luther P. Jackson, "The Early Strivings of the Negro in Virginia," *JNH* 24 (1940): 25-34; Lawrence W. Levine, "Slave Song and Slave Consciousness," in Tamara K. Hareven, ed., *Anonymous Americans* (Englewood Cliffs, N.J.: Prentice-Hall, 1971), 99-130; George P. Rawick, *From Sundown to Sunup; The Making of the Black Community* (Westport, Conn.: Greenwood Publishing Co., 1972); John W. Blassingame, *The Slave Community* (London: Oxford University Press, 1972); Ira Berlin, *Slaves Without Masters: The Free Negro in the Antebellum South* (New York: Pantheon Books, 1974); Eugene Genovese, *Roll, Jordan, Roll: The World the Slaves Made* (New York: Pantheon Books, 1974); Lawrence Levine, *Black Culture and Black Consciousness* (New York: Oxford University Press, 1977); and Kenneth K. Bailey, "Protestantism and Afro-Americans in the Old South: Another Look," *JSH* 41(1975): 451-472.

2. Two of the finest works in this new area are Gerald W. Mullin, *Flight and Rebellion: Slave Resistance in Eighteenth Century Virginia* (London: Oxford University Press, 1972); and Peter H. Wood, *Black Majority: Negroes in Colonial South Carolina from 1670 Through the Stono Rebellion* (New York: Alfred A. Knopf, 1974).

3. Alex Haley, *Roots* (Garden City, N.Y.: Doubleday & Co., 1976); Geoffrey Parrinder, *West African Religion,* 2d ed. (London: Epworth Press, [1949] 1961); and Geoffrey Parrinder, *West African Psychology* (London: Lutterworth Press, 1951).

4. Parrinder, *Psychology,* 17-18.

5. Philip D. Curtin, *The Atlantic Slave Trade: A Census* (Madison: University of Wisconsin Press, 1969), 72-75, 157 (discussed below, Chapter 2).

6. Frazier, *Negro Church,* 1-19; Timothy Smith, "Slavery and Theology: The Emergence of Black Christian Consciousness in 19th Century America," *Church History* 41 (1972): 497-512.

7. J. L. Dillard, *Black English: Its History and Usage in the United States* (New York: Random House, 1972).

Chapter 1

1. Thomas Luckman, *The Invisible Religion: The Problem of Religion in Modern Society* (New York: Macmillan Co., 1967), 52, 53, 54, 61; Peter L. Berger, *The Sacred Canopy* (Garden City, N.Y.: Anchor Books, 1969); Peter L. Berger and Thomas Luckman, *The Social Construction of Reality* (London: Penguin Press, 1966).

2. Luckman, *Invisible Religion,* 18, 19, 53, 55, 70.

3. Luckman and Berger do not deal specifically with traumatic change or clashing world views. Their outlook is oriented to an analysis of contemporary society and the gradual change that has taken place in the Sacred Cosmos over the last 200 years.

4. Joseph H. Greenberg, *Language, Culture and Communication* (Stanford, Calif.: Stanford University Press, 1971), 126-127; Joseph H. Greenberg, *The Languages of Africa* (Bloomington: Indiana University Press, 1966); Joseph H. Greenberg, "Africa as a Linguistic Area," in William R. Bascom and M. J. Herskovits, eds., *Continuity and Change in African Cultures* (Chicago: University of Chicago Press, 1959), 15-27.

5. Marcel Griaule, *Conversations with Ogotemmêli: An Introduction to Dogon Religious Ideas* (Oxford: Oxford University Press, 1965); Basil Davidson, *The Africans: An Entry to Cultural History* (London: Longmans Green & Co., 1969), 169; Marcel Griaule, "The Idea of Person Among the Dogon," in Simon and Phoebe Ottenberg, eds., *Culture and Societies of Africa* (New York: Random House, 1960), 365-371.

6. Melville J. Herskovits had a "classic" experience with Afro-American "indirection." See his account of playing an African game with a St. Vincent expert who originally claimed never to have heard of the pastime. *The Myth of the Negro Past* (Boston: Beacon Press, 1941), 155.

7. Ogotemmêli presented the symbolism while Griaule commented on the dimensions. "For the word 'symbol' he [Ogotemmêli] used a composite expression, the literal meaning of which is 'word of this lower world.' " Griaule, *Conversations,* 37, 49, 58-59, 159.

8. On the parallel Sacred Cosmos of the Fon of Dahomey, see P. Mercier, "The Fon of Dahomey," in Daryll Forde, ed., *African Worlds: Studies in the Cosmological Ideas and Social Values of African Peoples* (Oxford: Oxford University Press, 1954), 190-209. On other cosmos, see Y.D.Y. Peel, "Understanding Alien Belief Systems," *British Journal of Sociology* 20 (1969): 73-75; E. W. Smith, ed., *African Ideas of God,* 2d ed. rev. (London: Edinburgh House Press, 1961); Meyer Fortes and Germaine Dieterlen, eds., *African Systems of Thought* (London: Oxford University Press, 1965); S. F. Nadel, *Nupe Religion* (New York: Free Press of Glencoe, 1954); Terence O. Ranger and Isaria N. Kimambo, eds., *The Historical Study of African Religion* (Berkeley: University of California Press, 1972); Wilfrid D. Hambly, *Source Book for African Anthropology* (Chicago: Field Museum of Natural History, 1937), 541-585. Germaine Dieterlen, "The Mande Creation Myth," in Elliott P. Skinner, ed., *Peoples and Cultures of Africa* (Garden City, N.Y.: Doubleday/Natural History Press, 1973), 634-653.

Peter Morton-Williams has raised doubts about the "conventional hierarchic model" of Yoruba religious systems, as analyzed by Parrinder and as accepted in this book. He suggests a more complex tripartite division of the cosmos into sky, world, and earth, each with its relevant "denizens" but all interrelated. See Morton-Williams "An Outline of the Cosmology and Cult Organization of the Oyo Yoruba," in Skinner, ed., *Peoples and Cultures,* 654-677.

9. John S. Mbiti, *African Religions and Philosophy* (London: Heineman, 1969), 16.

10. Mbiti's excellent study, *African Religions,* is organized around this concept of time. On time in Africa, see Alexis Kagame, "The Empirical Apperception of Time and the Conception of History in Bantu Thought," in L. Gardet, et al., eds., *Cultures and Time* (Paris: UNESCO Press, 1976), 89-116; Meyer Fortes, *Time and Social Structure and Other Essays* (New York: Humanities Press, 1970).

11. Leonard E. Barrett, *Soul Force: African Heritage in Afro-American Religion* (Garden

City, N.Y.: Anchor Books, 1974), 13–40. considers the African heritage in a unified overview. His book traces the African view into captivity but follows it into the Caribbean and has little to say about North America.

12. Mbiti, *African Religions*, 27, 59, 61. Mbiti details rituals, sacrifices, prayers, offerings, and maxims to or about God among many African peoples. E. E. Evans-Pritchard, *Nuer Religion* (London: Oxford University Press, 1956), 22 (punctuation altered). On the Ashanti understanding of God, see R. S. Rattray, *Ashanti* (Westport, Conn.: Negro Universities Press, [1923] 1969), 140; on the Akan, see J. B. Danquah, *The Akan Doctrine of God* (London: Frank Cass & Co., 1968); and on the Mende (Sierra Leone), see W. T. Harris and Harry Sawyer, *The Springs of Mende Belief and Conduct* (Freetown: Sierra Leone University Press, 1968). Herskovits raised serious doubts about the idea of a single High God among the Dahomeans, a group most important in the slave trade, in *Dahomey: An Ancient African Kingdom* (Evanston, Ill.: Northwestern University Press, 1967), 2 vols., II, 292. He maintains that "it is seriously doubted whether this principle [of High God] can be abstracted from Dahomean belief, except through the application of a logic which would be incomprehensible to the natives themselves." Herskovits does recognize that the God Mawu "symbolizes the first executive force in the universe," but he suggests that Dahomeans, when pressed, believe he was created, too. I think Herskovits' own analysis suggests that there was an earlier concept of some First Creator, but it has been absorbed and essentially lost in the developing mythology. All data suggest belief in creation, although it can be pushed back further and further in time. P. Mercier's views confirm this interpretation. He suggests that the Dahomeans did indeed once believe in a Creator God, although He is not now consciously worshiped. Mercier, "The Fon," 218; Rattray, *Ashanti*, 140–144; Geoffrey Parrinder, *West African Religion*, 2d ed. (London: Epworth Press, 1961), 14, 15, 17.

13. Danquah totally rejects the idea that Onyame is a sky god, viewing this as a false Western interpretation. He suggests that the root *NYM* may be related to the root *I AM*, as in the Hebrew *JHWH*. See Danquah, *Akan*, 31–40, 36–37, 44. On altars, see Mbiti, *African Religions*, 59.

14. Mbiti, *African Religions*, 97, gives the Ashanti myth of the pestle and the Mende myth of "bothering." See Harris and Sawyer, *Mende Belief*, 6, for details on the myths of the Mende (of Sierra Leone) as to how man bothered God, causing him to go away. Yoruba and Mawu sources are quoted in Parrinder, *Religion*, 18, 20; Robin Horton, "Type of Spirit Possession in Kalabari Religion," in John Beattie and John Middleton, eds., *Spirit Mediumship and Society in Africa* (London: Routledge & Kegan Paul, 1969), 17. (I am adopting the terms *divinities* and *spirits* for all but the Supreme or High God and will consider spirits in two classes: spirits "proper" and recent dead or "living dead" after Mbiti's usage, explained below.) Parrinder, *Religion*, 24–25.

15. Father J. Henry, *L'ome d'un Peuple Africain, Les Bombaras* (1910), 26–28, cited by G. Parrinder, *West African Psychology* (London: Lutterworth Press, 1951), 14; Mercier, "The Fon," 220. Considerations of the idea of spirit can be found in Parrinder, *Psychology*, 14; Mbiti, *African Religions*, 197; Herskovits, *Dahomey*, II, 170; and Meyer Fortes, *Oedipus and Job in West African Religion* (Cambridge: Cambridge University Press, 1959). Ogotemmêli is cited by Griaule, *Conversations*, 107–108.

16. Davidson, *The Africans*, 171, 173; Griaule, *Conversations*, 156–158. For a remarkably parallel modern understanding of the duality of the soul, see Carl G. Jung, *The Collection Works of Carl G. Jung* (London: Routledge & Kegan Paul, 1971), IX, 11–12, XI, 29–31, 42–43, 476. On duality among the Fon, see Mercier, "The Fon," 231; Mbiti, *African Religions*, 88. On the belief in souls among the Ashanti, Ga, Fon, Yoruba, and Ibo, see Parrinder, *Religion*, 21, 97, 113–114. On the Dogon, see Griaule, "The Idea of Person Among the Dogon," in Simon and Phoebe Ottenburg, eds., *Cultures and Societies of Africa* (New York: Random House, 1960), 366–368; Parrinder, *Psychology*, 24, 31; G. Van Der Leeuw, *Religion in Essence and Manifestation* (New York: Harper & Row, 1963), 284; Danquah, *Akan*, 82; Griaule, *Conversations*, 113; Mbiti, *Afri-*

can Religions, 118.

17. Genesis 17:1,5; Exodus 3:13–15; 6:2–3; 32:32; 33:12–17.

18. Mercier, "The Fon," 225; Parrinder, *Religion*, 81, 102–103; Mbiti, *African Religions*, 116, 121, 176.

19. Osadolar Imasogie, "African Traditional Religion and Christian Faith," *Review and Expositor* 70 (1973): 289; Melville and Frances Herkovits, *Dahomean Narrative: A Cross-Cultural Analysis* (Evenston, Ill.: Northwestern University Press, 1958), 36; Pierre Verger, "Trance and Convention in Nago-Yoruba Spirit Mediumship," in Beattie and Middleton, eds., *Spirit Mediumship*, 51; Mbiti, *African Religions*, 81–83, 166, 171. The phrase "living dead" means something quite different for the Dogon, for whom they are descendants of the first ancestor who was impure at death because he did not have a cult to consecrate his soul. Those who were alive when the first death occurred— and who consecrated that body— were not initiates of any cult prior to that time. They were impure when they handled the dead body as the cult just then came into being. Their descendants remained impure *in life* or "living dead," and all their spiritual descendants were impure. These people play a crucial role in society: what they "eat" at rituals placates the dead who have no altars. But when they die, and "when the family sets up an altar, they become ancestors." Hence, the Dogon "living dead" are "dead" until they are in the grave and have their own altars. Ogotemmêli, in Griaule, *Conversations*, 184–185. Danquah, *Akan*, 82; Herskovits, *Dahomey*, II, 295. "Mawu, says the Dahomean, holds living beings as her first care, and as an expression of this has revealed to them the system of Fa which interprets for men what has angered the gods and how they may be appeased."

20. Mbiti, *African Religions*, 17, 22–29, 95. While Mbiti did his field work with the East Africans, Greenberg maintains that these languages are part of the same Niger-Congo and Kurdofanian language family found in West Africa as well. Parrinder, *Religion*, 22; Parrinder, *Psychology*, 100; John Atkins, *A Voyage to Guinea* (London: 1735), in Elizabeth Donnan, *Documents Illustrative of the History of the Slave Trade to America* (New York: Octagon Books, [1935] 1969), II, 282.

21. Davidson, *Africans*, 70–72, 134; Griaule, *Conversations*, 151; Harris and Sawyer, *Mende Belief*, 103; Mbiti, *African Religions*, 208, 213–214; Danquah, *Akan*, 85.

22. Parrinder, *Religion*, 75–76, and *Psychology*, 133; Mbiti, *African Religions*, 126, 161: "In a sample of 114 societies representing all parts of sub-Saharan Africa, 82% exhibited institutionalized forms of dissociational states, 81% some type of possession belief and 66% possession trance." Erika Bourguignon, "Ritual Dissociation and Possession Belief in Caribbean Negro Religion," in Norman E. Whitten, Jr., and John F. Szwed, eds., *Afro-American Anthropology: Contemporary Perspectives* (New York: Free Press, 1970), 91; M. J. Field, "Spirit Possession in Ghana," in Beattie and Middleton, eds., *Spirit Mediumship*, 3, 9; Sheila S. Walker, *Ceremonial Spirit Possession in Africa and Afro-America* (Leiden: E. J. Brill, 1972), 81. The Walker evidence is contemporary but is based insofar as possible on traditional cults. Verger, "Trance," 50, 51, referring to the Nago-Yoruban and Fon of Dahomey. Robin Horton, "Types of Spirit Possession in Kalabiri Religion," in Beattie and Middleton, eds., *Spirit Mediumship*, 17–22.

23. Parrinder, *Religion*, 8; Griaule, *Conversations*, 141, 168.

Chapter 2

1. On neo-African forms in the Catholic faith, see Melville J. Herskovits, "African Gods and Catholic Saints in New World Negro Belief," *American Anthropologist* 39 (1937): 635–643.

On the slave trade, see Philip D. Curtin, *The Atlantic Slave Trade: A Census* (Madison: University of Wisconsin Press, 1969), 72, 83; Curtin, "The Slave Trade and the Atlantic Basin," in Nathan I. Huggins, Martin Kilson, and Daniel M. Fox, eds., *Key Issues in the Afro-American Experience* (New York: Harcourt Brace Jovanovich, 1971), 74–93. In 1969 Curtin estimated the total North American import figure at 430,000 slaves. Fogel and Engerman suggest that the work of Henry Carey, a source used by Curtin, contained errors and that as a result Curtin's overall estimates of black population and the import figures for the 1760 to 1810 period were too low. The Fogel and Engerman figure is 596,000 total black "immigrants," almost half of whom they believe arrived between 1780 and 1810. (In 1969 Curtin suggested that the imports peaked in the period 1740-1760.) Robert William Fogel and Stanley L. Engerman, *Time on the Cross: The Economics of American Slavery* (Boston: Little, Brown & Co., 1974), 2 vols., I, 24, II, 28-31.) In a personal communication (March 16, 1977), Curtin indicates that he accepts the upward revision as probably correct. Given the upward revision of import figures for 1830-1850, Curtin now believes that there were probably two nearly equal peak importation periods.

The African origins of 81 percent of Virginia's slaves are emphasized by Herbert Klein, "Slaves and Shipping in 18th Century Virginia," *Journal of Interdisciplinary History* 5 (1975): 383-412. "Direct from Africa" figures are also suggested by W. Robert Higgins, "The Geographical Origins of Negro Slaves in Colonial South Carolina," *South Atlantic Quarterly* 70 (1971): 34-47. All of the above rely heavily on the excellent four-volume compilation made by Elizabeth Donnan, *Documents Illustrative of the History of the Slave Trade to America* (New York: Octagon Books, [1935] 1969). Curtin has published some revisions of his figures (made in light of more recent research, such as Postman's, below) in "Measuring the Atlantic Slave Trade," in Stanley L. Engerman and Eugene Genovese, eds., *Race and Slavery in the Western Hemisphere: Quantitative Studies* (Princeton, N.J.: Princeton University Press, 1975), 107-128. Peter H. Wood has analyzed the slave arrivals in South Carolina in *Black Majority: Negroes in Colonial South Carolina from 1670 Through the Stono Rebellion* (New York: Alfred A. Knopf, 1974), and in "More Like a Negro Country: Demographic Patterns in Colonial South Carolina, 1700-1740," in Engerman and Genovese, eds., *Race and Slavery,* 131-171. See in particular the tables of Africans who arrived in Charleston during 1735-1740, 167-171. Johannes Postman, "The Origin of African Slaves: The Dutch Activities on the Guinea Coast 1675-1795," in Engerman and Genovese, eds., *Race and Slavery,* 33-50.

2. Curtin, *Slave Trade,* 73 (page 74 for nineteenth-century illegal immigration); W.E.B. DuBois, *The Suppression of the African Slave Trade to the United States 1638-1870* (New York: Longmans, Green & Co., 1896); Harvey Wish, "The Revival of the African Slave Trade, 1855-1860," *MVHR* 27 (1941): 569-588. Roger Anstey suggests a somewhat different British slave distribution from that posited by Curtin. Anstey, "The Volume and Profitability of the British Slave Trade 1761-1807" in Engerman and Genovese, eds., *Race and Slavery,* 13.

3. Curtin, *Slave Trade,* 109, 111, 123, 129, 144, 157. By 1718, 56 percent of Virginia's slave purchases were coming directly from Africa. In Georgia, direct importation began in 1766 and rose rapidly, while in South Carolina direct importation began earlier and rose dramatically. See Wood, "More Like a Negro Country," 145-164; Klein, "Slaves and Shipping," 392.

4. Melville J. Herskovits, *The Myth of the Negro Past* (Boston: Beacon Press, 1941), 33; Marion Kilson, "West African Society and the Atlantic Slave Trade, 1441-1865," in Huggins, et al., *Key Issues,* 48; Cf. Gerald Mullin, *Flight and Rebellion: Slave Resistance in Eighteenth Century Virginia* (London: Oxford University Press, 1972), 174, note citing M. G. Smith, "The African Heritage in the Caribbean" (and George E. Simpson's reply), in Vera Rubin, ed., *Caribbean Studies: A Symposium* (Seattle: University of Washington Press, 1960), 34. Vansertima suggests that North American folklore features East African or Bantu archetypes, while the black Caribbean lore uses West African images, particularly Annancy, the Spider. He believes this indicates that American blacks were not from the West Coast of Africa, but only transshipped through there. "Most African slaves of the American South were from the Lower Congo, whose people were largely in the Bantu culture complex." Ivan Vansertima, "African Linguistic and Mythological Structures in the New World," in Rhoda L. Goldstein, ed., *Black Life and Culture in the United States* (New York: Thomas Y. Crowell Co., 1971), 32; Donnan, *Documents,* Captain William Smith, *A New Voyage to Guinea* (London: 1744), 28, cited by J. L. Dillard, *Black English: Its History and Usage in the United States* (New York: Random House, 1972), 73.

5. Francis Moore, *Travels in Africa* (1730–1735), in Donnan, *Documents,* II, 395. Donnan comments that "The Bumbrongs and Petcharias or Patcharis, two primitive negro tribes of the middle valley of the Gambia, were dominated in the eighteenth century by the Mandingoes," II, 295n.8.

6. Donnan, *Documents,* IV, 615n.7, 622n.25, 412n.7, 438n.5, 422n.6, 373n.3, 316–318, 359, 368. (Correspondence) Henry Laurens to Smith and Clifton, St. Christopher's Island, July 17, 1775, IV, 326; Laurens to Wells, May 27, 1755, IV, 320; Laurens to P. Funnell, Jamaica, September 3, 1755, IV, 317n.3; Laurens to John Knight, May 28, 1756, IV, 351.

7. "The Life of Olaudah Equiano," in Arna Bontemps, *Great Slave Narratives* (Boston: Beacon Press, 1969), 35 (emphasis added). Grant suggests that it was the Fula who were least able to adjust to slavery but that their Moslem faith kept them from suicide. Cf. Douglas Grant, *The Fortunate Slave* (New York: Oxford University Press, 1968), 70 and infra.

8. Donnan, *Documents,* IV, 234n.66, 160; *Boston Gazette,* 1726, III, 29; *Boston Gazette,* 1762, III, 68; *Virginia Gazette,* November 5, 1736, April 21, 1735, August 17, 1739, December 8, 1768, January 15, 1767, August 13, 1772, December 31, 1772, N, 234n.66. See Wood, *Black Majority,* 179n.40, on similar South Carolina advertisements.

9. Reverend Jonas Michaelius, in J. F. Jameson, ed., *Narratives of New Netherlands* (1628), 129, reprinted in Donnan, *Documents,* III, 405; John Mereweather, January 6, 1736, II, 455; John Atkins, *A Voyage to Guinea* (London: 1735), II, 282; Daniel Wescomb, February 23, 1721, II, 256; Tyndall and Assheton, November 13, 1729, II, 382. "Considerations on the Present Peace, as far as it is relative to the Colonies and the African Trade" (London: 1763), II, 516. Francis Moore described the Pholes as a "People of a Tawney Coulor . . . . much like the Arabs, which language they most of them speak . . . . They are industrious and frugal, and raise much more Corn and Cotton than they consume . . . . To have a Pholey Town in the Neighbourhood, is by the Natives reckon'd a blessing." From *Travels in Africa,* 1730–1735, in Donnan, *Documents,* II, 400. Jamaican documents substantiate island planters' similar classifications and judgments. See eighteenth-century Jamaican sources cited by Ulrich B. Phillips, *American Negro Slavery* (Baton Rouge: Louisiana State University Press, [1918] 1969), 42.

10. Donnan, *Documents,* I, 398n.25; Phillips, *Negro Slavery,* 36, 42. In *A Voyage to Guinea,* John Atkins wrote of his 1721 travels on the "black continent"; see Donnan, *Documents,* II, 282. Angola slaves varied widely in value: often sold in South Carolina noted as "of no value in Martinico," they were taken to St. Dominique where they were sold rapidly. Cf. South Sea Co. to Mr. Stratford, December 17, 1724, in Donnan, *Documents,* II, 320. On the high value of Gold Coast or Angola slaves in "plantations," see Daniel Wescomb, February 23, 1871, II, 256; and Tyndall and Assheton, November 13, 1729, II, 382.

11. Calendar of State Papers, Colonial, 1706–1708, 758, 760, reprinted in Donnan, *Documents,* IV, 21n.20.

12. *South Carolina Gazette,* June 4, 1741, and June 12, 1736, cited by Wood, *Black Majority,* 176, 179–180, 254; Mullin, *Flight and Rebellion,* 34–82. When Olaudah Equiano landed in the West Indies, in about 1756, he met "Africans of all languages" but managed to understand part of what they said. Curtin, *Africa Remembered* (Madison: University of Wisconsin Press, 1967), 97. See Curtin, "Atlantic Basin," 68. On Hausa as a trade language, see Joseph H. Greenberg, *Language, Culture and Communication* (Standord, Calif.: Stanford University Press, 1971), 126, 131; on Woloff, see David Dalby, *Black Through White: Patterns of Communication in Africa and the New World* (Bloomington: Indiana University Press, 1970), and Douglas Grant, *The Fortunate Slave,* 84; Dillard, *Black English,* discusses the likelihood of and evidence for Portuguese-pidgin, etc., in Africa. Wood, *Black Majority,* 179; Joseph Greenberg, "The Deciphering of the 'Ben-Ali Diary'," *JNH* (1940): 372–375. Thomas Bluett, "The Capture and Travels of Ayuba Suleiman" (1734), in Curtin, *Africa Remembered,* says Job (Ayuba Suleiman) journeyed in Africa accompanied by a servant-interpreter, who was enslaved together with him. Grant, *Fortunate Slave,* 84, recounts that in Maryland in 1731 a black "man who could speak Joloff" and English was brought to translate for Job, a Fula Muslim from Gambia.

13. Cf. John Atkins, *A Voyage to Guinea*, in Donnan, *Documents*, II, 381. Olaudah Equiano (whose Portuguese owners warned him that if the English captured him, they would eat him), in Curtin, *Africa Remembered*, 97, 331; Grant, *Fortunate Slave*, and Thomas Bluett, "Ayuba Suleiman," 23–59. The deposition is from a letter of Captain Joseph Harrison of Barbados, February 28, 1758, quoting "The Deposition of John Dawson, Mate of the Snow Rainbow," in relation to the "Suppos'd Murder of . . . Comer . . . ," in Donnan, *Documents*, IV, 371. On the high status of linguists in Africa, where they were often employed on a permanent basis by companies or trading stations, see Margaret Priestly in Curtin, *Africa Remembered*, 104–105, referring to Cudjo Caboceer of the Cape Coast who was a linguist around 1725–1776.

14. Peter L. Berger, *The Sacred Canopy* (Garden City, N.Y.: Doubleday & Co., 1969), 21–22; Mungo Park, *Travels* (1799), 320, cited by Grant, *Fortunate Slave*, 51. Each of the captives in Curtin's *Africa Remembered* recalled great grief and depression on capture; see 85–92, 297–298. Charles H. Nichols, *Many Thousands Gone: The Ex-Slaves' Account of Their Bondage and Freedom* (Leiden: E. J. Brill, 1963), 6.

15. Sadiki, cited in "Documents," *JNH* 21 (1936): 55, emphasis added.

16. Wood, *Black Majority*, 168; Niles Newbell Puckett, *Folk Beliefs of the Southern Negro* (New York: Negro Universities Press, [1926] 1968), 52; Herbert G. Gutman, *The Black Family in Slavery and Freedom, 1750–1925* (New York: Pantheon Books, 1976).

17. Donnan, *Documents*, III, 416, reprints a deposition relating to the branding of slaves in Africa in 1652. Slaves were branded on the breast with the initials of the different traders to whom they belonged.

Gutman, *Slave Family*, 244, suggests that by the 1780s "most slaves had surnames and so many so early had surnames different from their owners." Gutman concludes that this "shows a powerful *eighteenth-century Afro-American* desire to define immediate slave families in ways that symbolically separated them from their owners." I suspect Gutman errs in this conclusion since slaves did take their original owners' names as their own (and their families) and kept these names when sold. Gutman, in order to make his point, should show that the differing names were not those of a previous owner. That they were simply different from the slaves' owners is important but does not prove symbolic separation from owners. Slaves did want names of their own, names that remained theirs no matter where they went. In a sense this ownership of their own names made them symbolically equal to their owners: They, too, were men with a "title."

Church records for slaves generally recorded first names only—as Sarah, property of Dr. Smith, or Dr. Smith's Sarah. In many cases, however, a last name other than the owner's was recorded, as was the case with John Taylor, member of the First Baptist Church, Washington, D.C., and owned by James R. Miller. Miller had no respect for his slave's use of a surname, stating he "calls himself . . . John Taylor or John Edwards." Miller simply called him John. Manuscript minutes, First Baptist Church, Washington, D.C., November 7, 1834; December 12, 1834; and November 7, 1839. (Available on microfilm at HCSBC.)

Free blacks were also recorded without surnames, as was "Hanibel, a free man." (Manuscript minutes, Welsh Neck First Baptist Church, Welsh Neck, South Carolina, April 5, 1782, microfilm at HCSBC.) In the early period, brother and sister were generally appended to both the slaves and free blacks' "Christian" names, as in "Sister Hannah, a black woman" in the manuscript minutes of the Sandy Creek Primitive Baptist Church, Sandy Creek, South Carolina, September 19, 1825 (microfilm at HCSBC). In rare cases, no name was recorded for blacks baptized and accepted into a church, as at Little River Baptist Church, Fairfield, South Carolina, March 8 and August 10, 1817: "Rec'd Margaret Capo and three blacks by letter." "Baptised one black." (Manuscript minutes, microfilm at HCSBC.) Nevertheless, this same church kept a list of "male member blacks" with last names: "John Long, Abel Gibson," etc. A free black, known to the Nashville First Baptist Church as James, without a surname, is recorded as owning Brother Isham McLundy. (Manuscript minutes, First Baptist Church, Nashville, March 20, 1833, microfilm at HCSBC.)

Blacks were generally referred to as "blacks," "colored" or "coloured," and "Negro," as "Jersey, a black, the property of . . . .," or "Robert (Judge Ewan's)" or "a Negro man Ahmed James Laid under the sensure [sic] of the Church for Disagreeable Bad Conduct." (Little River Baptist Church, Fairfield County, South Carolina, manuscript minutes, December 10, 1808, microfilm at HCSBC.) Letters of dismission were written with these names in these forms, especially "Slade, belonging to . . . ." See the papers of Cushing Biggs Hassell, Primitive Baptist preacher in Williamstown, North Carolina, 1840–1880, whose "Letterbook, 1841–48" lists "Negro members" baptized and ordained. Southern Historical Collection, University of North Carolina at Chapel Hill, Chapel Hill, North Carolina. All the minutes listed in A Note on Sources below include names of blacks, often in separate listings, but interspersed throughout the minutes. For example, the forms:

"bro. Ben Smyth . . . ."
"Abbey belonging to the Knoxs estate . . . ."
"James a free man . . . ."
"Hannah Susk, a colored member . . . ."
"Major, a man of colour . . . ."
"Sister Rachel, a servant . . . ."
"Samuel Taylor, a blackman . . . ."

can all be found in the manuscript minutes of the First Baptist Church, Nashville, September 18, 1833, December 9, 1836, May 1, 1839, and January 7, 1841. (Microfilm at HCSBC.) Names are discussed further in Chapter 8, note 10.

18. Guion G. Johnson, *A Social History of the Sea Islands* (Chapel Hill: University of North Carolina Press, 1930), 77, 131. On "wangateurs," a term still used in Louisiana in reference to "occult" practitioners or "conjure doctors," see Puckett, *Folk Beliefs*, 19.

19. Advertisement in *Louisiana Gazette*, January 4, 1816; reprinted in Lyle Saxon, Edward Dreyer, and Robert Tallant, *Gumbo Ya-Ya: A Collection of Louisiana Folk Tales* (Boston: Houghton Mifflin Co., 1945); *South Carolina Gazette*, September 3, 1753, advertisement for a runaway placed by Henry Laurens: reprinted in Wood, *Black Majority*, 250. Cf. H. A. Wieschoff, "The Social Significance of Names Among the Ibo of Nigeria," *American Anthropologist* 43 (1941): 212–222; Richard and Sally Price, "Saranaka Onomastics: An Afro-American Naming System," *Ethnology* 11 (1972): 311–367; Mullin, *Flight and Rebellion*, 46; Richard Jones, Union, South Carolina, 1936 WPA interview reprinted in Norman R. Yetman, ed., *Life Under the "Peculiar Institution": Selections from the Slave Narrative Collection* (New York: Holt, Rinehart & Winston, 1970), 192.

20. William Stevens Perry, *Historical Collections Relating to the American Colonial Church* (New York: AMS Press, [1870–1878] 1969), 5 vols., I, 283, 293. Perry reprints the following relevant documents: Mr. Forbes, Upper Parish Isle of Wight, July 21, 1724, I, 327; on the desire to convert young American-born blacks and their general language difficulties, see Bartholomew Yates, Christ Church Parish, Virginia, 1724, and Alexander Scott, Overworton Parish, Virginia, 1724, I, 297, 312; J. Donaldson, King and Queen Parish, Maryland, 1724; A. Williamson, St. Paul's Parish, Kent County, Maryland; R. Sewell, Shrewsbury, Maryland, IV, 192, 222, 225. William Le Neve, pastor, James City Parish, Virginia, 1724, I, 264 (emphasis added). Blacks from Africa, as compared to those "born among us," were considered "much more indocile." Mr. Forbes, Upper Parish, Isle of Wight, July 21, 1724, I, 344.

21. In a personal letter (March 6, 1977), Philip D. Curtin commented on the high slave trade of 1830–1850. "Slave Narratives," I, 30, cited by B. F. Jones in "A Cultural Middle Passage: Slave Marriage and Family in the Antebellum South," Ph.D. dissertation, University of North Carolina, 1965, 134. Jones also cites other records of African languages spoken in "Slave Narratives," II, 7, 20; XVI, 1, 14. Charleston, South Carolina, newspapers carried advertisements for blacks who spoke "broken," "bad," or "little" English. Wood, *Black Majority*, 176n.25, cites the *South Carolina Gazette*, November 4, 1732, February 15, 1735, January 22,

1737. Allen W. Read, "The Speech of Negroes in Colonial America," *JNH* 24 (1939): 247–258; William A. Steward, "Sociolinguistic Factors in the History of American Negro Dialects," in V. P. Clark, P. A. Eschholtz, and A. F. Rosa, eds., *Language: Introductory Readings* (New York: St. Martin's Press, 1972). Mullin, *Flight and Rebellion,* 46, maintains, that during the first half year in the country most Africans spoke very little English; after six months, their proficiency generally rose dramatically, and after three years, he believes most were conversant. Donnan, *Documents,* III, 460, IV, 244. Winthrop D. Jordan, *White Over Black: American Attitudes Toward the Negro 1550—1812* (Chapel Hill: University of North Carolina Press, 1968), 184n.15; Eugene Genovese, *Roll, Jordan, Roll: The World the Slaves Made* (New York: Pantheon Books, 1974), 431–441.

    22. Phillips, *Negro Slavery,* 478; Herbert Aptheker, *American Negro Slave Revolts* (New York: International Publishers, 1943), 268, 668; John W. Lofton, *Insurrection in South Carolina: The Turbulent World of Denmark Vesey* (Yellow Springs, Ohio: Kent State University Press, 1964); Robert S. Starobin, ed., *Denmark Vesey: The Slave Conspiracy of 1822* (Englewood Cliffs, N.J.: Prentice-Hall, 1970); John O. Killens, ed., *The Trial Record of Denmark Vesey* (Boston: Beacon Press, 1970). G.S.S., "Sketches of the South Santee," *American Monthly Magazine* 8 (1836), reprinted in Eugene L. Schwaab, ed., *Travels in the Old South* (Lexington, Ky.: University of Kentucky Press, 1973), 2 vols., I, 11.

    23. "An affidavit of Stephen Dean (Deaux) of the *Brittania* that Finda Lawrence, a free black woman who is a trader on the Gambia, has come to Georgia for a sojurn, is in the archives of Georgia, Bills of Sale, 1772-1775." See American History Association, *Annual Report* I (1903), 445; Donnan, *Documents,* IV, 625n.5; Dillard, *Black English,* 78, 174n.21 (Dillard cites the 1692 Salem witch trial evidence of Tituba; the 1704-1705 *Journal* of Sarah Kemble Knight and Cotton Mather's 1721 *Treatise on Small Pox,* all of which quote the Pidgin English of blacks.) Commenting on Read's article, "The Speech of Negroes in Colonial America," which took evidence from eighteenth-century advertisements stating a slave "speaks good English," Dillard notes this may have meant *"for a slave"* or that those who spoke most like whites ran away more often. Dillard, *Black English,* 84, 85, 89-93, 97, 98.

    24. On the moving of sacred bones, see Marcel Griaule, *Conversations with Ogotemmêli: An Introduction to Dogon Religious Ideas* (Oxford: Oxford University Press, 1965); Zora Hurston, "Hoodoo in America," *JAF* 44 (1931), simply asserts "Ghosts cannot cross water," 397. "Victims" must be brought to the ghosts!

    25. Mullin, *Flight and Rebellion,* 43. Mullin cites the June 29, 1729, report to the Board of Trade made by Governor Sir William Gooch, which tells of fifteen Africans who ran away from a plantation on the James River in 1727. "They attempted to reconstruct familiar social and political arrangements. But shortly after building huts and sowing crops they were recaptured." Colonial Office Papers, 5/1322, 19 (Virginia Colonial Records Project, Microfilm); John W. Blassingame, *The Slave Community* (New York: Oxford University Press, 1972), 25; Herbert Aptheker, "Maroons Within the Present Limits of the United States," in Richard Price, ed., *Maroon Societies* (New York: Anchor Books, 1973), 151-168; Alex Hewitt, *An Historical Account of the Rise and Progress of the Colonies of South Carolina and Georgia* (1779), 347-348, printed in B. R. Carroll, ed., *Historical Collection of South Carolina,* I (1842); *Memoir of Mrs. Chloe Spear, A Native of Africa . . . Died in 1815, aged 65 by a Lady of Boston* (1815), 17; Charles Ball, *Slavery in the United States* (1837), 219-222; and the analysis of Roger Bastide, *African Civilisations in the New World* (London: Citturust & Co., 1967), 46. Hewitt, Spear, Ball, and Bastide are cited in Gutman, *Black Family,* 332 and 606n.6, in his discussion of the belief that spirits returned to Africa.

    26. George P. Rawick, *From Sundown to Sunup: The Making of the Black Community* (Westport, Conn.: Greenwood Publishing Co., 1972); Gutman, *Black Family,* 196.

    27. The Muslim faith was reacted to in a significantly more positive manner than "fetishistic" or "polytheistic" tribal faiths, indicating that the nature of black faith was a challenge to

Anglican tolerance as well. Grant, *Fortunate Slave,* 82–86. See March 19, 1716, entry in Frank J. Klingberg, ed., *The Carolina Chronicle of Dr. Francis Le Jeau* (Berkeley: University of California Press, 1956), 174; and James Gignillat of Santee, South Carolina, who wrote in May 28, 1710, that "all other slaves do laugh at them [the converts]." Cited by Ralph Klingberg, *An Appraisal of the Negro in Colonial South Carolina: A Study in Americanization* (Washington, D.C.: Associated Publishers, 1941), 24n.

28. Puckett, *Folk Beliefs,* 187, citing Mary A. Owen, suggests that in Missouri, much as in Louisiana, participants prepared themselves by nine days of near fasting. The dance itself was ecstatic, involving howling and jumping and, most crucially, a snake. A hodgepodge of data, much of it relevant, can be found in Langston Hughes and Arna Bontemps, *The Book of Negro Folklore* (New York: Dodd, Mead & Co., 1958), 183–209.

29. William Wells Brown, *My Southern Home* (Boston: A. G. Brown & Co., 1880), 71. See A. M. Bacon, "Conjuring and Conjure Doctors," *Southern Workmen* 14 (1895): 193, 209; Louis Hughes, *Thirty Years a Slave* (Milwaukee, Wis.: South Side Printing Co., 1897), 13–22; Puckett, *Folk Beliefs,* 214. See the testimony of ex-slave Rias Body, Georgia, who was nineteen at war's end. He recalled that witches and wizards were respected and looked up to, but that he gave them a "wide birth," "Slave Narratives," Georgia, IV, 89. Jordan, *White Over Black,* 343, reports twenty slaves were executed for poisonings in Virginia between 1772 and 1810. Wood reports increasing poisonings in South Carolina after 1751; *Black Majority,* 289. Clara Barton, in Saxon, et al., *Gumbo Ya-Ya,* 248.

30. South Carolina attempted to outlaw Negro doctoring, but given the black attitude toward conjurers, this bill had little effect; 1751 Statutes, VII, 422–423, cited by Wood, *Black Majority,* 290. As late as 1886, the New Orleans Board of Health tried to suppress Voudou doctors; Phillip A. Bruce, *The Plantation Negro as a Freeman* (Williamstown, Mass.: Corner House Publishers, [1889] 1970), 125. See Bacon, "Conjuring and Conjure Doctors," 191–198; R. Steiner, "Observations on the Practice of Conjuring in Georgia," *JAF* 14 (1901); J. A. Hall, "Negro Conjuring and Tricking," *JAF* 10 (1897).

31. Robert Carter, manuscript letter in the Carter Papers, Virginia Historical Society, cited by Phillips, *Negro Slavery,* 323; Puckett, *Folk Beliefs,* 280–284, 304; Blassingame, *The Slave Community,* 49; "Slave Narratives," IV, 32.

32. Willie Lee Rose, ed., *A Documentary History of Slavery in North America* (London: Oxford University Press, 1976), 249–250. One of the Kalabari possession rituals is comparable to the Georgia experience of the Heards: "To secure the services of an *Oru Kuro* woman, one goes to her house and tells her that one wants to talk to her spirit. She then takes a bottle of palm gin and a shilling or two, goes to the spirit's shrine and calls upon it to mount her . . . . Before long, she becomes drowsy. Then the spirit mounts her, jumps up and comes to confront its client." Robin Horton, "Types of Spirit Possession in Kalabari Religion," in John Beattie and John Middleton, eds., *Spirit Mediumship and Society in Africa* (London: Routledge & Kegan Paul, 1969), 29. Witchcraft and possession are discussed further in Chapter 3. Nat Turner mentions his birthmarks in his *Confessions,* reprinted in Henry Irving Tragle, ed., *Nat Turner's Slave Revolt 1831* (New York: Grossman Publishers, 1971), 306–307.

33. Elizabeth Brandon's reports of conjuring in southwest Louisiana in 1954 in Richard M. Dorson, *Buying the Wind* (Chicago: University of Chicago Press, 1964), 261. Dorson reminds us that there was a strong white folk medicine tradition. Cf. Puckett, *Folk Beliefs,* 166, 190; Norman E. Whitten, Jr., "Contemporary Patterns for Malign Occultism Among Negroes in North Carolina," *JAF* 75 (1962): 319. Whitten suggests that, by comparing black beliefs with those of whites (as outlined in Tom P. Cross, "Witchcraft in North Carolina," *Studies in Philology* 16 [1919]: 217–287), it can be shown that the ideas of the blacks are derivative. Descriptions of white faith healers in Arkansas and Michigan can be found in "The Power Doctors," in Vance Randolph, *Ozark Superstitions* (New York: Columbia University Press, 1947), 121–142, and in "Bloodstoppers," in Richard M. Dorson, *American Negro Folktales* (New York: Fawcett,

[1956] 1968), 150–165. Dorson maintains that of sixty-seven modern American black tales he has studied, fifty-five are related to European rather than African sources; that there is only a 10 percent correspondence with West African motifs. As will be suggested below, it is not the quantity of African motifs that determines the significance of African values in the world view. It will be suggested that African values and modes of thought more or less controlled the choice, use, and understanding of European folklore. See Dorson, the "Introduction" to *American Negro Folktales*, 12–18, and "Africa and Afro-American Folklore: A Reply to Bascom and other Misguided Critics," *JAF* 88 (1975): 151–164.

34. "Slave Narratives," Rachel Adams, Celestia Avery, Georgia, IV, 2. In 1564 or 1565, phrases such as "Raw head" and "bloudibone the ouglie" were used in England in the play, "The Bugbears." B. J. Whiting, *Proverbs in the Earlier English Drama* (Cambridge, Mass.: Harvard University Press, 1938), 360; Richard M. Dorson, *American Folklore and the Historian* (Chicago: University of Chicago Press, 1971), 40; Dorson, *American Folklore* (Chicago: University of Chicago Press, 1959), 159, 186, 188; Dorson, *American Negro Folktales*, 147–148; Puckett, *Folk Beliefs*, 110, 116–120, 115, 128; Zora Hurston, "Hoodoo in America," *Journal of American Folklore* 44 (1931): 317–417.

35. Jessie Collins in Hughes & Bontemps, eds., *Negro Folklore*, 163–210; Puckett, *Folk Beliefs*, 120; "Slave Narratives," Georgia, IV, 38.

36. Puckett, *Folk Beliefs*, 110, 117, 118, 125–128, 151, 243, 359. According to Puckett, Mrs. Virginia F. Boyle (white) of Memphis, Tennessee, tells of her old black nurse making a rag image of Virginia's mother and sticking pins in it while calling her mother's name. Virginia later found an image of herself under her mattress. Puckett also reports that an old Georgia man "claims to possess two spirits—one that prowls around and one that stays in the body."

37. Zora Hurston, "Hoodoo," 317–417; Herskovits, *The Myth*, 246–248; Sidney Mintz, introduction to Alfred Metraux, *Voodoo in Haiti* (London: Andre Deutsch, [1959] 1972), 8; Curtin, *Slave Trade*, 79, 88, 144, 192–195. Curtin suggests a 2 to 8 percent natural increase in the slave population of St. Dominique during 1681–1790.

38. Hurston, "Hoodoo," 326, 327. Hurston cites the birth records at St. Louis Cathedral, New Orleans, stating that Leveau was the natural daughter of Marie Leveau and Christophe Glapion. See also Hurston, *Mules and Men* (New York: Negro Universities Press, [1935] 1969), 239. Metraux, as Herskovits before him, concluded from practices and verbal sources (including the Haitian use of Fon and Yoruba terms for religious rituals and meanings) that the Dahomean roots of Voudou are the basic ones, although many other African deities and practices were incorporated in the Haitian religion. The Dahomean religion was already "functioning" in Haiti when later practices from the Congo and Angola were assimilated into it. Metraux, *Voodoo in Haiti*, 40, 88n.29.

On Voudou, see Herskovits, *The Myth*, 246; Herskovits, *Life in a Haitian Valley* (New York: Alfred A. Knopf, 1937); Maya Deren, *Divine Horsemen: The Living Gods of Haiti* (London: Thames & Hudson, 1935), 82–83; S. Culin, "Reports Concerning Voodooism," *JAF* 2 (1889): 233; Alice Fortier, "Customs and Superstitions in Louisiana," *JAF* I (1888): 138; Robert Tallant, *Voodoo in New Orleans* (London: Collier, Macmillan, [1946] 1974); Harold Courlander, "The Gods of the Haitian Mountains," *JNH* 29 (1944): 339–372; Metraux, *Voodoo in Haiti*, cites Saint Mery (writing in 1798), 36, 35; Genovese, "Slave Religion in Hemispheric Perspective," in *Roll, Jordan, Roll*, 168–183.

39. Leveau held weekly sessions in her home on St. Anne Street or on Bayou St. John's, while a special annual dance was held on the eve of the Catholic holy day of St. John's, around June 24. See Puckett, *Folk Beliefs*, 181; Hurston, *Mules and Men*, 241; Hurston, "Hoodoo," 326, 348–349, 359, 362, 363. Leveau is quoted according to the oral tradition as in Hurston "Hoodoo," 328–329, 369–371. Luke Turner is cited in Hurston, *Mules and Men*, 243. On page 297, Hurston explains that Catholic Voudouist Kitty Brown allowed her to participate in a "death request," along with "the most inner circle." For Catholic allusions in the Leveau tradi-

tion, see Hurston, "Hoodoo," 329, 336, 341, 344, 345, 350, 357. For Hurston's listing of saints' powers, 413, cf. Herskovits, "African Gods and Catholic Saints in New World Negro Belief," *American Anthropologist* 39 (1937): 635–643.

40. H. E. Sterkx, *The Free Negro in Ante-Bellum Louisiana* (Teaneck, N.J.: Fairleigh Dickinson University Press, 1972), 265, cites the *New Orleans Daily Delta,* July 31, 1850. He also cites the *New Orleans True Delta,* June 29, 1850, as reporting that during the same summer a New Orleans Voudou meeting was held at the house of a free black named Fostin and that the participants were found nude, dancing around an idol (266).

41. Cf. incantation for a death made by Anatol Pierre, New Orleans, in Hurston, *Mules and Men,* 261. Hurston concludes, "and the man died," with no comment on the morality of the act. For Leveau's curse, see Hurston, "Hoodoo," 357 (emphasis added).

42. See the possession experiences of Maya Deren, *Divine Horsemen,* who came to observe Haitian Voudou and stayed to participate; and Hurston, "Hoodoo."

Chapter 3

1. Peter L. Berger, *The Sacred Canopy* (Garden City, N.Y.: Anchor Books, 1969), 111; Thomas Luckman, *The Invisible Religion: The Problem of Religion in Modern Society* (New York: Macmillan Co., 1967), 58–59; Keith Thomas, *Religion and the Decline of Magic* (London: Weidenfeld & Nicholson, 1971), 47, 51, 635.

2. Maryland passed an "Act for Encouraging the Importation of Negroes and Slaves into this province" in 1671 and reenacted it in 1681, noting that owners have "Neglected to instruct them in the Christian faith or to Endure or permit them to Receive the holy Sacrament of Baptism for the Remission of their Sinns upon a mistake and ungrounded apprehension that by becoming Christians they and the Issue of their bodies are actually manumitted and made free." Elizabeth Donnan, *Documents Illustrative of the History of the Slave Trade to America* (New York: Octagon Books, [1935] 1969), 4 vols., IV, 9. For the unwillingness of slaveowners to have their slaves converted, see Thomas Dell, Virginia, June 1, 1724; George Robertson, Bristol Parish, Virginia, 1724; Henry Collings, St. Peter's Parish, Virginia, 1724; John Brunskill, Wilmington Parish, Virginia, June 18, 1724; Juo. Cargill, Southwark Parish, Virginia 1724—all reprinted in William Stevens Perry, ed., *Historical Collections Relating to the American Colonial Church* (New York: AMS Press, [1870] 1969), I, 255, 267, 269, 277, 306. See also V, 43, and I, 315, wherein John Bagg of St. Ann's Parish, Virginia, states in 1724 that owners disapproved of slave conversion, "being led away by the notion of their being and becoming worse slaves when Christians." H. R. McIlwaine, ed., *Journals of the House of Burgesses, Virginia, 1695–1702,* 174, cited by Winthrop P. Jordan in his excellent discussion of the development of white views in "The Souls of Men," in *White Over Black: American Attitudes Toward the Negro 1550–1812* (Chapel Hill: University of North Carolina Press, 1968), Ch. 5. For the Virginia Act of 1667, see William Waller Henning, *The Statutes at Large: Being a Collection of All the Laws of Virginia . . . .* (Richmond, Va.: 1809–1823), II, 260.

3. The following documents are reprinted in Perry, *Colonial Church:* Reverend John Lang seemed to feel conflicting emotions, but not unduly so. "There is one thing (tho') in which we must confess we are blameworthy, both Pastors and People, in that greater care is not taken about the Instruction of the Negroes. It cannot be denied but that they are a part of our cure, and that we shall be accountable to God for the discharge of our duty to them. But, on the other side, it cannot be expected that we should become Schoolmasters and Tutors to them any more than to others." A sermon by the rector of St. Peters in New Kent, Virginia, June 24, 1730 (IV, 292). Long to the bishop of London, February 7, 1725–1776 (I, 347). Charles Bridges to the bishop of London, Hanover, Virginia, October 19, 1738 (I, 361). Mr. Forbes, Upper Parish, Isle of Wight, July 24, 1724 (I, 344). Also see the plan of James Blair, February 12, 1699–1700 (I, 112). Edmund S. Morgan's data on tithes differ somewhat from the references made by James

Blair. Morgan states that from 1680 to 1705 Africans were subject to be tithed from age twelve and in 1705 from age sixteen. See *American Slavery American Freedom: The Ordeal of Colonial Virginia* (New York: W. W. Norton, 1975), 310, citing Henning, *Statutes of Virginia,* II, 479–480, III, 258–259. Morgan's discussion of the means by which Virginia "nourished an increasing contempt for blacks" provides an important backdrop for the religious interaction. See *American Slavery,* 295–337. Cf. Wesley Frank Craven, *White Red and Black: The Seventeenth Century Virginian* (Charlottesville: University of Virginia Press, 1971).

    4. The following documents are reprinted in Perry, *Colonial Church:* Hugh Neill, Dover, Bristol Parish in the upper part of James River, Virginia, 1724 (I, 267); Peter Fontaine, Virginia, 1724 (I, 272); Dan'l Claylor, rector, Blissland Parish, New Kent City, Virginia (I, 280); Thomas Crawford, Kent County, Pennsylvania, August 31, 1708 (V, 18); classes held by Fontaine (I, 281); Emmanuel Jones, Pettsworth, Virginia, 1724 (I, 287); William Black, Accomoko on the Eastern Shore, Virginia (I, 301); Giles Rainsford of St. Paul's Parish, Prince Georges County, Maryland (1724); and J. Frazier of King George's Parish on the Potomack River (Annapolis), Maryland. Rainsford and Frazier recorded many black baptisms (IV, 201, 204). Anthony Gavin, St. James, Goochland, Virginia, 1737 (I, 360).

    5. The following documents are reprinted in Perry, *Colonial Church:* Hugh Neill, Dover, Delaware, 1751 (V, 97). On March 5, 1782, Samuel Tingley of Sussex County, Delaware, reported that over the last six years "several thousand" had been baptized, "among which were many Blacks, from sixty years to two months old" (V, 138). Hugh Jones, William and Mary Church, Charles County, Maryland (V, 321, 331). Among the churchmen who had difficulty finding godparents for blacks were John Warden, Lawn's Creek in Jeury County; James Blair, Bruton Parish, Williamsburg, Virginia (I, 289, 299); and Thomas Crawford, Delaware (1706), (V, 1, 3). By "An Act for the Service of Almighty God, and Establishment of Religion in this Province, according to the Church of England," all births, marriages, and burials were required to be officially registered in the "Register of the Vestry," but the law specifically stated *"Negroes and Mallatos [sic] excepted."* (IV, 41, 45).

    6. Brooke Zach, St. Paul's Parish in Hanover, Virginia (1724); Forbes, Upper Parish Isle of Wight (1724); Lang, St. Peter's Parish, Virginia (1725–1726)—in Perry, *Colonial Church* (I, 263, 324, 346). In 1701, "there were only 50 ministers of the Church of England in the Colonies, nearly all of whom were in Virginia and Maryland." By 1776, there were no more than 250 ministers and 300 churches. See Luther A. Weigle, *American Idealism* (New Haven, Conn.: Yale University Press, 1928), 75.

    The "low tenor" of Anglicanism until about 1700 (when the Society for the Propagation of the Gospel improved the situation somewhat) is discussed in Sydney E. Ahlstrom, *A Religious History of the American People* (New Haven, Conn.: Yale University Press, 1972), 134, 188–198, 217–219, 227–228; Elizabeth H. Davidson, *The Establishment of the English Church in the Continental American Colonies* (Durham, N.C.: Duke University Press, 1936).

    Devereux Jarratt (1733–1801) was an important exception to the Anglican pattern. He was an emotional revival preacher, and both blacks and whites in Virginia and North Carolina responded to his missionary appeal. See Wesley Gewehr, *The First Great Awakening in Virginia, 1740–1790* (Durham, N.C.: Duke University Press, 1930), 138–166. H. Shelton Smith, Robert T. Handy, and Lefferts A. Loetscher, eds., *American Christianity: An Historical Interpretation with Representative Documents* (New York: Charles Scribner's Sons, 1960), 2 vols., I, 14–16, 52–54, 247–249, 366–371, which includes extracts from *The Life of the Reverend Devereux . . . Written by Himself* (Baltimore, Md: 1806); G. MacLaren Brydon, *Virginia's Mother Church* (Richmond, Va.: Virginia Historical Society, 1947), I, 123, 125, 190, 225.

    7. See documentation in Perry, *Colonial Church:* I, 225, 362, 264, 267, 269, 271, 273, 276, 277, 280, 281, 283, 285, 287, 289, 293, 295, 297, 299, 301, 304, 306, 308, 310, 312, 327, 344, 361; IV, 194, 201, 208, 212, 216, 225, 296, 304–306; V, 43, 54, 110. George P. Jackson, *White and Negro Spirituals* (Locust Valley, N.Y.: J. J. Augustin, n.d.), 17. William Tibbs, St. Paul's Parish,

Baltimore County, Maryland (1724), is quoted in Perry, *Colonial Church,* IV, 190. Significantly, by the 1720s, most Maryland ministers were referring to "Mullatoes," while Virginia Anglicans wrote only of "Negroes."

8. Smith, et al., *American Christianity,* I, 191, 249; Brydon, *Virginia's Mother Church,* I, 218; Edgar A. Knight, ed., *A Documentary History of Education in the South Before 1860* (Chapel Hill: University of North Carolina Press, 1949), I, 62–177; Henry P. Thompson, *Thomas Bray* (London: S.P.C.K., 1954). D. Francis LeJeau, in C. F. Pascoe, *Two Hundred Years of the S.P.G.: An Historical Account of the Society for the Propagation of the Gospel in Foreign Parts, 1701–1900* (London: The Society . . ., 1901); C. E. Pierre, "The Work of the Society for the Propagation of the Gospel in Foreign Parts Among the Negroes of the Colonies," *JNH* 1 (1916): 349–357; Edgar L. Pennington, "Thomas Bray's Associates' Work Among Negroes," *American Antiquarian Society Proceedings,* New Series 58 (1938): 334–381; Thad W. Tate, *The Negro in 18th Century Williamsburg* (Williamsburg, Va.: Colonial Williamsburg Foundation, 1965), 65–91. The manuscripts of Dr. Bray's Associates, Archives of the Society for the Propagation of the Gospel in Foreign Parts (reprinted in part in Knight, *A Documentary History*) are available on microfilm from the Colonial Williamsburg Foundation, Williamsburg, Virginia.

On Elias Neau, a white who converted to Anglicanism specifically so that he might run the New York City SPG black school from 1704 through 1722, and his successors, see Knight, *A Documentary History,* 15, 16, 22, 38, 39. Brydon, *Virginia's Mother Church,* 8; Theodore Bratton, *Wanted! Leaders* (New York: Department of Missions . . . of the Episcopal Church, 1922), 181. At Abingdon Parish, Virginia, (1677 to 1761), 950 blacks and 2,818 whites were baptized; at Old Bruton Parish (1746 to 1797), 1,122 blacks; and at St. Paul's, King George County, more blacks than whites. "Instructions to Missionaries" are given in Pascoe, *The S.P.G.,* 838–839.

9. P. Mercier, "The Fon of Dahomey," in Daryll Forde, ed., *African Worlds: Studies in the Cosmological Ideas and Social Values of African Peoples* (Oxford: Oxford University Press, [1954] 1970), 233–234.

10. *Virginia Gazette,* Williamsburg, October 7, 1773, in Gerald Mullin, *Flight and Rebellion: Slave Resistance in Eighteenth Century Virginia* (London: Oxford University Press, 1972), 40.

11. Richard M. Dorson, *American Negro Folktales* (New York: Fawcett, [1956] 1968), 141–142; and "Old Master Gets the Better of John," 145–152. "The Conjur That Didn't Work," in B. A. Botkin, *Lay My Burden Down* (Chicago: University of Chicago Press, 1945), 34; Niles Newbell Puckett, *Folk Beliefs of the Southern Negro* (New York: Negro Universities Press, [1926] 1968), 301, citing P. Smiley, "Folklore from Virginia, South Carolina, Georgia, Alabama and Florida," *JAF* 32 (1919): 365.

12. *Daily True Delta,* New Orleans, May 29, 1852, as reprinted in Lyle Saxon, Edward Dreyer, and Robert Tallant, *Gumbo Ya-Ya: A Collection of Louisiana Folk Tales* (Boston: Houghton Mifflin Co., 1945), 243–244, 249. On the faith of slaves in Voodoo, see Louis Hughes, *Thirty Years a Slave* (Milwaukee, Wis.: South Side Printing Co., 1897); Frederick Douglass, *My Bondage, My Freedom* (New York: Miller, Orton & Mulligan, 1855), Henry Bibb, *Narrative of the Life and Adventures of Henry Bibb, An American Slave* (New York: The Author, 1849), 22–35, reprinted in Willie Lee Rose, *A Documentary History of Slavery in North America* (London: Oxford University Press, 1976), 457–462. The belief in conjuring, which runs through the "Slave Narratives," is discussed further in Chapter 5.

13. Puckett, *Folk Beliefs,* 309–310. Gladys-Marie Fry, *Night Riders in Black Folk History* (Knoxville: University of Tennessee Press, 1975), 45–58.

14. "Slave Narratives," Rias Body, Georgia, IV, 89. E. E. Evans-Pritchard, *Nuer Religion* (London: Oxford University Press, 1956), 37.

15. Interrogation by Reverend Samuel Parris, in Winfield S. Nevins, *Witchcraft in Salem Village in 1692* (New York: Burt Franklin, [1916] 1971), 119. "The tradition is that . . . two girls,

[daughters of Rev. Samuel Parris] with perhaps a few other children of the neighborhood, used, during the winter of 1691–1692, to assemble in the minister's kitchen and practice tricks and incantations with Tituba." Tituba, their servant, was half West Indian and half Negro. She and her husband, "John Indian," were brought as slaves from the West Indies by Reverend Parris. "Tituba professed to know how to discover witches . . . but denied she was one herself." She claimed she had helped the girls identify local witches. Tituba was not tried, but she gave testimony in other cases; she was imprisoned and later sold "for her fees." Nevins, *Witchcraft*, 46, 49, 50, 68. (Twenty-two of the thirty-two "witches" executed in America were killed at Salem, Massachusetts, between February 1692 and January 1693.)

16. The source of the hag story was an ex-slave, quoted by Robert Carr, Columbus, Mississippi, in Puckett, *Folk Beliefs*, 152. Dorson recounts the encounter with a witch in *American Negro Folktales*, 239–249. Cf. Brandon on the use of the term *Gris Gris* in southwest Louisiana, in Richard M. Dorson, *Buying the Wind* (Chicago: University of Chicago Press, 1964), 269. Job's selling of *Gris Gris* in Africa is reported in Douglas Grant, *The Fortunate Slave* (New York: Oxford University Press, 1968). Techniques for protection from ghosts can be found in Puckett, *Folk Beliefs*, 99, 140, 161; haunts, 97–99, 101–102; animals talking, 32. Ghosts and hags can be found in Dorson, *American Negro Folktales*, 120 ff.; WPA, Georgia Writers' Project, *Drums and Shadows: Survival Studies Among the Georgia Coastal Negroes* (Athens, Ga.: 1940), 6, 16, 24, 34, 44–45, 59–60, 95–96, 108. Puckett, *Folk Beliefs*, 146, 151–153, 154, 163–165.

17. On "no-counts," see the discussion in Eugene Genovese, *Roll, Jordan, Roll: The World the Slaves Made* (New York: Pantheon Books, 1974), 622–636. Mullin, *Flight and Rebellion*, 45; Berger, *Sacred Canopy*, 14; Peter L. Berger and Thomas Luckman, *The Social Construction of Reality* (London: Penguin Press, 1966), 108.

18. For superstitions and signs, see Henry D. Spaulding, *Encyclopedia of Black Folklore and Humor* (Middle Village, N.Y.: Jonathan David, 1972), 536–541. Bernard DeVoto, *Mark Twain's America* (Boston: Houghton Mifflin Co., 1951), 67–73, provides a concise summary of nineteenth-century white knowledge of the black spirit world.

19. Celestia Avery, in "Slave Narratives," Georgia, IV, 75; Jack Atkinson, Georgia, IV, 17. Tricks are discussed in Puckett, *Folk Beliefs*, 231, 234, and by Henry F. Pyles, Tulsa, Oklahoma, born in August 15, 1865, in Jackson, Tenn., in Botkin, *Lay My Burden Down*, 30–31. For Hoodoo experiences, see "Slave Narratives," William Adams, Texas; Abram Sells, Texas; Henry F. Pyles, Tennessee; H. B. Holloway, Arkansas; Jake Green, Alabama; Orleans Finger, Alabama; Annie Page, Alabama; Maggie Perkins, Arkansas; William Adams, Texas (reprinted in Botkin, *Lay My Burden Down*, 29–36). Rebecca Fletcher is quoted in Saxon, et al., *Gumbo Ya-Ya*, 250. For "Some Slave Superstitions," see *The Southern Workman* 41 (1912): 246.

20. W. T. Harris and Harry Sawyer, *The Springs of Mende Belief and Conduct* (Freetown: Sierra Leone University Press, 1968), 105. The baptism is recorded on the Ethnic Folkways Record, *Negro Folk Music of Alabama* (FE 4417), Side 2, Band 9.

21. Pidgin and Gullah are discussed in J. L. Dillard, *Black English: Its History and Usage in the United States* (New York:Random House, 1972), 109; Wood, *Black Majority*, 185; Lorenzo Dow Turner, *Africanisms in the Gullah Dialect* (New York: Arno Press, [1949] 1969); David Dalby, "The African Element in American English," in Thomas Kochman, ed., *Rappin' and Stylin' Out* (Urbana: University of Illinois Press, 1972), 170–186. For examples of black English, see Puckett, *Folk Beliefs*, 21; Turner, *Africanisms*; William Allen, *Slave Songs of the United States* (New York: Peter Smith, [1967] 1951), XXIV. On meaning in life, see Carl G. Jung, *Man and His Symbols* (London: Aldus Books, 1964), 89.

Chapter 4

1. Erskine Caldwell, *Deep South* (New York: Weybright & Talley, 1968), 254.
2. Brief but excellent summaries of Baptist history can be found in H. Shelton Smith,

Robert T. Handy, and Lefferts A. Loetscher, eds., *American Christianity: An Historical Interpretation With Representative Documents* (New York: Charles Scribner's Sons, 1960), I, 143-146, 170-172, 200, 268-271, 313-314, 360-365, and in Sydney E. Ahlstrom, *A Religious History of the American People* (New Haven, Conn.: Yale University Press, 1972). For more detailed background, see R. G. Torbet, *A History of the Baptists* (Philadelphia: Judson Press, 1950); N. H. Pius, *An Outline of Baptist History* (Nashville, Tenn.: National Baptist Publication Board, 1911); David Benedict, *A General History of the Baptist Denomination in America and Other Parts of the World* (New York: Lewis Colby & Co., 1848); Jesse L. Boyd, *A History of the Baptists in America Prior to 1845* (New York: American Press, 1957); Robert A. Baker, *The Southern Baptist Convention and Its People, 1607-1972* (Nashville, Tenn.: Broadman Press, 1974); W. W. Sweet, *Religion on the American Frontier* (4 vols.), Vol. 1, *The Baptists 1783-1830* (New York: Henry Holt & Co., 1931).

3. Keith Thomas, *Religion and the Decline of Magic* (London: Weidenfeld & Nicolson, 1971), IX, 449, 638, infra. Citing Richard Napier's casebooks, Thomas notes that between 1600 and 1639, he had 120 cases in which the patient believed witchcraft to be the cause, and that William Lilly's casebooks for 1644-1666 record 50 such cases. See also Alan A. McFarlane, *Witchcraft in Tudor and Stuart England* (London: Routledge & Kegan Paul, 1970). MacFarlane found that witchcraft cases dominated the life in the three towns in his study and that there was "a background of complex and widely distributed beliefs about witchcraft" (251).

4. Increase Mather, *Remarkable Providences*, 114-118; John Winthrop, *Journal*, II, 344-346; Cotton Mather, *Wonders...*, 80-84, 161, all reprinted in Richard M. Dorson, *America Begins: Early American Writings* (Greenwich, Conn.: Fawcett, 1950), 348-349, 353-356, 362-366. Emphasis on *a small black man* added.

5. Thomas, *Religion and Magic*, 126. Ephesians 4:11; I Corinthians 12:10; I Corinthians 14; Ephesians 5:21.

6. Baker, *Southern Baptist Convention*, 15-58; Ernst Troeltsch, *The Social Teaching of the Christian Churches* (New York: Harper & Brothers, 1960), II, 697; H. Wheeler Robinson, *The Life and Faith of the Baptists* (London: Methuen & Co., 1927); Charles Williams, *The Principles and Practices of the Baptists* (London: Baptist Tract Society, 1879); Sweet, *The Baptists;* Sweet, *Revivalism in America: Its Origin, Growth and Decline* (New York: Charles Scribner's Sons, 1944), 133; Sweet, "The Churches as Moral Courts of the Frontier," *Church History* 2 (1933): 3-21. Ahlstrom, *Religious History*, 171-173. Jacob Arminius (1560-1609) was a Dutch Calvinist who believed that Christ died for all men in a *general* atonement.

7. The six principles refer to those listed in Hebrews 6:1-2. In 1707, the Philadelphia Association adopted the 1677 English Baptist adaptation of the Westminster Confession. Ahlstrom, *Religious History*, 131, 175.

8. For a review of the revival, see Sweet, *Revivalism*. Excellent regional studies are Edwin S. Gaustad, *The Great Awakening in New England* (Chicago: Quadrangle Books, 1957); C. C. Goen, *Revivalism and Separatism in New England 1740-1800* (New Haven, Conn.: Yale University Press, 1962); Charles H. Maxson, *The Great Awakening in the Middle Colonies* (Chicago: University of Chicago Press, 1920); Wesley M. Gewehr, *The Great Awakening in Virginia 1740-1790* (Durham: University of North Carolina Press, 1930). Bernard Weisberger cogently analyzes this and the subsequent revivals in *They Gathered at the River* (Boston: Little, Brown & Co., 1958).

9. The citation is from Robert B. Semple, *A History of the Rise and Progress of the Baptists in Virginia* (Richmond, Va.: John Lynch, 1810), 15-16, commenting on the Baptist revival in Virginia in 1770.

10. See Louis F. Benson, *The English Hymn, Its Development and Use in Worship* (New York: Hodder & Stoughton, 1915), 196 ff.; George Pullen Jackson, *Spiritual Folk-Songs of Early America* (New York: J. J. Augustin, 1937); Jackson, *White and Negro Spirituals* (Locust Valley, N.Y.: J. J. Augustin, n.d.), 38-63; Annabel Morris Buchanan, *Folk Hymns of America* (New

York: J. Fischer & Brother, 1938). The first Baptist song book to appear in America was *Divine Hymns,* edited by Joshua Smith and published in several editions between 1784 and 1803. (The eleventh edition was published by Sterry & Porter in Norwich, Connecticut, 1803.)

11. An excellent picture of early Southern Baptist life can be found in David Benedict, *Fifty Years Among the Baptists* (New York: Sheldon & Co., 1860). The volumes by Robert Baker, *The Southern Baptist Convention and the First Southern Baptists* (Nashville, Tenn.: Broadman Press, 1966) and *A Baptist Source Book, with Particular Reference to Southern Baptists* (Nashville, Tenn.: Broadman Press, 1966), provide a fine introduction to the factual material by a committed Baptist. Also see William L. Lumpkin, *Baptist Foundations in the South* (Nashville, Tenn.: Broadman Press, 1961), and B. F. Riley, *A History of the Baptists in the Southern States East of the Mississippi* (Philadelphia: American Baptist Publication Society, 1898).

Southern Baptist history has been analyzed most carefully in separate state studies, among them: J. M. Carrol, *A History of Texas Baptists* (Dallas, Tex.: Baptist Standard Publishing Co., 1923); John T. Christian, *A History of Baptists of Louisiana* (Shreveport: Louisiana Baptist Convention, 1923); Hosea Holcombe, *Baptists in Alabama* (Philadelphia: King & Beard, 1840); M. A. Huggins, *A History of North Carolina Baptists 1727-1932* (Raleigh: General Board, North Carolina State Convention, 1967); E. Earl Joiner, *A History of Florida Baptists* (Jacksonville: Florida Baptist Convention, 1972); Joe M. King, *A History of South Carolina Baptists* (Columbia: General Board of South Carolina Baptist Convention, 1964); R. A. McLemore, *A History of Mississippi Baptists, 1780-1790* (Jackson, Miss.: Baptist Convention Board, 1971); Frank M. Masters, *A History of Baptists in Kentucky* (Louisville: Kentucky Baptist Historical Society, 1953); George W. Paschal, *History of North Carolina Baptists* (Raleigh: General Board, North Carolina Baptist State Convention, 1930, 1955), 2 vols.; J. S. Rogers, *History of Arkansas Baptists* (Little Rock: Executive Board of the Arkansas Baptist Convention, 1948); Garnett Ryland, *The Baptists of Virginia 1699-1926* (Richmond: Virginia Baptist Board of Missions & Education, 1955); Robert B. Semple, *History of the Baptists in Virginia;* C. Penrose St. Amant, *Short History of Louisiana Baptists* (Nashville, Tenn.: Broadman Press, 1948); Leah Townsend, *South Carolina Baptists 1670-1805* (Florence, S.C.: Florence Printing Co., 1935).

12. On Stearns, see G. W. Paschal, ed., *"Morgan Edwards": Materials Towards a History of the Baptists in the Province of North Carolina,* as reprinted in Smith, et al., *American Christianity,* I, 362-365; Baker, *Southern Baptist Convention,* 46, 52-57; Lumpkin, *Baptist Foundations,* 147ff.; Gewehr, *Great Awakening,* 109.

13. "Address to the Anabaptists," Dawson MSS, cited in Gewehr, *Great Awakening,* 130. See Walter B. Posey, "The Baptists and Slavery in the Lower Mississippi Valley," *JNH* 61 (1956): 117-130, which surveys the varying attitudes of Baptists over time, running from antislavery through accommodation and acceptance. William T. Thom, *The Struggle for Religious Freedom in Virginia: The Baptists* (Baltimore, Md.: Johns Hopkins University Press, 1900) is very cursory in relation to the blacks but gives an adequate picture of Baptist persecution in this period. See also Lewis P. Little, *Imprisoned Preachers and Religious Liberty in Virginia* (Lynchburg, Va.: J. P. Bell Co., 1938), and James Birkitt, *Carving Out a Kingdom: A History of Carmel Baptist Church and Persecuted Baptists of Caroline County, Virginia, 1773-1865* (Richmond, Va.: Christian Enterprises, 1965). A general discussion can be found in Smith, et al., *American Christianity,* 364ff.; Gewehr, *Great Awakening,* 167-177, and Ryland, *Baptists of Virginia.* Cf. Winthrop S. Hudson, ed., *Baptist Concepts of the Church* (Philadelphia: Judson Press, 1959) for a discussion of church policy and associations. On page 129 in *Revivalism,* Sweet comments:

> By the eighteen-twenties the whole settled portion of the West was covered with a network of Baptist Associations . . . . The meetings of these Associations corresponded somewhat to the camp meetings. It became the custom to hold them in the woods where the general public was invited, and it was not uncommon for many thousands to be in attendance.

Gilbert H. Barnes, *The Anti-Slavery Impulse (1830–1844)* (New York: Appleton-Century-Crofts, 1933), 18-19. Cf. the antislavery statement of the Ketocton Association of Virginia, *Minutes* (1787).

14. Baker, *Source Book*, 40-42, quoting from John Leland, *Works*, and Gewehr, *Great Awakening*, 239-241, also citing Leland, *Works*, 51. This is a slight variant of the statement in the *Minutes* of the General Committee (1789), 7. Robert Carter, "Day Book," in Vol. XVI (beginning in May 1784), 76. The Carter manuscript is in Perkins Library, Duke University, Durham, North Carolina, in the Manuscript Division. Carter, who had been an Anglican, soon became a Swedenborgian, but Baptist antislavery appeals were clearly of direct influence. See Louis Morton, *Robert Carter of Nomini Hall* (Williamsburg, Va.: Colonial Williamsburg Foundation, 1941).

A plea for manumission was made in the Washington, D.C., First Baptist Church. See the manuscript minutes, August 8, 1817. (Microfilm available at HCSBC.)

15. *Minutes*, Shaftsbury Association of New York (1972), reprinted in John Rippon, *The Baptist Annual Register* (London: Dilly, Button & Thomas), II (1794-1797). 198. For evidence of anti-Baptist feeling, see Gewehr, *Great Awakening*, 115. Baptist rejection of Anglican theology can be found in a letter of John Watts, et al., to Thomas Clayton, March 11, 1699, rejecting *any* Anglican overture. Reprinted in Smith, et al., *American Christianity*, 268-271.

For surveys of white churches' reactions to blacks and their participation in abolitionist activity, see Willis D. Weatherford, *American Churches and the Negro* (Boston: Christopher Publishing House, 1957); Thomas E. Drake, *Quakers and Slavery in America* (New Haven, Conn: Yale University Press, 1950); Donald G. Mathews, *Slavery and Methodism: A Chapter in American Morality, 1780–1845* (Princeton, N.J.: Princeton University Press, 1965); James Shaw, *The Negro in the History of Methodism* (Nashville, Tenn.: Parthenon Press, 1954); Andrew Murray, *Presbyterians and the Negro—A History* (Philadelphia: Presbyterian Historical Society, 1966); Robert O. Fife, *Teeth On Edge* (Grand Rapids, Mich.: Baker Book House, 1971) on Disciples and blacks; John T. Gillard, *The Catholic Church and the American Negro* (Baltimore, Md: St. Joseph's Society Press, 1929); Barnes, *The Anti-Slavery Impulse;* Timothy Smith, *Revivalism and Social Reform in Mid-Nineteenth Century America* (New York: Abingdon Press, 1957).

16. Morgan Edwards, *Materials Toward a History of American Baptists*, 12 vols. Four volumes were published in Philadelphia (1770-1792); the rest are in manuscript, available at the American Baptist Historical Society, Rochester, New York, and on microfilm at HCSBS, "North Carolina," manuscript, 45; Benedict, *Fifty Years*, 163; Baker, *Southern Baptist Convention*, 49; Ryland, *Baptists of Virginia*, 142. A good published study of a Stearns' revival church is that of James Donovan Mosteller, *A History of the Kiokee Baptist Church in Georgia* (Ann Arbor, Mich.: Edwards Brothers, 1952).

17. *Minutes*, General Committee of Virginia (1793), 4; *Minutes*, Dover Association, Virginia (1797), 10th question. Antislavery leader Robert B. Semple was then moderator. Ahlstrom, *Religious History*, 321, 432, 441. Regular and Separatist Baptists in Kentucky united in 1801. A similar union took place in North Carolina in 1788, while in South Carolina and Georgia unity was gradually achieved without any formal act. Baker, *Southern Baptist Convention*, 93-192. When the Arminian and Particular Baptists united in the Elkhorn Association of Kentucky (1801), their creedal statement was a hybrid allowing for both views: (#5) "That the saints will finally preserve through grace to glory," and also (#9) "That the preaching Christ tasted death for everyman shall be no bar to communion." Reprinted in Sweet, *The Baptists*, 23-24; Benedict, *General History*, 252-253; Catherine Cleveland, *The Great Revival in the West 1797–1805* (Chicago: University of Chicago Press, 1916); Charles A. Johnson, *The Frontier Camp Meeting* (Dallas, Tex.: Southern Methodist University Press, 1955).

18. William James, *Varieties of Religious Experience* (New York: Modern Library, [1902] 1929), 99. Luther, *Werke*, ed. by Walch, XLLC, 2525: "The grace of God 'is the rule of the Spirit

in directing and governing the human will . . . . Accordingly, all the actions which are afterwards done are truly said to be wholly his'." Calvin, *Institutes*, II, 15, and XV, 4. Luther and Calvin cited by Bernard Citron, in *New Birth: A Study of the Evangelical Doctrine of Conversion in the Protestant Fathers* (Edinburgh: University Press, 1951), 68, 118.

19. Perry Miller, *The New England Mind: The Seventeenth Century* (New York: Macmillan Co., 1939), 3. See also Miller, *The New England Mind: From Colony to Province* (Cambridge, Mass.: Harvard University Press, 1953), 70; and Peter G. Mode, *Source Book and Bibliographic Guide for American Church History* (Boston: J. S. Canner, [1921] 1964), 66 on the Presbyterians' use of experience. "The Answer of the Elders and Other Messengers of the Churches, Assembled at Boston in the Year 1662," *The Results of Three Synods* (Boston: 1725), 50–51 is reprinted in Smith, et al., *American Christianity*, I, 203–204.

20. Alan Heimart and Perry Miller, eds., *The Great Awakening* (New York: Bobbs-Merrill Co., 1967), xxviii; Perry Miller, *Jonathan Edwards* (New York: Meridian Books, 1959), 209.

21. David Brainerd, in Jonathan Edwards and Sereno E. Dwight, eds., *Memoirs of the Reverend David Brainerd* (New Haven, Conn.: 1822), 45–47, reprinted in James, *Varieties of Religious Experience*, 209–210, and another visionary experience, 245. Also see Brainerd, *Memoirs*, 217, reprinted in Smith, et al., *American Christianity*, I, 337, 339; Weisberger, *They Gathered at the River*, 58. A highly critical report of Davenport was printed in the *Boston Evening Post*, July 5, 1742.

22. *Testimony* reprinted in Weisberger, *They Gathered at the River*, 29; Weisberger, 47, also cites Lorenzo Dow, *Autobiography*, I, 9–10, 147, 150. Devereaux Jarratt (1733–1801), *The Life of the Reverend Devereaux Jarratt* . . . . (Baltimore, Md.: 1806) cited by Sweet, *Revivalism*, 86–87, and Smith, *American Christianity*, I, 366ff. Henry Alline (1748–1784), *The Testimony of the Reverend Henry Alline* (Boston: 1806), 25–26, is reprinted in James, *Varieties of Religious Experience*, 156. Background on Alline's mission can be found in Maurice W. Armstrong, *The Great Awakening in Nova Scotia 1776–1809* (Hartford, Conn.: American Society of Church History, 1948). Charles G. Finney's testimony is from *Memoirs of Reverend Charles Grandison Finney* . . . (New York: 1876), 18–21, reprinted in Weisberger, *They Gathered at the River*, 92. For the conversions of James Finley, Peter Cartwright, Jacob Young, and Stephen Bradley, see Weisberger, 48. J. H. Noyes, *Confessions of John Humphrey Noyes*, Part I (Oneida, N.Y.: n.p., 1849), 18, re: February 29, 1834. Noyes experienced a third rebirth to sinlessness or perfection. The volume *Twice Born Men*, compiled by Hy. Pickering, includes the conversion experiences of 100 men, including Abraham Lincoln, 119; the American preachers R. A. Torrey, 106; Charles G. Finney, 117; and William Wilberforce, 24. James C. Hefley, *Living Miracles* (Grand Rapids, Mich.: Zondervan Publishing House, 1964) contains the conversional experiences of twenty-nine Baptists.

23. Jabez Swann, *The Evangelist or Life and Labors of the Reverend Jabez Swann* (Waterford, Conn.: W. L. Peckham, 1873), 50–51. Jacob Knapp, *Autobiography of Elder Jacob Knapp* (New York: Sheldon & Co., 1868), 14. See also Weisberger, *They Gathered at the River*, 136; Charles Cole, Jr., *The Social Ideas of the Northern Evangelists (1826–1860)* (New York: Columbia University Press, 1954), 33–36.

24. Cf. Gaustad, *Great Awakening*, 25, 49. For a report of the excesses in the wake of Davenport's sermons, see the *Boston Evening Post*, July 5, 1742. Weisberger, *They Gathered at the River*, 25, asks why only ten people were saved at the most excited of sessions at Red River, Kentucky [June, 1800]. Cf. O. W. Taylor, *Early Tennessee Baptists 1769–1832* (Nashville, Tenn.: HCSBC, 1957), 156–175; Frederick Davenport, *Primitive Traits in Religious Revivals* (Westport, Conn.: Negro Universities Press, [1905] 1960); Charles A. Johnson, *The Frontier Camp Meeting* (Dallas, Tex.: Southern Methodist University Press, 1955). Samuel Davies, writing from Hanover, Virginia, to a Dr. Doddridge, October 2, 1750, is cited in William Perry, ed., *Historical Collections Relating to the American Colonial Church* (New York: AMS Press [1870] 1969), 369. Perry notes that during 1748–1750 Davies baptized about forty people, "7 or 8 of whom are ad-

mitted into full communion and partake of the Lord's Supper." See Samuel Davies, *The State of Religion Among the Protestant Dissenters in Virginia* (Boston: S. Kneeland, 1751) and Davies, *The Duty of Christians to Propagate Their Religion Among Heathens Earnestly Recommended to the Masters of Negroe Slaves in Virginia, Hanover, January 8, 1757* (London: J. Oliver, 1758). Other evidence of black participation in revivals can be found in *George Whitefield's Journals* (London: Banner of Truth Trust, 1960), 422; *The Journal and Letters of Francis Asbury*, (London: Epworth Press, 1958), 3 vols.; John Marrant, "A Narrative of the Lord's Wonderful Dealings with John Marrant, a black . . . ." (1802), reprinted in Dorothy Porter, ed., *Early Negro Writing, 1760–1837* (Boston: Beacon Press, 1971), 427–447; W. P. Harrison, *The Gospel Among the Slaves* (Nashville, Tenn.: Methodist Episcopal Church South, 1893), 53, 63, 92, 126, 134; Isaac Backus, "An 18th Century Baptist Tours Virginia on Horseback," *Virginia Baptist Register* 2 (1963): 64–85; Johnson, *Frontier Meeting*, 46; Holcombe, *Baptists in Alabama*, 45ff.; Weisberger, *They Gathered at the River*, 31ff.; Paschal, *North Carolina Baptists*, 240ff.; Joseph Tracy, *The Great Awakening* (Boston: Tappan & Dennet, 1842), 117; Jackson, *White and Negro Spirituals*, 35, 174; Ulrich B. Phillips and John R. Commons, *A Documentary History of the American Industrial Society* (Cleveland, Ohio: American Bureau of Industrial Research, 1910–1911), II, 284–286; Carter G. Woodson, *The History of the Negro Church*, 2d. ed. (Washington, D.C.: Associated Publishers, 1921), 63. Richard Dozier, "Historical Notes Concerning the Planting of Baptist Principles in the Northern Neck of Virginia," manuscript, 1771, typed copy, 36 (available at the Virginia Baptist Historical Society, Richmond, Virginia); Jean Russell, *God's Lost Cause: A Study of the Church and the Racial Problem* (London: SCM Press, 1968), 46. Russell suggests that segregation was general at Methodist camp meetings, but it was not "stated policy" until 1864 when the Methodist Episcopal Church, South, "recommended segregated facilities."

25. Ulrich Phillips, *American Negro Slavery* (Baton Rouge: Louisiana State University [1918] 1969), 316.

Chapter 5

1. Thomas Luckman, *The Invisible Religion: The Problem of Religion in Modern Society* (New York: Macmillan Co., 1967), 69.

2. Francis W. Titus, *Narrative of Sojourner Truth: A Bondswoman of Olden Times* (Battle Creek, Mich.: F. W. Titus, 1878); Jacqueline Bernard, *Journey Toward Freedom: The Story of Sojourner Truth* (New York: Dell Publishing Co., 1967), 18–19. On her mother's African concepts of a High God and Sojourner's understandings, see 21, 38, 48, 53, 102, 114, 188.

3. James Jefferson Watson, "The Religion of the Negro," Ph.D. dissertation, University of Pennsylvania, 1912, 51.

4. See the various studies by Morgan Edwards in "Materials towards a history of the Baptists in Maryland, Virginia, North Carolina, South Carolina and Georgia" (1972), unpublished manuscripts in the library of the Baptist Historical Society, Rochester, New York. (Microfilm copies available at HCSBC.) Edwards reports that the 1758 Separatist revival at the Dan River, Virginia Church brought eleven blacks into the congregation. In 1779, eighty-one blacks were members of the new, weak, and persecuted Delaware Baptist churches. Edwards, III, 59.

For black Baptist sources, much of the extensive literature is cited below, in relation to particular individuals, churches, and issues. However, no single volume adequately surveys the prewar history of black Baptists inasmuch as all historians working in this area accepted the thesis that the institution was hidden.

For general guides to the relevant literature on black Baptists, consult the bibliographies appended to A Note on Sources. A brief bibliography of basic materials is given in Note 1 of the Introduction. A selected list of basic readings on blacks in the prewar period should also include the following recent interpretations: Leonard E. Barrett, *Soul-Force: African Heritage in Afro-*

American Religion (New York: Anchor/Doubleday, 1974); William L. Banks, *The Black Church in America* (Chicago: Moody Bible Institute, 1972); "The Black Experience and the Church," *Review and Expositor* 70, no. 3 (1973); Harold A. Carter, *The Prayer Tradition of Black People* (Valley Forge, Pa.: Judson Press, 1976); Albert B. Cleague, Jr., *The Black Messiah* (New York: Sheed & Ward, 1969); Charles V. Hamilton, *The Black Preacher in America* (New York: William Morris & Co., 1972); William R. Jones, *Is God a White Racist?* (New York: Anchor/Doubleday, 1973); Emmanuel McCall, ed., *The Black Christian Experience* (Nashville, Tenn.: Broadman Press, 1972); Henry Mitchell, *Black Preaching* (Philadelphia: J. B. Lippincott, 1970); Henry Mitchell, *Black Belief* (New York: Harper & Row, 1975); M. Nelson, R. Yokley, and A. K. Nelson, *The Black Church in America* (New York: Basic Books, 1975); Gayraud S. Wilmore, *Black Religion and Black Radicalism* (New York: Anchor/Doubleday, 1973).

5. Robert B. Semple, *A History of the Rise and Progress of the Baptists in Virginia* (Richmond: John Lynch, 1810), 22-23. *South Carolina Gazette,* April 24, 1742, as reprinted in Winthrop D. Jordan, *White Over Black: American Attitudes Toward the Negro 1550-1812* (Chapel Hill: University of North Carolina Press, 1968), 85-86.

6. George Whitefield, reprinted in William W. Sweet, *Revivalism in America* (Gloucester, Mass.: P. Smith, [1944] 1965), 109. John Marrant, "A Narrative of the Lord's Wonderful Dealings with John Marrant, a Black . . . .," (London, 1802), reprinted in full in Dorothy Porter, ed., *Early Negro Writing 1760-1837* (Boston: Beacon Press, 1971), 431, 446.

7. George Liele, letter from Kingston, Jamaica, December 18, 1791; Liele and David George, quoted in a letter from Reverend Joseph Cook of Euhaw, South Carolina, September 15, 1790. Liele wrote at length of his religious experience. He noted that he did not know his father well, but he was told by both whites and blacks "that my father was the only black person who knew the Lord in a spiritual way in that country [Virginia]." Letters published in John Rippon, ed., *The Baptist Annual Register* (London: Dilley, Button & Thomas), I (1790-1793): 332, 474-475, and reprinted in "Letters Showing the Rise and Progress of the Early Negro Churches of Georgia and the West Indies," *JNH* 1 (1916): 69ff. See also Edward A. Holmes, "George Liele: Negro Slavery's Prophet of Deliverance," *Baptist Quarterly* (1964): 340-350. Holmes suggests that the church to which Liele, his owner Henry Sharpe, and preacher Mathew Moore belonged was probably Big Buckhead Creek Baptist Church. John W. Davis, "George Liele and Andrew Bryan, Pioneer Negro Baptist Preachers," *JNH* 3 (1918): 119-127. David Benedict, *A General History of the Baptist Denomination in America* (Boston: Lincoln & Edwards, 1813), 2 vols., II: 189ff.; W.E.B. DuBois, *The Negro Church* (Atlanta, Ga.: Atlanta University Press, 1903), 190. B. F. Riley, *A History of the Baptists in the Southern States East of the Mississippi* (Philadelphia: American Baptist Publication Society, 1898), 312; W. P. Harrison, *The Gospel Among the Slaves* (Nashville, Tenn.: Methodist Episcopal Church, South, 1893), 59.

8. On Marshall, Burton, and the Kiokee Church, see James Donovan Mostellor, *A History of the Kiokee Baptist Church in Georgia* (Ann Arbor, Mich.: Edwards Brothers, 1952).

9. Hosea Holcombe, *A History of the Rise and Progress of the Baptists in Alabama* (Philadelphia: King & Beard, 1840), 61-62; Charles C. Jones, *The Religious Instruction of the Negroes in the United States* (Savannah, Ga.: T. Purse, 1842), 125. On Jones, see Robert M. Myers, ed., *The Children of Pride: A True Story of Georgia and the Civil War* (New Haven, Conn.: Yale University Press, 1972), and the critical comments in Appendix H, "The Sunbury Baptist Association and the Association for the Religious Instruction of the Negroes in Liberty County, Georgia." Robert Ryland, "Reminiscences of the First African Church, Richmond, Virginia by the Pastor," *American Baptist Memorial* (1855): 265. See the conversion experiences of Israel Campbell, *An Autobiography: Bond and Free* (Philadelphia: I. Campbell, 1861), 76ff.; J. H. Magee, *The Night of Affliction and Morning of Recovery: An Autobiography* (Cincinnati: J. H. Magee, 1873), 30-31.

10. A. P. Watson and Clifton H. Johnson, eds., *God Struck Me Dead: Religious Conversion Experiences and Autobiographies of Negro Ex-Slaves* (Philadelphia: Pilgrim Press, 1969). Two

informants explicitly state they were not slaves (100 and 172). Watson does not provide bio-graphical data beyond what is in the narratives. Vision experiences are recounted in many narra-tives, cited below. See "Narratives of Religious Experience," in Lorenzo Dow Turner, *Africanisms in the Gulluh Dialect* (New York: Arno Press, [1949] 1969), 271–281.

11. On the terminology "sinner," etc., see John W. Work, *American Negro Songs and Spirituals* (New York: Bonanza Books, 1940), 54.

12. Watson and Johnson, *God Struck Me Dead*, 19–150. William Francis Allen, *Slave Songs of the United States* (New York: Peter Smith, [1867] 1951), 49.

13. Watson and Johnson, *God Struck Me Dead*, 20, 45, 63, 61, 94. See also 123 and 146 on dancing. A black Baptist convert noted:

> I was a wild thing when I was young. Why I was more on dancing than my old Missy, and she taught me to dance. But after I joined the church, I didn't have the desire to dance no more. For a long time, you know, I could not git ahold of religion, cause I wanted to dance, but now I know what my religion did for me. It cleared me soul for all eternity. Dancing was an injury to me, I see it now.

In the Fisk University Archives, cited by Alan Lomax, *The Folk Songs of North America* (Gar-den City, N.Y.: Doubleday & Co., 1960), 467.

Allen, *Slave Songs*, 14. See also "I coud't hear Nobody Pray" and "Steal Away and Pray," in Work, *Negro Songs*, 72–77. Comments on private praying places run through the "Slave Nar-ratives"; see Andrew Moss, Knoxville, Tennessee:

> One ting dat's wrong widdis world today, is dat dey a'n got no 'prayer grounds'! Down in Georgia, whar I was born, dat was 'way back in 1852—us colored folks cleaned out knee-spots in de cane breaks. Cane, you know, grows high and thick and colored folks could hide de 'seves in dar, and nobody could see and pester em. (George P. Rawick, *From Sundown to Sunup: The Making of the Black Community* [Westport, Conn.: Greenwood Publishing Co., 1972].)

Rawick cites many references to praying places in the published version of the narratives. See Rawick, ed., *The American Slave: A Composite Autobiography* (Westport, Conn.: Greenwood Press, 1973), 17 vols. The narratives are very carefully indexed in Olli Alho, *The Religion of the Slaves; A Study of the Religious Tradition and Behaviour of Plantation Slaves in the United States 1830–1865* (Helsinki: Academia Scientiarum Fennica, 1976), Appendix 1, 278ff. Watson and Johnson, *God Struck Me Dead*, 15–151. Voices were heard by almost every candidate. Only one individual suggested that the voice heard was that of "conscience" (14).

14. On God "killing,": See Watson and Johnson, *God Struck Me Dead*, 59–169; on hang-ing over hell, 15–143; on blackness, 21–149 (emphasis added); on the little me, 63–151. On Edwards, see "Sinners in the Hands of an Angry God" (July 1741), reprinted in G. Grob and R. N. Beck, eds., *American Ideas* (New York: Free Press, 1963) 19, as well as the imagery of Charles Chauncy (1741): "There is nothing betwixt you and the place of blackness or dark-ness but a poor, frail, uncertain life. You hang, as it were, over the bottomless pit, by a slender thread of life, and the moment that snaps asunder, you sink down into perdition." Cited by Edwin Gaustad, *The Great Awakening in New England* (Chicago: Quadrangle Books, 1957), 86. On African concern with the spider, see G. Parrinder, *West African Religion*, 2d ed. (London: Epworth Press, 1961), 16, 19; and Harold Courlander, comp., *A Treasury of African Folklore* (New York: Crown Publishers, 1975), 60ff., 135ff., 313ff.

15. Rawick interprets the guide as Legba and Holy Spirit, mixed together (*From Sundown to Sunup*, 48). See Lawrence Levine "Some Go Up and Some Go Down: The Meaning of the Slave Trickster," in Stanley Elkins and Eric McKitrick, eds., *The Hofstadter Aegis* (New York: Alfred A. Knopf, 1974), 94–124. On the little guide, see Watson and Johnson, *God Struck Me*

Dead, 63–148; and on the "deed" to one's name, 21–147. See also Work, *Negro Songs,* 137. Sometimes the individual's name is written on a "ticket" as for a train, or for permission to leave a plantation.

16. Watson and Johnson, *God Struck Me Dead,* 64–173.

17. Parrinder, *Religion,* 18, 28, 47. John S. Mbiti, *African Religions and Philosophy* (London: Heineman, 1969), 212. In 1959, a Guinean dance troup, Les Ballets Africaines, visiting New York, portrayed "evil" as black-draped figures and "good" as white draped. Cited by Harold R. Isaacs, *The New World of Negro Americans* (New York: John Day & Co., 1963), 77. Henry Spaulding, *Encyclopedia of Black Folklore and Humor* (Middle Village, N.Y.: Jonathan David Publishers, 1972), 166.

18. See the songs "New Born Again" and "Good Lor I Done Done Done," in Work, *Negro Songs,* 151, 160. Watson and Johnson, *God Struck Me Dead,* 50–169. Also see James Jefferson Watson, "The Religion of the Negro," Ph.D. Dissertation, University of Pennsylvania, 1912, 51.

19. Benjamin Quarles, *The Negro in the American Revolution* (Chapel Hill: University of North Carolina Press, 1961); Jupiter Hammon, "An Address to the Negroes in the State of New York" (1787), reprinted in full in Porter, *Early Negro Writing,* 321.

Nichols cites a sermon preached by a black preacher, Williams, to the slaves in Richmond during a cholera epidemic in which he compared the white deaths to the havoc wrought by the plagues, when the Egyptians would not let God's people go. Charles H. Nichols, *Many Thousands Gone: The Ex-Slaves' Accounts of Their Bondage and Freedom* (Leiden: E. J. Brill, 1963), 97.

20. Watson and Johnson, *God Struck Me Dead,* 152, 169. Song sung by Horace Sprout (about sixty-five years old in 1954) on "trabelin"; see Folkways Record FP 656, "Music from the South: Elder Songsters," vol. 7, Side 2, #8; and Work, *Negro Songs,* 55, 86. E. E. Evans-Pritchard. *Neur Religion* (London: Oxford University Press, 1956), 26.

21. Spaulding, *Black Folklore,* 28, source not given (emphasis added). See "Bye & Bye and "Poor Me," in Work, *Negro Songs,* 63, 67. Watson and Johnson, *God Struck Me Dead,* 23–169.

22. Marcel Griaule, *Conversations with Ogotemmêli: An Introduction to Dogon Religious Ideas* (Oxford: Oxford University Press, 1965).

23. Watson and Johnson, *God Struck Me Dead,* 73, 149, 111. On abandoned Banjos, see Lomax, *Folk Songs,* 468. "Lord I want to be a Christian, I want to be more Loving," in Work, *Negro Songs,* 76, 90. Watson and Johnson, *God Struck Me Dead,* 13–145.

See the conversion experience of John, an African converted by Lott Carey in Sierra Leone in about 1825. John used to "cus and fight," but after dying and being reborn: "Suppose a man cus me this time—me cant cus 'im no more . . . . light come in my heart . . . . make me lover everybody." Solomon Peck, "History of the Missions of the Baptist General Convention . . . .," in *History of American Missions to the Heathens* (Worcester, Mass.: Spooner & Howland, 1840), 441.

24. Work, *Negro Songs,* 51. Parrinder, *Religion,* 16, 23. "Any priest will say that his god is a son of the supreme God and that God speaks through his sons."

25. Griaule, *Conversations,* 141. Mbiti, *African Religions,* 85. The latest work with hypnosis and fertility tends to bear out this notion; apparently, a large percentage of infertility is psychologically determined.

26. Parrinder, *African Traditional Religion* (London: Hutchinson's Universal Library, 1954), 49ff.; Parrinder, *Religion,* 44–50; Melville J. Herskovits, *The Myth of the Negro Past* (New York: Harper & Row, 1941), 232, 235. Work, *Negro Songs,* 78, 91, 174. Watson and Johnson, *God Struck Me Dead,* 108, 174. Richard Jolla, "Elder Songsters"; Allen, *Slave Songs,* 55. Richard A. Long and Eugenia W. Collier, eds., *Afro-American Writing* (New York: New York University Press, 1972).

27. James Bolten, in "Slave Narratives," Georgia, IV, 97. Watson and Johnson, *God Struck Me Dead,* 19–170. The use of the biblical image of Jacob's ladder is reminiscent of the Dogon image.

28. Cf. the Jungian discussion of lonely journeys by Joseph L. Henderson and M. L. Von Franz on Jung and dream voices in Carl G. Jung, *Man and His Symbols* (London: Aldus Books, 1964), 151, 198, 280.

29. Timothy Smith, "Slavery and Theology: The Emergence of Black Christian Consciousness in 19th Century America," *Church History* 41 (1972): 497, 498, 501.

30. George Liele in a letter dated December 18, 1791, in Rippon, *Annual Baptist Register,* I, (1790-1793): 332-337.

31. Sydney Ahlstrom, *A Religious History of the American People* (New Haven, Conn.: Yale University Press, 1972), 373, 443. On black Methodists, see James B. F. Shaw, *The Negro in the History of Methodism* (Nashville, Tenn.: Parthenon Press, 1954); George A. Singleton, *The Romance of African Methodism* (New York: Exposition Press, 1952); W. P. Harrison, *The Gospel Among the Slaves* (Nashville, Tenn.: Methodist Episcopal Church, South, 1893).

32. Israel Campbell, *Autobiography,* 82-86. Elizabeth Ross Hite, born a slave on a Louisiana plantation, in Lyle Saxon, Edward Dryer, and Robert Tallant, eds., *Gumbo Ya-Ya: A Collection of Louisiana Folk Tales* (Boston: Houghton Mifflin Co., 1945), 242.

33. To a certain extent, the fine study by Eugene Genovese, *Roll, Jordan, Roll, The World the Slaves Made* (New York: Pantheon Books, 1974), suffers from overdependence on the narratives and is thereby skewed toward being a study of the last period of slavery. However, the analysis of this last period is a major contribution.

34. Ruth Miller, ed., *Blackamerican Literature* (Beverly Hills, Calif.: Glencoe Press, 1971), 9, 10. Wheatley's poetry was published in England in 1773. See in particular her poem on the death of Whitefield (1770), 532-534. See also Saunders Redding, "Phillis Wheatley" in Edward T. James, ed., *Notable American Women,* IV (Cambridge, Mass.: Belknap Press, 1971), 573-574.

35. Jupiter Hammon, "A Dialogue Entitled the Kind Master and the Dutiful Servant," (1777?), in Miller, *Blackamerican Literature,* 7-9, and "Penetential Cries," (1760), in Porter, *Early Negro Writing,* 313. When blacks prayed "I'm going to pray for you," it might mean "that they were going to ask God to exact retribution." Earle Thorpe, *The Mind of the Negro* (Baton Rouge, La.: Ortlieb Press, 1961), 81. Sojourner Truth in Titus, *Sojourner Truth,* and Bernard, *Journey Toward Freedom,* 99; see Redding, "Sojourner Truth," in James, *Notable American Women,* IV, 479-481.

36. On Lemuel Haynes, see Sidney Kaplan, *The Black Presence in the Era of the American Revolution, 1770-1800* (Greenwich, Conn.: New York Graphic Society, 1973), 102-108.

Richard Allen (1760-1831), the father of the African Methodist Episcopal Church, has been widely written about. See in particular: Charles H. Wesley, *Richard Allen, Apostle of Freedom* (Washington, D.C.: Associated Publishers, 1935), Carol V. R. George, *Segregated Sabbaths; Richard Allen and the Emergence of Independent Black Churches 1760-1840* (New York: Oxford University Press, 1974), and Milton C. Sernett, *Black Religion and American Evangelicalism* (Metuchen, N.J.: The Scarecrow Press, 1975).

Samuel Ringold Ward (1817-1866?), born a slave, became a preacher to whites at Congregational churches at South Butler and Cortland, New York. Ward was an active abolitionist. See his *Autobiography of a Fugitive Negro* (London: John Snow, 1855). Henry Highland Garnet (1815-1882) was also born a slave and, like Ward, was later educated at the Oneida Institute. He became a Presbyterian minister and served in Troy, New York. He served blacks as a missionary in Jamaica, returned to a Washington, D.C., pulpit, and was appointed U.S. ambassador to Liberia in 1881. See William Brewer, "Henry Highland Garnet," *JNH* 13 (1928): 36-52.

37. Daniel Boyd, "Free Born Negro: The Life of John Chavis," B.A. Thesis, Princeton University, January 1947; M. B. DesChamps, "John Chavis as a Preacher to Whites, *North Carolina Historical Review* 32 (1955): 165-172; W. S. Savage, "The Influence of John Chavis and Lunsford Lane," *JNH,* 25 (1940): 14-24; Benjamin Brawley, *Negro Builders and Heroes* (Chapel Hill: University of North Carolina Press, 1937), 49; August Meir and Elliott M. Rudwick, *From Plantation to Ghetto* (New York: Hill & Wang, 1966), 75; Woodson, *Negro Church, 67-69;*

DuBois, *Negro Church*, 35.

38. Leonard L. Haynes, *The Negro Community in American Protestantism 1619-1844* (Boston: Christopher Publishing House, 1953), 58; Harrison, *The Gospel*, 138; DuBois, *Negro Church*, 36.

New Hope Baptist Church, Gates County, North Carolina (constituted in 1856) and Pleasant Plains Church, Hertford County, North Carolina (constituted circa 1850) were both for free blacks *only*, and New Hope would not admit former slaves after the war. Elam Church in Charles City, Virginia, which broke away from Gillfield African in 1810, was for free blacks only. (Cf. Appendix I.)

39. These individuals, and other black Baptists working with whites, are discussed in Chapter 7.

40. This is the view of Reverend Charles O. Walker, pastor, First Baptist Church of Jasper, Georgia, as given in an interview, Nashville, Tennessee, in May 1974.

Chapter 6

1. When taught in a Baptist Sunday School, blacks were instructed by means of a simple catechism similar to that used for children, with emphasis on duties and obedience, but with a full range of Baptist beliefs included. See the catechism by a white Baptist preacher to the blacks, Robert Ryland, *A Scripture Catechism for the Instruction of Children and Servants* (Richmond, Va.: Harrold & Murray, 1848), and that of a Presbyterian, Charles C. Jones, *A Catechism for Colored Persons* (Charleston, S.C.: Observer Office Press, 1834).

Whites also had a mystical association with living water. See G. Van der Leeuw, *Religion in Essence and Manifestation* (New York: Harper & Row, 1963), 344.

2. Atlantic Records, No. 1346, "Southern Heritage Series," Side 1, Band 2.

3. Sheila S. Walker, *Ceremonial Spirit Possession in Africa and Afro-America* (Leiden: E. J. Brill, 1972), 53; Erika Bourguigon, "Ritual Dissociation and Possession Belief in Caribbean Negro Religion," in Norman E. Whitten, Jr., and John F. Szwed, eds., *Afro-American Anthropology: Contemporary Perspectives* (New York: Free Press, 1970), 94; John Horton, "Types of Spirit Possession in Kalabari Religion," M. J. Field, "Spirit Possession in Ghana," and Pierre Verger, "Trance and Convention in Nago-Yoruba Spirit Mediumship," all in John Beatie and John Middleton, eds., *Spirit Mediumship and Society in Africa* (London: Routledge & Kegan Paul, 1969), 8, 17, 50.

4. *Boston Evening Post*, July 5, 1742, cited by Edwin Gaustad, *The Great Awakening in New England* (Chicago: Quadrangle Books, 1957), 39. Singing was early used to restore order as well as to work up excitement. Devereaux Jarratt, an Anglican who led an ecstatic revival in Virginia, was upset by the confused exhortation and babel of religious excitement at a chapel in Dinwiddie County, in May 1776. "I went into the pulpit and began to sing, adding short exhortations and prayers. The confusion ceased: several spirits were revived and some mourners comforted." Letter from Jarratt, May 7, 1776, in H. Shelton Smith, Robert T. Handy, and Lefferts A. Loetscher, eds., *American Christianity: An Historical Interpretation with Representative Documents* (New York: Charles Scribner's Sons, 1960), 2 vols., I, 365.

5. Bernard Weisberger, *They Gathered at the River* (Boston: Little, Brown & Co., 1958), 24, 35, citing McGready. See the seminal discussion of black influences on white revival activity in Melville Herskovits, *The Myth of the Negro Past* (New York: Harper & Row, 1941), 229-230.

Marcel Griaule, *Conversations with Ogotemmêli* (Oxford: Oxford University Press, 1965), 50, 64; Walker, *Spirit Possession*, 15, 27; Newbell Niles Puckett, *Folk Beliefs of the Southern Negro* (New York: Negro Universities Press, [1926] 1968), 60; Thomas Wentworth Higginson, *Army Life in a Black Regiment* (New York: Collier Books, 1962), 41; William F. Allen, *Slave Songs of the U.S.* (New York: A. Simpson & Co., 1867), XIII-XIV. Allan Lomax, *The Folk Songs of North America* (Garden City, N.Y.: Doubleday & Co., 1960), 463; Margaret D. Cate,

Early Days of Coastal Georgia (New York: Golley Press, 1955), 145; W.E.B. DuBois, *Souls of Black Folk* (1903), reprinted in H. M. Nelson, R. Yokley, and A. K. Nelson, eds., *The Black Church in America* (New York: Basic Books, 1971), 29.

6. W.E.B. DuBois, *The Negro Church* (Atlanta, Ga.: Atlanta University Press, 1903), 93; Robert Ryland, "Reminiscences of the First African Church, Richmond, Virginia, by the Pastor," *American Baptist Memorial* 14 (1855): 289, 290; John F. Watson, "Methodist Error . . . ." (Trenton, N.J.: 1819), reprinted in Eileen Southern, *Readings in Black American Music* (New York: W. W. Norton, 1971), 63.; Daniel A. Payne, *Recollections of 70 Years* (New York: Arno Press, [1888] 1969), 250, 253–254.

In the correspondence of the First African Presbyterian Church, Philadelphia, a letter of April 16, 1839, signed by five members (both male and female) and sent to the session of the First Presbyterian Church, related that the new singing school was being harshly criticized and belittled by some *older* members. The writers asked for aid and "protection from those whose age is an invulnerable shield behind which they place themselves with the most perfect security and heap upon us scumillity, abuse and insult with the utmost impunity." Manuscript, Presbyterian Historical Society, Philadelphia.

7. John Work, *American Negro Songs and Spirituals* (New York: Bonanza Books, 1940), 145; Philip Foner, ed., *The Life and Writings of Frederick Douglass* (New York: International Publishers, 1950), 4 vols., I, 14. David Benedict, *A General History of the Baptist Denomination in America and Other Parts of the World* (New York: Lewis Colby & Co., 1848), 730n.2; Annie McLean, "A Town in Florida," in DuBois, *Negro Church,* 67.

8. A. P. Watson and C. Johnson, eds., *God Struck Me Dead: Religious Conversion Experiences and Autobiographies of Negro Ex-Slaves* (Philadelphia: Pilgrim Press, 1969), 16–145; Frederika Bremer, *Homes of the New World* (New York: 1854), II, 144, 156–160, reprinted in Southern, *Black American Music,* 106. Work, *American Negro Songs.* 61–66.

9. Lomax, *Folk Songs,* 462–463; no date, place, or time given.

10. Zora Hurston, *Mules and Men* (Philadelphia: J. B. Lippincott, 1935), 305, describes experience meetings and the very similar Methodist "love feasts." Puckett, *Folk Beliefs,* 574–575, citing A. E. Gonzales, "With Aesop along the Black Border." Lorenzo Dow Turner, *Africanisms in the Gullah Dialect* (New York: Arno Press, [1949] 1969); Charlotte Forten, *The Journal of Charlotte Forten: A Free Negro in the Slave Era* (New York: Collier, 1953); Guion G. Johnson, *A Social History of the Sea Islands* (Chapel Hill: University of North Carolina Press, 1930); Guion G. Johnson, *Ante-Bellum North Carolina: A Social History* (Chapel Hill: University of North Carolina Press, 1934); William R. Riddell, "The Baptism of Slaves on Prince Edward Island," *JNH* 6 (1921): 307–309; Samuel Miller Lawton, "The Religious Life of South Carolina Coastal and Sea Island Negroes," Ph.D. dissertation, George Peabody College for Teachers, Nashville, Tennessee, 1939; Cate, *Early Days of Coastal Georgia;* Mason Crum, *Gullah: Negro Life in the Carolina Sea Islands* (Durham, N.C.: Duke University Press, 1940). Harriet Ware's description cited in Willie Lee Rose, *Rehearsal for Reconstruction* (New York: Vintage Books, 1967), 91. (I have relied heavily on Willie Lee Rose and Guion Johnson for the background to the Civil War period on the Islands.) Frederick Douglass, as cited by Charles H. Nichols, *Many Thousands Gone: The Ex-Slaves' Accounts of Their Bondage and Freedom* (Leiden: E. J. brill, 1963), 94.

Cousin, brother, and sister were often shortened into Cus; Bro', Si', or T' for Titty. Allen, *Slave Songs,* XXIX. See Herbert Gutman, *The Black Family in Slavery and Freedom, 1750–1925* (New York: Pantheon Books, 1976), 216, 220, for a discussion of "fictive kin."

Puckett, *Folk Beliefs,* 110–111, 167, 333, 524. On white Georgians' superstitions, see Johnson, *Ante-bellum North Carolina,* 48–51.

11. "Not Weary Yet," collected on Port Royal Island in Allen, *Slave Songs,* 12.

12. The *Alabama Baptist Advocate* of February 13, 1850, pleased at the efforts to convert blacks, noted: "We rejoice at the efforts now making [sic] to Christianize the sable sons of Africa and turn them away from their dance around the Devil Bush." Cited by James B. Sellers, *Slavery*

in Alabama (University, Ala.: University of Alabama Press, 1950), 316.

Comment of white Joseph Cook of Euhaw on his black contemporary, Andrew Marshall, in John Rippon, *The Baptist Annual Register* (London: Dilly, Button & Thomas) I, (1790-1793): 540-541.

13. "You no holy" is found in Marriet Martineau, *Views of Slavery and Emancipation* (New York: Piercy & Reed, 1837), 37. Dillard's comments are in *Black English: Its History and Usage in the United States* (New York: Random House, 1972), 104. See Sir Charles Lyell, *A Second Visit to the United States of North America*, II, 15-16, cited by Puckett, *Folk Beliefs*, 21.

14. J. B. Danquah, *The Akan Doctrine of God* (London: Frank Cass & Co., 1968), 195; Lomax, *Folk Songs*, 474-475.

15. This covenant was apparently sent to the *London Baptist Repository* by Liele's church which had moved to Jamaica. It was published in London in 1805 and brought to light by G. W. Rusling in "A Note on Early Negro Baptist History," in *Foundations*, 2 (1968): 362-368. (Liele's account was originally published by Adam Taylor, ed., in *Supplement to the General Baptist Repository* 1 (1805): 289-300, mislabeled 229-240.) As the covenant was often read aloud, there is a strong likelihood that it was essentially unchanged from its earliest redaction.

16. "Living Water" song, as sung on Ethnic Folkways Record FP655, "Music of the South," Vol. 6, Side 10. See also Harold Courlander, in introductory notes to Ethnic Folkways Record *Negro Folk Music of Alabama*, FE4417 and 4418 (1956, 1960); The "moan" quoted is on Vol. 4, Side 1, Band 1.

17. Frederick P. Jackson, reprinted in Southern, *Black American Music*, 28, 110. W. P. Whalum, "Black Hymnody," in *Review and Expositor* 70, no. 3 (1973): 347-348, comments: "They [black Baptists] virtually threw out the meter signature and rhythm . . . .The melody sung in parallel intervals, fourths and fifths, sometimes thirds and sixths at cadence points, took a rather crudely shaped line which floated melismatically along, being held together primarily by the deacon who raised and lined it." John F. Szwed, "Afro-American Musical Adaptation," in Whitten and Szwed, eds., *Afro-American Anthropology*, 222; Allen, *Slave Songs*, Introduction.

18. Harold Courlander, *Negro Folk Music, USA* (New York: Columbia University Press, 1963), 27. See dialogue sermons in Langston Hughes and Arna Bontemps, eds., *The Book of Negro Folklore* (New York: Dodd Mead & Co., 1958), 243-245, 248-249; sermon on "Sampson" in Lomax, *Folk Songs*, 465, citing John Henry Faulk, "Negro Folk Sermons," Ph.D. dissertation, University of Texas; William H. Pipes, *Say Amen, Brother! Old-time Negro Preaching: A Study in American Frustration* (New York: William Frederick Press, 1951); Frederick Law Olmsted, *The Cotton Kingdom* (New York: Alfred A. Knopf, 1966), 240-247; sermons by Israel Campbell, *An Autobiography: Bond and Free* (Philadelphia: I. Campbell, 1861); "Folk Sermons," in Ruth Miller, ed., *Blackamerican Literature* (Beverly Hills, Calif.: Glencoe Press, 1971), 115-135; Henry Mitchell, "Black Preaching," *Review and Expositor* 70, no. 3 (1973): 331-340; Henry Mitchell, *Black Preaching* (Philadelphia: J. B. Lippincott, 1970). Sermons of Uncle Jack in Williams White, *The African Preacher* (Philadelphia: Presbyterian Board of Publications, 1849); of Jacob Knapp, who stormed the Northeast and Midwest in the 1830s and 1840s, in *The Autobiography of Elder Jacob Knapp* (New York: J. Knapp, 1868), 272, 274. John Jasper in William E. Hatcher, *John Jasper: the Unmatched Negro Philosopher and Preacher* (New York: Fleming H. Revell Co., 1908), and reprinted in Willie Lee Rose, *A Documentary History of Slavery in North America* (New York: Oxford University Press, 1976), 471.

19. On "pie in the sky," see Gold Refined Wilson, "The Religion of the American Negro Slave: His Attitude Toward Life and Death," *JNH* 8 (1923): 71. On Christianity asserting black manhood, see William H. Becker, "The Black Church: Manhood and Mission," *Journal of the American Academy of Religion* 40 (1972): 317.

20. Anthony Burns wrote to the Baptists in Virginia, who had expelled him when he ran away: "God made me a man—not a slave, and gave the same right to myself that he gave the man who stole me to himself," cited in Charles E. Stevens, *Anthony Burns, A History* (Boston:

J. P. Jewett & Co., 1856). Eugene Genovese, *Roll, Jordan, Roll: The World the Slaves Made* (New York: Pantheon Books, 1974), 163, discusses Christianity as a form of control. William W. Sweet, *Revivalism in America* (Gloucester, Mass.: P. Smith, [1944] 1965), 154; T. W. Yonker, "The Negro Church in North Carolina, 1700-1900," Ph.D. dissertation, Duke University, 1955, 8, 11. Freeborn Garrettson (who manumitted his own slaves in 1775) openly acknowledged that in 1777 he spoke of physical freedom to slaves in *The Experience and Travels of Mr. Freeborn Garrettson, Minister of the Methodist-Episcopal Church in North-America* (Philadelphia: Joseph Crukshank, 1791). Cf. David Reimers, *White Protestantism and the Negro* (London: Oxford University Press, 1965). For a brief bibliography of Protestant abolitionist activity, see Chapter 4, note 15.

21. Gayraud Wilmore, *Black Religion and Black Radicalism* (New York: Anchor Press, 1973), 5-10; Henry Bibb, *Narrative of the Life and Adventures of Henry Bibb, An American Slave* (New York: H. Bibb, 1849), 102. Advertisements for several runaway preachers are in "Eighteenth Century Slaves as Advertised by Their Masters," *JNH* 1 (1916): 202-205. Slave J. Hammon implied that there would be black superiority in Heaven. See "A Dialouge . . .," in Miller, *Blackamerican Literature*, 7. See also May in Watson and Johnson, *God Struck Me Dead*, 161: "In them days it [slavery] was hell without fires.This is one reason why I believe in a hell. I don't believe a just God is going to take no such man as that [master] into his kingdom."

22. David was sent to preach by the Countess of Huntingdon, who owned slaves in Georgia. Evidence from "Letters of James Habersham" (1775), cited by Winthrop D. Jordan, *White Over Black: American Attitudes Toward the Negro* (Chapel Hill: University of North Carolina Press, 1968), 209. Walter B. Posey, *The Baptist Church in the Lower Mississippi Valley, 1776-1845* (Lexington: University of Kentucky Press, 1957), 91.

23. Herbert Aptheker, *A Documentary History of the Negro People in the United States* (New York: Citadel Press, 1951), I, 9, 11; Wilmore, *Black Religion and Black Radicalism*, 108; William H. Hester, *Twelfth Baptist Church: One Hundred and Five Years of Faith* (Boston: n.p., 1946), 18, which also discusses Leonard Grimes. *Minutes*, Hudson River Association of New York (1834), 19. Blockley African Church, Philadelphia, "Deplores Slavery," in *Minutes*, Philadelphia Association, Pennsylvania (1854), 32. On Reverend Duke William Anderson, see George W. Williams, *A History of the Negro Race in America* (New York: Bergman Publishers, [1882] 1968), II, 476-503. On Israel Campbell, see *Autobiography* . . ., 288-289; Nathaniel Paul, "An Address on the Abolition of Slavery in New York, delivered in Albany, New York," (July 5, 1827), 17—see Aptheker, *Documentary History*, I, 87, 147; Benjamin Quarles, *Black Abolitionists* (London: Oxford University Press, 1969), Ch. 4.

24. "Song of Martyrs," Campbell, *Autobiography*, 288. "David Walker's Appeal in Four Articles," Boston (1829 edition), in Miller, *Blackamerican Literature*, 78; see also, for the last paragraph cited (altered by Walker in the 1830 or third edition), John B. Duff and Peter M. Mitchel, eds., *The Nat Turner Rebellion: The Historical and the Modern Controversy* (New York: Harper & Row, 1971).

25. W.E.B. DuBois, "Negro Owners of Slaves," *JNH* 29 (1944): 109-125. Reverends Andrew Marshall and Joseph Willis were black Baptists who owned slaves. Cf. Winfred E. Garrison and Alfred T. DeGroot, *The Disciples of Christ* (St. Louis, Mo.: Christian Board of Publication, 1958), 473-474; Glen Greene, *House Upon a Rock: About Southern Baptists in Louisiana* (Alexandria, La.: Executive Board of the Louisiana Baptist Convention, 1973), 531.

26. John T. Christian, *A History of the Baptists of Louisiana* (Shreveport: Executive Board of Louisiana Baptist Convention, 1923), 139. On Jack, see DuBois, *Negro Church*, 36-37. Reverend Dr. William Bright is quoted in William J. Simons, *Men of Mark* (New York: Arno Press, [1887] 1968), 323. Ferrill is cited for his dedicated work with whites during the cholera epidemic of 1833, during which his wife died. James M. Simms, *First Colored Baptist Church in North America, Constituted Savannah, Georgia, January 20, 1788* (Philadelphia: J. B. Lippincott, 1888), 69. Genovese, *Roll, Jordan, Roll*, infra.

27. Joseph Ernest, *The Religious Development of the Negro in Virginia* (Charlottesville, Va.: Michie Co., 1914), 58–59; Gerald W. Mullin, *Flight and Rebellion: Slave Resistance in Eighteenth Century Virginia* (New York: Oxford University Press, 1972), 159–160. Benjamin Mays, *The Negro's God as Reflected in His Literature* (Boston: Chapman & Grimes, 1938), Chs. 2–3; Gold Refined Wilson, "The Religion of the American Negro Slave," *JNH* 8 (1923), 41–71. On the general question of the role of religion in revolts, see John Lovell, "The Social Implications of the Negro Spiritual," *Journal of Negro Education* 8 (1939): 634–643; Vincent Harding, "Religion and Resistance Among Antebellum Negroes 1880–1860," in A. Meir and E. Rudwick, eds., *The Making of Black America* (New York: Atheneum Press, 1969), I, 179–197; Wilmore, *Black Radicalism*, 43–45.

28. Jack, Monday, Ned, and Peter were all church members; the last two were class leaders. (Each Methodist church was divided into small classes, led by one responsible member. These classes generally met weekly to discuss the members' moral development.) Cf. John Killens, ed., *The Trial Record of Denmark Vesey* (Boston: Beacon Press, 1970), infra; see especially the testimony of Benjamin Ford, a white, aged fifteen or sixteen, and the confession of Rolla, an associate (64; 45, 136).

29. Herbert Aptheker, *Nat Turner's Slave Rebellion* (New York: Humanities Press, 1966); Duff and Mitchell, *Nat Turner . . .;* Henry Irving Tragle, *The Southhampton Slave Revolt of 1831: A Compilation of Source Materials* (Amherst: University of Massachusetts Press, 1971); Stephen B. Oates, *The Fires of Jubilee: Nat Turner's Fierce Rebellion* (New York: Harper & Row, 1975).

30. Zora Hurston, *Mules and Men* (Philadelphia: J. B. Lippincott, 1935), 38. Many folktales are about false calls to preach like that of hearing a mule and mistaking it for God; or asking for a negative sign such as: "If you don't roll me over this log, God, I'll know I'm called."

31. The terminology on the license was usual for both whites and blacks; Dover Association of Virginia, *Summary of Church Discipline,* 1824, which summarizes licensing, ordination, and constitution procedures. (Available at HCSBC.) David Benedict, *Fifty Years Among the Baptists* (New York: Sheldon & Co., 1860), 96. Many church minutes confirm that it was common practice to license blacks. See manuscript minutes of the following churches for examples: First Baptist Church, Minden, Louisiana (November 1849, March 1850); First Baptist Church, Charleston, South Carolina (September 8, 1851, August 14, 1854, September 11, 1854); First Baptist Church, Nashville, Tennessee (June 6, 1849, March 9, 1853); First Baptist Church, Washington, D.C. (August 8, 1828). (Microfilm copies of minutes available at HCSBC.)

Preacher Harry Cowan (born 1810), slave of Thomas L. Cowan in North Carolina, was given "privilege papers" legally drawn up by his owner in 1828 which read: "This is to certify that whosoever is interested about my man Harry he has the privilege to preach and marry also; to baptize anyone who makes a profession of faith." J. A. Whitted, *A History of the Negro Baptists of North Carolina* (Raleigh, N.C.: Edwards and Broughton, 1908), 11.

Cf. B. F. Riley, *A History of the Baptists in the Southern States East of the Mississippi* (Philadelphia: American Baptist Publication Society, 1898), 319.

32. For records of black ordinations, see ordination of Nelson Merry, manuscript minutes, First Baptist Church, Nashville, Tennessee, November 29, 1833, on microfilm at HCSBC; ordination of Andrew Bryan by A. Marshall on January 19, 1788, in letter of Marshall in *JNH* 1 (1916): 78; ordination of Gardiner and Farrell by John Michaels, 1774, in L. A. Black, *Sketch of the Centennial Anniversary of the First Baptist Church, Petersburg, Virginia* (Petersburg, Va.: Index-Appeal Publishing House, 1879), 6–11; ordination of Harley Housten, 1864, *Minutes, Sunbury Baptist Association, Georgia* (1866), 8. Re Loudin Ferrill, *Minutes,* Elkhorn Association, Kentucky (1821) 7, (1822) 4; Simons, *Men of Mark,* 322; J. Lansing Burrows, ed., *American Baptist Register for 1852* (Philadelphia: American Baptist Publication Society, 1853), 116.

33. Miles Mark Fisher wrote of his grandfather in *His Master's Slave, John Fisher* (Philadelphia: Hudson Press, 1922), 9. On exhortation, see Jerry L. Tarver, "Exhortation Among

Early Virginia Baptists," *Virginia Baptist Register* 5 (1966): 228–236. Unlicensed exhorting was common among whites in Virginia where exhorters "engaged in a widespread and uniform type of pulpit address." However, exhorters were sometimes licensed for this role. Tarver cites such cases (1772–1812) as well as situations in which individuals were criticized for overstepping the bounds of exhortation and actually preaching.

Arrie Binns (born on a plantation in Lincoln County, Georgia, aged fifteen or sixteen in 1865), "Slave Narratives," Georgia, IV, 77; James Bolton, 92.

34. Thomas R. Gray, ed., *The Confessions of Nat Turner, the leader of the late insurection in Southhampton, Va. . . .* was originally published by Gray (Baltimore: Lucas & Deaver, 1831). It has been widely reprinted: see Aptheker, *Nat Turner,* 132; Tragle, *Southhampton Slave Revolt,* 300–320; Duff and Mitchell, eds., *Nat Turner,* 21–30. The citations in this book come from the Duff & Mitchell edition.

Six "members of the court," justices of the peace, including Justice James Parker who had interrogated Turner, signed a statement that Turner had heard and acknowledged this confession. The court heard only a report on Turner's interrogation as summarized by Justice Samuel Trezevant. See Tragle's excellent compilation (244). Oates, *Fires of Jubilee,* 123, also accepts the likelihood that the confession was substantially Turner's. (Jerusalem, Virginia, is now called Courtland.)

35. Tragle, *Southhampton Slave Revolt,* 221–224; "Confessions . . .," in Duff and Mitchell, *Nat Turner,* 15–16; Oates, *Fires of Jubilee,* 11.

36. See *Constitutional Whig,* Richmond, August 29, 1831, reprinted in Tragle, *Southhampton Slave Revolt,* 51–52. "Confessions," in Duff and Mitchell, *Nat Turner,* 17, 18 (emphasis in both selections added). As suggested above, I rely on Gray's recounting of Turner's words, but Turner apparently did acknowledge them and they do fit in with the folklore of Turner's life as afterwards talked of in the neighborhood.

37. Anonymous letter dated Jerusalem, Virginia, September 17, 1831, published in the *Constitutional Whig,* Richmond, September 26, 1831. Perhaps the source was Thomas Trezevant, postmaster at Jerusalem, the county seat of Southhampton, who promised to keep the editor of the *Constitutional Whig* informed and who had several signed letters published. Tragle, however, suggests that the writer may have been Thomas Gray, while Oates suggests it was Attorney William C. Parker of Jerusalem. Tragle, *Southhampton Slave Revolt,* 92, 400, 408; Oates, *Fires of Jubilee,* 155.

38. "Confessions," in Duff and Mitchell, *Nat Turner,* 18, 19. Blacks took care of black membership in many mixed churches. See manuscript minutes, First Baptist Church, Nashville, Tennessee; First Baptist Church, Washington, D.C. (Available on microfilm at HCSBC.)

Citation from a letter published after the revolt while Nat Turner was in hiding. Letter unsigned, dated Jerusalem, September 21, 1831, published in the *Richmond Enquirer,* September 27, 1831; anonymous letter of September 17, 1831; anonymous letter from a man who claimed to have watched and heard Nat Turner as he was examined by the magistrates after his arrest, dated Southhampton, November 1, 1831, and published in the *Richmond Enquirer,* November 8, 1831—all reprinted in Tragle, *Southhampton Slave Revolt,* 92, 99, 136.

39. Trial Record, Southhampton, November 5, 1831, reprinted in Tragle, *Southhampton Slave Revolt,* 221-222, 233. Also the anonymous letter of September 17, 1831, op. cit., 93.

40. Ulrich B. Phillips, *American Negro Slavery* (Baton Rouge: Louisiana State University Press, [1918] 1966), 469.

41. Ben Woolfolk at the trial of G. Smith, in the Executive Papers, Virginia, September-December 1800 (Virginia State Library, Richmond), cited by Mullin, *Flight and Rebellion,* 159. See the summary published by authority of the City Council, in Killens, *The Trial Record of Denmark Vesey,* 15, 76–84 (emphasis added). The notation "born in Africa" runs throughout this document. Williams reports the Gullah Society met once a month; he is referring either to the Methodist class group or to Jack's band.

42. Puckett, *Folk Beliefs*, 63. Sometime after the Vesey plot in South Carolina, the president of the Baptist State Convention in South Carolina, Richard Furman, issued an "Exposition" for Governor Wilson in order to explain his stand on slavery. He affirmed that he believed in freedom for those who were prepared for it, but that "general emancipation to the Negroes in this country would not, in present circumstances, be for their own happiness, as a body; while it would be extremely injurious to the community at large in various ways." He could still maintain "that the interest and security of the State would be promoted by allowing under proper regulations, considerable religious privileges to such of this class, as known how to estimate them aright, and have given suitable evidence of their own good principles, uprightness, and fidelity." Richard Furman, *Exposition of the Views of the Baptists* (Charleston: A. E. Mille, 1833), 11, 15.

Minutes, Portsmouth Baptist Association (1832), include a similar statement, which was also published in I. M. Allen, ed., *Baptist Register 1832* (Philadelphia: T. W. Ustick, 1833), 139.

43. Israel Campbell, writing in 1861 of whites putting down a supposed rebellion and "killing blacks," said that the blacks arrested were "steam doctors and colored preachers." "The party who were making arrests endeavored to get hold of every steam doctor and colored preacher they could; and once in their grasp, there was very little mercy shown them." I. Campbell, *Autobiography,* 73–74.

Constitutional Whig, Richmond, August 29, 1831, *Richmond Enquirer,* August 36, 1831; reprinted in Tragle, *Southhampton Slave Revolt,* 46–52.

On Virginia Governor John Floyd's attack on black preachers after the rebellion, see Oates, *The Fires of Jubilee,* 130–131.

44. Garnett Ryland, *The Baptists of Virginia 1699-1926* (Richmond: Virginia Baptist Board of Missions, 1955), 64, referring to James Ireland, itinerant Separatist Baptist. Wesley Gewehr, *The First Great Awakening in Virginia 1740-1790* (Durham, N.C.: Duke University Press, 1930), 118. Abrams, quoted in Robert Ryland, "Reminiscences," 354. On Sanders, see William Hicks, *History of Louisiana Baptists, 1804-1914* (Nashville, Tenn.: National Baptist Publication Board, n.d.), 26; Wilmore, *Black Radicalism,* 103ff.

Campbell, *Autobiography,* 87 (emphasis added). Sunday meetings were held with owner approval; late night weekday meetings, without. On persecution, see Nichols, *Many Thousands Gone,* 46; John R. Commons and Ulrich B. Phillips, eds., *Documentary History of American Industrial Society* (Cleveland, Ohio: American Bureau of Industrial Research, 1910-1911), II, 150. In Millegeville, Georgia, September 13, 1831, the marshall was to look for assemblies of Negroes and break them up.

Helen Catterall, ed., *Judicial Cases Concerning American Slavery and the Negro* (New York: Octagon Books, 1968), V, 243, reports a case where blacks were whipped on the way home from an orderly white-attended church service. It was maintained that the patrol went outside its proper area to whip the blacks. The court accepted the above as facts but did not punish the patrol (July 1854, Marion Township, Arkansas). "A negro preacher was allowed by his master to fill a distant appointment. Belated once, and returning home after the hour forbidden for slaves to be abroad, he was caught by the patrol and cruelly whipped. As the blows fell, his words were 'Jesus Christ suffered for righteousness sake; so kin I.' " J. Allen, cited by Ivane McDougle, *Slavery in Kentucky 1792-1865* (Lancaster, Pa.: New Era Printing Co., 1918), 83.

45. Patrick H. Thompson, *The History of Negro Baptists in Mississippi* (Jackson, Miss.: Baily Printing Co., 1898), 12, 32, 95; Peter Randolph, *From Slave Cabin to the Pulpit* (Boston: James H. Earle, 1893), 202–203; on the Ashbie Plantation, Virginia, see Norman Yetman, *Life Under the "Peculiar Institution": Selections from the Slave Narrative Collection* (New York: Holt, Rinehart & Winston, 1970), 177; Miles Mark Fisher, *Negro Slave Songs in the U.S.* (New York: Russell & Russell, [1953] 1968), 66–87.

46. Lyle Saxon, Edward Dreyer, and Robert Tallant, eds., *Gumbo Ya-Ya: A Collection of Louisiana Folk Tales* (Boston: Houghton Mifflin Co., 1945), 242. Clara Young (age ninety-five

when interviewed in Mississippi), Lucretia Alexander and Anthony Dawson, in Yetman, *Life Under the "Peculiar Institution,"* 12, 95, 355. Edgar Garfield Thomas, *The First African Baptist Church of North America* (Savannah, Ga.: E. G. Thomas, 1925), 78–79; Benedict, *General History* (1848), 730; C. C. Jones, *The Religious Instruction of the Negroes in the U.S.* (Savannah, Ga.: T. Purse, 1842); *Minutes,* Sunbury Association, Georgia, 1843–1846, especially 1843, 7, and 1846, 5. See also Appendix II, below, for details.

47. Patrick Thompson, *Negro Baptists in Mississippi,* 32. George P. Rawick, *From Sundown to Sunup: The Making of the Black Community* (Westport, Conn.: Greenwood Publishing Co., 1972), 39, 43, citing Sidney Mintz (who has a manuscript in preparation). Peter Randolph, *Slave Cabin,* 202–203. Randolph left the South after gaining his freedom. He was licensed by the black Joy Street Church, Boston, and traveled as a missionary, serving both races. In 1855, he accepted a call to the New Haven black Baptist Church; he was ordained at Williamsburgh, Brooklyn, in 1856. He served at Newburgh, New York, after 1858, and during the war he went South as a chaplain. See Louis Jordan, *Negro Baptist History USA 1750-1930* (Nashville, Tenn.: Sunday School Publishing Board, 1930), 78. *Minutes,* ABMC (1855), 17. L. A. Alexander, in Yetman, *Life Under the "Peculiar Institution,"* 13.

48. On Virginia, see Silas Jackson, black Baptist preacher in Yetman, *Life Under the "Peculiar Institution,"* 177; on Mississippi, see Thompson, *Negro in Mississippi,* 32, and Weisberger, *They Gathered at the River,* 147ff.; on white brush arbors, see Benedict, *General History* (1848), 778, and Benedict, *Fifty Years,* infra.

49. Herbert G. Gutman, *The Black Family in Slavery and Freedom 1750-1925* (New York: Pantheon Books, 1976), 51, 102, 116.

50. Testimony of Robert Smalls, cited by Gutman, *Black Family,* 70–71.

51. Guion G. Johnson, *Antebellum North Carolina: A Social History* (Chapel Hill: University of North Carolina Press, 1937), Ch. VII. Anne Firor Scott, *The Southern Lady: From Pedestal to Politics, 1830-1930* (Chicago: University of Chicago Press, 1970), 3–79. Genovese, *Roll, Jordan, Roll,* 458ff.

Marriages Registers, Archives of Virginia, State Library Clerk's Offices, cities and counties, contain marriage records of free blacks, as cited by Jackson, *JNH* 25 (1940): 29. For example, thirty-two such marriages took place in Petersburg in 1856. In contrast, the record books kept by Reverend Hassell in North Carolina (dating from February 1844) record numerous black baptisms but no marriages until November 15, 1866. Cushing Biggs Hassell (1809–1880), Primitive Baptist Preacher in Williamstown, North Carolina, in his "Diary" (1840–1880), "Letter Book," and "List" of those baptized and married, 1844–1880, in the Southern Historical Collection, Duke University, Durham, North Carolina. Vesey was reputed to have seven wives. Cf. Killens, *Trial Record.*

52. On the issues of marriage and adultery in Africa, see A. R. Radcliffe-Brown and Daryll Forde, eds., *African Systems of Kinship and Marriage* (London: Oxford University Press, 1950); P. H. Gulliver, "Jie Marriage," in Simon and Phoebe Ottenberg, eds., *Culture and Societies of Africa* (New York: Random House, 1960), 190–198 (The quotation in the text is from Ottenberg's Introduction, 58). E. E. Evans-Pritchard, *Kinship and Marriage Among the Nuer* (London: Oxford University Press, 1951); Laura Bohannan, "Dahomean Marriage: A Revaluation," *Africa* 19 (1949): 273–287; Jomo Kenyatta, "Marriage System," in Elliott P. Skinner, ed., *Peoples and Cultures of Africa* (Garden City, N.Y.: Doubleday/Natural History Press, 1973), 280–296.

The wide range of African marriage patterns is suggested in the following: M. G. Smith, "Secondary Marriage in Northern Nigeria," *Africa* 23 (1953): 198–323; Jean-Claude Muller, "Preferential Marriage Among the Rukuba of Benue-Plateau State, Nigeria," *American Anthropologist* (1969): 1057–1061; Walter H. Sangree, "Going Home to Mother: Traditional Marriage Among the Irigwe of Benue-Plateau State, Nigeria," *American Anthropologist* (1969): 1046–1057. E. E. Evans-Pritchard, *Man and Woman Among the Azande* (London: Faber &

Faber, 1974), 33, 194; Evans-Pritchard, *Kinship and Marriage,* 68, 70, 120.

A very interesting comparative analysis of marital relationships and their meaning in England (or the West) and Africa can be found in Evans-Pritchard, *The Position of Women in Primitive Societies and Other Essays* (New York: Free Press, 1965), 37–58.

The range of premarital sex mores in Africa is very wide. On acceptance of premarital promiscuity among the Fulani Bororo, see Marguerite Dupre, "Woman in a Pastoral Society," in Skinner, ed., *People and Cultures,* 297–303, especially 302–303. A young girl, "Having complete sexual freedom at this period of her life, under the one condition that certain partners must be avoided, . . . feels no shame in expressing her feelings and is full of [sexual] initiative and audacity." "These premarital relationships do not usually last very long, because the girl knows that she is destined to marry her fiance."

On the other hand, Kenyatta, "Marriage System," (287) in writing of Gikuyu sex mores, notes: "The guestion of physical virginity is very important and parents expect their daughters to go to their husbands as physical virgins. This must be reported to the parents of both sides." Among the Jie, "Adultery was traditionally reckoned as grave a crime as homicide, involving the death of the man concerned or a compensation payment equal to that for murder." Among the Nyakyusa, a husband was wont to use magic against an adulteress. See Godfrey Wilson, "An African Morality," in Ottenberg, eds., *Culture and Society,* 345–364.

Gutman makes a very important contribution in his identification and analysis of patterns of slave exogamy. See *Black Family,* 88–91.

On white interference and black marriages, see Chapter 8, note 10.

53. Watson, *Black Music,* 77; Tempie Herndon, in Yetman, *Life Under the "Peculiar Institution,"* 164. G. Johnson, *Antebellum North Carolina,* 191; Baker, "Slave Narratives," Georgia, IV, 38. (Baker was eighty-seven at the time of the interview.)

54. *Minutes,* Wood River Association (1858), 6.

A number of the individual clergy men who spoke at the meeting . . . reported the practice of their sessions *was to treat involuntary separation as equivalent to death,* and to allow remarriage. Several of them indicated that the same practice obtained in churches of other denominations in their neighborhood . . . . But the Committee that reported on this question "suggested" that this was a questionable practice and that influence should be used to stop owners from breaking up Christian marriages.

Haven P. Perkins, "Religion for Slaves: Difficulties and Methods," *Church History* 10 (1941): 238.

55. At Casey's Fork Church, 1822, "misconduct reported to this Church by Brother Thd. Alexander and Brother Mass about sister Patty A Woman of Coulour the property of Brother Thd. Alexander about her having Children, and no husband and likewise trateing the Church with contempt." On March 3, 1822, "the Church found her guilty and she was excommunicated." One of the investigators, Brother Mass, was also black. Casey's Fork Church Book, January 3 and March 3, 1822, 29–30. See manuscript minutes, First Baptist Church, Rome, Georgia, March 21, April, 10, 1852. (*HCSBC*)

Manuscript, "Church Record Book," Gillfield Church, Petersburg, Virginia, March 13, 1819, property of the church and available on microfilm at the Alderman Library, University of Virginia, Charlottesville, Virginia, and manuscript, "Church Record Book," First African Baptist Church, Petersburg, Virginia, February 13, 1848, property of the church. Simm, *First Colored Baptist Church,* 44. Loudin Ferrill supposedly included the words "united until death or distance do them part" in his slave marriage services. Simons, *Men of Mark,* 326.

56. I. Campbell, *Autobiography,* 290. Israel Campbell was born in about 1815 in Mississippi and was later taken to a plantation near Winchester, Tennessee. He was converted in 1837 and licensed in 1839. He was a trusted and capable slave, owning, according to his own account, a horse and cash property. Campbell ran away to Canada and became an active and popular abolitionist speaker. He preached at the Free Mission Baptist Convention in Lafayette, Ohio, in

1853 and in 1856, was moderator of the Ambersburg Baptist Association, Canada West. By 1856, he was pastor of the fledgling Sandusky City (Ohio) Baptist Church, and he also organized a church in Toledo, Ohio. See also A. W. Pegues, *Our Baptist Ministers and Schools* (New York: Johnson Reprint Co., [1892] 1970), 100.

57. For black concern with sex and marriage practices, see the following manuscript minutes: First Baptist Church, Nashville, Tennessee, August-September 1836; First Baptist Church, Charleston, South Carolina, October 1848, July 22, 1849; Welsh Neck, South Carolina, August 2, 1828, February 1829, First Baptist Church, Washington, D.C., February 7, 1807, May 11, 1813, October 11, 1816, March 7, 1817, September 9, 1831. (Available at HCSBC.)

Chapter 7

1. E. Franklin Frazier suggests that George I. Bragg, writing in 1922, was the first to use the phrase "the hidden institution." Since that time, most historians have accepted this view of the black church. Cf. Frazier, *The Negro Church in America* (New York: Schocken Books, 1964), 16; John Hope Franklin, *From Slavery to Freedom,* 3d ed. (New York: Alfred A. Knopf, 1967), 162, 227; Joseph R. Washington, *Black Religion* (Boston: Beacon Press, 1964), 34, 213, 296; Edward Wheeler, "Beyond One Man: A General Survey of Black Baptist History," in *Review and Expositor* 70 (1973): 313. Wheeler maintains that "in order to worship as they desired, blacks in the South were forced to meet in secret, continually aware that severe punishment or death could be the penalty if they were discovered."

The available records of over 200 black Baptist churches are tabulated in Appendix I, and the sources are listed in the notes to Appendix I.

2. In 1824, the Dover Association published a "summary of Church Discipline" which suggested this manner of church formation (8). (Available at HCSBC.) On early Baptist practice, and for practices outside the United States, see H. Wheeler Robinson, *The Life and Faith of the Baptists* (London: Methuen & Co., 1927), 103; Charles Williams, *The Principles and Practices of the Baptists* (London: Baptist Tract Society, 1879), 1, 92–93.

3. The church statistics as cited reflect some overlapping. In the South, sixty-six black churches were in mixed or "white" associations. Of these, two churches were also in a black association and five in the ABMC. In the North, fifteen churches were in mixed associations, but ten of these were also in the ABMC. Thirty-three other Northern black churches were only affiliated with black associations.

Very few cases of association rejection are on record. In 1855, the Union Association, Texas, rejected a black church in Anderson, Grimes County. J. M. Carroll, *A History of Texas Baptists* (Dallas, Tex.: Baptist Standard Publishing Co., 1923), 258.

On the role of deacons and the plantation churches, see James P. Wesberry, *Baptists in South Carolina Before the War Between the States* (Columbia, S.C.: R. L. Bryan Co., 1966), 69; H. A. Tupper, *Two Centuries of the Baptist Church of South Carolina* (Baltimore, Md.: R. H. Woodward & Co., 1889), 315; *Minutes,* Sunbury Association, Georgia (1850), 13, where in answer to a written query in relation to the duties of a deacon, St. Mary's African was informed that "While it is not the duty of a Deacon to assume the office of a Minister, and hold public meetings, we can see no impropriety in his holding private or social meetings, where and when the approbation of the owners can be obtained."

4. Cf. Hosea Holcombe, *A History of the Rise and Progress of the Baptists in Alabama* (Philadelphia: King & Beard, 1840), 300; David Benedict, *A General History of the Baptist Denomination in America and Other Parts of the World* (New York: Lewis Colby & Co., 1848), 124; Jesse L. Boyd, *A History of the Baptists in America Prior to 1845* (New York: American Press, 1957), 188. Boyd suggests that the black congregation in Mobile, Alabama, dates from 1806. Carter G. Woodson, *The History of the Negro Church,* 2d ed. (Washington, D.C.: Associated Publishers, 1921), 118. Woodson, without citing sources, is the only one to maintain that this was

a mixed congregation until 1839, "when blacks separated." What seems more likely, since blacks kept their own church building, is that the few whites, who until then may have attended the black-dominated mixed church, opted to start a white Baptist church. Woodson's excellent early survey is marred by its lack of documentation.

5. Reverend Thomas S. Malcom, quoted in Benedict, *General History* (1848), 817, 832; *Minutes,* Long Run Association, Kentucky (1842), 4 (1850–1861) infra, when the First Colored Church was represented by the Walnut Street Church.

6. Malcom in Benedict, *General History* (1848), 832; *Minutes,* Elkhorn Association, Kentucky (1855), 2, (1861), 2. *Minutes,* Long Run Association, Kentucky (1859). Shelbyville mixed church was listed as having 134 blacks in 1859, but no record of a black branch was officially submitted. *Minutes,* First Colored Baptist Association, Kentucky (1869).

On Simpsonville, Kentucky, see Elijah P. Marrs, *Life and History of Reverend Elijah P. Marrs* (Louisville, Ky.: Bradley & Gilbert Co., 1885), 14; Long Run Association, Kentucky, *Minutes* (1860), 8.

On Zion Church, Hampton, Virginia, see *Minutes,* Virginia State Convention Colored, First Annual Meeting (1868), n.p. This black church may have grown out of Hampton Church, Dover Association, Virginia. *Minutes,* Dover Association (1859), 15, lists 960 blacks and 214 whites as members. On W. B. Taylor, see ABMC *Minutes* (1849), 15.

On "private" churches, see, for example, the church of "Uncle" Perry Hinson in Maryland. Hinson, a free black, built and owned the church and generally preached there. There was no other black or white control, although whites occasionally checked on the services. See the reminiscences of a black Methodist bishop, L. J. Coppin, who attended Hinson's church services: L. J. Coppin, *Unwritten History* (Philadelphia: AME Book Concern, 1919), 44–46. The Third Colored Baptist Church in Washington, D.C., "belonged" to the pastor. Albert Bouldin, from its origin in September 1857 until he conveyed it to a board of trustees on April 4, 1864. Helen Catterall, ed., *Judicial Cases Concerning American Slavery and the Negro* (New York: Octagon Books, 1968), IV, 209.

The black missionary association, the American Baptist Missionary Convention (1840), is discussed in Appendix III.

7. Benjamin Quarles, "Ante-bellum relationships Between the First African Baptist Church of New Orleans and White Agencies," *Chronicle* 18 (1955): 26–36.

On the Virginia developments, see above. Ralph Ellison, *Invisible Man* (New York: Random House, 1947), 7, 9.

8. Luther P. Jackson suggested a somewhat different periodization: 1750 to 1790, 1790 to 1830, and 1830 to 1860. However, the outreach to the blacks at the time of the Second Great Awakening (circa 1800) was such that I feel it must be included in the first period; and I feel that the events cited demarcate the periods better than the decades used by Jackson. "Religious Development of the Negro in Virginia," *JNH* 16 (April 1931): 168–239.

For Baptist statistics and a discussion of the origin of the Southern Baptist Convention, see Robert Andrew Baker, *The Southern Baptist Convention and Its People* (Nashville, Tenn.: Broadman Press, 1974), 161; *Relations Between Northern and Southern Baptists* (Fort Worth, Tex.: Marvin D. Evans Printing Co., 1954); *A Baptist's Source Book, with Particular Reference to Southern Baptists* (Nashville, Tenn.: Broadman Press, 1966).

9. In this first period, one Southern black church was created out of a mixed congregation. In 1779, white Reverend Elhanan Winchester constituted an African church at Welsh Neck, South Carolina. In 1782, he was replaced by another white preacher, Edmund Botsford; who disbanded the black church and *partially* readmitted the black congregation to his mixed church. See Appendix I and the manuscript minutes of Welsh Neck Baptist Church, Welsh Neck, South Carolina, 1779–1782. (Microfilm copy available at HCSBC.) See Appendix IA for a list of the churches constituted prior to 1800.

10. David George left an excellent autobiographical account, reprinted in John Rippon,

The Baptist Annual Register (London: Dilly, Button & Thomas, 1790–1793), I, 473. See Walter H. Brooks, *The Silver Bluff Church* (Washington, D.C.: Press of R. L. Pendleton, 1910), infra. For George's work in Canada, see Pearleen Oliver, *A Brief History of the Colored Baptists of Nova Scotia 1782-1953* (n.l.: Pearleen Oliver, 1953), 20–24.

On Peter, see Benedict, *General History,* (1813), II, 193; Boyd, *History of the Baptists,* 145; letter of Jonathan Clarke, Savannah, Georgia, December 22, 1792, in Rippon, *Annual Register,* I, 541; Lewis G. Jordan, *Negro Baptist History, USA, 1750-1930* (Nashville, Sunday School Publication Board, 1930), 49; B. D. Ragsdale, *The Story of Georgia Baptists* (Atlanta: Executive Committee of the Georgia Baptist Convention, 1938), 3 vols., I, 65.

On the Savannah First Colored Church, see Rippon, *Annual Register,* I, 341, wherein Clark writes of Marshall's activity, documenting the church's constitution. Thomas Burton's role is also mentioned, but no date is given for his visit. It is possible that Burton officiated at the 1777 constitution, when Liele was made preacher. David George and many of the fifty or so slaves he brought to Savannah from Silver Bluff joined the Savannah church where George preached as well. Liele refers to members David George, Jessy Gaulsing (i.e., Peters), and Mrs. Liele. Brooks, in *Silver Bluff,* 372, argues that the Silver Bluff congregants were the great majority of the Savannah church, but they chose Liele as preacher rather than George because he was older and had good relations with the British. See Edward A. Holmes, "George Liele: Negro Slavery's Prophet of Deliverance," *Baptist Quarterly* (1964): 340–350; John W. Davis, "George Liele and Andrew Bryan, Pioneer Negro Baptist Preachers," *JNH* 3 (1918): 119–127; B. F. Riley, *A History of the Baptists in the Southern States East of the Mississippi* (Philadelphia: American Baptist Publication Society, 1898), 312; W. P. Harrison, *The Gospel Among the Slaves* (Nashville, Tenn.: Methodist Episcopal Church, South, 1893), 59.

There has been a lengthy and ascerbic debate on the origin of the church with both the Bryan church and the First African, Savannah, claiming the earliest date. See James M. Simms, *First Colored Baptist Church in North America, Constituted Savannah, Georgia, January 20, 1788* (Philadelphia: J. B. Lippincott, 1888); Edgar G. Thomas, *The First African Baptist Church of North America* (Savannah, Ga.: E. G. Thomas, 1925); G. W. Rusling, "A Note on Early Negro Baptist History," *Foundations* 2 (1968): 362–368. Liele's own account was originally published by Adam Taylor, ed., in *Supplement to the General Baptist Repository* 1 (1805): 289–300 (mislabeled 229–240).

Bryan's letter of December 23, 1800, is in Rippon, *Annual Register,* III (1798–1801), 367. Bryan is memorialized in the *Minutes,* Savannah River Association (1812). Bryan's extensive work is widely known. (This includes his conversion of white Thomas Polhill, son of an Episcopal minister; see the manuscript minutes of North Newington Church [1887] available at the Georgia Baptist Historical Society, Macon, Georgia.) Reports can be found in Boyd, *History of the Baptists,* 145; Davis, "George Liele and Andrew Bryan," 119–127; Riley, *Baptists in the Southern States,* 313; Jordan, *Negro Baptist History,* 46–48; DuBois, *The Negro Church,* 19.

11. The roles of black deacons are evidenced in the manuscript minutes of the mixed churches. See manuscript minutes, Welsh Neck, South Carolina (August 5, 1826, January 7 and 14, 1827, March 7 and 21, April 3, June 6, 1830, July 17, 1836); Dahlonega, Georgia (June 1, 1847); First Baptist Church, Washington, D.C. (December 12, 1817, December 18, 1819, August 9, 1820, July 8, 1825—all available on microfilm at HCSBC).

On black preachers around 1770, see T. W. Yonker, "The Negro Church in North Carolina, 1700–1900," Ph.D. dissertation, Duke University, 1955, 6.

12. The manuscript records of the Gillfield Baptist Church (1827–1939), 7 vols., are owned by the Petersburg, Virginia, church. They can be seen at the church library, or on microfilm at the manuscript department of the Alderman Library, University of Virginia, Charlottesville.

See Luther P. Jackson, *A Short History of the Gillfield Baptist Church of Petersburg, Virginia* (Petersburg, Va.: Virginia Print Co., 1937); William H. Johnson, comp., *A Short History of the Gilfield Baptist Church of Petersburg, Virginia . . .* (Petersburg, Va.: A. Owen, 1903).

Robert B. Semple, *A History of the Rise and Progress of the Baptists in Virginia* (Richmond, Va.: John Lynch, 1810), 361; Garnett Ryland, *The Baptists of Virginia, 1699–1926* (Richmond: Virginia Baptist Board of Missions and Education, 1955), 157; Reuben Jones, *A History of the Virginia Portsmouth Baptist Association* (Raleigh, N.C.: Broughton, 1881), 224; Benedict, *General History . . .* (1848), 664, n.5; *Minutes,* Portsmouth Association (1794, 1801, 1810, 1811 1813, 1817, 1840). Israel Decoudry was variously recorded as De Courdry, Decudra, or D. Coudre. Jackson states that he represented the church at the association in 1796 and 1798, while Daniel lists 1797, 1800, and 1801. The *Minutes* of the Portsmouth Association for the years 1796–1798 are not in the Virginia Baptist Archives, but in the available minutes of May 23, 1801, D. Cudre is listed as a messenger of the 165-member Davenport Church. See Jackson, *Gillfield Church,* 5; W. Harrison Daniel, "Virginia Baptists and the Negro in the Early Republic," *The Virginia Magazine of History* 80 (1972): 61.

13. See the Pleasant Plains Church, North Carolina, 1850, Appendix IB, no. 102. On social stratification in Northern churches, see W.E.B. DuBois, *The Philadelphia Negro* (New York: Schocken Books, [1899] 1967), 203–204.

14. Thomas Paul was the constituting preacher at Boston's Joy Church in 1805. He remained there at least through 1813. Benedict, *General History . . .* (1813), I, 412; N. H. Pius, *An Outline of Baptist History* (Nashville, Tenn.: National Baptist Publication Board, 1911), 59; Boyd, *History of the Baptists,* 188. On the history of the Abysinnian Church, see Appendix IB, no. 17.

15. Bishop may have been the "Jacob(N)" (for Negro) listed in Asplund's *Register* for Lower Northampton, 1791, and perhaps the same Jacob who came from the eastern shore of Virginia with M. Bacon in 1789 and preached in Richmond County. This Jacob was described by Dozier as "a most wonderful preacher." John Asplund, *The Annual Register of the Baptist Denomination in North America to the First of November 1790* (Southhampton County, Va.: n.p., 1791), 30; Richard Dozier, "Historical Notes Concerning the Planting of Baptist Principles in the Northern Neck of Virginia," Westmoreland County, Va., 1771, typescript available at the Virginia Baptist Historical Society, Richmond. See George J. Hobday, "Historical Sketch of the Court Street Baptist Church, Portsmouth, Virginia," in *The Centennial of Court Street Baptist Church, 1889* (Philadelphia: Jas. B. Rodgers, 1889), 30. The early minutes of the Court Street Church were not preserved. In 1848, Benedict (*General History,* 693) reported, "The Portsmouth Church was founded in 1798 with 68 members. Reverend Thomas Armistead was the first pastor; after him, . . . they had Josiah Bishop, a man of color." If the church was founded in 1798 (as Benedict reported) and Bishop was second pastor, his pastorate lasted less than four years. Woodson (*Black Church,* 54) states that Bishop arrived in Portsmouth in 1795 and that blacks later considered creating a separate church around Bishop, although they abandoned the idea. In the official history written by Zion Baptist Church, the black daughter church formed in 1865, Jacob Bishop's pastorate is recorded as from 1792 to 1802. See *Zion Baptist Church: An Authentic History* (Portsmouth, Va.: Zion Baptist Church, 1949), 7. Both Adamson and Hobday, official Court Street historians, later denied that Bishop served the full church; it was claimed that he served the blacks separately. N. E. Adamson, *History of the Court Street Baptist Church of Portsmouth Virginia* (Portsmouth, Va.: Print Craft Press, Inc., 1939), 8; and Hobday, *Court Street Church,* 30. Ryland, in support of his claim that Bishop was pastor, notes that Bishop was the church delegate to the Portsmouth Association in 1798. Records are not available. Ryland, *Baptists of Virginia,* 156.

16. Semple, *History of the Rise of Baptists in Virginia,* 170; Rappahannock Association, "Sketches of the History of the Baptist Churches Within the Limits of the Rappahannock Association in Virginia" (Richmond, Va.: Harold & Murray, 1850), 57. Lemon is noted as "Pastor of Pettsworth" from at least 1797, "maybe earlier," until 1801. *Minutes,* Dover Association, Virginia (1801), 4. Both Semple (*History of the Rise of Baptists in Virginia,* 170) and Ryland (*Baptists of Virginia,* 156) state that Lemon was a delegate to the Dover Association in 1797, 1798,

and 1801. (Minutes of earlier years not located.) The manuscript minutes of the First Baptist Church, Washington, D.C., June 5, 1803, confirm that Lemon had signed a letter of dismission as the "Pastor" of Pettsworth Church. (Microfilm at HCSBC.) For the history of the church, see Appendix IB, no. 78.

17. Glen Greene, *House Upon a Rock: About Southern Baptists in Louisiana* (Alexandria, La.: Executive Board of the Louisiana Baptist Convention, 1973), 53; Leah Townsend, *South Carolina Baptists 1670–1805* (Florence, S.C.: Florence Printing Co., 1935), 216. Bethel Association, *Minutes* (1791, 1799).

Willis's contemporaries definitely thought of him as part Negro. His descendants, however, among whom are many prominent white Baptists, have gone to great lengths to prove that Willis's father was "a prominent North Carolina English citizen" and his mother an Indian. Older sources maintain that she was a slave and that Willis was considered a mulatto. It is established that there was Indian blood in at least one of his four wives. See Appendix to Green, *House Upon a Rock*, 325–326, for both nineteenth- and twentieth-century comments on Willis's race. See C. Penrose St. Amant, *A Short History of Louisiana Baptists* (Nashville, Tenn.: Broadman Press, 1948), 17–18 for a twentieth-century denial of Willis's blackness. Baker, in his authoritative study of Southern Baptists, refers to Willis without comment on his race, which leaves the reader to infer that he was white, as in other cases color is noted (*Southern Baptist Convention*, 12). Woodson states that Willis was born in South Carolina in 1762, and he apparently incorrectly suggests that Willis organized a Mississippi church, Mound Bayou, in 1805 (*Negro Church*, 86). Leonard Haynes, *The Negro Community Within American Protestantism* (Boston: Christopher Publishing House, 1953), 64; Benedict, *General History* (1848), 376, 778, n.9; *Minutes*, Mississippi Baptist Association (1810–1817); *Minutes*, Louisiana Association (1818–1854); William Hicks, *History of Louisiana Negro Baptists, 1804–1914* (Nashville, Tenn.: National Baptist Publication Board, n.d.), 17–19, 31; *Negro Year Book* (1818–1819), 236.

18. "Uncle Jack," cited by William Spottswood White in *The African Preacher* (Philadelphia, Penn.: Presbyterian Board of Publication, 1849), 20, 33, 72. The dates of Jack's birth in Africa and arrival in America are uncertain. He died on April 6, 1843, at an advanced age. See also Woodson, *Negro Church*, 55–56; and DuBois, *Negro Church*, 36–37.

19. Charles Bowles (born in Boston, 1761) was a pastor of mixed churches in Vermont, Massachusetts, and Rhode Island, areas where Baptists were still quite unpopular; yet, he converted many whites between 1808 and 1817. See John Weld Lewis, *The Life, Labors and Travels of Elder Charles Bowles, of the Free Will Baptist Denomination* (Watertown, Mass.: Ingalls & Stowell's Steam Press, 1852). Bowles' mother may have been white; his father was a slave.

Slave Lewis [Brockenbrough] was a preacher to mixed congregations at the Carter Estates, Virginia, between 1782 and 1794. The (white) Carter overseer, Richard Dozier, praised him very highly, claiming "His gift exceeded many white preachers." Richard Dozier, "Historical Notes Concerning the Planting of Baptist Principles in the Northern Neck of Virginia, 1771," 12, 32; typescript available at the Virginia Baptist Historical Society, Richmond, which also has Dozier's "Textbook," May 1782–August 1786 and his "Journal."

Well-established ex-slave Thomas Blacknall was deacon at the First Baptist Church of Franklin, North Carolina, and "frequently led the congregation composed largely of white men and women in a prayer service." T. W. Yonker, "The Negro Church in North Carolina, 1700–1900," Ph.D. dissertation, Duke University, 1955, 18 n.54. John Hope Franklin, in *The Free Negro in Carolina 1790–1860* (New York: W. W. Norton, [1943] 1971, 176, says that Blacknall purchased his freedom prior to 1830 (no year is given) and apparently became a slaveowner himself. See Williams, *Baptists in North Carolina*, 162, where Blacknall is called Thomas Blackwell.

Thomas Lemley, an Arkansas black, preached at the mixed Point Remove Church sometime after 1853; and James Staryman, a slave, preached to the mixed congregation at the First Baptist Church, Pine Bluff, Arkansas (1854). Orville W. Taylor, *Negro Slavery in Arkansas* (Durham, N.C.: Duke University Press, 1958), 177.

Cyrus Chin preached to mixed congregations at Deacons Woods, Tennessee, around 1838, where the white people "thought a great deal of him." Israel Campbell, *An Autobiography: Bond and Free* (Philadelphia: The author, 1861), 89.

George Bently was paid a salary of $600 per year. He may have actually opted to remain a slave as he would have been unprotected as a free black and subject to exile from the state. T. O. Fuller, *History of the Negro Baptists of Tennessee* (Memphis, Tenn.: Haskins Print Co., 1936),

John Jones, a free black, was frequently called upon by whites to preach at Shreveport, Louisiana, First Baptist Church. He, as the others, was recognized as in possession of "wonderful gifts." John T. Christian, *A History of the Baptists of Louisiana* (Shreveport: Executive Board of the Louisiana Baptist Convention, 1923), 139.

Joe Strater worked with the Wyandotte between 1859 and 1864; he founded the Kansas City Baptist Church in 1864. Edward A. Freeman, *The Epoch of Negro Baptists and the Foreign Mission Board* (Kansas City, Kans.: Central Seminary Press, 1953), Appendix I, infra.

20. Henry Adams was ordained at the Mt. Lebanon Louisiana Church on July 8, 1837, installed by Reverends John Mill and Henry Adams, white. He remained in this pulpit until 1839 and moved to Kentucky around 1840. Christian, *Baptists of Louisiana,* 73; Benedict, *General History* (1848), 814; Burrows, *Baptist Register,* 120; *Minutes,* Kentucky Colored Baptist Association (1866, 1869), 2; Baker, *Southern Baptist Convention,* 142.

21. Deer Creek Church, Black Methodist Episcopal, 1815(?) to 1823. DuBois, *Negro Church,* 93. Walter H. Brooks, "The Evolution of the Negro Baptist Church," *JNH* 7 (1922): 21.

22. Medaris, quoted in Taylor, *Slavery in Arkansas,* 180. Clements was brought to Arkansas prior to 1850. He was a slave of the Clements family until he was emancipated by the Civil War, after which continued to work for them.

23. Records of whites preaching at black funerals can be found in the manuscript minutes of Welsh Neck, South Carolina, First Baptist Church (May 6, 1827); manuscript minutes of the First Baptist Church, Washington, D.C. (May 12, 1850). Whites preached at the funerals of Joseph Abrams in Richmond, Virginia, and Andrew Bryan in Savannah, Georgia. See the narrative of Robert Shepherd in Norman R. Yetman, ed., *Life Under the "Peculiar Institution": Selections from the Slave Narrative Collection* (New York: Holt, Rinehart & Winston, 1970), 266. George Pullen Jackson, *White and Negro Spirituals: Their Life Span and Kinship* (New York: J. J. Augustin, n.d.), 46, citing Baptist songbooks, *A New Collection of Hymns and Spiritual Songs* (1793), and Harvey, *Hymns and Spiritual Songs* (1806). James Bolton, in "Slave Narratives," Georgia, IV, 92. See Genovese, *Roll, Jordan, Roll,* 196–201, for an analysis of slave funerals.

24. Robert Shepherd, quoted in Yetman, *Life Under the "Peculiar Institution,"* 266; White, *First Baptist Church, Richmond,* 136–138; Lyle Saxon, Edward Dreyer, and Robert Tallant, eds., *Gumbo Ya-Ya: A Collection of Louisiana Folk Tales* (Boston: Houghton Mifflin Co., 1945), 244. Newbell Niles Puckett, *Folk Beliefs of the Southern Negro* (New York: Negro Universities Press [1926] 1968), 94, 104. The N'debele, an African people, bury bodies east to west, but the Dogon follow a north to south pattern. John S. Mbiti, *African Religions and Philosophy* (London: Heineman, 1969), 149–150; Marcel Griaule, *Conversations with Ogotemmêli: An Introduction to Dogon Religious Ideas* (Oxford: Oxford University Press, 1965), 49. For additional information on black funerals see Margaret D. Cate, *Early Days of Coastal Georgia* (New York: Galley Press, 1955), 207–213.

25. William E. Hatcher, *John Jasper; The Unmatched Negro Philosopher and Preacher* (New York: Fleming H. Revell Co., 1908), 38. Jasper was born in Richmond, Virginia, in 1812, the last child in a family of twenty-four. He had been a fieldhand but was working as a tobacco factory worker at the time he was suddenly converted. His most famous sermon, "De Sun Do Move," given in Hatcher, has been widely reprinted. Cf. Ruther Miller, ed., *Blackamerican Literature* (Beverly Hills, Calif.: Glencoe Press, 1971), 128–135. For other conversion experiences, see A. P. Watson and Clifton H. Johnson, eds., *God Struck Me Dead: Religious Conver-*

sion Experiences and Autobiographies of Negro Ex-Slaves (Philadelphia, Penn.: Pilgrim Press, 1969), 95–154.

26. Ernest Kirby, *UR Drama* (New York: New York University Press, 1975), Ch. 1. For a more limited view of the role of Shamans, see Mircea Eliade, *Shamanism* (Princeton, N.J.: Princeton University Press, 1972). Cf. I. M. Lewis, *Ecstatic Religion* (Harmondsworth, England: Penguin Books, 1971); Cate, *Early Georgia*, 215; White, *First Baptist Church, Richmond*, Appendix II, 131ff., "The Night Funeral of a Slave."

Boston Herald, May 7, 1887, reprinted in Puckett, *Folk Beliefs*, 102. Puckett suggests African funeral "games" may have survived on the Sea Islands. Occasionally, blacks remembered cooking food for the spirits of the dead or contacting them in physical ways, such as feeling a dead father's slap on the face.

As an example of an elaborate and expensive funeral, see the description of the 1849 funeral arranged by William Johnson, a free and rich black man in Natchez, for his mother. Edwin A. Davis and William R. Hogan, *The Barber of Natchez* (Baton Rouge: Louisiana State University Press, 1954).

Luther P. Jackson, "The Early Strivings of the Negro in Virginia," *JNH* 24 (1940):33.

27. John O. Killens, ed., *The Trial Record of Denmark Vesey* (Boston: Beacon Press, 1970), 15.

The whites who left the First Baptist Church, Norfolk, Virginia, in 1816 founded the Cumberland Street Baptist Church. White Reverend James Mitchell stayed on with the black congregation. *1800-1950, Sesquicentennial Jubilee Norfolk's First Baptist Church* (Norfolk, Va.: First Baptist Church, 1950).

Mitchell resigned in 1845. However, it was not until Mitchell's death in 1849 that the black congregants supposedly founded a new church, Bute Street. This "new" church was founded in Mitchell's old home. In 1862, it reverted to its old name, the First Baptist Church. A large number of blacks left the First Baptist Church of Norfolk when it came under attack. Membership fell from 400 in 1839 to 199 in 1840, when a new, acceptable black church, the Bell Church, under white pastor Robert Gordon, was constituted. The Bell Church joined the Portsmouth Association and became known as the First Baptist Church in 1840. By 1851, 643 blacks were members, while only 250 were in the Bute Street Church (the successor to Mitchell's "disorderly" First Baptist Church). While it was not until the postwar period that the Mitchell church regained its original name and prominence, it never closed. A black, Lewis Tucker, was preaching at the First Baptist Church from 1845 on, but he did not become official preacher until 1862. Cf. Lewis Tucker, manuscript, "Family and Church Record Book, kept at Norfolk, Virginia, c. 1822–1833," in the Manuscript Division, Library of Congress, Washington, D.C., C. D. Woodson Papers; and *1800-1950, Sesquicentennial Jubilee Norfolk's First Baptist Church*.

28. *Minutes*, Sunbury Association, Georgia (1834). Thomas Campbell (1763–1854), an Irish seceder Presbyterian, arrived in the United States in 1807 and was disturbed by the closed communion of his denomination in America. In response, he formed the Christian Association of Washington County, Pennsylvania (1809). The goal of the association was the union of all Christians on the apostolic pattern. His son Alexander (1788–1866) was the major leader of the movement, taking his followers into Baptist churches. However, conflicts with many Baptists led the Campbellites to secede and merge with the followers of Presbyterian Barton W. Stone (1772–1844) in the formation of the Disciples of Christ (1832). See H. Shelton Smith, Robert T. Handy, and Lefferts A. Loetscher, *American Christianity: An Historical Interpretation with Representative Documents* (New York: Charles Scribner's Sons, 1960), I, 562-563, 576–586. Winthrop S. Hudson, *Religion in America* (New York: Charles Scribner's Sons, 1965), 179, characterizes the Disciples as "combining a Presbyterian heritage with Methodist doctrines and Baptist polity and practice." Winfred E. Garrison and Alfred DeGroot, *The Disciples of Christ: A History* (St. Louis, Mo.: Christian Board of Publication, 1958), 472. Blacks formed a separate black Disciples church in Kentucky; they were the majority at the Nashville, Tennessee, Disciples

Church and were members, in large numbers, in six Kentucky mixed churches; four in North Carolina and Tennessee, two in Texas and Virginia; one in Kansas, Missouri, and Louisiana. At Cheyneyville, Louisiana, two blacks were preaching. See Robert O. Fife, *Teeth on Edge* (Grand Rapids, Mich.: Baker Book House, 1971), 58–65. Marshall's life history is widely recounted: see James Simms, *First Colored Baptist Church in North America* (Philadelphia: J. B. Lippincott, 1888), 80-89; Garrison, *The Disciples,* 473-474; Samuel Boykin, *A History of the Baptist Denomination in Georgia* (Atlanta, Ga.: Jas. P. Harrison & Co., 1851), 49; *Minutes,* Sunbury Association (1843), 13. Marshall died in December 1856 "while returning from the North," and is memorialized in *Minutes,* Sunbury Association (1857), 7. There is a fine description of a Marshall sermon given by Charles Lyell and reprinted in Leslie Fishel and Benjamin Quarles, *The Negro American* (New York: William Morrow & Co., 1967), 135–136. On Marshall's conflict with the association, see *Minutes,* Sunbury Association (1839), 2; (1841), 9. The black minority that had conformed to the association demands stayed in the old building. They became known as the Third African or First Bryan Church. Both this church and the church led by Marshall now claim descent from the eighteenth-century Savannah church. *Minutes,* Sunbury Association (1834).

29. The original constitution of the Sunbury Association, giving all member churches voting rights, can be found in the *Minutes* of 1823. Black members are listed in all the early reports, summarized in *Minutes* (1843), 13; (1839), 7; (1856), Appendix. By the 1830s, blacks were "timidly" voicing their opinions. (Simms, *First Colored Church,* 112). The changed constitution of the mid-1840s, eliminating all black voting rights, is printed with the 1854 *Minutes,* 14, no. III. In 1843 and again in 1846, the association objected to black "innovations": sending bread and wine to the plantations in the hands of deacons. See *Minutes* (1843), 7, and (1846), 5. Sunbury policy was to try to have small white minorities control the large black churches, wherever possible, but they did not feel they were having marked missionary success. Presbyterian minister C. C. Jones, through the Liberty County Association, supported interdenominational plantation preaching stations; and the Great Ogeechee black Baptist Church was essentially run by the local Presbyterian church, until 1855, when the white Baptists disavowed the relationship. See Appendix II.

30. *Minutes,* Sunbury Association (1852), report by A. Harmon, 16, (1855), 16, 20; (1863), 9; (1866), 8. On the Sunbury goal of church independence, see Appendix II, above.

After the war, White Bluff joined the Zion Colored Association. In 1868 it was pastored by Reverend H. Handy (*Minutes,* Zion Colored Association [1868], 13).

31. Ira Berlin identifies Old Captain as a Virginia-born freed black "who moved to Kentucky with his former master." *Slaves Without Masters: The Free Negro in the Ante-Bellum South* (New York: Pantheon Books, 1974), 70.

The best biographical material on Ferrill is in William J. Simons, *Men of Mark* (New York: Arno Press, [1887] 1968), 321–323. (Simons was a minister at the same Lexington church in the second half of the nineteenth century.) Ferrill was a slave of Anna Winston in Hanover County, Virginia. At twelve years of age, when he was saved from drowning, he had a religious experience. While still in Virginia, Ferrill was a baptized preacher, and he had married and had been trained as a house-joiner prior to his move to Lexington. See also *Minutes,* Elkhorn Association (1821), 7, (1822), 4, (1861), n.p.; and Benedict, *General History* (1848), 813.

32. Cromwell in DuBois, *The Black Church* (1903), 35 (emphasis added). Stephen B. Oates, Oates, *The Fires of Jubilee: Nat Turner's Fierce Rebellion* (New York: Harper & Row, 1975), 159, n.4.

33. Puckett, *Folk Beliefs,* 5. Zora Hurston, *Mules and Men* (Philadelphia: J. B. Lippincott, 1935). Alexander Young, "Ethiopian Manifesto" (1829), reprinted in Herbert Aptheker, *A Documentary History of the Negro People in the United States* (New York: The Citadel Press, 1966), I, 92. Nathaniel Paul, July 4, 1827; reprinted in Eric Foner, ed., *America's Black Past: A Reader in Afro-American History* (New York: Harper & Row, 1970), 41.

34. Josiah Henson, *The Life of Josiah Henson* (Boston, 1849), 12, reprinted in Gold Refined Wilson, "The Religion of the American Negro Slave: His Attitude Toward Life and Death," *JNH* 8 (1923): 52. Lily Y. Cohen, *Lost Spirituals* (Freeport, N.Y.: Books for Libraries Press, [1928] 1972), 41–42.

35. See above, note 12. Official minutes for the year 1837 were either kept secretly or destroyed. The available manuscript version ends just before White's selection; it picks up after he left Virginia.

The adult life of Sampson White can be outlined as follows:

1837:   Pastor at Gillfield Church, Petersburg, Virginia.
1838:   Possibly in Norfolk, Virginia.
1839:   Very active at the First Baptist Church (mixed), Washington, D.C., leading a "rebellious group" out of the church.
1839–40:   Pastor, First Colored Baptist Church, Washington, D.C.
1848:   Pastor, Abyssinian Baptist Church, New York City.
1848–49:   Pastor, Concord Street Church, Brooklyn, New York.
1849:   Corresponding Secretary ABMC.
1851:   Pastor, Philadelphia Union Church, Philadelphia, Pennsylvania.
1855:   Pastor, First Colored Baptist Church, Washington, D.C.
1860:   Pastor, Concord Street Church, Brooklyn, New York.
1868:   Pastor, African Church, Lynchburg, Virginia.

Johnson, *Gillfield*, 14; Jackson, *Gillfield*, 45; variant spelling by the authors. Manuscript minutes of Gillfield Church, available at the church or at the Manuscript Division, Alderman Library, University of Virginia, on microfilm. Manuscript Minutes of the First Baptist Church, Washington, D.C., available on microfilm at HCSBC. *Minutes*, Philadelphia Association (1840), 3, 8, 15; (1851), 2; *Minutes*, Hudson River Association, New York (1849), 2; *Minutes*, ABMC (1849), 2, 5, (1855), 17, (1860), 20; *Minutes*, Virginia Baptist State Convention (1868), 2.

36. Citation from manuscript minutes, Gillfield, July 6, 1851. Peter Valentine, an exhorter, was expelled for fighting, and Deacon Walker made confession of using the terms *liar* and *foul*. See entries of June 2, October 6, 1827 and May 22, 1842.

For the role of deacons and the customs and rituals at Gillfield, see the manuscript minutes of July 6, 1851, July 1, 1846, March 15, 1857, and the introduction written in 1973.

In 1827, ten black members of the Gillfield Church were expelled for fighting and three members for sexual misbehavior. For these and other expulsion cases, see manuscript minutes, Gillfield, June 2, August 3, 1827; September 1834; July 3, June 10, August 22, September 18, October 2, 1842; September 5, 1845; and July 6, 1851.

A list of "Grants to Marry" can be found in the Gillfield minutes of April 8, 1850.

For remarriage cases, see manuscript minutes, Washington, D.C., September 5, 1845. The case of R. Hampton is noted August 9, 1806, February 7, 1807, and June 13, 1807. See also Jones, *Virginia Portsmouth Association*, 226.

37. Harrison W. Daniel, "Virginia Baptists and the Negro in the Antebellum Era," *JNH* 56 (1971): 1-16.

Jackson, "Religious Development," 229. At Richmond's First African, the pastor was chosen by the white business meeting, but this was not the usual state of affairs.

38. This church, begun in 1773 or 1780, was originally called Buruss and then Carmel. Records in Virginia Baptist Historical Society; *Minutes*, Dover Association, Virginia; H. A. Tupper, *The First Century of the First Baptist Church of Richmond, Virginia* (Richmond, Va.: McCarthy, 1880), 247–272.

See also *Minutes*, Dover Association (1838), 4. Benedict, *General History* (1848), 661–662 n.5. On the 1823 plan, see Richard C. Wade, *Slavery in the Cities* (New York: Oxford University Press, 1964), 166–167, 309 n.58. Wade cites the "Petition of Slaves and Free Negroes for Church," petitions of the City of Richmond to the State Legislature, December 23, 1823, manuscript in the State Library, Richmond. The petition claimed 700 blacks wanted to build a church and to chose teachers, " 'subject to the mayor's approval.' "

Jeremiah B. Jeter, *The Recollections of a Long Life* (Richmond, Va.: Religious Herald Co., 1891), 209. The blacks were given the old First Baptist church building when, in the fall of 1841, the whites built themselves a new $40,000 structure. *Minutes, Dover Association* (1845), 5, (1859), 15.

Robert Ryland, "Reminiscences of the First African Church, Richmond, Virginia, by the Pastor," *American Baptist Memorial* 14 (September through December 1855): 211, 262–263. Ryland claimed that the white overseers served as a protection for the congregants—for example, blacks in the church could appeal to the white committee to overrule the black deacons. However, "Their decision [the whites] is to be final." Jeter did not recall any cases in which the blacks were overruled. Jeter, *Recollections*, 211.

39. Ryland, "Reminiscences," 264–265, 323–325, 356. Jeter commented on Ryland's selection as pastor to the blacks: "As his afternoons (Saturdays and Sundays) were unoccupied, and the pastorate would make no great draft on his intellectual powers, he was unanimously selected for the important post." Jeter, *Recollections*, 211, 212. In praising Ryland, Jeter claimed that the colored people "were emotional" and would have been "pleased" with a "superficial" preacher. Ryland, however, would not placate their passions. He wanted them to "think rather than to feel"; in this he was "eminently successful."

Ryland blamed the church crisis on a black convict whom, he claimed, collected fees for his contacts and plans to help slaves run away, and then, for a larger fee, revealed their plans to their owners. Ryland, "Reminiscences," 323.

On Reverend James Holmes, see *Minutes*, Virginia State Baptist Convention, Colored (1868), 25. The church population totaled 4,148.

40. See, for example, the manuscript minutes of the First Baptist Church, Nashville, Tennessee (available on microfilm at HCSBC). Brother and Sister were titles used for all members prior to the 1830s, although slave status and color were always noted in the minutes. By the late 1830s these terms were rarely used for blacks, although they were retained as a mark of honor for blacks who were preachers. Within a few years they were dropped for whites as well, but whites were then called Mr. and Mrs., while blacks were generally called by their first names (December 27, 1840, January 7, 1841, January 1842).

For evidence of black activity in mixed churches, see the manuscript minutes of the First Baptist Church, Washington, D.C.; First Baptist Church, Jackson, Louisiana; First Baptist Church, Minden, Louisiana; Welsh Neck Baptist Church, Welsh Neck, South Carolina; First Baptist Church, Nashville, Tennessee (all available on microfilm at HCSBC).

James Jefferson Watson spoke with many ex-slaves who had been alive in this period, and on the basis of evidence they provided, he outlined a picture of branch churches in "The Religion of the Negro," Ph.D. dissertation, University of Pennsylvania, 1912, 34–35.

41. Manuscript minutes, First Baptist Church, Charleston, South Carolina, 1849–1859, especially January 15, 1850, September 8, 1851, July 1859 (available on microfilm at HCSBC). See also H. A. Tupper, *Two Centuries of the First Baptist Church of South Carolina* (Baltimore, Md.: R. H. Woodward & Co., 1889). See Appendix IB for details on branch churches.

42. The best sources of information on the growth of this black subcongregation are the manuscript minutes of the First Baptist Church, Washington, D.C. (available from the founding in 1803 through 1865 at HCSBC). See also John Cromwell, "First Negro Churches in the District of Columbia," *JNH* 7 (1922): 64–106.

On August 8, 1828, Butler was admitted to the Washington, D.C., church on the basis of a letter of dismission from the United Baptist Church, Whitecook Meeting House. "The letter . . . states he had been indulged to exercise his gifts in the ministry, whereupon it was agreed that he be permitted the same privilege."

For evidence of the black-white troubles in the Washington church, see manuscript minutes, First Baptist Church, Washington, D.C., August 8, December 12, 1817; October 8, December 10, 1819; December 12, 1817; December 11, 1835; December 7, 1838; letter dated November 30, 1838, read into minutes of January 11, 1939; June 7, 1839; September 13, 1839. *Minutes,* Philadelphia Association (1840), 3, 8, 15.

43. A white committee investigated the blacks' exclusion of Wormly and led Wormly to express sorrow. He was then reinstated by the blacks on January 7, 1848.

Leonard had come from the Meeting Street Church in Providence, Rhode Island (1855), and from the Union Baptist Church in Maryland (1856–1858) where he had been the principal of a Baptist school for Negroes. Active in the ABMC, he was a very energetic Baptist missionary preacher after the war. See *Minutes,* ABMC (1855), 17, and *Minutes,* Philadelphia Association (1860), 5.

See manuscript minutes, First Baptist Church, Washington, D.C., infra, especially June 1852, when the white membership was tallied at eighty-eight and the black at forty-seven. In 1862, there were ninety-seven whites and eight blacks.

44. See Appendix IA.

45. On black associations, see Appendix III.

Circular letter of Elder T. J. Shores; see *Minutes,* Colored Baptist Association, Wood River, Illinois (1844), 6–7.

46. See *Minutes,* ABMC (1840–1854). See *Minutes,* ABMC (1859), 13, for motion introduced by Sampson White.

Societies and individuals from Virginia, Louisiana, Missouri, Georgia, as well as from Washington, D.C., through Massachusetts were members of the ABMC—(1849), 16, (1860), 20.

See Appendix III. In addition to the church associations, black Baptists formed missionary and social welfare societies. The best known, and perhaps most significant, was the mixed African Baptist Missionary Society of Richmond, Virginia, begun in 1815. (See Chapter 8, note 12, below.)

A missionary society was formed at Blockley Church, Philadelphia, on July 4, 1827. See David Spencer, "Annals of Philadelphia Baptists" (unpublished typescript, American Baptist Historical Society, Rochester, New York), 261.

By 1849, there were two societies in Norfolk, Virginia: the Sons and the Daughters of the Baptist Convention. Similar societies then existed at the First Colored Church, Washington, D.C.; Union Church, Philadelphia; and Shiloh, Philadelphia. By 1860, there were societies at the First Colored Church, Baltimore, Maryland; Abyssinian, New York City; 12th Street Church, Boston; Second Colored, New Bedford, Massachusetts; and Oak Street Church, West Philadelphia. See *Minutes,* ABMC (1849), 5, and (1860), 20.

Conclusions

1. Twi maxim in J. B. Danquah, *The Akan Doctrine of God* (London: Frank Cass & Co., 1968), 196.

2. Alexis Kagame, "The Empirical Apperception of Time and the Conception of History in Bantu Thought," L. Gardet, et al., eds., *Culture and Time* (Paris: UNESCO Press, 1976), 89–116.

3. See discussion in Chapter 2. At least 45,088 slaves came directly from Africa to Virginia between 1710 and 1769; at least 65,466 came directly to South Carolina during 1733–1785. See Philip D. Curtin, *The Atlantic Slave Trade: A Census* (Madison, Wis.: University of Wisconsin Press, 1969), 143; Melville Herskovits, *The Myth of the Negro Past* (New York: Harper & Row, 1941), 48; and sources cited in Chapter 2, notes 1–3.

4. Ivan Vansertima, "African Linguistic and Mythological Structures in the New World," Rhoda L. Goldstein, ed., *Black Life and Culture in the United States* (New York: Thomas Y. Crowell Co., 1971), 21–22.

5. Sydney E. Ahlstrom, *A Religious History of the American People* (New Haven, Conn.: Yale University Press, 1972), 707. Ahlstrom suggests that one-eighth to one-sixth of the black population was churched. Other estimates have suggested that one in four blacks was churched.

6. In 1754, two runaway slaves taken into custody in Virginia were asked to identify their owner; they reported "their father's name is Davis but he is now dead." *Virginia Gazette,* July 19, 1754, cited by Gerald W. Mullin, *Flight and Rebellion: Slave Resistance in Eighteenth Century Virginia* (London: Oxford University Press, 1972), 45.

Several letters written by ex-slaves (emigrants to Africa) to their former owner, John McDonogh, begin with the salutation "Dear Father" or "Parent." Some letters are signed "affectionate son" or "beloved Son until death." Some eighty of McDonogh's slaves had emigrated to Liberia in 1842. Of the eight individuals whose letters (1845-1849) are reproduced in Robert S. Starobin's *Blacks in Bondage: Letters of American Slaves* (New York: New Viewpoints, 1974), 173-188, four retained the surname of McDonogh.

See the discussion of surnames in Herbert Gutman, *The Black Family in Slavery and Freedom, 1750-1925* (New York: Pantheon Books, 1976), 230-256, and below, note 10

7. John Killens, ed., *The Trial Record of Denmark Vesey* (Boston: Beacon Press, 1970), 165n.25.

8. Eugene Genovese, *Roll, Jordan, Roll: The World the Slaves Made* (New York: Pantheon Books, 1974), 216, quoting from "'Tatler' on the Management of Negroes," *Southern Cultivator* 9 (1851): 84-85.

9. W.E.B. DuBois, *The Negro Church* (Atlanta, Ga.: Atlanta University Press, 1903), 22ff. Secret societies, i.e., societies which were known of but whose meetings were secret, were ubiquitous in the black South. Nat Turner organized a "society," as did Vesey. The Sea Islands had myriad societies in 1861 and, to a great extent, every black church was a society; or if it was too large, it was divided into bands or societies. On the role of secret societies in Africa, see Kenneth K. Little, "The Role of the Secret Society in Cultural Specialization," in Simon and Phoebe Ottenberg, eds., *Culture and Societies of Africa* (New York: Random House, 1960), 199-213.

10. There is some evidence of owner interference in slave social life. See, for example, the case of John Hartwell Cocke (1780-1866), who was trying to stimulate black independence on his new Alabama plantation. In 1848, he became extremely upset at the "shocking state of moral depravity among the people," and he "commanded . . . . that they be married forthwith or be punished and sold." As a result, nine couples were joined by a Baptist clergyman. "Diary of John Hartwell Cocke, January 26, 1848," reprinted in Willie Lee Rose, *A Documentary History of Slavery in North America* (London: Oxford University Press, 1976), 446-448.

Henry Bland, born in 1851, remembering his plantation life in "Slave Narratives," Georgia, IV, 80, recalled "No promiscuous relationships allowed."

Jomo Kenyatta, "Marriage System," in Elliott P. Skinner, ed., *Peoples and Cultures of Africa* (Garden City, N.Y.: Doubleday/Natural History, 1973), 281.

As is suggested above (Chapter 2, note 17), and in the recent works of Genovese and Gutman, many blacks had surnames. These surnames often differed from those of their owners, although they may well have been those of previous owners or of their parents' owners. Gutman suggests that whites did not widely know these surnames. However, church records indicate that whites did know and use these names, although practices varied widely. In the records of the First Baptist Church of Nashville (as in most Southern churches), slaves were generally referred to by first name only, as "Sister Tillar [first name] (belonging) to Sister Watbase [surname]," or "Brother Ben belonging to Mr. Lythe." One slave who was referred to with a surname was owned by a black without one: "Brother Isham McLundy, prop. of James (a free man of color)."

Quite a few free blacks in the Deep South had their surnames recorded (as Samuel Taylor, Hannah Susk, or Brother Reuben Butcher), but in Nashville even some free blacks were known by one name only. Nashville records indicate that the whites recognized only a few slaves as having surnames that differed from their owners. (In December 1842, Eliza Davis was recorded as "The property of Mrs. H. Badwin.") In stark contrast, the manuscript minutes kept by whites of the First Baptist Church in Washington, D.C., reveal that there many slaves were known and recorded as having their own last names, entirely different from those of their owners. All the black members, both slaves and free blacks, were officially recorded with two names, although in the early business sessions, blacks were most often referred to by their first names only. (Even Rhoday Hampton, an active member from June 1803, was at first called Brother Rhoday. By the 1820s, he was referred to as Rhoda Hampton.)

The detailed Washington, D.C., church minutes reveal many cases in which slaves had their own (different) names: Abraham Smith, servant of John Lyon (1813), Nelly Baker, servant of Col. Troop (1814), Milly Jackson, servant of Mr. Bergman (1824), Susan Grant, servant of Mr. Custis (1824), Betsy Orr, servant of Andrew Ramsey (March 1826), Lewis Manning, servant of Mr. Payloe (1826), Delpy Harris, servant of Mr. Curtis (1827), Dorcas White, servant of Mr. Pibbs (1827), Stately Webster and James Fenwick, servants of Mr. Forsyth (1831). These names were recorded by whites.

When, in 1834, James R. Miller complained about the behavior of his "servant John . . . who calls himself either John Taylor or John Edwards," the black discipline committee responded to the owner's plea and "worked with" him, but they blatantly called him "John Edwards" and not John Miller. The white recording secretary followed their usage.

The Federal Census of 1790 did not widely record black surnames. Most free blacks were listed with one name only. Census takers were local people and may well have written down black names as they knew them rather than as blacks thought of themselves.

On black names, see Gutman, *Black Family,* 196, 230-256; Genovese, *Roll, Jordan, Roll,* 444-450; MSS *Minutes,* First Baptist Church, Nashville, Tenn. (available at HCSBC), May 1, 1831, March 28, 1822, December 9, 1836, May 1, 1839, March 13, 1841, November 13, 1841, December 1842, January 11, 1844. MSS *Minutes,* First Baptist Church, Washington, D.C. (available at HCSBC), December 26, 1813, July 9, 1824, March 12, 1826, June 9, 1826, July 7, 1826, March 11, 1827, November 7; December 12, 1834. Debra Nelson, comp., *List of Free Black Heads of Families in the First Census of the United States, 1790* (Washington, D.C.: National Archives, 1973).

11. *Minutes,* Sunbury Association, Georgia (1843), 7; (1852), 6; (1860), 6.

On July 4, 1826, a collection for Africa was made in the black gallery of the First Baptist Church, Washington, D.C. The same was done in Matagorda Church, Texas, in 1848 and in the First Baptist Church, Charleston, South Carolina, on January 10, 1853. Blacks on the plantation of J. Grimke Drayton raised a "missionary crop" and sold it for $16 which they gave to the African mission. See manuscript minutes, First Baptist Church, Washington, D.C., June 18, 1826; First Baptist Church, Charleston, South Carolina, January 19, 1853 (both available on microfilm at HCSBC). See also J. M. Carroll, *A History of Texas Baptists* (Dallas, Tex.: Baptist Standard Publishing Co., 1923), 259-260.

12. The black Baptist emigration to Africa began as early as the 1790s with the missions of Hector Peters, Samuel Calvert, David George, and over 1,000 followers; in the 1820s, Lott Carey, Colin Teague, Colston Waring, and John Lewis; in the 1830s, John Day and A. L. Jones; in the 1840s, Samuel Ball; and in the 1850s, J. T. Bowin. By 1852, sixteen of the seventeen missionaries in Africa supported by the Southern Baptist Convention were blacks, and Southern black churches had many missionary societies. See Chapter 7, note 46.

See Lewis Jordan, *A Brief Record of Negro Baptist Missionaries* (Nashville, Tenn.: L. Jordan, n.d.); James B. Taylor, *Elder Lott Carey* (Baltimore, Md.: Armstrong & Berry, 1837); Miles Mark Fisher, "Lott Carey," manuscript, typed copy available at the American Baptist Historical Society, Rochester, New York; William A. Poe, "Lott Carey: Man of Purchased Freedom," *Church History* 39 (1970): 49-61; Solomon Peck, "History of the Missions of the

Baptist General Convention," in *History of American Missions to the Heathen* (Worcester, Mass.: Spooner & Howland, 1840), 441–446. Peck reprints a letter Carey wrote from Africa: "There has never been an hour, or a minute, no, not even when the balls were flying around my head, when I could wish myself again in America."

On general black attitudes to Africa, see Robert G. Weisbord, *Ebony Kinship: Africa, Africans and the Afro-American* (Westport, Conn.: Greenwood Press, 1973), Ch. 1; Rodney Carlisle, *The Roots of Black Nationalism* (Port Washington, N.Y.: Kennikat Press, 1975).

On black emigration under the white aegis, see P. J. Stadenraus, *The American Colonization Movement 1816–1865* (New York: Columbia University Press, 1961).

13. Miles Mark Fisher, letter to Dr. Ray Billington, February 25, 1948, in the archives of the American Baptist Historical Society, Rochester, New York.

Lott Carey, quoted in Carlisle, *The Roots of Black Nationalism,* 36. Carey took on an important leadership role in Liberia. He helped stage a bloodless rebellion against the American Colonization Society that led Carey's black group to have more direct participation in the government of Liberia and gained for them more extensive rights. His role was known to blacks in America.

Jacob Walker is quoted in David Benedict, *A General History of the Baptist Denomination in America* (New York: Lewis & Co., 1848), 730.

The anonymous author of "A Call Upon the Church for Progressive Action to Elevate the Colored American People," a twelve-page tract published in 1847, objected strongly to the term *Colored Americans,* even though he used it in his title. (Tract available at Pennsylvania Historical Society.)

The thankful African can be found in L. Richmond (1772–1827), *The Negro Servant* (London: Religious Tract Society, c. 1822), 17.

14. Charles A. Valentine, "Deficit, Difference and Bi-Cultural Models of Afro-American Behavior," *Harvard Education Review* 41 (1971): 137–157. Valentine uses Steven Polgar's term, *biculturation,* by which he means people "are simultaneously enculturated and socialized in two different ways of life."

15. Elsie Clews Parsons, *Folklore of the Sea Islands, South Carolina* (Cambridge, Mass.: American Folk-Lore Society, 1923), 61–63; Henry Bibb, *Narrative of the Life and Adventures of Henry Bibb, An American Slave* (New York: H. Bibb, 1849), 22–35. Both are reprinted in Rose, *Documents,* 249, 459–460.

16. William F. Allen, *Slave Songs of the United States* (New York: A. Simpson & Co., 1867), XII; Zora Hurston, *Mules and Men* (Philadelphia: J. B. Lippincott, 1935), 44.

17. Gutman, *Black Family,* 60–67, 78–79. See above, Chapter 6, note 52, for a discussion of marriage and adultery in Africa. During the period of the slave trade, the Africans had been increasingly concerned with adultery; many peoples had held public legal hearings or "woman palavers" on this issue, often selling the "guilty" into slavery. See Walter Rodney, *West Africa and the Atlantic Slave-Trade* (Nairobi: East African Publishing House, 1967), 10.

On white Baptist social life around 1800, see David Benedict, *Fifty Years Among the Baptists* (New York: Sheldon & Co., 1860).

18. Eight white men and one white woman constituted the First Baptist Church, Washington, D.C. (Manuscript minutes are available on microfilm at HCSBC.) On R. Hampton, see June 5, 1803. By June 1803, there were eleven black members, but only six were in the roll book, along with twenty-six whites. On the compact, see March 7, 1802. Blacks joined by letter from Hedgerman River, Goucester, Upper Essex, Hammonds Branch, and Old Seneca Church.

Among the slave members were two of President Monroe's servants, Kitty and Susan; see June 1812, May 7, 1819. On R. Hamilton's marital difficulty, see August 9, 1806, February 7, 1807, June 13, 1807, September 3, 1810. On Hamilton's family, see May 7, 1830,

January 11, 1839, September 13, 1839. (He died in December 1829.)

Between 1802 and 1838, during which 73 blacks had joined the church, 36 were excluded (10 of whom were later restored). Of the 235 whites who had joined, 46 were excluded and 16 restored. The black exclusion rate was somewhat higher than that of the whites. Minutes, infra, especially September 6, 1839.

The church suggested marriage to Nancy Colbert, a "free woman of colour," (October 10, 1817). Re Johnson, see November 9, 1832, December 7, 1832; re Kitty Monroe, see May 1813.

19. Black marriage is discussed above in Chapter 6. See manuscript minutes, First Baptist Church, Charleston, South Carolina, July 22, 1849, October 1848. Remarriage or adultery was the most common cause for black exclusion in the First Baptist Church, Nashville, Tennessee (see August–September 1836). See the following manuscript minutes, available at HCSBC: Welsh Neck, South Carolina (1819, infra), August 2, 1828, February 1829; First Baptist Church, Washington, D.C., October 11, 1816, March 7, 1817, September 1831; Gillfield Baptist church, Petersburg, Virginia, March 13, 1819; Church Record Book (manuscript) at the church, First African Baptist Church, Richmond, Virginia, cited by Luther Jackson, *JNH* (1940): 29.

The detailed manuscript minutes of Mother Bethel African Methodist Episcopal Church, Philadelphia, Pennsylvania, 1760-1874, indicate that a similar concern with morals dominated community meetings among the black Methodists of Philadelphia. The minutes are extraordinarily detailed. They can be seen at the Historical Society of Pennsylvania, Philadelphia, with the approval of the church.

20. Genovese, *Roll, Jordan, Roll,* 246-247; John S. Mbiti, *African Religions and Philosophy* (London: Heineman, 1969), 211, 213; Basil Davidson, *The Africans: An Entry to Cultural History* (London: Longmans Green & Co., 1969); Henry Faulk, "Negro Folk Sermons," Ph.D. dissertation, University of Texas, reprinted in Allan Lomax, *The Folk Songs of North America* (New York: Doubleday & Co., 1960), 468; Bernard Weisberger, *They Gathered at the River* (Boston: Little, Brown & Co., 1958); John W. Work, *American Negro Songs and Spirituals* (New York: Bonanza Books, 1940), 90. Manuscript minutes, First Baptist Church, Washington, D.C. (November 7, 14, 1808; September 4, 1809). Available at HCSBC.

21. Robert A. Baker, *The Southern Baptist Convention and Its People 1607–1972* (Nashville, Tenn.: Broadman Press, 1974), 49; *Minutes,* ABMC (1840-1860); manuscript minutes, Gillfield Baptist Church, available on microfilm at Manuscript Department, Alderman Library, University of Virginia, Charlottesville.

22. A. P. Watson and Clifton Johnson, eds., *God Struck Me Dead: Religious Conversion Experiences and Autobiographies of Negro Ex-Slaves* (Philadelphia: Pilgrim Press, 1969), 69-70. J. F. Magee, *The Night of Affliction and Morning of Recovery: An Autobiography* (Cincinnati: The author, 1873), 32; Starobin, *Blacks in Bondage,* 57.

23. Israel Campbell, *An Autobiography: Bond and Free* (Philadelphia: The author, 1861), 83; John Jasper in William E. Hatcher, *John Jasper, The Unmatched Negro Philosopher and Preacher* (New York: Fleming H. Revell Co., 1908), 31.

In addition to the "royal" blood discussed above, in Chapter 7, note 32, in relation to Ferrill and Nat Turner, the AME bishop, Henry Turner (born in South Carolina in 1833 of free parents) "was descended from an African Chief." See Kenneth LaTourette, *A History of the Expansion of Christianity,* IV, *The Great Century in Europe and the U.S.A.: AD 1800–AD 1914* (New York: Harper & Row, 1941), 353.

24. Data on these preachers have been collected from published sources and the manuscript minutes of the churches. A large number of these pastors are listed with their churches in Appendix I. Most ordinations were performed by whites. However, in 1856, Reverend L. A. Black (a black man) ordained Randolph King in Brooklyn, New York, while

Richard DeBaptiste was ordained by a racially mixed council in Mt. Pleasant, Ohio, in 1860, and J. Barnett was ordained by blacks at Shiloh Church, Philadelphia, in 1858. Nine men were ordained while still possibly slaves: W. J. Campbell, Farrell, the three Gardiners, David George, Simon Harper, Ulysses L. Houston, and James Staryman. All of these men had been slaves, but they may have become free prior to ordination. See above, Chapter 6, note 32.

Peter Randolph, *From Slave Cabin to the Pulpit* (Boston: James H. Earle, 1893), 51; Jeremiah Asher, *An Autobiography with Details of a Visit to England* (Philadelphia: The author, 1862), 217; William J. Simons, *Men of Mark: Eminent, Progressive and Rising* (New York: Arno Press, [1887] 1968), 353.

25. One African, apparently converted at the ABMC's mission, came to America several times. This was J. Barnett, born in Sierra Leone and ordained in Philadelphia in 1858. He returned to Africa in 1859 and was back in Philadelphia in 1862 where he served the Oak Street Baptist Church, *Minutes,* ABMC (1858-1862); Lewis Jordan, *Negro Baptist History USA, 1750-1930* (Nashville, Tenn.: Sunday School Publishing Board, 1930), 80; Asher, *Autobiography,* 217.

On Uncle Jack, see William Spottswood White, *The African Preacher* [Uncle Jack] (Philadelphia: Presbyterian Board of Publications, 1849). On Job Davis, see Hosea Holcombe, *A History of the Rise and Progress of the Baptists in Alabama* (Philadelphia: King & Beard, 1840), 227; James B. Sellers, *Slavery in Alabama* (Birmingham: University of Alabama, [1950] 1964), 307; Jordan, *Negro Baptist History,* 95. See, as well, Venture Golphin, Appendix IB, additions, 127A.

26. On Meachum, see Willis Weatherford, *American Churches and the Negro* (Boston: Christopher Publishing House, 1957), 125; Allen, *Baptist Register,* 278-279; R. S. Duncan, *A History of the Baptists in Missouri* (St. Louis, Mo.: Scammell & Co., 1882), 755-756; John B. Metchum, *An Address to All Colored Citizens of the United States* (Philadelphia: 1846).

27. For Uncle Link and Brother George, see manuscript minutes, First Baptist Church, Minden, Louisiana (March 1850), available on microfilm at HCSBC.

On Moses Gift, Busch River, South Carolina, October 1794; Brother Titus, Cedar Spring, South Carolina, November 1804; Black Bill, Tyger River, South Carolina, October 1804, see Joe M. King, *A History of South Carolina Baptists* (Nashville, Tenn.: General Board of the South Carolina Baptist Convention, 1964), 128.

On Simon, see Garnett Ryland, *The Baptists of Virginia 1699-1926* (Richmond: Virginia Baptist Board of Missions, 1955), 155.

28. Baptist preachers known to have escaped from slavery included Israel Campbell, circa 1840, Jan Young, 1850, John Sella Martin, 1855, and Joe Strater, circa 1859.

29. George Washington Williams, *A History of the Negro Race in America* (New York: G. P. Putnam's Sons, 1882), II, 161-162. Azzie Koger, *Negro Baptists of Maryland* (Baltimore, Md.: The author, 1946), 6, 42. *Minutes,* Maryland Union Association (1861).

30. On class structure, see the 1802 division of the Savannah, Georgia, churches, where the Second Colored was for the elite, while Great Ogeechee was for slaves. (A geographical division may have been a factor—city versus plantation). See James M. Simms, *First Colored Baptist Church in North America* (Philadelphia: J. B. Lippincott, 1888), 55-59.

An anonymous paper, dated 1847, "A Call Upon the Church for Progressive Action to Elevate the Colored American People," 9, recognized class divisions and class feelings as being very strong within black churches.

31. Jordan, *Negro Baptist History,* 83; Koger, *Negro Baptists in Maryland,* 76; Ira Berlin, *Slaves Without Masters: The Free Negro in the Antebellum South* (New York: Pantheon Books, 1974), 304-305.

32. *Minutes,* Philadelphia Association (1832, 1850), 25; *Minutes,* ABMC (1849), 5; Benedict, *General History* (1848), 621.

33. Manuscript minutes, First Baptist Church, Washington, D.C. (June 7, 1839,

March 9, 1832, June 7, 1839, January 11, 1839).

34. The fact that Asher left in 1850 suggests that while reactions to the Fugitive Slave Act contributed to the weakening of his church, his absence also played a role. See Asher, *Autobiography*, Benedict, *General History* (1848), 458; Jordan, *Negro Baptist History*, 82-83; *Minutes*, ABMC (1849), 5, (1865), 5.

35. Anderson, the Wood River Association's first moderator, was later in Washington, D.C., and was a trustee of Howard University. Williams, *Negro Race*, 476-503; Benedict, *General History* (1848), 863, 957.

36. See Appendix IB for a record of the churches they served.

37. James W. Busch, *The Beaufort Baptist Church* (Beaufort, S.C.: Beaufort County Historical Society, n.d.), 27; Willie Lee Rose, *Rehearsal for Reconstruction: The Port Royal Experiment* (New York: Vintage Books, 1964), 7, 315; William Allen, *Slave Songs of the United States* (New York: A. Simpson & Co., 1867), XII.

38. Miles Mark Fisher, "The History of the Olivet Baptist Church of Chicago," M.A. thesis, University of Chicago Divinity School, 1922, 5-7, 15; *Minutes*, Wood River Association (1861), 4, (1862), 5, (1864), 8. *Minutes*, ABMC (1859), in Jordan, *Negro Baptist History*, 70; Patrick Thompson, *The History of the Negro Baptists in Mississippi* (Jackson, Miss.: Daily Print Co., 1898), 60.

39. W.E.B. DuBois, *The Philadelphia Negro* (New York: Schocken Books, [1899] 1967), 25, 205; Fisher, "Olivet Church," Appendix G; Simons, *Men of Mark*, 353; A. W. Pegues, *Our Baptist Ministers and Schools* (Springfield, Mass.: Wiley & Co., 1892), 153-165.

40. Raymond Julius Jones, *A Comparative Study of Religious Cult Behavior Among Negroes* (Washington, D.C.: Howard University, 1939).

41. Genovese, *Roll, Jordan, Roll*, infra.

42. J. B. Danquah, *The Akan Doctrine of God* (London: Frank Cass & Co., 1968), 193; Calvin, in Bernhard Citron, *New Birth: A Study of the Evangelical Doctrine of Conversion in the Protestant Fathers* (Edinburgh: University Press, 1951), 148, 150; "visions" in Watson and Johnson, *God Struck Me Dead*, 144.

43. Watson and Johnson, *God Struck Me Dead*, 13, 18, 149.

44. Robert Tallant, *Voodoo in New Orleans* (New York: Collier Books, [1946] 1974), 93; Niles Newbell Puckett, *Folk Beliefs of the Southern Negro* (New York: Negro Universities Press, [1926] 1968), 151; H. W. Turner, *African Independent Church (Aladura)* (Oxford: Clarendon Press, 1967), II, 137; Watson and Johnson, *God Struck Me Dead*, 22-150.

45. Blacks recounted being protected by Jesus from conjurers: Celestia Avery and Jack Atkinson, "Slave Narratives," Georgia, IV, 17. Black Baptists were expelled for "doctoring": Jack (Nettles) by the Hephzibah Church, April 16, 1825, cited in Orville W. Taylor, *Negro Slavery in Arkansas* (Durham, N.C.: Duke University Press, 1958), 134; Cupid, expelled by the Welsh Neck Church, manuscript minutes, October 1832; Betty Orr expelled by the Washington, D.C., First Baptist Church, manuscript minutes, June 11, 1830. (Minutes available on microfilm at HCSBC.) See Minutes, 8th Annual Colored Missionary.

Watson and Johnson, *God Struck Me Dead*, 127; Puckett, *Folk Beliefs*, 168.

See *Minutes*, 8th Annual Colored Missionary Baptist Convention, Alabama (1875), 13, for a lament concerning the continuing superstitions.

46. Watson and Johnson, *God Struck Me Dead*, 156; Lomax, *Folk Songs*, 464.

Richard Jolla, recorded on "Music from the South, Elder Songsters," Folkways Record FP 656, Vol. 7, Side 2, Band 7.

A NOTE ON SOURCES _____

To draw up and then return what one had drawn . . . that is the life of the world.

Ogotemmêli, elder of the Dogon

The extensive published bibliographies on black history and church history provide the student and researcher with introductions to a significant portion of the known materials. Following is a selected list of bibliographies and a discussion of the lesser known manuscript sources for black Baptist history. (See Introduction, note 1, and Chapter 5, note 4, for selected secondary sources.)

By far the richest sources for the social history of black Christians, including the inner life of the churches, are found in the narratives of ex-slaves, written both during the antebellum era and long after the end of slavery. While many are cited at different points in this text, John W. Blassingame, *The Slave Community: Plantation Life in the Ante-Bellum South* (New York: Oxford University Press, 1972), 227–238, has compiled a bibliography of a large body of these writings.

The most extensive single collection of ex-slave narratives, the Federal Writers Project, "Slave Narratives: A Folk History of Slavery in the U.S. . . ." (Washington, D.C.: Library of Congress, 1941), has been edited by George P. Rawick and published as Volumes 2–17 of *The American Slave: A Composite Autobiography* (Westport, Conn.: Greenwood Press, 1973). For critical evaluations of the use of such sources, see C. Vann Woodward, "History from Slave Sources," *American Historical Review* 79 (1974): 470–481, and John W. Blassingame, "Using the Testimony of Ex-Slaves: Approaches and Problems," *Journal of Southern History* 41 (1975): 473–482.

Olli Alho, in *The Religion of the Slaves: A Study of the Religious Tradition and Behaviour of Plantation Slaves in the United States 1830–1865* (Helsinki: Academia Scientiarum Fennica, 1976), 278–303, has thoroughly indexed the slave narratives and spirituals. This index of religious beliefs and practices should prove an excellent tool for further analysis.

The printed minutes of the "white" Baptist church associations attest to the membership of all-black churches in these associations and of black individuals in mixed churches. The most extensive microfilm collection of these minutes can be found at the Southern Baptist Historical Society, Nashville, Tennessee. This is the most comprehensive collection of records of Baptist activities in the United States. Its holdings reveal the extent of black participation in Baptist life, although there is very little that is overtly recorded as "Black history." Black history must be sought out, but this archive holds the basic materials for this research.

The major Northern archive is that of the American Baptist Historical Society, housed at Colgate-Rochester University, Rochester, New York. Its holdings supplement those of the Southern Baptist Historical Society in regard to specific association minutes and are far more extensive in regard to all-black association records.

Both of these archives hold both originals and copies of the manuscript minutes of church meetings which every Baptist church was expected to keep. These contain an extraordinary wealth of social history. The lives of churches and of the individuals who belonged to them can be reconstructed through their use. The words of black ministers, deacons, and members are often cited at length. (See, for example, the manuscript minutes of the First Baptist Church, Washington, D.C.) The problems and responses of individuals and institutions are their constant concern. These minutes have provided some of the key evidence for the analysis in this work. (A list of the minutes researched, that include data on blacks, is appended below.)

Other archives have extensive collections of contemporary Baptist journals and tracts, many of which reflect concern with blacks. Private diaries of Baptist preachers and letters of promi-nent Baptists are preserved. In these, many reactions to black religion, descriptions of black ser-vices, and lists of black baptisms are still in safekeeping. See, for example, the fascinating details of black church life in Robert Ryland's "Reminiscences of the First African Church, Richmond, Virginia, By the Pastor," *American Baptist Memorial* 14 (1855): 262–265, 289–292, 321–327, 353–358.

White commentaries, for example those of Fredrika Bremer and Frederick Olmsted, have often been cited in the writing of black religious history. In addition, there is a large body of other contemporary (white) commentaries on black religion that is little known. These are the writings of religious men such as David Benedict, whose church recordkeeping was of great im-portance. In 1860, Benedict published a memoir entitled *Fifty Years Among the Baptists* (New York: Sheldon & Co., 1860). Here, as in his other writings, Benedict provided personal reactions to black church life. (He promised to devote a book to this issue, and some archive may well have the papers he was saving to this end. The American Baptist Historical Society has a large collec-tion of his papers; others are scattered at Brown and Harvard Universities, but none that I have seen includes this special collection.)

In sum, the two major Baptist archives contain an exceptionally rich collection of materials for the writing of black history. When supplemented by (1) other records, diaries, and letters in the major Southern history collections (including those at the University of North Carolina at Chapel Hill, Duke University, Louisiana State University, and the Colonial Williamsburg Foun-dation), by (2) data from the collections of the individual state Baptist historical societies (espe-cially those at Richmond, Virginia, and Macon, Georgia), as well as by (3) the major collections of black history (the Schomberg Collection, New York City Public Library, the Fisk University Collection, Nashville, Tennessee, and the Howard University Archives, Washington, D.C.), pre-war black church history *can* be documented.

One of the reasons why the scholarly community had heretofore accepted the "hiddenness" of the antebellum church was the paucity of records kept by black churches. To my knowledge, the only extensive black church minutes extant are those of the Gillfield Church, Petersburg, Virginia, the First African Baptist Church, Richmond, Virginia, and the Mother Bethel African Methodist Episcopal Church, Philadelphia, Pennsylvania. (The Gillfield minutes, 1827, are in the church library and can be seen there. A microfilm copy is also on file at the Alderman Li-brary, University of Virginia, Charlottesville. The Bethel records (1760-   ) can be seen, on church approval, at the Historical Society of Pennsylvania, Philadelphia.)

It is highly probable that other early black church records exist and may yet come to light, although many have no doubt been lost or burned or simply disregarded. (Even the well-preserved Gillfield minutes were used as a scrapbook in the 1920s. Someone pasted newsclip-pings over precious entries from the midnineteenth century, making it impossible to transcribe them.) While extensive black church minutes have yet to be found, taken all together there is a substantial amount of material written by blacks that attests to the institutional reality of the Afro-Christian church.

Black churches wrote and published covenants. We have, for example, that of the Liele church in Georgia (1777) and the "Articles of Faith and Covenant" of the Shiloh Baptist Church,

Philadelphia (1861). Black churches kept records of membership and contributions which they sent to the associations; these have been recorded in the associations' minutes. (The holdings of the Historical Society of Pennsylvania include a "Penny Collection Book" of the First African Baptist Church, Philadelphia, January 1834–. These collections ranged from 8 to 98 cents. Southern churches recorded tithing slaves a half-penny a month, and many Southern black churches recorded contributions to African missions.)

From a very early period, black churchmen wrote letters about themselves and their congregations. The very first issue of the *Journal of Negro History* reprinted an important collection of Georgia letters ("Letters Showing the Rise and Progress of the early Negro Churches of Georgia and the West Indies," *Journal of Negro History* I [1916]: 61ff.) Others can be found in contemporary English Baptist journals, reprinted in narratives, and scattered in archival holdings. See, for example, the letters of John Gloucester, William Gray, Robert Ralston, Robert Burch, and Shandy Young in the collection of the Historical Society of Pennsylvania. In these letters, blacks often wrote of their inner feelings and analyzed their life experiences, revealing both personal and church problems.

Lewis Tucker's "Family and Church Record Book" is preserved in the Carter G. Woodson papers in the manuscript collection at the Library of Congress, Washington, D.C. Tucker, a black Baptist preacher, was born in Norfolk County, Virginia, in March 1822; converted in August 1837; joined the First Baptist Church of Norfolk in July 1842; was called to preach in January 1845; was licensed in April 1859; and was ordained in 1863. He remained pastor at the Norfolk First Baptist Church through 1870. This personal history can be reconstructed through his own record book and the records left by his church, in particular a "Sesquicentennial Jubilee" pamphlet printed in 1950.

Biographies of several hundred black churchmen can be reconstructed in some detail by combining the white churches' prewar records with those of the black churches in the postwar period. Long after the war, black churches often printed pamphlets memorializing their prewar histories. These provide important clues and data as to their early history and social life, as an oral history was handed down. See, for example, Charles H. Brooks, *Official History of the First African Baptist Church* (Philadelphia: 1922).

Some sermons and sermon topics presented by black preachers have been preserved. We have either the written words of, or detailed reports on, the sermons of Jupiter Hammon, Israel Campbell, Jeremiah Asher, Samuel Ball, Charles Bowles, Lott Carey, Andrew Marshall, John Chavis, John Day, and Richard DeBaptiste, among others.

The folk traditions of oral history, story, song, and music are increasingly being investigated by historians and cultural anthropologists interested in the roots of religious behavior. See Morton Marks, "Uncovering Ritual Structures in Afro-American Music," in Irving I. Zaretsky and Mark P. Leone, eds., *Religious Movements in Contemporary America* (Princeton, N.J.: Princeton University Press, 1974, 60–132).

In all of these materials, church records, narratives, diaries, letters, newspapers, journals, and oral and written folklore as well as in types of documents not discussed (such as legal records, municipal and state records, and census returns), much relevant data await retrieval and analysis. The collections cited above and others, in particular the Genealogical Collection in Salt Lake City, Utah, hold vast treasure-troves. Notwithstanding all the fine work that has been done in this area, we have just begun to explore the possibilities of writing black religious history.

SELECTED BIBLIOGRAPHIES———

Allison, William Henry. *Inventory of Unpublished Material for American Religious History in Protestant Church Archives and Other Repositories.* Washington, D.C.: Carnegie Institution of Washington, 1910.

Burr, Nelson R. *A Critical Bibliography of Religion in America.* 2 vols. Princeton, N.J.: Princeton University Press, 1961.

Hampton Institute. *A Classified Catalog of the Negro Collection in the C. P. Huntington Library, Hampton Institute,* Hampton, Va.: Hampton Institute, 1940.

Historical Records Survey. *Guide to the Manuscripts in the Southern Historical Collection of the University of North Carolina at Chapel Hill.* Chapel Hill: University of North Carolina, 1941.

Historical Society of Pennsylvania. *Afro-Americana 1553–1906: Author Catalogue of the Library of Philadelphia and the Historical Society of Pennsylvania.* Boston: G. K. Hall & Co., 1973.

McPherson, James M., C. B. Holland, J. M. Banner, Jr., et al. *Blacks in America: Bibliographical Essays.* New York: Anchor Books, 1971.

New York Public Library. *Dictionary Catalog of the Schomburg Collection of Negro Literature and History.* 9 vols. Boston: G. K. Hall, 1962. 2-volume supplement 1968.

Porter, Dorothy B. *The Negro in the United States of America, Selected Bibliographies,* Washington, D.C.: Library of Congress, 1970.

Southern Baptist Historical Commission. *Microfilm Catalog: Basic Baptist Historical Materials.* Nashville, Tenn.: Southern Baptist Church, 1977.

Starr, Edward Caryl. *A Baptist Bibliography.* 6 vols. Philadelphia: Judson Press, 1947-1958.

Williams, Ethel L., and Clifton L. Brown. *Afro-American Religious Studies.* Metuchen, N.J.: Scarecrow Press, 1972.

Work, Monroe N. (ed.). *Bibliography of the Negro in Africa and America.* New York: Argosy-Antiquarian, [1928] 1966.

Manuscript Church Minutes Researched

Unless otherwise indicated, copies of the following handwritten minutes are available on microfilm at the Southern Baptist Historical Society, Nashville, Tennessee.

Georgia:
   Crawfordville Baptist Church, Taliaferro County, 1831-1865.

Sandy Creek Primitive Baptist Church, Jackson, Butts County, 1824-1844, 1825-1858, 1866-1875.

First Baptist Church, Rome, 1835-1864.

Kentucky:

Boone's Creek Baptist Church (formerly Boggs Fork Baptist Church), 1795-1865.

Casey's Fork Baptist Meeting House, 1818-1856.

First Christian Church, Louisville, 1830-1840.

Sandy Creek Baptist Church, 1805-1865.

Louisiana:

First Baptist Church, Minden, 1844-1865.

First Baptist Church, Jackson, 1835-1865.

Mississippi:

Beulah Baptist Church, Tippah County, 1848-1865.

Clear Creek Baptist Church, Washington, 1835-1865.

North Carolina:

Sawyer's Creek Baptist Church, 1815-1872 (Southern Historical Collection, University of North Carolina at Chapel Hill).

Pennsylvania:

Mother Bethel African Methodist Episcopal Church, Philadelphia, Historical Records, 1760-1874 (Historical Society of Pennsylvania, Philadelphia).

First African Methodist Episcopal Church Minutes. Philadelphia (Historical Society of Pennsylvania, 1815).

First African Presbyterian Church, Philadelphia, Expenses, 1842-1891 (Historical Society of Pennsylvania).

First African Presbyterian Church, Philadelphia, Minutes of the Sunday School, December 8, 1836 (Historical Society of Pennsylvania).

South Carolina:

Antioch Baptist Church, Enoree, 1835-1865.

Arrowood Baptist Church, Chesness, 1843-1865.

Catfish Creek Baptist Church, Dillon County, 1802-1865.

Coronaca Church, Coronaca, 1845-1865.

Euha Baptist Church, Euha, 1831-1865. (*Euha Baptist Church Book, October 1831-1907* [Columbia: University of South Carolina Press, 1934].)

First Baptist Church, Charleston, 1806-1864.

First Baptist Church or Lower Duncan's Baptist Church, Whitmire, 1841-1865.

Little River Baptist Church, Fairfield County, 1794-1820.

Providence Baptist Church, Greenwood County, 1845-1865.

Sweetwater Baptist Church, Edgefield County, 1832-1865.

Welsh Neck Baptist Church, Darlington County, 1837-1865.

Tennessee:

First Baptist Church, Nashville, 1820-1865.

Garrison Fork Baptist Church, Beach Grove, 1809-1865.

Virginia:

Antioch Church (originally Boar Swamp), 1787-1828 (Virginia Baptist Historical Society).

Gillfield Church (black), Petersburg, 1827-1864. (Alderman Library, University of Virginia, Charlottesville).

Washington, D.C.:

First Baptist Church, 1802-1866.

Nova Scotia, Canada:

Digby Black Baptist Church, 1799-1895 (Manuscript Department, Perkins Library, Duke University, Durham, North Carolina).

INDEX OF NAMES

SUBJECT INDEX